Artistic
WEB DESIGN
Using Adobe® Dreamweaver® and Photoshop®

An Introduction

Vickie Ellen Wolper

JONES & BARTLETT
LEARNING

World Headquarters
Jones & Bartlett Learning
40 Tall Pine Drive
Sudbury, MA 01776
978-443-5000
info@jblearning.com
www.jblearning.com

Jones & Bartlett Learning
Canada
6339 Ormindale Way
Mississauga, Ontario L5V 1J2
Canada

Jones & Bartlett Learning
International
Barb House, Barb Mews
London W6 7PA
United Kingdom

Jones & Bartlett Learning books and products are available through most bookstores and online booksellers. To contact Jones & Bartlett Learning directly, call 800-832-0034, fax 978-443-8000, or visit our website, www.jblearning.com.

Substantial discounts on bulk quantities of Jones & Bartlett Learning publications are available to corporations, professional associations, and other qualified organizations. For details and specific discount information, contact the special sales department at Jones & Bartlett Learning via the above contact information or send an email to specialsales@jblearning.com.

Production Credits

Publisher: Cathleen Sether
Associate Editor: Melissa Potter
Editorial Assistant: Molly Whitman
Production Director: Amy Rose
Associate Production Editor: Tiffany Sliter
Associate Marketing Manager: Lindsay White
V.P., Manufacturing and Inventory Control:
  Therese Connell
Cover and Title Page Design: Kristin E. Parker

Composition: Glyph International
Cover Images: Background abstract: © Evgeniy Perov/Dreamstime.com; Background code: © Fourthexposure/Dreamstime.com; Laptop: © Photocrea Michael Bednarek/ShutterStock, Inc.; Website: © Macrocozm/Dreamstime.com; Arrow: © Arenacreative/Dreamstime.com; Color lights: © Elgris29/Dreamstime.com; Color wheels: © Gines Valera Marin/Dreamstime.com.
Printing and Binding: Courier Kendallville
Cover Printing: Courier Kendallville

Library of Congress Cataloging-in-Publication Data
Wolper, Vickie Ellen.
  Artistic web design using Adobe Dreamweaver & Photoshop : an introduction / Vickie Ellen Wolper.
    p. cm.
  Includes index.
  ISBN-13: 978-0-7637-8594-9 (pbk.)
  ISBN-10: 0-7637-8594-6 (ibid)
  1. Dreamweaver (Computer file) 2. Adobe Photoshop. 3. Web sites—Design. I. Title.
  TK5105.8885.D74W64 2010
  006.7'8—dc22
                        2010023495

6048

Printed in the United States of America
14 13 12 11 10   10 9 8 7 6 5 4 3 2 1

This book is dedicated to Razz
and the special bond that we shared.

Contents

Preface

Artists are visual: visual in their work, and visual in their learning style. I have written *Artistic Web Design Using Adobe® Dreamweaver® and Photoshop®: An Introduction* with this principle as its foundation. Throughout this text, rather than simply stating fundamental web design principles, such as "use web safe fonts," my philosophy for this and other essential concepts is to illustrate the *why* behind a recommendation through providing visual samples of the problem, coupled with visual solutions.

Learning any new software can be difficult. As an educator, I have found that oftentimes users of other types of graphics software are particularly challenged by the unique characteristics specific to Dreamweaver. Being sensitive to that, I have designed each new chapter to build on the previous one, noted similarities with other programs the reader may already be familiar with, and provided numerous hands-on exercises that culminate with a completed workable website. To accommodate the diversity of its readers and further aid in the learning process, all of the software content has been customized to address users of each of the Adobe Creative Suite® versions—CS3, CS4, and CS5.

Readers who choose to do so can further reinforce their learning by building their own websites simultaneously, guided through the process chapter by chapter, from initial conception to the final upload process.

I have designed the format of this book around my personal teaching experience. When new concepts are presented in a step-by-step format and are balanced with ample opportunities to reinforce those concepts through practical applications, software training transcends to software comprehension, and ultimately its real life application.

Acknowledgment

I would like to thank all of my colleagues, friends, family, and students who encouraged me to write this book, with special thanks to David Pallai for the opportunity to pursue my dream of dreams.

Introduction

This book is designed to guide readers through their introduction to the unique design considerations of the Web, following a "building block" teaching style tailored to provide a solid foundation in Dreamweaver. To reduce the initial learning curve required to take command of this new software, correlational tips on similarities between Dreamweaver and the concepts readers are already familiar with in Photoshop (and other graphics programs) are noted whenever applicable. Learning web design should be an exciting and inviting adventure, not one that is dreaded or threatening!

Not a Photoshop user? Readers with experience in Adobe Illustrator® will find that the Save for Web dialog box, as well as many other graphics software features utilized in this text are similar, and oftentimes identical, to those of Photoshop.

A CD-ROM with full-color images, web pages, practice files, completed project samples, and more accompanies the book.

> **For Instructors**
> Quizzes, solutions, printable illustrations of key concepts, and Microsoft® PowerPoint® slides for lectures are available for qualified instructors at http://www.jblearning.com/catalog/9780763785949/. Designated instructors' materials are for qualified instructors only. Jones & Bartlett Learning reserves the right to evaluate all requests.

Overview of Helpful Features

The following are used throughout the text to provide power-user tips, help out when something may have gone wrong, and detail features unique to CS3 or CS5:

- **Tip Icon:** Provides helpful suggestions, such as ways to complete a task or remember to do one.

- **What Happened Icon:** When something may have gone wrong, seeing this icon will offer comfort by explaining what error might have occurred and how to avoid or correct it.

- **CS5 Icon:** When a feature in Dreamweaver is new and available only in Dreamweaver CS5.

- **For CS3 Users' Box:** These smartly placed boxes will appear when a feature is new or different in CS4 and CS5 vs. CS3, and will explain how to achieve the desired outcome using CS3.

The Design Phase—
Before Launching
Dreamweaver

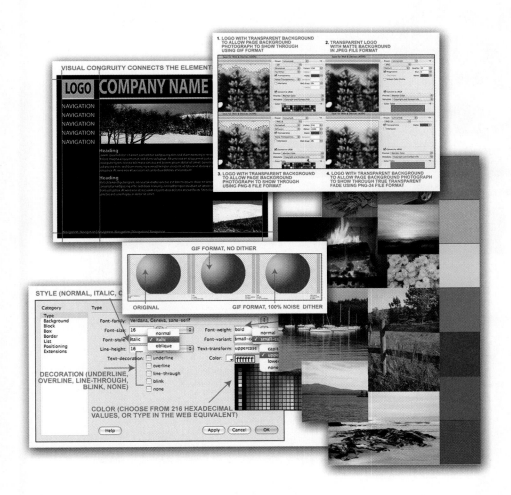

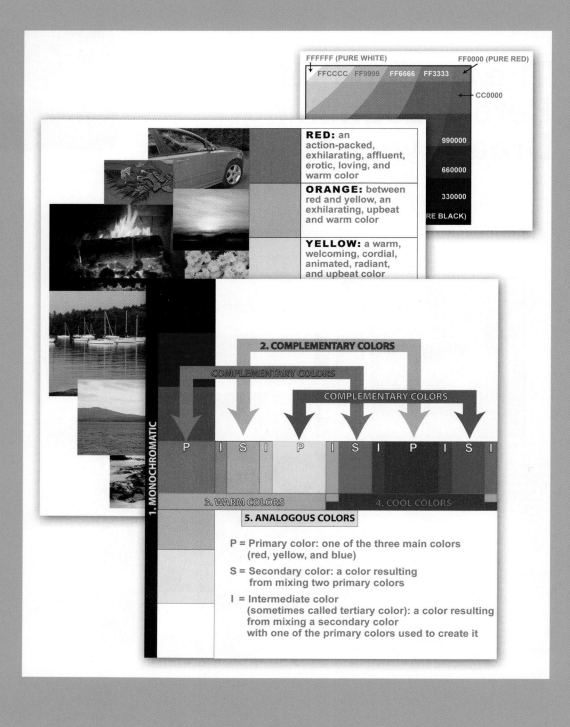

Part 1

FFFFFF (PURE WHITE)   FF0000 (PURE RED)

FFCCCC   FF9999   FF6666   FF3333

← CC0000

990000

660000

330000

RE BLACK)

RED: an action-packed, exhilarating, affluent, erotic, loving, and warm color

ORANGE: between red and yellow, an exhilarating, upbeat and warm color

YELLOW: a warm, welcoming, cordial, animated, radiant, and upbeat color

2. COMPLEMENTARY COLORS

COMPLEMENTARY COLORS

COMPLEMENTARY COLORS

P   P S I   P   P S I   P   P S I

1. MONOCHROMATIC

3. WARM COLORS   4. COOL COLORS

5. ANALOGOUS COLORS

P = Primary color: one of the three main colors
     (red, yellow, and blue)

S = Secondary color: a color resulting
     from mixing two primary colors

I = Intermediate color
     (sometimes called tertiary color): a color resulting
     from mixing a secondary color
     with one of the primary colors used to create it

Creating the Critical First Impression of Your Site

1

In This Chapter

- Collect website samples
- Understand web colors
- Review the fundamentals of color theory
- Utilize the emotional impact of color in your work

Great design begins by recognizing great design. This chapter will begin by training your eye to recognize and learn from existing websites. When learning about color, our discussions will encompass web safe, web smart, and web equivalent colors, followed by a look at the subliminal psychological influence colors have on viewers and how to capitalize on those important characteristics of color to maximize the effectiveness of your websites.

You are about to embark on a journey into the world of web design, culminating with the creation of your own custom-designed site. It's an exciting challenge, and one that will be educational, rewarding, and most importantly … fun! Let's get started!

Surfing the Web from an Artist's Perspective

The first step in web design is to learn to appreciate good design. Taking a critical look at existing websites as an artist, and taking note of design ideas that appeal to you, is a great place to start.

1.1.1 Building an Idea Book

What is an idea book, anyway? It's a name I have given to a very special kind of book … your own personal book of inspiring ideas that can help to create and brainstorm, as well as learn what *not* to do. Whether it is for print design or web design, new ideas spawn from looking at existing ideas. As a graphic artist, you may have already been creating an idea book, perhaps under a different name. When working in print design, you may have torn pages out of magazines, saved flyers that came in the mail, etc., and compiled them all into a notebook that you saved to use for future inspiration. Some of your most unique designs may have resulted from the culmination of bits and pieces of those ideas blended together with your own creativity. On a whole page there may have only been one small part of it that you noticed and thought: "That's cool. I could use that idea somehow in another layout sometime." My name for the process, building an *idea book*, is my own; however, this concept is not a new one. You may prefer to think of your idea collection as a resource notebook, or maybe an inspiration book. Whatever the name, its purpose is to provide the stimulation and birth of *ideas*; therefore, welcome to the idea book, a.k.a. the inspiration book.

Collecting Screen Shots of Existing Websites   One of the hardest first steps in beginning to learn web design is addressing the questions: I know I want to build a website, but now what? Where do I start? It is amazing that we have all used the Web and been to innumerable sites for whatever reason, but because we were going to those sites for something very specific, most of us most of the time, and certainly all of us some of the time, probably didn't think much about the *design* of the site, just its content. However, the artist who created that site *did* think about design, and its initial impression on you, the visitor. Especially when you first arrived at the home page, he/she strove to initially engage you with the site's design so that you would visit long enough to delve into its content, and not click out and on to the next one as quickly as you arrived. The first stage of the web design learning process is to surf the Web, without concern for the *content* of the sites you visit. This critical stage is the one that requires you to see beyond the obvious into what gives a site its decision-making "street appeal" (whether the visitor stays to investigate or clicks out)—to study it strictly through the eyes of an *artist*. When collecting print ideas, it is simply a matter of slipping the flyer or part of a page into a folder. To collect ideas in web design, I recommend taking a screen shot instead of printing the whole web page. One reason is that you may get unexpected results when you print the page. Most importantly, it is often just a small part of the page

FIGURE 1-1 On a Mac, the pointer becomes crosshairs when taking a screen shot.

that catches your eye, and that part is the only thing you want to save for future design inspirations.

To take a screen shot on an Apple® Mac®, press Command+Shift+4 to initiate the process. This changes the mouse pointer to crosshairs, as shown in **FIGURE 1-1**.

Move the pointer to place the crosshairs on the upper-left corner of the area you want to capture. Press the mouse button and drag from the upper left to the lower right to select the area. The resulting full-color screen shot will be automatically placed on your desktop with the extension .png. It can be renamed and saved in a digital folder, or printed and added to a hard copy folder.

To take a screen shot on a PC, press the Print Screen key, which is usually at the far right of your keyboard. Press the Alt key at the same time (Print Screen+Alt) if you have multiple windows open and want to capture only the active window in your screen shot. On a PC, when the image is captured, it is placed on the Clipboard, not the desktop. You will now need to open an image-editing program (Photoshop for example) and choose File>New. The size in the New Document dialog box will automatically be representative of your current content on the Clipboard. When opened, followed by choosing Edit>Paste, the screen shot will be placed in Photoshop ready for editing. Now, it can be cropped to display only the "cool" part that initially attracted you in the page, and saved to a digital folder or printed and stored in a hard copy folder.

The Art of Page Design vs. Visitor Usability   So, now that you know you should be saving ideas, the next questions are: What kind of ideas? What characteristics should a site have to make it worth saving? All web pages function, meaning that they allow you to get from point A to point B within the site, but there is a huge range of how well the pages allow this to happen. Most importantly at this stage of exploration, when the visitor arrives at the site, how does the art of the page keep the user engaged in the site? In Chapter 3, we will examine a website's navigational components: their designs, their effectiveness, and their usability. Our focus now is not on navigation or visitor usability; it is on the art of page design.

This is where the artist in you takes center stage. Search the Web for something someone did that was *out of the ordinary*, some unique way that an image, text, or background design was displayed/overlapped, combined, faded, etc. It is *not* time to look at a page and say, "That's cool, but I have no clue how it would be done, so forget it." It is only time to say, "Hey, I like that idea." If it is a photograph that overlaps the page border, maybe in your site it will be a flower that overlaps your headline text or part of your navigation; it is simply the concept of overlapping that may appeal to you. Think creativity. Think design. Think possibilities. Screen shots, screen shots, and more screen shots … but from what kind of sites?

For this exercise, categories of sites to study are not important. In fact, if anything, a broader range is better. All types of sites will surprise you, as long as you "think outside the box" while you search, and do not allow yourself to be limited to only certain types of sites.

This sample list will help you get started:

- airlines
- car dealerships
- day care centers
- garden centers
- online stores
- photographers
- restaurants
- sports teams

Got the idea? Limiting yourself to only certain types of sites that you think you should visit will limit the versatility of your idea book: you will discover that great design ideas are not limited to specific subject areas.

Stimulating Your Creativity: The Art of Inspiration   To help you hone in on your search, let's take a closer look at a couple of examples. **FIGURE 1-2** shows the home page of the Nashville Zoo.

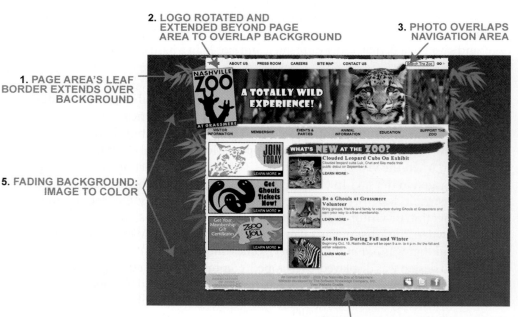

FIGURE 1-2   Nashville Zoo home page. (Courtesy of the Nashville Zoo at Grassmere, http://www.nashvillezoo.org.)

Although you should save screen shots of sites even if they have just one artistic feature that catches your eye, this page has several:

1. The addition of the leaf effect around the outer edge of the page area designed to overlap the background
2. The rotation of the company logo and its extension beyond the page onto the background
3. The overlapping of the navigation area with an image at the top of the page
4. The creation of a jagged edge around the outside of the page area
5. The use of a photograph that gradually transforms into a solid color from top to bottom for the background

Before you begin your research, let's look at one more site. The following site is the official tourism site for the state of Missouri. When you arrive at this site, it immediately gives the street appeal of friendly, informal, and fun, as shown in FIGURE 1-3.

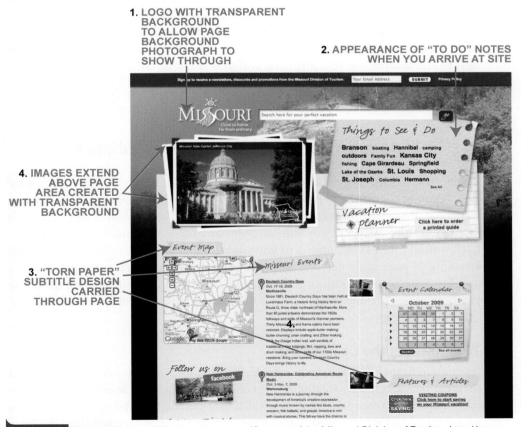

FIGURE 1-3 Missouri Division of Tourism home page. (Courtesy of the Missouri Division of Tourism, http://www.visitmo.com.)

A closer look reveals some cool effects that contribute to creating that initial street appeal:

1. The state logo has been created with a transparent background, so that when placed against a background photograph, the photograph shows through it.

2. The torn paper appearance has been used to create reminder "to do" notes that appear to be "taped up" (with the rings of the paper also allowing the background photograph to appear through them).

3. The additional appearance of torn paper "notes" for the subject titles, with one angled, carries the casual "tacked up" theme even further.

4. Images are extended above the defined white area of the page.

An Important Reminder of the Purpose of an Idea Book   Before you begin, remember that you will be collecting design *ideas*, not designs: your book must always be an *inspiration* book, not a copy book! Never copy someone's work! Your idea book must *always* be used as the starting point, never the ending point of the design process. First and most importantly as an artist, you will always want your designs to be your own unique designs. Second, copying someone's work is just plain illegal: plagiarism is fraud. Now that you understand *what* to look for, and *how* to use it later, are you inspired? Did you get your creative engines fired up? Take some time now to surf and save to your idea book!

Tailoring Your Site to Your Future Audience

An effective website design is one that is tailored to its audience. This goal is achieved by remaining cognizant of your future visitors throughout the site design process, but is particularly important in the initial design stage. Take time now to clearly identify who you expect your audience will be by determining the ages, interests, backgrounds, and expectations of your potential visitors. Gaining a solid understanding of your audience will help you make informed decisions regarding the graphics you create, the colors and fonts you choose, and the formality of the layout you design—all the ingredients that combine to create the street appeal of that critical first impression.

1.2.1 Surfing the Competition

It will help to surf the Web again, narrowing the topic of your web search this time to target sites specifically created by your competition. It is not to criticize them or to copy them, but to compare what is included in them and how it is presented, making note of concepts you like and don't like to help you design your website.

1.2.2 The Power of Brainstorming

Brainstorming is a process used to generate multiple ideas and solutions. Brainstorming, both alone and with others, can be extremely helpful throughout the website design process and can be particularly helpful with the design task. The input of friends and colleagues can help provide a fresh objective look at the specifics of your intended audience, and the backgrounds and interests of your visitors, that you may not think of on your own. Ideally, try to even brainstorm with actual future visitors to your site, asking them what they expect the site to include. A successful website is one that effectively blends design with functionality: one that began by defining its audience during the initial design stage and continued to keep the audience as the main focus throughout the development process.

1.2.3 The Principle of the Fold

The principle of the fold (originally a newspaper term for placing the critical information above the fold of the paper) became popular in web design when most monitors had substantially smaller viewing areas than their counterparts today. The principle states that when designing a website, be sure that critical content is in the top 400–500 pixel viewing area of the page to reduce the necessity of the visitor having to scroll down to locate that content. This is not about horizontal scrolling: current practices in web page design have minimized the need to scroll to the right to read page content. The fold refers to the vertical scrolling issue, whether page content should require or not require the visitor to scroll down for it. Sometimes, sites will limit vertical scrolling on the home page, but incorporate it into link pages, depending on their content, after the visitors have immersed themselves in the site. Because monitor dimensions and resolutions keep increasing and browser designs vary, rather than define any specific pixel height limit, a good rule of thumb is to simply remain steadfast to your original design goal: use street appeal to attract your visitors. If the top area of your page has valuable content and engages them, your visitors will scroll down to keep reading!

1.3 Engaging Your Visitors Through Color

Color is everywhere, so much so that we often take its powerful influence on us for granted. However, creating a website requires that the designer make effective critical decisions on the colors he/she selects and the resulting impact those choices will have on the site's visitors.

1.3.1 Choosing Web Equivalent, Web Smart, or Web Safe Colors

When designing for the Web, all images used must be in the RGB color mode, with all graphics, backgrounds, and text created using hexadecimal values: the name given to a color's web equivalent comprised of a combination of six letters and numbers consisting of A–F and 0–9. When creating web graphics in Photoshop, clicking on a color in the toolbox will automatically open the Color Picker. Here, you may select a color by clicking the color slider, then choosing the value of the color in the large box to the left of the slider. If you happen to know its RGB, CMYK, or hexadecimal values, and enter any one of those values into its specific area of the Color Picker dialog box, Photoshop will automatically generate the equivalent color values for the other options. Because current monitors have the ability to display millions of colors, Photoshop gives you two options for your web color choice. In **FIGURE 1-4**, the top dialog box illustrates a color picked by using the color slider and value area, with Photoshop generating the web equivalent, but warns with the "cube" that the color is not one of the safe 216 colors. The dialog box below it shows that if the cube

CHOOSING ANY RGB COLOR IN THE COLOR PICKER
CUBE INDICATES COLOR IS NOT WEB SAFE

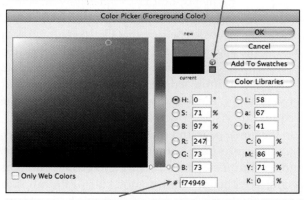

PHOTOSHOP DETERMINES THE WEB EQUIVALENT FOR YOU

COLOR CONVERTED TO ONE OF 216 WEB SAFE COLORS

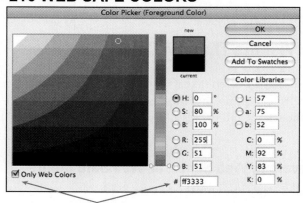

COLOR IS NOW ONE OF 216 WEB SAFE COLORS

FIGURE 1-4 Select one of the 216 web safe colors.

is clicked, or the Only Web Colors box at the bottom of the palette is checked, the same color will be shifted as needed to comply with the 216 web safe color palette.

Understanding the Web Safe Palette   Colors are defined in web design by a hash symbol (#) followed by the hexadecimal value of the color chosen. The term *web safe* is the name for a limited group of 216 colors that have been determined to look exactly the same on any computer monitor. Because monitors are RGB, the 216 colors are percentage combinations of red, green, and blue. When you see a web safe color, the *FF* indicates that the red, green, or blue (in that order) component of that RGB color is at 100%; *00* indicates that the color contains 0% of the particular RGB component. Because RGB colors are *additive* colors, 100% of all components (red, green, and blue) equals pure white. As a web safe color, white is therefore defined as #FFFFFF. Following that same logic, #FF0000 is pure red, #00FF00 is pure green, #0000FF is pure blue, and #000000 contains none of the three components and therefore represents black.

The "full" percent is displayed as FF and the "zero" percent is displayed as 00. The following additional identifiers are used to represent the percentage of the RGB colors— red, green, and blue, in that order—that are used to name the 216 web safe colors:

CC = 80%

99 = 60%

66 = 40%

33 = 20%

FIGURE 1-5 illustrates how these identifiers are logically used to name the colors of the web safe palette.

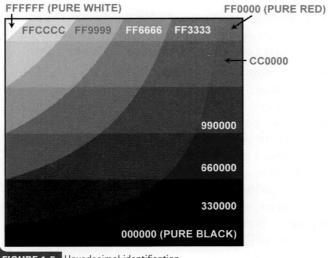

FFFFFF (PURE WHITE)   FF0000 (PURE RED)

FFCCCC   FF9999   FF6666   FF3333

CC0000

990000

660000

330000

000000 (PURE BLACK)

FIGURE 1-5 Hexadecimal identification.

Web Safe vs. Web Smart Colors   Web smart colors are a newer concept that evolved out of the desire for more safe colors than the original 216. They include all of the color combinations using the A–F and 0–9 hexadecimal values that have double identical letters or digits—such as 0077DD—therefore offering 4,096 colors instead of only 216. If you search the Web for web smart colors, you will find a variety of sites that will convert your selected color into both its web safe and web smart alternatives to help you choose the hexadecimal option you feel is most appropriate for your design application. Is it necessary to choose web safe or web smart colors vs. web equivalent colors when designing for today's visitors? Although there is much debate on this issue, web safe or web smart colors still remain viable options. The decision, once again, should be based on your audience. By researching your future visitor's needs and/or limitations, you will be able to make an informed decision about the need to use web safe, web smart, or simply web equivalent colors when designing a website for them.

1.3.2 Determining the Color Scheme for a Site

Choosing a color scheme for a website may be totally out of your control. If you are given a mandatory color scheme based on an existing corporate color identity, then the color decisions for the site have already been made for you—good or bad. However, if you are designing one for yourself, or have been given the opportunity to make the color decisions for a client's website, those decisions should be based on the fundamentals of color theory, combined with the knowledge of how your color scheme will impact future visitors when they arrive at the site.

Choosing a Color Scheme Based on the Fundamentals of Color Theory   Print layout requires you to incorporate the fundamentals of color theory to maximize the effectiveness of a printed page. Let's take a few minutes to review those fundamentals because they are also relevant to web page design. **FIGURE 1-6** illustrates the essential components of color theory.

Just as color schemes that are composed of related colors can be effective in print design, they are also effective in web design. Those schemes are monochromatic colors, complementary colors, warm colors, cool colors, and analogous colors.

- **monochromatic colors:** A monochromatic color scheme is a common choice in websites. With "mono" referring to one, it is the combined use of one color with colors created by adding varying amounts of black and white to the original color for contrast.
- **complementary colors:** There are three main sets of complementary colors, and each incorporates a primary color with the corresponding secondary made from the remaining two primary colors. When placed next to each other, the complementary colors will appear brighter, which can be very effective for accents or used to draw attention to particular critical areas in web pages. A great example of the use of complementary colors in a website is shown in **FIGURE 1-7**. This web page's main color is

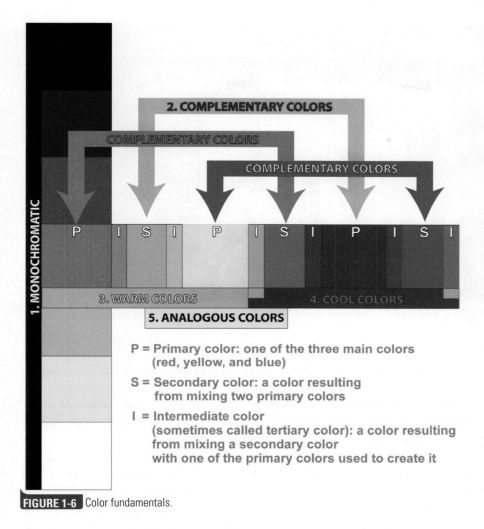

P = Primary color: one of the three main colors
    (red, yellow, and blue)

S = Secondary color: a color resulting
    from mixing two primary colors

I = Intermediate color
    (sometimes called tertiary color): a color resulting
    from mixing a secondary color
    with one of the primary colors used to create it

FIGURE 1-6 Color fundamentals.

blue because its theme is space exploration. However, it also incorporates orange, the complement of blue, applied behind its headline area and in some of the site's navigation. Used together, especially in the headline area, the brilliance and impact of both colors are maximized, drawing the visitor immediately to the name of the Discovery Center.

- **warm colors:** The colors included in this scheme are easy to remember by associating them with fire; they are red, red–orange, orange, yellow–orange, and yellow, but can also include yellow–green and red–violet because those particular intermediate colors border them on each side, respectively.

- **cool colors:** These colors are easy to remember by associating them with water; they are blue–violet, violet, blue, blue–green, and green, but can

FIGURE 1-7   McAuliffe-Shepard Discovery Center home page. (Courtesy of the McAuliffe-Shepard Discovery Center, http://www.starhop.com.)

include yellow–green and red–violet because those particular intermediate colors border them on each side, respectively.

- **analogous colors:** An analogous color scheme is one that starts with any color and includes the three to five colors adjacent to it when referencing its position on a traditional color wheel.

Choosing a Color Scheme Based on the Psychological Influence of Color   Color influences how we feel and affects our decisions. Faber Birren (1900–1988) spent his life studying and implementing what is referred to as the *psychology of color*. His work was founded on research at that time, which documented a correlation between blood pressure and color: notably, red and the warm colors associated with it increase blood pressure and blue, with its accompanying cool colors, decrease it.[1]

Since that time, the individual emotional impact of each color has been more specifically identified. A general overview of the implications of the main colors is shown in **FIGURE 1-8**.

All of the accompanying photographs in Figure 1-8 illustrate either the environmental influences that helped define the current color associations or the application of some of those associations to our daily lives:

- the excitement of red cars
- the romantic implications of red roses
- the warmth of a fireplace

RED: an action-packed, exhilarating, affluent, erotic, loving, and warm color

ORANGE: between red and yellow, an exhilarating, upbeat, and warm color

YELLOW: a warm, welcoming, cordial, animated, radiant, and upbeat color

GREEN: a cool, tranquil, soothing, peaceful color associated with foliage and germination

BLUE: a cool refreshing color that is relaxing and soothing, yet also steadfast and reliable

PURPLE: a cool, passionate, luxurious, regal, and first-class color

BROWN: a genuine, trustworthy, dependable color related to soil and rural terrain

FIGURE 1-8 The influence of color.

- the dawning of a new day
- the welcoming, upbeat aura of yellow flowers
- the shades of green and the peacefulness of nature and its foliage
- the cool, refreshing characteristics of water
- the earth tones of sand and the solidness of rocks

In addition to the basic color wheel, the psychological associations of the colors black, gray, and white can be used to influence both print and web viewers.[2] **FIGURE 1-9** lists some of the more common associations.

BLACK: opulent, dignified, chic, respected, polished, fine, convincing	**GRAY:** authoritative, accomplished, constant, stable, dependable, refined	**WHITE:** flawless, fresh, wholesome, spacious, virgin, lucid, plain, straightforward

FIGURE 1-9 Psychological associations of black, gray, and white.

Let's take a look at a few sites and their intentional implementation of the influential quality of color into their color schemes.

Red is an action-packed, exhilarating color that is often applied to the automotive industry. The home page for Ferrari of Houston, shown in **FIGURE 1-10**, focuses on the power of this color in its headline, chosen images, and accent text.

Sandwiched between the action-packed color of red and the welcoming color of yellow on the color wheel, orange is a blend of both colors. Tyler Walker used this to his advantage when designing his website's home page, shown in **FIGURE 1-11**. The site greets the visitor with a fun, inviting, upbeat, and ambitious psychological implication of color that subliminally states: "I can and will create whatever you need!"

Let's take a look at an effective application of the color blue by Advanced Eyecare of Manhattan Beach in **FIGURE 1-12**. The power of blue helps establish a relaxing,

FIGURE 1-10 Ferrari of Houston home page. (Courtesy of Ferrari of Houston, http://www.ferrariofhouston.com.)

FIGURE 1-11 Graphic Geek home page. (Courtesy of Tyler Walker, student, Grantham, NH.)

soothing, initial street appeal that also implies that the company is reliable and steadfast in its commitment to its patients.

Combining the Psychological Influence of Colors   Can you combine the psychological influence of multiple colors to your advantage? The answer to that question is *yes*. In **FIGURE 1-13**, Speer's Fine Jewelry combines the powerful implications of four colors in its home page design.

1. The color black sets a tone of style, fashion, and opulence.
2. The color red evokes love.
3. The color purple sets a tone of regality and class.
4. The color brown suggests that the company is a dependable, trustworthy jeweler.

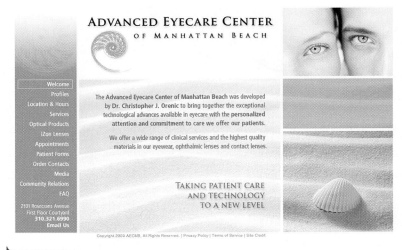

FIGURE 1-12 Advanced Eyecare Center of Manhattan Beach home page. (Courtesy of Advanced Eyecare Center of Manhattan Beach, http://advancedeyecarecenter.net. Website design by Summa Marketing, http://summamarketing.com.)

As these examples have shown, harnessing the power of color and its subliminal influence on the viewer can significantly enhance the critical first impression of a site. However, once again, you must know your audience and design accordingly for it. The color associations discussed in this text are based on cultural data for the Western world. If you are designing with an international audience in mind, research the associations of the colors you want to use with all your future audiences before

FIGURE 1-13 Speer's Fine Jewelry home page. (Courtesy of Speer's Fine Jewelry, http://www.speersfinejewelry.com.)

making a final decision to ensure that the color(s) you choose will positively, not negatively, influence the *majority* of your visitors.

Combining Color Theory with the Psychological Influence of Color The choice of a website's color scheme, such as monochromatic, warm, cool, etc., often begins with a decision to apply the psychology of color to the site design. We have seen that cool colors are calming colors, and that warm colors can be exciting. By having an understanding of both color theory and color psychology, you will be able to decide what color(s) you will use to create your desired emotional impact, and then incorporate those colors into your design using an effective color scheme.

What We Have Learned

Maintaining an idea book should become an ongoing process: by training your eye to see unique treatments of design elements, you are able to push your own creativity to new heights. Whether you need to use web safe, web smart, or simply web equivalent colors is relative to your audience, which you must become familiar with before beginning to design a website. Lastly, we learned that, in addition to considering the fundamentals of color theory when making your decisions, another critical consideration is the effect your color choices will have, consciously and unconsciously, on your visitors, and how to tailor your site accordingly.

Reinforcing Your Knowledge

Project 1

Search the Web for samples of the following items to add to your idea book:
- Find five web pages with attractive background designs that enhance the overall appearance of the page.
- Find 10 sites with unique artistic features. Circle the effect.
- Find five sites that have applied the psychology of color effectively to enhance their street appeal.
- Find five additional sites that have employed any of the following color schemes: monochromatic, warm, cool, analogous, or complementary. Identify which color scheme was used in each of your samples.

Project 2

Create three website color schemes based on the fundamentals of color theory. When creating your layouts, create an RGB document in Photoshop that is 750 × 200 pixels, with blocks of color on individual layers. You will learn to always think in pixels throughout this text, for its application to the Web.

- Create a monochromatic color scheme for a law firm using only a web safe color.
- Create a complementary color scheme for a pizza shop using web smart colors.
- Create an analogous color scheme for a bank using web equivalent colors.

Project 3

Define a color scheme that combines the fundamentals of color theory with the psychological influence of color using web safe colors only:

- Using a fictitious financial investment company named StableRock-Investments.com, create an RGB document in Photoshop that is 750 × 200 pixels, with blocks of colors on individual layers.
- Create a variety of colored shapes incorporating your choice of a monochromatic, warm, cool, complementary, or analogous color scheme, with that scheme specifically composed of colors known to psychologically influence viewers based on the type of business.

Project 4

Following the same procedure used in Project 3 to complete the layouts in Photoshop, create web safe color schemes for each of the three following additional fictitious companies. Create one using a monochromatic color scheme, one using an analogous color scheme, and one using warm, cool, or complementary colors. In each case, also consider the psychological impact of the colors you choose for your layouts.

- DistinctionRestaurant.com (a restaurant specializing in fine dining)
- MumazYumaz.com (pastries, candies, and whatever might be homemade and yummy!)
- Cuddluvs.com (a baby product website)

1.6 Building Your Own Website

This is the first of 16 chapters that will guide you through the complete construction process of your own personal site. Each of these exercises is designed to help you tailor the information presented in the chapter to fit your own website design needs. Let's start building!

1. Study several existing sites with similar product or service needs that your site will encompass. Note each one's color scheme, and pay special attention to the similarities and differences in how each one presents the same information or product. Be particularly cognizant of specific aspects of the sites that you liked and didn't like, detailing what it was that appealed to you or detracted from its appeal.

2. Now, determine the emotional impact you want to create for your visitors upon their arrival at your site, and choose a color scheme that will relay your message effectively.

3. Create an RGB document in Photoshop that is 750×200 pixels. This will eventually become the headline of your website. For now, it will be your drawing board. Fill the background with one of the colors you have chosen.

4. Add shapes and colors or values on additional layers, organizing the general layout that your headline will have for its name, logo, etc., and then name it scheme_1. Should you use web safe, web smart, or web equivalent colors? Have you studied your audience and their viewing needs?

Only you can decide which route to go, remembering that colors are identified as web safe because you can be assured they will be viewed as designed.

5. Repeat this process by creating two (or more) additional mock layouts using new color schemes or variations of your original. You are brain-storming as you are creating. Title and save these, respectively, as scheme_2, etc., or give them more descriptive names for identification purposes. You have started to create your own website!

1.7 Endnotes

1. Birren, Faber. 1961. *Color Psychology and Color Therapy: A Factual Study of the Influence of Color on Human Life.* Whitefish, MT: Kessinger Publishing.

2. Eiseman, Leatrice. 2006. *Color: Messages and Meanings, A Pantone Color Resource.* Gloucester, MA: Hand Books Press.

WEB SAFE FONTS
SAFE BUT NONVERBAL

John Doe   John Doe   John Doe   John Doe   John Doe
Verdana   Comic Sans MS   Trebuchet MS   Courier   Times New Roman

↓

VERBAL SAMPLES

JOHN DOE   *John Doe*   John Doe
Machine   Edwa

FIVE V

John Doe   **John Doe**
Ex Ponto Regular   Script MT Bold

FIN

Jo

Your Complete Source for
Fish Products & Information
HOME | PRODUCTS

**Welcome to Fishluvrz...
aquarium needs!
Supplies? WE'VE GOT
Questions? WE'VE GOT**

Lorem ipsum dolor sit amet, consetetur sadi
nonumy eirmod tempor invidunt ut labore et

Standard font: Arial 16   Select...

1. FONT SIZE SET TO PIXELS
USER DEFAULT SETTING 16

Your Complete Source for
Fish Products & Information
HOME | PRODUCTS

**Welcome to Fishluvrz...
aquarium needs!
Supplies? WE'VE GOT
Questions? WE'VE GOT**

Lorem ipsum dolor sit amet, consetetur s
diam nonumy eirmod tempor invidunt ut

Standard font: Arial 16   Select...

2. FONT SIZE SET TO EMS
USER DEFAULT SETTING 16

Your Complete Source for
Fish Products & Information
HOME | PRODUCTS

**Welcome to Fishluvrz...
aquarium needs!
Supplies? WE'VE GOT
Questions? WE'VE GOT**

Lorem ipsum dolor sit amet, consetetur sadi
nonumy eirmod tempor invidunt ut labore et

Standard font: Arial 24   Select...

3. FONT SIZE SET TO PIXELS
USER DEFAULT SETTING 24

Your Complete Source for
Fish Products & Information
HOME | PRODUCTS

**Welcome to Fish
for all your fish
Supplies? WE'V
Questions? WE**

Standard font: Arial 24   Select...

4. FONT SIZE SET TO EMS
USER DEFAULT SETTING 24

Custom font looks great

This is what the visitor may see instead

The NH Lupine
Restaurant
The Ultimate Dining Experience
HOME   MENU   LOCATION   RESERVATIONS
Welcome to the finest restaurant in New Hampshire!

Typography for the Web vs. the Printed Page

2

In This Chapter

- Typographical terminology for print vs. the Web
- Maximize the readability of type on the Web
- Understand web safe fonts and how to work around their limitations
- Learn to employ the emotional influence of type in your sites
- Combine the influential qualities of both color and type in web design

A graphic artist enters web design with a toolbox of typography rules. The problem is that many of those rules don't apply here! In this chapter we will compare and contrast the rules and sort out the essentials needed for effective web design. The second half of the chapter will teach you how to design and create type that speaks to the viewer by transcending the limitations of web safe fonts, allowing you to design the heading you demand for the impact you need to create on your visitors.

2.1   A Graphic Designer's Introduction to the Differences Between Typography for the Printed Page vs. Type for the Web

One of the hardest adjustments a graphic artist must make when moving from traditional print layout to web layout is to learn how to adapt his/her typographical experience to the unique characteristics and challenges of web typography. This chapter's goals are to provide a general overview of typographical terminology and to clarify, at the early stages of the design process, the specific similarities and differences that exist when incorporating type into print vs. the Web, in order to maximize your effectiveness when designing for the Web.

2.2   Comparing and Contrasting Typographical Terminology for Print vs. the Web

Let's begin by discussing the typographical features that are relative to both mediums, and how the names and methods of applying them compare.

▪ 2.2.1 Type Properties

One of the major typographical differences between print design and Web design is also one of the most fundamental elements of typography: type size.

Size   In print, type is measured in points, with one point equaling 1/72 of an inch. Typically, body text, which is the name given to the main content section of the text, is set at 12 points in print design. When designing for the Web, Dreamweaver offers multiple options for type measurement for the Web, most commonly pixel and em, as shown in **FIGURE 2-1**.

Graphic designers making the transition from print to the Web often choose points for their type for the Web, understandably as that is their familiar unit of measurement. Although points is an option for web type, the pixel and em options are the most common units of measure for web design, and there is tremendous debate about which option is better.

Pixel is a font measurement based on screen pixels. For graphic designers familiar with points, 12 points equals 16 pixels. Pixel units are easy to understand, and allow the designer complete control in web layout.

Understanding the Em   The em in print typography originally derived its name from the size of the letter *M* and is a relative measurement based on the type's size. The em in web typography is a font measurement relative to the default font size of the current browser. For example, if the browser font size is set to 12 points (16 pixels), 1 em will be equal to 12 points: 12 points = 16 pixels = 1 em. The em

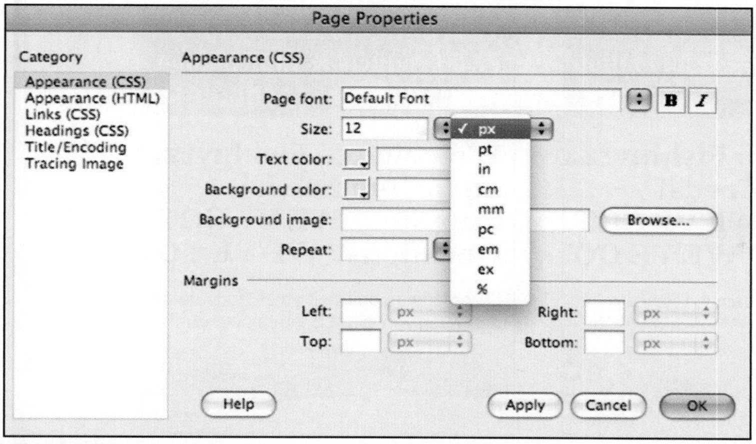

FIGURE 2-1 Units used to measure type size in Dreamweaver.

measurement unit differs from the pixel unit in that it is scalable: if 1 em is equal to 12 points, 3 em will be equal to 36 points, or three times the current font size, based on the user's default browser size. If a user changes his/her browser default font settings, and the fonts in the web page were set in the em type unit, the text will automatically adjust/scale proportionately. In **FIGURE 2-2**, the same page is shown in a browser with the web page created first in pixel units and then in em units.

Note the differences among the settings:

1. In this sample, the type was created in pixels, with the browser default setting at 16.

2. In this sample, the type was created using the em and appears almost identical to the pixel sample when the browser setting is 16.

3. Here, the browser default has been changed to 24. However, because this sample was created in pixels, the type size is identical in appearance to that of the type in sample one: the browser default had no effect on the web page's type.

4. In this final sample, because the type was created using the em measurement, it has scaled proportionately to the browser setting. Notice that the images, created in pixels, have not scaled up with it. Can images also be created in ems? Because images are pixel based, conversion is possible, but care must be taken to retain the quality of the original image as they are resized. Using ems for the conversion of graphics is beyond the scope of this book.

There is much debate about whether to use pixel or em units to set the type size when creating for the Web. As an introduction to web design, which is a pixel-based medium, this text will work exclusively in pixel units when determining font size. It is easier to understand, and the most predictable for the beginning web designer.

1. **FONT SIZE SET TO PIXELS**
   USER DEFAULT SETTING 16

2. **FONT SIZE SET TO EMS**
   USER DEFAULT SETTING 16

3. **FONT SIZE SET TO PIXELS**
   USER DEFAULT SETTING 24

4. **FONT SIZE SET TO EMS**
   USER DEFAULT SETTING 24

FIGURE 2-2 Font sizes in pixels vs. ems.

Alignment   Text *alignment* describes how type flows on a page or within a column of a page. This definition, as it is stated, applies equally to both print design and web design. There are four types of text alignment available for both design mediums: left, right, center, and justified. It is important to note that this chapter addresses text alignment only: visual alignment, which encompasses the relationship of both text and graphic elements on a page, will be explored in Chapter 3.

- **left alignment:** In this type of alignment, text is flush on the left and staggers on the right. This is the default alignment in both mediums, following the rule that when people are reading, they scan left to right "by default." Because of this, coupled with the urgency of the "click-and-go" nature of visitor web searches, most websites have this type of alignment incorporated into both the navigation and body content areas of their pages.

- **center alignment:** In this type of alignment, text staggers equally on both its left and right sides as it flows down the page or column. In print layout, it is used more for some types of print documents, such as wedding invitations, than for newsletters or other types of print documents. In web design, although left alignment is the predominant layout used, center alignment is also used for the body content area of the page as well as the various navigational schemes of the page. One unique twist to this, however, is that many web pages will use center alignment for the footer navigation at the bottom of the page, even if the body content and the rest of the page's navigational schemes are set to a different type of alignment.

- **right alignment:** In this type of alignment, text is flush on the right and staggers on the left. Although used less commonly than left alignment in both print and web layouts, it can be very effective when seeking a unique solution to the problem. When visiting a web page that uses a right-aligned structure, you may not even know what it was that caught your eye as you came to the page, but the subliminal change is what may have attracted you. In Chapter 1, the web page in Figure 1-12 employed the power of color in its website theme of blue. If you study this company's home page closer, you will see that it also incorporates right alignment in its navigation and body text. As you continue to expand your knowledge of web design, you will notice that many times more than one design tool has been applied to a website to build the overall professional and inviting initial street appeal.

- **justified alignment:** This type of alignment is flush on both sides of the page or column, creating clear visual delineations between columns of text. When applied to print, justified alignment is used most commonly in newspapers and magazines. Although some page layout programs include an option to *force justify*, which spreads the last line of text across the entire page or column no matter how few words it contains, in most instances where text is justified, all lines of the text will have the justify property applied to them, with the exception of the last line, which is usually left aligned if it does not fill the column width completely. While not commonly used in web design, justify is also an available option for web text. However, when using justified type, for either print or web, caution is required when applying it to narrow columns of text: columns with less than eight to ten words per line. **FIGURE 2-3** exemplifies how "airy," awkward, and most importantly from a visitor's perspective, more difficult to read the justified web sample appears vs. the common standard left-aligned column.

Vertical Spacing/Leading   It is possible to adjust the vertical spacing of lines of type in both print and web layout. In print, leading is defined as the distance between lines of type in a paragraph. Although auto leading will set the distance based

We're in your Neighborhood!	**We're in your Neighborhood!**
Lorem ipsum dolor sit amet, consetetur sadipscing elitr, sed diam nonumy eirmod tempor invidunt ut labore et dolore magna aliquyam erat, sed diam voluptua. At vero eos et accusam et justo duo dolores et ea rebum. Stet clita kasd gubergren, no sea takimata sanctus est Lorem ipsum dolor sit amet. Lorem ipsum dolor sit amet, consetetur sadipscing elitr, sed diam nonumy eirmod tempor invidunt ut labore et dolore magna aliquyam erat, sed diam voluptua. At vero eos et accusam et justo duo dolores et ea rebum. Stet clita kasd gubergren, no sea takimata sanctus est Lorem ipsum dolor sit amet.	Lorem ipsum dolor sit amet, consetetur sadipscing elitr, sed diam nonumy eirmod tempor invidunt ut labore et dolore magna aliquyam erat, sed diam voluptua. At vero eos et accusam et justo duo dolores et ea rebum. Stet clita kasd gubergren, no sea takimata sanctus est Lorem ipsum dolor sit amet. Lorem ipsum dolor sit amet, consetetur sadipscing elitr, sed diam nonumy eirmod tempor invidunt ut labore et dolore magna aliquyam erat, sed diam voluptua. At vero eos et accusam et justo duo dolores et ea rebum. Stet clita kasd gubergren, no sea takimata sanctus est Lorem ipsum dolor sit amet.
LEFT ALIGNMENT	**JUSTIFIED ALIGNMENT**

FIGURE 2-3   Type alignment for the Web.

on 120 percent of the font size used, it is common for professional designers to adjust the leading up or down to create more effective readability of the text depending on its size and application. In web design, the corresponding term for adjusting the distance between lines of type is *line-height*.

Horizontal Spacing/Tracking   Although *kerning*, the distance between a pair of letters, is only available for print design, the space between all letters of a word or all words in a paragraph can be adjusted in both print and web layouts.

In print, space between characters can be changed for all letters of a selected word, or all letters and words of a selected paragraph by adjusting the tracking. *Tracking* is the process of uniformly increasing or decreasing the space between all the letters of a selection of text: increase the tracking value to spread the letters out or decrease it to tighten them. In web design, the same two effects can be created, increasing the space between letters of a word and increasing the space between the words of a paragraph; however, they are two separate type settings. In web design, *letter-spacing* is the term for adjusting the distance between each letter of selected words, and *word-spacing* is the term for adjusting the space between the words.

Indenting Text   First line indents can be created for paragraph text in web text as well as print text, including the ability to specifically assign an indent distance for the text, as well as the ability to indent an entire paragraph of text. When applying an indent to an entire paragraph in web design, it can be added with preset increments of indentation referred to as *block quotes*, or by entering a specific distance defined as text box *margins*.

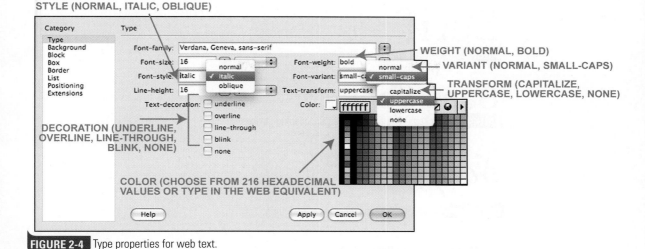

FIGURE 2-4 Type properties for web text.

Identifying Additional Print Type Properties that Can Be Set for Web Text
FIGURE 2-4 details more print page properties that can be set in web page design, their web category names, and their options. We will learn how to apply all of the type properties defined in Figure 2-4, as well as the rest of the type properties defined in this chapter, by using the text formatting features of Dreamweaver later in this book.

Paragraphs   A *paragraph* is a section of text beginning with a new line. When typing in print or web layout, both hard and soft returns can be applied to paragraphs, and work the same in each medium. When a new paragraph is needed, pressing the Enter/Return key, called a *hard return*, will end the current paragraph and begin a new one. When the Shift key is held down while pressing the Enter/Return key, a soft return is created, referred to in web design as a *line break*. The text following this type of return will be forced to a new line; however, the text will remain part of the previous paragraph.

2.2.2 Typeface Categories

Modern print layout allows the designer to be a "kid in a candy store" in the world of available typefaces. The choices have become so vast that general categories have been created to help delineate one basic letter design from another, with the two largest and most common categories being serif and sans serif.

A *serif* typeface, shown in **FIGURE 2-5**, has curly ends on each letter, often referred to as *finishing strokes*.

A *sans serif* typeface, shown in **FIGURE 2-6**, has no finishing strokes on the ends of the letter forms.

Whether the type is fancy or more casual, if it simulates handwriting, it is categorized as a *script* typeface, shown in **FIGURE 2-7**.

Serif

FIGURE 2-5   A serif typeface with a finishing stroke highlighted.

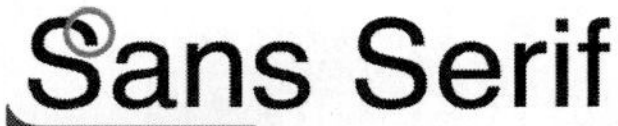

Sans Serif

FIGURE 2-6   A sans serif typeface has no finishing strokes.

Script

FIGURE 2-7   A script typeface simulates handwriting.

DECORATIVE

FIGURE 2-8   Decorative typefaces are used for headlines not for body text.

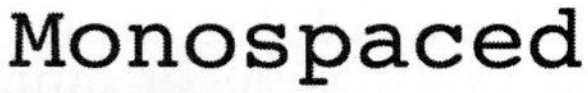

Monospaced

FIGURE 2-9   Monospaced typefaces display all letters using a single width.

FIGURE 2-10   Symbol typefaces create shapes instead of letters.

Decorative typefaces, shown in **FIGURE 2-8**, also referred to as *novelty* or *ornamental* typefaces, are used for headlines or other display purposes. They are not meant for body type because of readability.

Monospaced typefaces, shown in **FIGURE 2-9**, are also called *fixed-width* typefaces. They are "mono" meaning "single-width" letter forms in which each letter, no matter which letter of the alphabet it is, will occupy the same width when placed on a page: this means *i* and *m* use the same character width, as was the case in the old "typewriter" days.

Symbol typefaces, shown in **FIGURE 2-10**, are just as the name implies. They are not letters at all, but a variety of shapes, with each one corresponding to a specific key or combination of keys on the keyboard.

2.2.3 Readability of Type

In print and web layout, standard practice is to incorporate only two to three different fonts in a design: one for the heading, one for the body text, and sometimes a third one for special effects. When factoring the readability of type into this aspect of the design process, differences exist in the readability of body content type in print pages vs. web pages, and alterations are required to accommodate those differences.

Serif Font
Times New Roman: 10pt

Lorem ipsum dolor sit amet,
consectetuer adipiscing elit, sed diam
nonummy nibh euismod tincidunt ut
laoreet dolore magna aliquam erat
volutpat. Ut wisi enim ad minim
veniam, quis nostrud exerci tation
ullamcorper suscipit lobortis nisl ut
aliquip ex ea commodo consequat.

Sans Serif Font
Verdana: 9pt

Lorem ipsum dolor sit amet,
consectetuer adipiscing elit, sed diam
nonummy nibh euismod tincidunt ut
laoreet dolore magna aliquam erat
volutpat. Ut wisi enim ad minim
veniam, quis nostrud exerci tation
ullamcorper suscipit lobortis nisl ut
aliquip ex ea commodo consequat.

FIGURE 2-11 Font readability.

Serif vs. Sans Serif: Choosing Heading vs. Body Typefaces   In print design, it is typical to have headings in a sans serif font and body type in a serif font. As the Web has evolved, however, more and more sites have used sans serif fonts for body type to address the inherent problem of jagged edges created when small type is viewed on a monitor. The finishing strokes on serif fonts, which are said to make reading body text easier in print by helping the eye "flow" across the text, can, instead, add to the difficulty of reading small jagged type on the Web. Therefore, to add contrast in type design for the Web, if a sans serif font is used for the body type, it is common to apply a serif type to the headings to create the emphasis and delineation they require. Take a short break and peek at a few sites on the Web, focusing on fonts in your searches. The results may surprise you!

Let's examine two paragraphs of body type, thinking about the Web and readability. **FIGURE 2-11** displays one paragraph in a serif font and one paragraph in a sans serif font. To help emphasize the readability difference, the sans serif font on the right has even been set at a font size slightly smaller that the serif font on the left, yet is still more readable.

Perhaps, as a graphic designer with a print typography background, when you have surfed and studied sites on the Web in the past, you may have wondered why body text was often in a sans serif font, while headlines and subheads were in a serif font. Now you know why!

Sentence Case vs. Uppercase   Using uppercase, also referred to as *all caps*, is reserved for headlines, titles, and logos. This principle applies equally to print and web type. Although some fonts are worse than others, body text in all caps can be more difficult to read than type written in sentence case, which uses a capital letter for the first word of a sentence, plus any word(s) within that sentence that need to be capitalized such as a person's name, with the remaining words of the sentence in lowercase. The last thing you want as a web designer is for someone to arrive

Sans Serif Font: Arial 12 pt Sentence case

This sentence case type is set to 12 pt type with 14.4 pt leading.

Sans Serif Font: Arial 12 pt Uppercase

THIS UPPERCASE TYPE IS SET TO 12 PT TYPE WITH 14.4 PT LEADING.

FIGURE 2-12   Using sentence case vs. uppercase text.

at your site and have difficulty reading your information. In a click-and-go world, he/she may literally click and go … elsewhere! **FIGURE 2-12** illustrates this problem.

As you may have also noticed in this sample, another problem with using all caps is that they take more room on a page. As it relates to web design, that could lead to unnecessary scrolling.

Type Color vs. Background Color   Assuring that ample contrast exists between the type color and the background it is displayed on is of equal concern for both print and the Web. At its most basic level, black type placed on a white background creates the highest contrast, maximizing its readability. But do you want just black and white? What about company logo colors? Maybe you want to try complementary colors? The text shown in **FIGURE 2-13** clearly lacks enough contrast to be readable and effective in print or on the Web.

Although color contrast affects how eye-catching and readable your print pages and web pages look, there is more to color choice than its aesthetic quality. An additional important aspect of this particular readability issue, depending on your audience, is one that is unique to the Web: accessibility of your site for visitors with difficulty seeing text or colors. There are specific guidelines to follow if you want to ensure that your colors comply with the World Wide Web Consortium (W3C) standards (http://www.w3.org). These color standards are not mandatory, but should be considered if you know that your audience will be comprised of a significant number of visitors who would benefit from compliance with these standards. To help you meet these standards, several interactive websites can assist you in determining if your type vs. background color complies with these standards. These sites allow you to type in your hexadecimal choices (for both your type and its background), display your chosen text color against the background color, and identify the compliance or noncompliance of the color combination with accessibility standards.

This is a sample of type withuot enough contrast to be easily read, either as regular type or **BOLD type.**

FIGURE 2-13   Color contrast affects readability.

Type "Web colors for accessibility" into a web search engine to locate websites that offer this feature. You can experiment with a variety of companies and interactive formats to find one that you like the best.

2.2.4 Type Speaks to the Reader: The Influential Quality of Type

How does type "speak" to you? You may not even realize that you are influenced by it daily. Every font, based on its unique characteristics, such as width, special shape, angle, and design of its finishing strokes if it has them, evokes a different feeling, emotional response, mood, or tone (it speaks to you!) as you read it. In **FIGURE 2-14** the first row displays the word in various web safe fonts (fonts designated as safe to use because they are the ones most likely to be available on all computers: these fonts are safe, but nonverbal). However, as you read the name "John Doe" to yourself while you move your eyes across the second row, you may find yourself using different intonations as you read a powerful authoritative font like Machine, an elegant formal font such as Edwardian Script, or a more casual, whimsical font like Teenage Girl 2. So what do you use? Because you have just "heard" three distinctly different fonts, it will depend on what type of business the site is being designed for, and how you want to influence your visitors by the way your font speaks to them. Perhaps you are designing a website for a client's posh Victorian bed-and-breakfast. After beginning with three very different fonts, as shown in the Verbal Samples row, you decide that John Doe, your client's bed-and-breakfast, lends itself best to a script font. You copy and paste the name a few times, and choose a variety of formalities of script fonts until the right font speaks to you. In Figure 2-14, Zapfino spoke to me. Which one most effectively speaks of luxury to you?

Type has a powerful, influential quality that can set a mood, evoke an emotion, and, most importantly for web design, help to establish a company identity. Choosing the right font is an essential ingredient of effective web design and how your site will speak to your visitors. Using this method to help you choose your font selection when designing a print or web layout is a great way to find the right influential font for a company: a critical element of success in both design mediums. Type speaks to the reader. Can you hear it now?

2.2.5 Harnessing the Influence of Type for the Web: Understanding the Problem

Now that you understand the impact and influence type can have, the next step is to understand its limitations when applied to web design. Although there are as many fonts for print design as you have installed on your computer, caution must be used when choosing fonts in web design. The web safe list was generated because it designates the fonts identified as universally supported by computers and browsers. As both computers and browsers have evolved, the safe list has grown, but still remains relatively limited. Because we will be building web pages exclusively using Dreamweaver, **FIGURE 2-15** details the default font list in collections preselected for you in Dreamweaver CS4 and CS5.

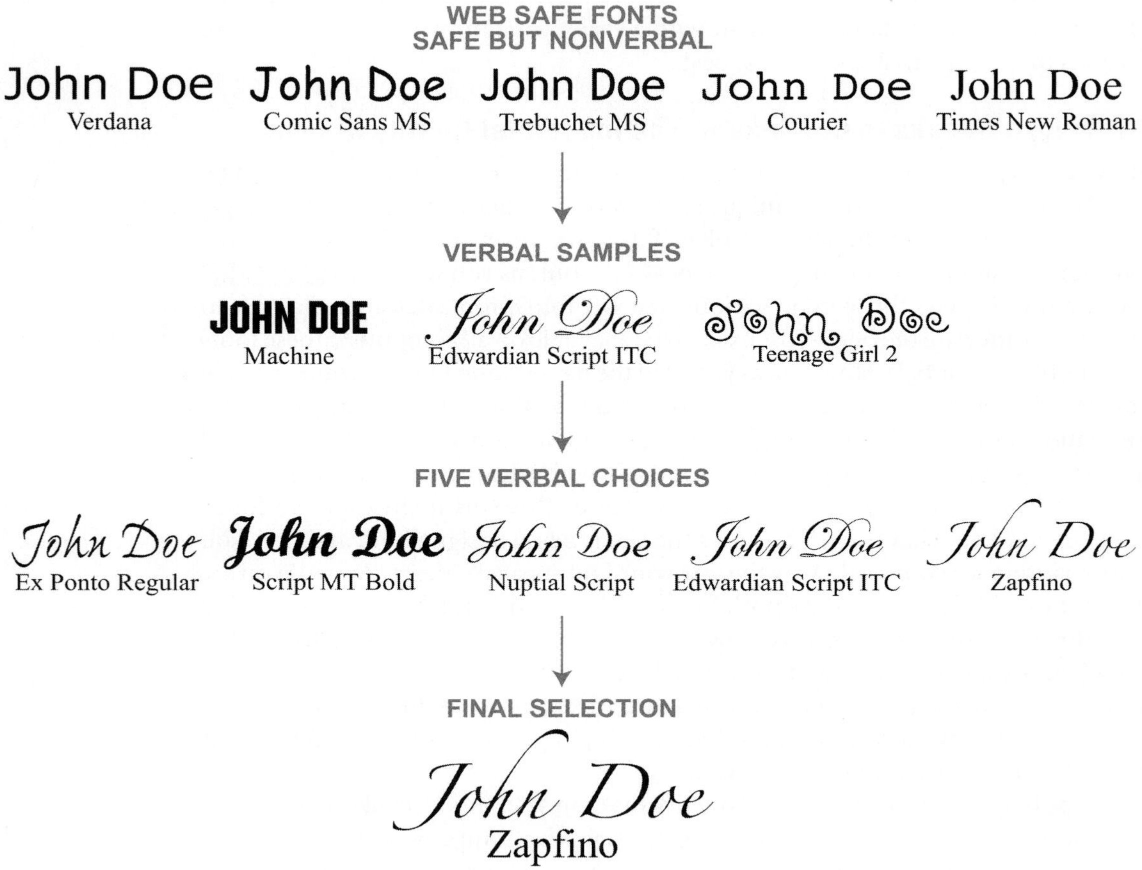

WEB SAFE FONTS
SAFE BUT NONVERBAL
John Doe
Verdana
John Doe
Comic Sans MS
John Doe
Trebuchet MS
John Doe
Courier
John Doe
Times New Roman
VERBAL SAMPLES
JOHN DOE
Machine
John Doe
Edwardian Script ITC
John Doe
Teenage Girl 2
FIVE VERBAL CHOICES
John Doe
Ex Ponto Regular
John Doe
Script MT Bold
John Doe
Nuptial Script
John Doe
Edwardian Script ITC
John Doe
Zapfino
FINAL SELECTION
John Doe
Zapfino

FIGURE 2-14 Select a typeface that speaks to your reader.

Page Properties
Category
Appearance (CSS)
Appearance (HTML)
Links (CSS)
Headings (CSS)
Title/Encoding
Tracing Image
Appearance (CSS)
Page font:
Default Font
Size:
px
Text color:
Background color:
Background image:
Repeat:
Margins
Left:
px
Right:
Top:
px
Bottom:
Help
Apply
✓ Default Font
Verdana, Geneva, sans-serif
Georgia, Times New Roman, Times, serif
Courier New, Courier, monospace
Arial, Helvetica, sans-serif
Tahoma, Geneva, sans-serif
Trebuchet MS, Arial, Helvetica, sans-serif
Arial Black, Gadget, sans-serif
Times New Roman, Times, serif
Palatino Linotype, Book Antiqua, Palatino, serif
Lucida Sans Unicode, Lucida Grande, sans-serif
MS Serif, New York, serif
Lucida Console, Monaco, monospace
Comic Sans MS, cursive
Edit Font List...

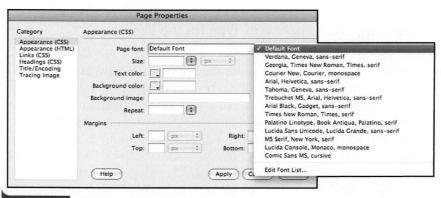

FIGURE 2-15 Default font choices in Dreamweaver.

The font collections are combinations that determine how the user's browser will display the particular text that has a font applied to it. The hierarchy determines how that font will be chosen, based on the fonts available on the user's computer. For example, if the "Arial, Helvetica, sans-serif" collection option is chosen, the first choice that will be used to display the text will be the Arial font. If the user's computer does not have the Arial font installed, then the browser will look for Helvetica, and lastly its installed generic sans serif font.

For CS3 Users

If you are working in CS3, when using the Dreamweaver CS3 corresponding Page Properties dialog box you will see that the available font collection list is shorter. Through the Edit Font List option, you can add fonts to the list of font choices. However, it is recommended that you add only more web safe fonts to your options, and avoid the temptation to add your favorites instead. How to add them is detailed in the next section of this chapter.

2.2.6 Custom Fonts vs. Substitution

The last item on the font group list is the Edit Font List option. This option not only allows you to add fonts or collections of fonts to your web design options from those available on your system, it also allows you to create them as a collection, and set the hierarchy of their selection by the viewer's browser based on availability, just as the rest of the font collections have been created. However, *availability* is the heart of the problem: font availability on your computer vs. the font availability on your website visitor's computer. As a graphic designer, you are most likely familiar with the dreaded missing font/substitution issue when creating a print document. If the receiver does not have the font, substitution comes into play and, at the very least, usually massacres your perfect layout. This same nightmare can occur in web page design as well. In the first example, shown in **FIGURE 2-16**, the restaurant headline

FIGURE 2-16 Restaurant headline uses a safe installed font.

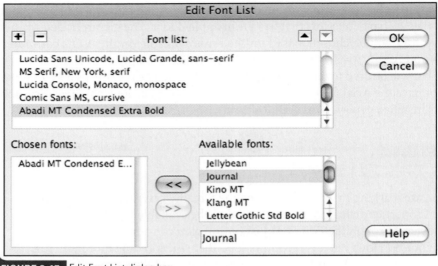

FIGURE 2-17 Edit Font List dialog box.

was created using a universal web safe font. Safe, it will display predictably in all browsers, but it's boring.

What kind of influence does this type have when you read it? Most graphic designers would be itching to add more emotional impact to the type in this headline, especially to help set the atmosphere for fine dining—if, in fact, this restaurant is supposed to be "the ultimate dining experience." The first thought is to use a more enticing font on your system through this option. After choosing the Edit Font List option from the drop-down menu, the dialog box shown in **FIGURE 2-17** appears, allowing you to choose a font from your computer's list of available fonts to add to the existing font collections available in Dreamweaver.

In this dialog box, if you select one of the font collections from the Font list section, when you choose a font from the Available fonts scrollable list of all the fonts installed on your computer on the right and click the corresponding arrow, it will be added to the font collection you chose from the Font list. Alternatively, you can create your own collection: the last option of the Font list section is Add fonts in list below, allowing you to click and choose the first font for your own collection (as shown with the font Abadi MT Condensed Extra Bold), with the second font you choose becoming the next option in the font collection hierarchy. Although this initially sounds like a great solution to the problem, it actually creates a new set of issues. To clearly understand how the look of your design can be affected by this process, **FIGURE 2-18** demonstrates how differently your design may end up displaying in a user's browser if that computer does not have your font installed on it, causing an automatic substitution of the browser's default font and size restrictions that are beyond the control of you, the designer.

Custom font looks great on your computer

This is what the visitor may see instead

FIGURE 2-18   Custom font might not display as intended.

2.2.7 The Artistic Alternative: Custom Headlines Created in Photoshop

With an understanding of the font dilemma, perhaps you are now wondering how some of the beautiful headlines were created in the web pages that you added to your idea book as you searched the Web. The easy, artistic, and predictable solution to this design issue is to create those headlines in Photoshop and bring them into your web page already made. The fonts will be converted to graphics so there will be no substitution issues. You will have the layout flexibility you were starving for, and the final professional look you wanted when you first designed the layout! In FIGURE 2-19, the same headline that we looked at using a default font, and then as a custom font with font substitution issues, was created in Photoshop and brought into the web page with the text built into the design of the headline. Because the type was already in place when it was imported into Dreamweaver, there were no

FIGURE 2-19   Special font headline created in Photoshop.

FIGURE 2-20 Graphic design headline created in Photoshop. (Courtesy of Christine Coll, student, Hooksett, NH.)

font substitution issues. Additional advantages of this method include the ability to easily arrange the font's placement and size more artistically as individual type layers in the original Photoshop layout, and the ease of incorporating multiple fonts into the design of the headline if desired.

The headline shown in **FIGURE 2-20** was created by student Christine Coll. By creating her title in Photoshop, she was not only able to use a font that speaks to her visitors, but was able to rotate her text to add to the impact of her design. Remember what we learned about the color brown? It says genuine, trustworthy, and dependable—a great color to promote her graphic design website!

Combining the Influence of Type with the Influence of Color

Earlier in this chapter, we noted that the Advanced Eyecare Center website incorporated the use of right alignment in addition to the influential use of color to create an effective home page. Carrying this concept further, let's examine two more sites that effectively combine the influence of type with the influence of color. The first one we will examine is the home page for Grace Limousine, shown in **FIGURE 2-21**. In this page, the power of violet and black create a feeling of royalty and sophistication that are combined with a font that speaks of elegance: together, they set the tone that a luxurious experience awaits you, as soon as you arrive at this site.

Let's examine one more website for now, the Good Mojo Dog Center, shown in **FIGURE 2-22**.

The emotional impact created by the use of yellow here is cheery and upbeat. The use of brown suggests the company is trustworthy and dependable. The font in the headline is whimsical and fun. Together they speak to the visitor, saying that this is a fun and safe place for his/her pet to visit.

Now that we have completed our first two chapters, as an artist, you may already never view the Web the same again. We have learned that multiple design elements combine together to establish a particular mood or tone as you enter a particular company's website.

FIGURE 2-21 Grace Limousine home page. (Courtesy of Grace Limousine, LLC, http://www.gracelimo.com.)

FIGURE 2-22 Good Mojo Dog Center home page. (Courtesy of Good Mojo Dog Center, http://goodmojodog center.com. Website design by Beechleaf Design, http://beechleafdesign.com.)

2.4 What We Have Learned

While there are many similarities between print typography and web typography, there are also many important differences. We have learned what they are and how to handle them. In learning about the powerful voice a font can have, we learned how you can still employ that voice by building the web page's headline in Photoshop, eliminating the restrictions of web safe fonts, and offering the flexibility you need. As we continued to expand our knowledge in web design, we learned to combine the design tools we have learned thus far: adding these newly learned type alternatives to web safe fonts, to the color theory, and the emotional impact of color we learned about in Chapter 1.

2.5 Reinforcing Your Knowledge

Project 1

Search the Web again, this time looking specifically at the company identification headline area of the web pages. Identify 20 that appeal to you, that you can tell were clearly created in a program such as Photoshop because of their unique font use, effects added to the font, layout of the font in the headline, or voice. Add these to your idea book. Although our focus here is headlines, now that you have learned that it is often a combination of design elements that make a site effective, note also the colors used in the pages containing the headlines that attract you, and how the font and color choices relate to the website's business. And remember: during this search, if you also discover any "cool" page effects along the way, because you learned to identify them in Chapter 1, add them to your idea book, too. Your idea book should be an ever-growing resource of all types of future web layout ideas!

Project 2

Using the fonts on your computer, create a blank page in Photoshop then find three fonts that you feel speak to each of the following business types. Type the name, then apply the font using the word for the category as the type you apply the font to, such as "Floral Shop," or come up with your own name such as "Burst of Sun Florist." Apply a color to the font based on your learning from Chapter 1. Tap into your creativity and make it fun!

- floral shop
- airlines
- sub shop
- hair salon
- commercial construction

Project 3

Using any three of the types of businesses listed in Project 2, choose the best font available for them, from the web safe font list provided here.

- Verdana
- Times New Roman
- Comic Sans MS

Project 4

Apply type to your mock headlines:

1. Open your StableRockInvestments.com project from Chapter 1. Add, reshape, or remove any of your existing layers as needed to design a mock headline for the company, and then create a type layer above all your layers.

2. Type the company name in a font with a voice you feel best expresses this site's service.

3. Choose a web safe color for the font appropriate to your color scheme defined in Chapter 1, considering the importance of contrast as learned in this chapter. Add a fictitious phone number, address, and slogan to this headline, using different complimenting fonts or sizes as needed.

4. Following these same steps, now use the color layouts you created for DistinctionRestaurant.com, MumazYumaz.com, and Cuddluvs.com to also apply verbal fonts and font colors to each of your layouts, converting each one to a mock headline that includes phone number, address, and applicable slogan.

 Be sure to keep all type and color shapes on separate layers and *never* flatten your Photoshop file because we will continue to work with these headlines, and you will want to keep the flexibility to rearrange, delete, etc. This is an important tip to remember for all web work created in Photoshop.

2.6 Building Your Own Website

1. Open your first color combination document created for your website in Chapter 1. Add your company name and slogan, if applicable, to the layout on separate layers above any color shape layers you may have. Add your URL or "samplenameofyourcompany.com" if you do not have it yet, because it is easier to build it in now if you want it to be an integral part of the headline than having to redesign the headline to add it later. Experiment with fonts on your computer until you find one that has the best voice for your company title. Remember that you can adjust text

sizes, use multiple fonts of your choice, and place and overlap the text any way you want because you are not bound by the restrictions of the Web!

2. Make color adjustments as needed to enhance contrast and readability of your company information.

3. Repeat this process with your other two color combinations from Chapter 1, each time choosing a different voice (font). Remember to be consistent with your original decision about using web safe, web smart, or web equivalent colors.

4. Mix and match, ask the advice of friends and colleagues, and then choose the best headline combination of colors, fonts, and overall effectiveness of your layout for emotional impact, voice, and overall professional appeal. Congratulations! You have a company identity headline for your website!

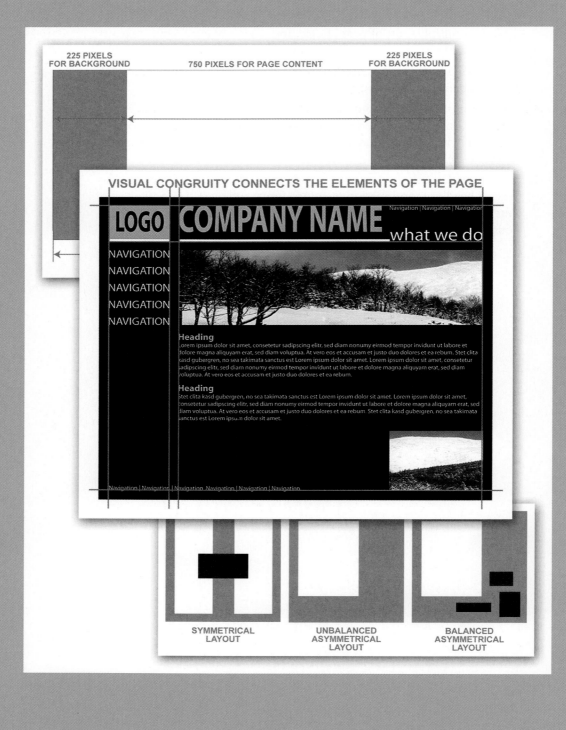

Designing the Layout of Your Website

3

In This Chapter

- Understand the principles of navigation
- Design to accommodate the limitations of your visitors' monitors
- Understand the design principles of the Web
- Brainstorm your first page designs through mock layouts

Effective navigation takes careful thought and planning. We will learn how to recognize it on the Web and how you can make your site's navigation effective. We will also explore layout options to accommodate monitor viewing area variations and learn about the unique design principles of the Web and how their inclusion or lack of them can impact your visitors. Lastly, we'll begin the process of putting our designs into action through visual brainstorming with mock layouts in Photoshop.

3.1 Keeping Visitors in Your Site: Designing an Effective Navigational Scheme

Learning to create your own effective navigational scheme begins by recognizing successful navigational schemes already on the Web and understanding what makes them effective.

3.1.1 Examining Navigational Layouts

In Chapter 1, you searched the Web for design ideas. In searching the Web you searched for unique graphic elements that had been incorporated into various types of sites. It was important at that time to not be concerned with what type of site it was, or how a graphic may have been created. Instead, you simply collected screen shots of sites that caught your eye to begin to build an idea book of resources, a process that should be an ongoing one, just as it most likely has always been in your print design career.

It is time now to study the Web from a different perspective: the navigational perspective. The word *navigation* is defined as the method of determining position, course, and distance traveled. When it comes to website navigation, it pertains specifically to creating a logical easy course for your visitors to follow within your site. After you have been given the topic to design a website for a client, or have decided to design a site for yourself, the next step is to do some "comparative traveling" so to speak. Search the Web again, looking this time for sites with the same or similar products or services as the website you will be creating. When doing so, the focus now is on the navigational layout of the sites. After analyzing what has been included on the home pages, search their links, noting how they interact with each other, and with the home pages. It will be helpful to review the sites using the following checklist, which has been divided into three general categories:

- **Home page information**

    What information is on the home page, the page designed with the critical street appeal, to engage the visitor to explore the site further?

    How in-depth is the information on the home page? Is the home page more of an introduction, with the critical information covered in more detail in specific linked pages?

- **Link pages**

    How many link pages are there?

    Does every link page clearly and logically return to the home page?

    Do you see an unnecessary number of link pages, that is, do some of them have information that would more logically be grouped together as one page?

How easy is it to find the specific information you are looking for, or feel is the most important information visitors will be searching for in the site?

How many clicks did it take to get there?

What types of links seem to be standard across all of the websites for similar products or services?

- **Navigational scheme(s) of the sites**

  Where is the main navigational scheme located on the page?

  Is there more than one navigational scheme on the page that will take you to the same links?

  Are the navigational scheme and the design of the navigation consistent on each page of the site?

  Is the site easy to navigate?

Navigational Guidelines   After learning about the content requirements of home pages vs. link pages, we will explore how current trends in web design address the unique navigational demands of these two types of pages.

Home Page Information   When studying the content presented on home pages, with the critical goal of getting your visitor engaged to stay within your site, there are no set rules for the amount of content that is included here. There is a wide range of depth presented on home pages, even those designed for the same type of product or service. So what should you do? You will be able to answer this question after you have determined all of the content you want or need to include in your site and have arranged it according to a logical web of link pages.

Link Pages   After a visitor has arrived at your site, the next goal is to keep him/ her in your site. Link pages should be logically woven together with the ability to consistently return to the home/index page. Link pages should also always contain effectual content. It is important not to irritate a visitor by sending him/her to a use-less, unnecessary page: it may become the deciding factor that will drive your visitor on to another site. Conversely, be sure not to have a variety of topics included on the same link page: clearly separate content into individual pages, allowing the visi-tor to go directly to the specific information he/she is searching for. In addition to *not* filling a site with unnecessary link pages to try to give the website more size and credibility, or forcing a visitor to scroll through unrelated information on a single page to find the content he/she wants, it is also important that material someone may want to find does not require several clicks to reach it. The rule of thumb is no more than three clicks to reach specific information.

Navigational Schemes   There are usually two ways to navigate on a web page; of-ten, there are more than two. Typically, there will be the main method of naviga-tion and text links repeating this main navigation at the bottom of the page. If you have scrolled down to read content, this bottom navigation allows you to move to the next page without having to scroll back up to use the main navigational scheme again.

There are a variety of types of main navigation: top, left, right, three column (the page is divided into three columns with each column containing navigation), and various combinations of these. The most common navigational schemes are top and left, based on the thought that people read top to bottom and left to right. However, following that same logic, if you want your visitors to see an important graphic first, incorporating a navigational scheme using the right side of the page instead will allow that image to take center stage. The McAuliffe-Shepard Discovery Center home page that we studied for its use of color in Chapter 1 (shown in Figure 1-7) is a great example of this: the use of right navigation allows their "The sky is no limit it's just the beginning" graphic to take visual priority when you reach their site.

There is also a relatively new trend in navigation design that groups large amounts of navigation, when needed, into "blocks" by categories, which are usually placed lower in the page, below the original "fold" area, but above the text links located at the bottom of the page. This subordinate navigation does not replace the main navigation or the text links in the footer area of the page, it is in addition to them. **FIGURE 3-1** exemplifies this trend.

Inclusion of a Site Map   A *site map page*, also called a *site index page*, is a special type of link page that is sometimes added to a site. This unique page serves two

FIGURE 3-1   Block navigation in Jay Peak's home page. (Courtesy of Jay Peak Resort, http://www.jaypeakresort.com.)

purposes. One purpose of a site map is to aid in search engine recognition, which can be an asset to sites of all sizes. The second use is to act as an index for the pages of the site (not to be confused with the *index.html* home page of the site). If a site has many link pages, especially pages that link off of another link, it can be a quick way for a visitor to find a particular page. The typical format of the site map page is to list general categories of information available in the site as titles that may or may not be links themselves, with all the link pages that pertain to those categories listed below them as text links for easy access. **FIGURE 3-2** exemplifies the use of a site map for indexing. The smaller image is the site's home page, which contains a text link at the bottom of the page to connect to its site map page. The larger illustration shows its site map page, listing all the pages of the site with single click access.

Navigation: Consistent and Hassle Free   Websites should always have a consistent navigational scheme. The last thing you want is for your visitor to be confused and wonder if he/she accidentally moved on elsewhere! Utah's Hogle Zoo uses

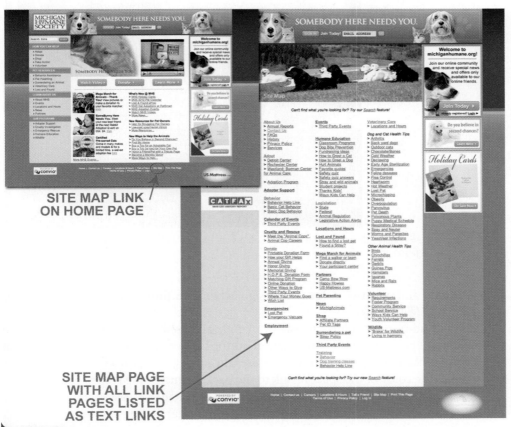

FIGURE 3-2 Michigan Humane Society home page and site map page. (Courtesy of the Michigan Humane Society, http://www.michiganhumane.org.)

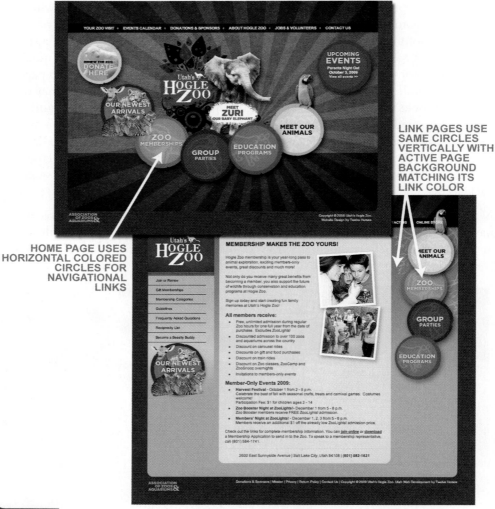

LINK PAGES USE SAME CIRCLES VERTICALLY WITH ACTIVE PAGE BACKGROUND MATCHING ITS LINK COLOR

HOME PAGE USES HORIZONTAL COLORED CIRCLES FOR NAVIGATIONAL LINKS

FIGURE 3-3 Utah's Hogle Zoo website navigation. (Courtesy of Utah's Hogle Zoo, http://www. hoglezoo.org.)

a unique and effective color and design scheme to unify the pages of its site, as shown in **FIGURE 3-3**.

The home page of this site uses overlapping colored circles in a horizontal layout across the page for its main navigation buttons. After the visitor has clicked one of the links, the corresponding link page uses the same buttons in a vertical design and applies the color of the specific link to the background of the respective page.

Along with consistency, navigation should be hassle free: easy to understand and easy to use. We have all been to sites that became aggravating when we tried to get to the content we wanted, and we simply moved on, even if that site probably had what we needed, because we got weary of trying to find it!

■ 3.1.2 Creating a Navigational Flowchart: Planning and Organizing Site Content

Certain general similarities existed among the navigational schemes of the sites you reviewed. Some navigational similarities were specific to the subject matter of the sites, whereas others were uniform across all types of sites. A detailed diagram of a website navigational system is called a *navigational flowchart*. Flowcharts help organize and strategically plan the link system of a site. Finding a site that you feel has a particularly effective link system, and drawing a navigational flowchart that details the hierarchy of that site, will help you understand this process and the types of link considerations that a site requires. The flowchart can be created in a graphic program or created as a rough pencil sketch. Its function is to create visible documentation of how the links of the site intertwine to check for logistics, feasibility, and simplicity. **FIGURE 3-4** illustrates the initial main link structure of a sample site.

After you understand the process, it is best practice to always create a navigational flowchart each time you plan to build a website. It really is no different than creating thumbnail sketches and comps for print design. Taking the time to carefully plan your "highway" can prevent wasted time further on in the website building process. Having to reinvent the wheel later, if you realize additional links or additional ways to link your pages are needed for efficient, logical, and systematic navigation

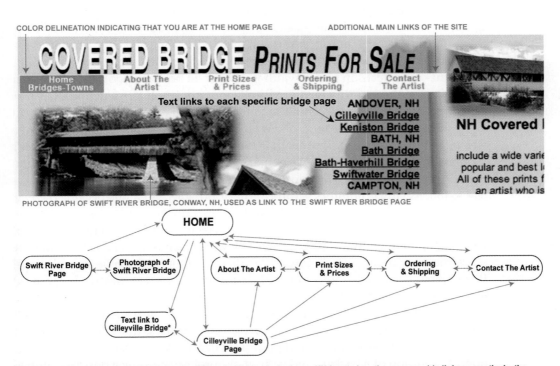

*Additional alphabetical text links below the Cilleyville Bridge in Andover, NH located on the map graphic link, respectively, the rest of the 30 bridge pages of the site, each bridge page linking back to the home page and to the rest of the main site link pages

FIGURE 3-4 Navigational flowchart.

through your site, is time wasted unnecessarily. Ouch! As a graphic artist, never forget the old saying, "Time is money." Web design, like any other graphic design medium, is about production time. Although this process may initially seem like a frivolous step and one you don't "need" to do, it is, instead, an effective planning strategy that will streamline the execution of your website design further on in the construction process.

After you design a website flowchart, test it. Show it to others, who do not have to be graphic artists, and ask them for feedback on your navigational hierarchy. It is easy to get too close to an idea and lose the perspective of a potential visitor. Ask for their input about whether there are unnecessary links, or even worse, important links you forgot to include. By having a visual reference, they can help you determine if you have considered all the necessary links, not only back to the home page, but also all the logical links among pages and any appropriate external links you plan to allow the visitor to choose as well. This is the time to plan a navigational scheme that is easy to use, easy to understand, and efficient in its structure.

3.2 Designing for Screen Resolutions

All stages of the design process should focus on the visitor. Remember that in cyberspace, an unhappy visitor will click out of your site and move on. One of the factors that can play a significant role in this is scrolling. We discussed the principle of the fold in Chapter 1, in relation to vertical scrolling: the issue here is horizontal scrolling. When making a decision on the width your site will be, it is important to consider the settings of the majority of your visitors' monitor resolutions, defined as *screen resolution*. Although it has become acceptable to scroll down a page if necessary, it is considered unacceptable to scroll *over* to see the rest of the horizontal width of a web page. If your web page is wider than the screen resolution setting of the viewer's monitor, the browser will add a horizontal scroll bar automatically. Screen resolution is always expressed in pixels as width × height. The original standard resolution was 640 × 480. As larger monitors became more affordable, 800 × 600 became the new standard. Many viewers now surf the Web using monitors with screen resolution capabilities of 1024 × 768 and higher. At what screen resolution will the majority of your visitors view your site? More specifically, what resolution will their monitors be set at (they may choose a lower setting than their monitors are capable of displaying)? If you know, you can design your pages accordingly. If you are unsure, designing at 800 × 600 is still very acceptable and very safe. This solution becomes even more appealing when the web pages are designed to automatically center on the visitor's screen. When centered, even if the visitor's screen capacity is much larger than your design, it can still be attractive and professional. A centered design also allows the popular addition of a background pattern or border to become a positive complement to your page, and add visual interest beyond the limitations of your actual page.

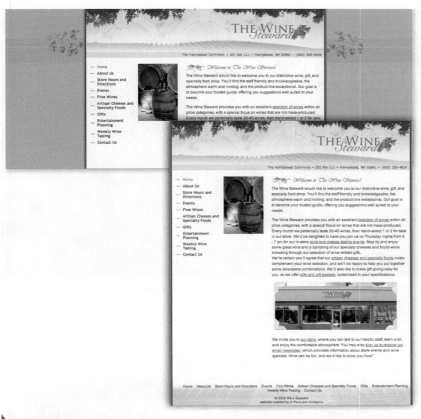

FIGURE 3-5 Using a background pattern. (Courtesy of The Wine Steward, http://www.thewinestewardnh. com.)

FIGURE 3-5 is the home page of The Wine Steward in Hampstead, NH. The top screen shot illustrates that as additional width is available, more of the striped background pattern becomes visible based on the monitor's viewing area. Conversely, if needed, the leaf patterns can be hidden to accommodate an even narrower viewing area of the page, as shown in the full-page sample below it.

As you search the Web, you will see this alternative effectively used for all types of sites. Another great example is the home page of the Fezzari Performance Bicycles website, as shown in **FIGURE 3-6**.

Here, the page is designed with a centered format safe for 800 × 600 screen resolution settings, with a sleek border design that extends as needed to fill any visible area beyond its main content width for visitors with broader viewing capabilities.

Another option is to design a site with a *liquid layout*, which is a percentage-based layout vs. a pixel-based one. This type of layout is called liquid because it will adjust automatically to the screen width provided, whether it is 640 × 480, 800 × 600, 1024 × 768, or higher. **FIGURE 3-7** is an excellent example of this flexibility.

1. NAVIGATION REMAINS SAME WIDTH IN BOTH LAYOUTS

2. VISIBILITY OF GRAPHIC ADJUSTS AS SPACE ALLOWS

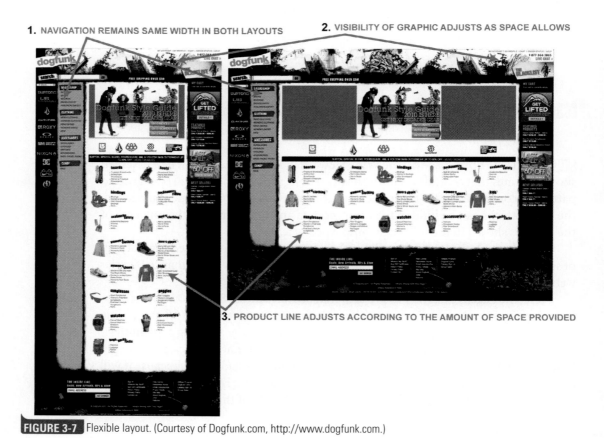

3. PRODUCT LINE ADJUSTS ACCORDING TO THE AMOUNT OF SPACE PROVIDED

This example shows the same page displayed narrow vs. wide if the viewing area allows. Let's take a closer look at how this website's flexible page works.

1. Notice that the left navigation is the same width in the narrow page and the wider page.

2. The graphic across the top of the page is the same size in both layouts. However, because more room is provided in the example on the right, more of the graphic is displayed.

3. As more space is provided for the width of the page, the products adjust automatically in their layout, changing gradually from two rows to five rows as more screen viewing area is provided. Now *that's* flexible! It is at this stage of the creative process that you should decide which site width alternative will best meet the needs of your visitors (once again, your audience) so that your layouts can be designed accordingly.

There is yet another method of layout, referred to as an *elastic layout*. This type of layout will also flex like a liquid layout. However, rather than being built in pixels or percentages, it is created using the scalability of the em unit. Our learning will focus on the fixed and liquid options for page layout.

 ## Design Principles of Web Layout

Having a solid understanding of the principles of design and applying them to a layout can dramatically improve the overall power of any page design, whether it is for print or the Web. In 1905, G. Woolliscroft Rhead wrote about the "the principles of ornament," naming nine "laws" that when combined create a successful design:

1. Symmetry and balance
2. Proportion and spacing
3. Subordination
4. Repose
5. Congruity
6. Radiation
7. Contrast
8. Repetition
9. Unity

Since that time, there have been numerous books and articles written on the principles of design, with as many different interpretations as to which combination of "laws" yield successful layouts. Although you may have experience with some of these principles as they relate to print design, our list has been tailored to the specific challenges inherent in web design. When you arrive at an aesthetically pleasing web page, an analysis of why it is successful will reveal its incorporation of the following design principles: symmetry and balance, repose, congruity, contrast, repetition, and unity.

3.3.1 Symmetry and Balance: Harmony in Form

While Rhead referred to the word *balance* as "creating the impression of symmetry with dissimilar forms," today, we would refer to that as asymmetrical, with the terms *symmetrical* and *asymmetrical* used to describe the two ways to achieve visual balance in design. When trying to remember which is which, it works well to think of symmetrical as "similar." In actuality, the definition of symmetrical is "made up of exactly similar parts facing each other or around an axis." In reference to web design, a web page containing two side-by-side columns of information that are equal in height and width, perhaps with a single graphic centered between them, would exemplify symmetry in its layout. Although this is safe and can be effective, many times it is also boring.

A design that has asymmetrical balance does *not* have exactly similar parts facing each other or around an axis, yet still seems to appear in harmony. Though it may be harder to create, if "balanced," it is often more visually interesting than a symmetrical one. This is accomplished by having a larger design element and/or lighter color on one side of the page, with several smaller and/or darker ones on the other half of the page that balance the larger shape on the page by their collective activity. After creating one, if your eyes can move comfortably around the page without getting visually "stuck" in any one area of the layout, you have succeeded at creating a balanced design, whether it is symmetrical or asymmetrical. Examples of symmetrical and asymmetrical balance are illustrated in FIGURE 3-8.

3.3.2 Repose: White Space/Negative Space

Rhead defined *repose* as adding simplicity when artwork was too busy. Today, we would refer to that as needing *white space*, also known as *negative space*. It is important to understand that "white" does not, in this situation, literally mean the color

SYMMETRICAL
LAYOUT

UNBALANCED
ASYMMETRICAL
LAYOUT

BALANCED
ASYMMETRICAL
LAYOUT

FIGURE 3-8 Balanced and unbalanced layouts.

white, although it can. It refers to empty space, or space on the page with inactivity or minimal activity. Sometimes, novice designers feel the need to fill every corner of a page with type and/or graphics. Letting an area be empty, and simply filled with the background layout color, can enhance the visual balance of the page, give it "breathing space," and allow the visitor to focus on the main content, without the page appearing too busy or cluttered. Busy and cluttered are layout errors that scream out "amateur" to a website visitor. A visitor may not even know what it is that makes the page appear that way, except that he/she will recognize that it does not have a professional appearance, which may prompt him/her to move on to another site.

◼ 3.3.3 Congruity: Consistency in Design

Congruity is having consistency in the relationship of the parts of a design: consistency in the placement of the content and consistency in the alignment of the content.

Content Congruity: Consistency in Content Placement   In *content congruity*, placing related elements together creates consistency and order in a design. For example, combining similar links together in the same area of a page creates a logical, orderly, and user-friendly navigation system for website visitors. A visitor should be able to find all the same type of links/information together, without having to fumble around and locate it in bits and pieces around the page. It's a fast click-and-go world. You need to capture your visitor and keep him/her clicking in your site without becoming frustrated and moving on to somewhere else in cyberspace. Having related content organized in a logical fashion will enhance your chances of doing just that.

Visual Congruity: Consistency in Graphic Alignment   It is important to realize in this application that alignment does not mean type alignment. *Visual congruity* refers to graphic alignment: how text and images are consistent in their alignment to each other, creating an "invisible connecting line" between them that enhances the unity of the page. Although the implementation of all of the principles of design together creates an effective page in print and web design, this principle alone immediately adds a professional touch when it is applied. The interesting thing is that your visitor may not be an artist and, therefore, may have no idea what he/she does not like about your page: but, the underlying reason may simply be the unprofessional appearance of a page that lacks visual congruity.

FIGURE 3-9 is the clock repair page of the Chelsea Clock Company in Chelsea, MA. The red arrows in the screen shot indicate the elements of the page that have been visually aligned. Notice how they create the appearance of lines running down the sides of the page, unifying the elements they appear to connect. In addition to the two areas that have been identified, there is also visual congruity evident in the relationship of the body text to the photograph above it.

We have learned that many times the effectiveness of a website is achieved through the utilization of a combination of design tools. This site's home page

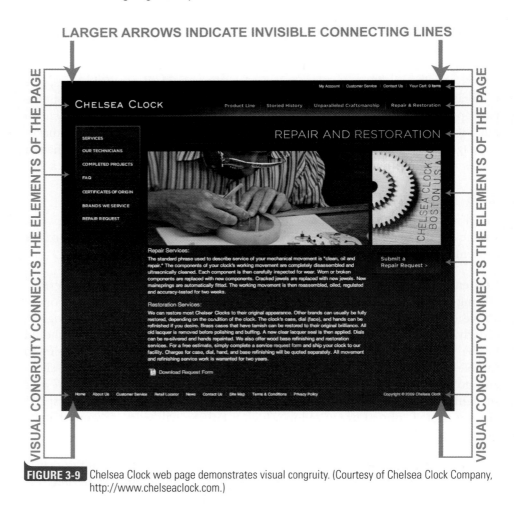

FIGURE 3-9 Chelsea Clock web page demonstrates visual congruity. (Courtesy of Chelsea Clock Company, http://www.chelseaclock.com.)

employs the psychology of color in its choice of black, as used on this page, with the additional color of gray to convey to its visitors that the company is respected, accomplished, and dependable.

3.3.4 Contrast: Enhancing a Design by the Juxtaposition of Opposing Elements

The effectiveness of this principle relies on the degree of the opposing elements in a design. Contrast can enhance a design and draw attention to an area of a page by creating emphasis, but only if it is strong enough to be viewed as such. If contrast is added, there must be no doubt that it has been added. Raising a font point size from 12 points to 14 points, or changing a color from light blue to medium blue, will in most cases *not* be enough contrast, and will look more like a mistake than the application of this design principle. Once again, remember the click-and-go

Lorem ipsum dolor sit amet, consectetuer adipiscing elit, sed diam nonummy nibh euismod tincidunt ut laoreet dolore magna aliquam erat volutpat.

Lorem ipsum dolor sit amet, consectetuer adipiscing elit, sed diam nonummy nibh

For more information, click here:

Lorem ipsum dolor sit amet, consectetuer adipiscing elit, sed diam nonummy nibh euismod tincidunt ut laoreet dolore magna aliquam erat volutpat.

Lorem ipsum dolor sit amet, consectetuer adipiscing elit, sed diam nonummy nibh

For more information, click here:

FIGURE 3-10 Creating contrast.

philosophy. Strong contrast when designing links and other important information through size and color can be used effectively to draw a visitor to a particular area of a page, keeping him/her searching *within* your site, rather than clicking out and moving on to someone else's. Notice the difference in contrast in **FIGURE 3-10**.

3.3.5 Repetition: Repeating Similar Decorative Units

This principle refers to repeating decorative elements within a page. This principle is applicable not only when creating an individual web page; it must also be consistent across the entire site. It is not limited to fonts and colors; it is any type of decorative element, graphic as well as typographic in nature, which is used repeatedly within a layout. It is one more way to assure your visitor that he/she is still in your site and aids in creating the continuity needed to do just that. **FIGURE 3-11**, the home page

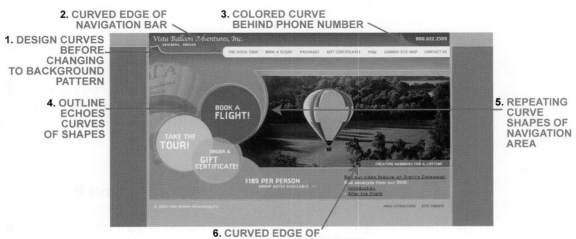

FIGURE 3-11 Vista Balloon Adventures contains repeating design elements. (Courtesy of Vista Balloon Adventures, Inc., http://www.vistaballoon.com.)

of the Vista Balloon Adventures company, is an excellent example of the use of a repeating design element on a page.

In this design, the curved element is repeated in a variety of ways throughout the page:

1. The curve follows the shape of the text before converting to the background border.
2. The navigation bar edge is curved at its left end.
3. The shape behind the phone number follows the curve shapes of the balloons.
4. The navigation shapes are outlined with an echoing curve.
5. The navigation shapes are repetitive curves.
6. The corners of the left edge of the text area background are rounded instead of square.

3.3.6 Unity: The Final Checklist

Unity is the coherence and completeness of a design, and the cooperation of all of the parts of a piece. Unity can actually be thought of as the final checklist of the design process. After creating a layout, use the following checklist when reviewing your design:

- Is your design balanced either symmetrically or asymmetrically?
- Does it contain some repose to give breathing space in the page?
- Is related content consistently placed together?
- Are text and graphics consistent in their alignment with each other?
- Where applied, is your contrast strong enough to create the emphasis it was designed to accomplish?
- Have you employed the repetitive use of colors, fonts, shapes, etc., to create continuity within the layout?

If you can say yes (objectively, of course) to each of the items in this list, *your page has unity*. In web design, this unity must now span across your entire site and all of its link pages to convince visitors that it is a credible, professional site.

 ## 3.4   Formulating the Layout Structure of Your Pages

The layout of an effective web page has its information divided into five major content areas. Let's examine those areas in more detail and see how mock layouts can be used to design logical, functional, user friendly, structured pages.

▣ 3.4.1 The Five Major Content Areas of a Web Page

Although, as a designer, you will want your pages to be unique, they still must conform to certain general content areas that have become the staples of successful web pages. Incorporating them effectively, coupled with your personal touch, is what will make your pages special. In your search for designs when building your idea book (remember that building an idea book should be an ongoing process), you collected design ideas and navigational schemes that caught your eye. One of the reasons they appealed to you, was their logical, user friendly layout structure, which is divided into within five major content areas:

- the headline area where the company name exists (always at the top of the page)
- the main navigational system area or areas, because there may be more than one on the page (top below the headline area, left, right, and sometimes left+center+right)
- the main body text content area
- the white/negative space area or areas (as we have learned, a critical part of any good design)
- the footer area (text link navigational area at the bottom of the page)

The challenge to you, as a web designer, is to build these components into an attractive, yet functional web page tailored to your visitor's specific needs.

▣ 3.4.2 Brainstorming Your Design Ideas Through Mock Layouts

Mock layouts are a great way to experiment with the organization of the components you will need to include in a web page. Using Photoshop, adding individual layers for each web page component you will need is a quick and effective method of brainstorming multiple layouts on the fly. In minutes, instead of hours, mock layouts can help you organize your page components using several different configurations. By drawing and labeling blocks of your chosen color scheme in the general size and location you will add actual text and graphics to later, you can create as many combinations as needed until you have a page framework that successfully meets the criteria of a unified page. Not only are these valuable for designing your own sites, they are excellent first-meeting layouts to present to your website clients to receive signed initial approval before beginning to build their sites in Dreamweaver.

In Photoshop, be sure to set your unit of measurement to pixels, so that you will be able to echo those dimensions when you convert your final idea into a page created through Dreamweaver. If you decide to build your site using a fixed width design at the 800 × 600 pixel dimensions, create a mock layout at 1200 pixels, with the 750 pixel design area in the middle, allowing you to explore various background options on either side of your page area, as shown in **FIGURE 3-12**. Using a center design area that is 750 pixels wide, with a total width of 1200 pixels, provides an easy-to-calculate

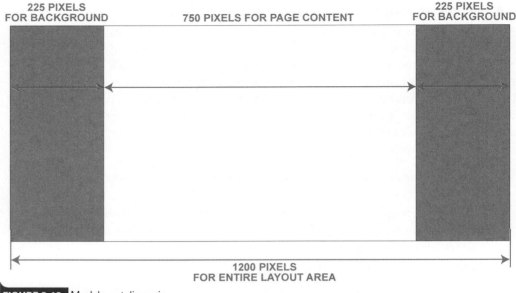

FIGURE 3-12 Mock layout dimensions.

drawing board or scratch area on both sides to test background colors or patterns and how they will affect the fixed, centered layout.

If you are considering a flexible layout viewable from 640 pixels to 1024+ pixels, it will be important to create two mock layouts for each concept: one with a page content width of 600 pixels and one with a width of 1200 pixels, adjusting the content in the larger sample as it would expand in a wider display.

3.4.3 Heights for Mock Layouts

The height you build into your mock layouts should be the height of your final web pages. When determining the pixel height to design your layouts, you should consider the "fold" for priority of content, and the typical height your visitor's monitor will display, if your goal is to eliminate or minimize vertical scrolling. If this is your goal, when creating a mock layout designed for a screen resolution of 800 × 600, a height of 500–600 pixels will work well.

In **FIGURE 3-13**, mock layouts were created by student Nicholas Moulton for the fictitious investment company, StableRockInvestments.com. They were designed as a centered, fixed layout for a screen resolution of 800 × 600.

How many variations of your design do you need? These mock layouts (also referred to as *comps*) are brainstorming on the fly. Notice the increase in sophistication and attention to detail in Nicholas's second layout vs. his first. Student Sarah Gaertner chose to work with the MumazYumaz bakery theme. When reviewing each of her layouts, placed in order of creation in **FIGURE 3-14**, it is clear that each one spawned additional ideas and idea refinements with each successive layout.

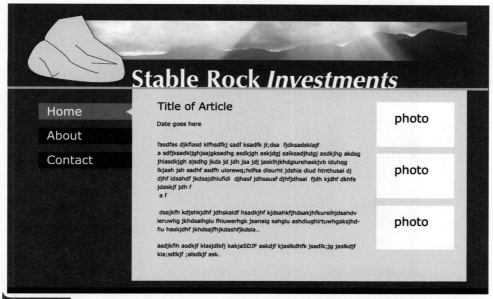

FIGURE 3-15 Stable Rock Investments detailed comp. (Courtesy of Adam Caron, student, Manchester, NH.)

3.5   What We Have Learned

In this chapter, we learned how careful planning of navigation ahead of time will eliminate problems later in the website construction process. In studying navigation, we learned the types available and incorporated them into mock layouts. We also examined each of the design principles of web pages individually and learned how their combined application creates a unified, aesthetically pleasing, professional web page.

3.6   Reinforcing Your Knowledge

Project 1

Surf the Web for five different website home pages that have principles of design you can identify. Create screen shots, print them, and then circle and label each of the principles on your print outs.

FINAL MOCK LAYOUT

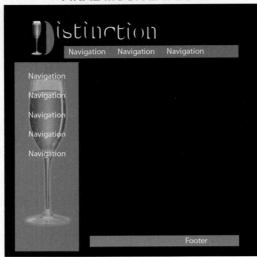

FINAL HOME PAGE

FIGURE 3-16 Distinction Restaurant mock layout and final web page. (Courtesy of Michael Andreo, student, Bedford, NH.)

Project 2

1. Create a new RGB document in Photoshop 1200 × 600 pixels. Add vertical guides at 225 pixels and 975 pixels to simulate a fixed page layout.

2. Open your favorite mock headline from any of the sites that you created in Chapter 2. Group and drag the layers into your new document and align the headline with the top and center of the page area between the vertical guides.

3. Fill the background layer of this document with one of the colors that you used in your chosen headline.

4. Continue to build a mock home page layout that indicates a navigational scheme containing four to six main links equally spaced horizontally across the page, or in a vertical configuration in the location of your choice. We will not add photos just yet. Complete this mock layout using only color and type, as shown in Figure 3-13. Apply the knowledge of web page layout you have learned thus far to your designs:

   - design principles of web layout
   - the major components of a web page
   - the influential power of color (from Chapter 1)
   - the voice of type (from Chapter 2)

6. Create three more centered, fixed mock layout variations for the same company name, changing the design and location of the navigation and other elements to make each one different, refining your ideas as you build your mock layouts. Label them Layout_1, Layout_2, and Layout_3.

Project 3

Surf the Web for a site that you like, with navigation that can be detailed clearly in a flowchart, as shown in Figure 3-4. This can be a neatly drawn and labeled pencil sketch, or you can create it in a graphic program if you would like. Submit a screen shot of the home page of the selected site with your sketch.

Project 4

Using your favorite mock layout from Project 2, draw a navigational flowchart for the chosen site based on the links you have created. Indicate all of its major links, the pages they would need to link to, and how all pages would link back to the home page.

3.7 Building Your Own Website

1. Create four mock layouts for the home page of your own personal site using the headline that you created in Chapter 2. Build two using the fixed width centered page format of 1200 pixels wide, with an actual centered page design area of 750 pixels. Create a third design as a flexible liquid web page layout by creating two mock layouts for it: one at 600 pixels wide and one with a width of 1200 pixels. When designing a liquid layout, plan a vertical navigation design vs. a horizontal one. You will not need the background 1200 pixel colored layer for these, because your flexible layout will be designed to fill the viewer's entire screen whatever its width.

2. Incorporate the following design criteria and determine the specific number of navigation buttons you will need:

   - design principles of web layout
   - the major components of a web page
   - the influential power of color (from Chapter 1)
   - the voice of type (from Chapter 2)

3. Choose your most effective design and create a navigational flowchart for it.

1. CHOOSE THE VIEW TO WORK IN

10. BLUE OUTLINE INDICATES SELECTED OPTIMIZATION

2. HAND
3. SLICE SELECT
4. ZOOM
5. EYEDROPPER
6. SELECTED COLOR
7. SLICE VISIBILITY

Original Optimized 2-Up 4-Up

Be SMART

Be SMART
BEFORE You START!

JPEG
10.86K
3 sec @ 56.6 Kbps

44 quality

Be SMART
BEFORE You START!

JPEG
5.611K
2 sec @ 56.6 Kbps

11 quality

Alpha: --   Hex: --   Index: --

Save

CENT

SLICE TOOL

SLICES FROM GUIDES OPTION

Style: Normal   Width: Height: Slices From Guides

3APPLES.jpg @ 100% (RGB/8#)

100%   Doc: 972.0K/972.0K

SLICES ARE CREATED FROM GUIDES ADDED FIRST AND ARE NUMBERED SEQUENTIALLY FROM UPPER LEFT TO LOWER RIGHT

Effects
Bevel and Em
products_u
home_u
faq_u
contact_u
ALL OVERS
info_o
products_o
home_o
faq_o
contact_o

Preset: [Unnamed]

GIF
Selective   Colors: 256
Diffusion   Dither: 100%
☑ Transparency   Matte:
No Transparency Di...   Amount:
☐ Interlaced   Web Snap: 0%
Lossy: 0

☑ Convert to sRGB
Preview: Monitor Color
Metadata: Copyright and Contact Info

Color Table

100% dither
Selective palette
54 colors

Preparing Graphics for the Web

4

In this chapter, we will explore your legal options for securing the images you need for your sites. After you have acquired your images, the next step is their optimization. This chapter takes you through each of the Save for Web file formats of Photoshop and when to use each format, including an understanding of when slicing may be the best alternative for a particular optimization requirement. The potential of the Save for Web feature is studied in more depth, including its ability to turn layers on and off as needed in one master file created in Photoshop, yielding multiple possible navigational states through this special asset of its Save for Web dialog box.

Acquiring Photographs for Web Design

Website photographs must be not only appropriate and viable, they must also be affordable and legal.

4.1.1 Acquiring Photographs Legally

Before we cover working with photographs, it is important, first of all, to discuss their acquisition. It is a common thought that photographs on the Web are free to download, just because you can right-click and choose Save Image As. Don't go there! In addition to the fact that there are legal ramifications of using photographs acquired in this way, ask yourself, would you want someone stealing your photographs? The reality is that it is not only unethical, it is illegal! The usage of photographs encompasses strict copyright laws designed to protect the photographer. In lieu of stealing, there are viable solutions to this dilemma.

Commission a Photographer with Expertise in Your Website Photography Needs   The obvious first solution is to pay to have the photographs taken. If you need the perfect shot, you can commission the expertise of a professional photographer who specializes in the type of photography you need for the website you are creating. However, in making the decision to do this, you must balance the need to use a professional vs. the costs incurred in your contract if you do. By default, he/she automatically owns the photographs; you don't. You will need a contract that clearly defines your usage rights of the photographs after they are taken. The degree or level of usage you secure will impact the price you pay for the work. This may be an expensive alternative; however, if you have researched photographers, and know that the professional quality will be there, it can be worth every penny.

Purchase Royalty-free Photographs   The next more affordable option is royalty-free photographs. It is a common misconception that royalty-free images are literally "free." What it actually means is that the photograph is licensed for multiple types of usage determined by the company you are purchasing it through. Thanks to competition and the Internet, this option continues to grow in popularity as an effective, valuable, and affordable solution. Searching the Web for "royalty free stock photos" will provide several companies to choose from and thousands of images. However, be sure to take the time to check out the licensing agreement of the company before choosing it. Most of them, when listing their allowed uses, will have website design as one of them. Many companies sell low resolution files for the Web, perhaps as low as one dollar for the lowest resolution/image size combination.

 Know the required dimensions of your desired photograph in both pixels and inches before you start searching at stock photography company sites. Some companies list them one way, some the other, and some as both. All of the photographs will be listed with a variety of size/quality options, with higher prices as the size and quality increase. Knowing ahead of time what your needs are will eliminate paying more for a photograph that is larger than you actually need for your site.

Free Stock Photographs   Free? Yes, there are some stock images available on the Web that really are free. There are a surprising number of companies on the Web already that offer free stock photos (and more pop up every day). Just type in an Internet search for "free stock photography" and presto! A wide variety of companies will come up for you to check. Some will simply ask you to register, while others won't even require that. When you do your Internet search, along with the list of free ones, you'll also see more royalty-free companies listed to purchase images from as well. That's OK. You can start your image search with the free companies, and move on to the companies that charge if you just can't find what you need for free. Just as with the royalty-free companies, when searching the free ones, remember to take the time to read their licensing agreement because it will be explicit regarding its allowance or restrictions on use for web design. The few minutes it will take you can be well worth it.

Make the Acquisition Part of the Fun: Take Them Yourself   Whenever possible, you may prefer to take the photographs yourself anyway. Try shooting your own first, and make the image acquisition part of the website design as fun as building the rest of the site. Just a few years ago, this option would have been much more difficult. At that time, it would have required lots of film, lots of developing, and lots of hope that one or two of your images would work as you designed. However, digital cameras are inexpensive and readily available with large memory cards and immediate preview. Fire away! Depending on your subject matter, set up a studio backdrop as needed and start shooting. Later, if you need to, you'll be able to use your talents in Photoshop to eliminate backgrounds, combine your photographs, etc. The beauty of a digital camera lies in the ability to shoot, look, and toss until you succeed at the shots you need. This alternative is inexpensive, effective, and safe. As a graphic artist, you already have an eye for composition and creativity, and with your editing skills in Photoshop, the task can become fun, free, and especially rewarding to see your own photographs on the website!

4.2 Understanding Web File Formats and Dithering

After you have secured your website images, they must be properly optimized for the Web.

4.2.1 General Information about Preparing Graphics and Photographs for the Web

Before we discuss specific file format features, let's cover a couple of important general tips regarding the preparation of your photographs.

Know Your Image Dimension Requirements and Background Color Where It Will Be Placed   We have discussed the importance of knowing your dimensions prior to purchasing photographs on the Web. Whether you purchase an image or create a graphic from scratch, you will need to determine your final dimensions and required background color prior to preparing the images/graphics for the Web, and check that it is in the RGB file format. If you have created mock layouts/comps as shown in Chapter 3, you have already determined the size requirements of your images and your background color. If you have not determined the image size and background color requirements, it should be done before proceeding to saving specific images for use in a web page.

Cropping Your Image Accurately   The fixed ratio crop feature in Photoshop can be very handy to apply the exact size you need to an image you want to use on a web page. To do this, be sure you are using pixels for its units of measurement setting and that your image is 72 ppi, choose the Crop tool, type your pixel dimensions in its Options bar, press the mouse button, and then drag the mouse over the area you need.

4.2.2 Save for Web Feature in Photoshop

After you have acquired the photographs you are going to use or created your graphics, use the Save for Web and Devices command (hereafter, simply referred to as Save for Web) in Photoshop to maximize the optimization of your images.

 This can never be said enough: *always keep your original images as .psd files* with all of their layers intact so that you will be able to re-work them later if necessary! The more intricate your images/graphics become, the more critical it will be to keep all your layers.

General Features of the Photoshop Save for Web Dialog Box   When you choose File>Save for Web, the features on the left half of the dialog box are applicable to all format choices. **FIGURE 4-1** details those options.

1. Here, you can choose to display two or four views of an image to help you make your optimization decision, with one of the views always displaying the original image. The Optimized tab displays the combination of options you have chosen. It is always good to carefully examine the optimization you have chosen if you have text in your graphic, because you will see degradation there before other areas of your photograph as you drop the quality.

2. This Hand tool will allow you to move around the selected window to check various areas of your image to compare quality with file size.

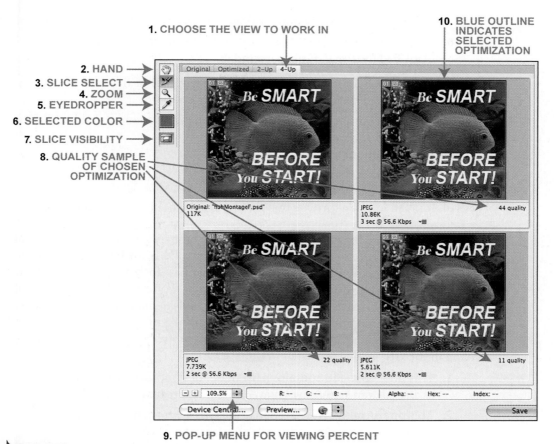

1. CHOOSE THE VIEW TO WORK IN

10. BLUE OUTLINE INDICATES SELECTED OPTIMIZATION

2. HAND
3. SLICE SELECT
4. ZOOM
5. EYEDROPPER
6. SELECTED COLOR
7. SLICE VISIBILITY
8. QUALITY SAMPLE OF CHOSEN OPTIMIZATION

Original: "fishMontageF.psd"
117K

JPEG
10.86K
3 sec @ 56.6 Kbps

44 quality

JPEG
7.739K
2 sec @ 56.6 Kbps

22 quality

JPEG
5.611K
2 sec @ 56.6 Kbps

11 quality

109.5%   R: --   G: --   B: --   Alpha: --   Hex: --   Index: --

Device Central...   Preview...   Save

9. POP-UP MENU FOR VIEWING PERCENT

FIGURE 4-1 Save for Web dialog box in Photoshop.

3. If you have sliced your image, the Slice Select tool will let you click to select the slice you want to save. You will only need to use this tool if you are saving individual slices, not when you are saving all of the slices at the same time.

4. This Zoom tool allows you to click or click and drag to increase the view of your selection. Press Alt/Option as you click to decrease the magnification of your selected optimization view.

5. This Eyedropper tool will allow you to select a color within your graphic.

6. This window displays the color you selected with the Eyedropper tool.

7. If your image has been sliced, this icon will let you toggle between viewing and hiding the slices.

8. Each view will display the resulting quality and download rate for the optimization option you have selected.

9. This menu will let you choose a preset magnification to view your selection.

10. When viewing the choices at 2-up or 4-up, your selected optimization is identified by a blue outline around it.

In conjunction with these general features, the right half of the dialog box allows you to choose one of five file formats to save your image in:

- GIF (usually pronounced like Ge̲orge, sometimes pronounced like G̲ail)
- JPEG (pronounced Jay Peg)
- PNG-8 (pronounced Ping)
- PNG-24
- WBMP (this is a black and white option for mobile devices only)

Let's discuss the four file formats that are applicable to full-color web graphics.

Choosing the GIF File Format   This format is best suited and most commonly used for web graphics that contain large areas of solid color because it is limited to a maximum of 256 colors. Typical uses of the GIF format are logos, buttons, etc., that do not have the continuous tone quality requirements of a photograph. GIF also allows transparency when application needs demand it. This format uses *indexed color*, meaning that each of its colors is given a number based on the total number of colors chosen in the Save for Web dialog box. The available options for saving in the GIF format are listed in **FIGURE 4-2**.

1. This pop-up menu contains a list of default optimization settings as well as any custom settings you have previously created and saved.

2. This option allows you to choose the GIF file format.

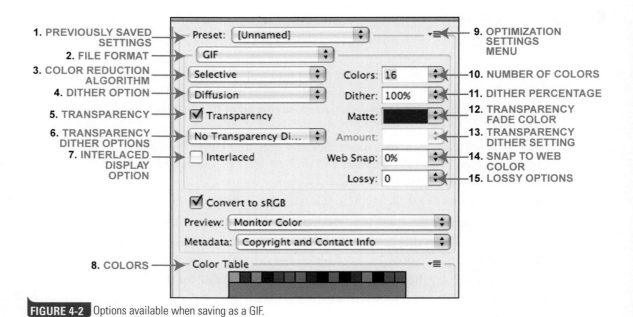

FIGURE 4-2 Options available when saving as a GIF.

3. This option determines how colors will be reduced: the default option is Selective.

4. This option allows you to apply dithering.

5. This option should be selected if you want to keep the background transparent: if left blank, the negative space will be automatically filled with the selected matte color.

6. If using transparency that must gradually appear (e.g., a drop shadow), choose dither to create the appearance of a fading edge.

7. The Interlaced option allows the image to gradually display clearer and clearer as it is loading: this is useful for large, slow-loading graphics.

8. This box displays the colors, as chosen from the Colors pop-up menu.

9. This pop-up menu allows you to save custom settings for use with future GIF files.

10. This pop-up menu sets the number of colors you want to be used in the file: always choose the fewest colors possible while maintaining the integrity of the image.

11. If adding dither, set the percentage here.

12. If fading to background using dithering, this option sets the color that will be used for the dithering to help the transition. Use the pop-up menu or click the color box to choose the color you want to use.

13. If setting a transparency dither option, set the percentage here.

14. This option converts the colors to their nearest web equivalents.

15. This option will cause some blurring by the setting chosen because it removes image data, but aids in reducing the size of the file. It defaults to *not* being applied and is not available when Interlaced or certain dithering options are selected.

Choosing the JPEG File Format   The Save for Web JPEG format is the format of choice for photographs, providing the best balance of color and file size. It creates the appearance of transparency for images with vignettes, drop shadows, etc., by adding a background color chosen to match the background of the destination page. **FIGURE 4-3** illustrates how the appearance of a fade to transparency is created for an image to be used in a web page designed with a blue background.

The background color chosen to represent the transparent area must be the exact color of the web page background where the image will be placed. This can be assured by typing the exact web equivalent values under the Matte option of the Save for Web dialog box. If it matches, the graphic will appear to fade seamlessly into the background when it is inserted into Dreamweaver. **FIGURE 4-4** identifies this option, with the rest of the optimization features available for the JPEG file format.

1. This pop-up menu contains a list of default optimization settings as well as any custom settings you have previously created and saved.

DROP SHADOW AGAINST
TRANSPARENCY

FAUX TRANSPARENT APPEARANCE USING
COLORED SAVE FOR WEB MATTE SETTING
TO MATCH BACKGROUND OF WEB PAGE

FIGURE 4-3 Faux transparency.

2. This option allows you to choose the JPEG file format.
3. These are the general settings for the quality of the image with the options of Low, Medium, High, Very High, and Maximum. The higher the quality you choose, the larger your resulting file will be.

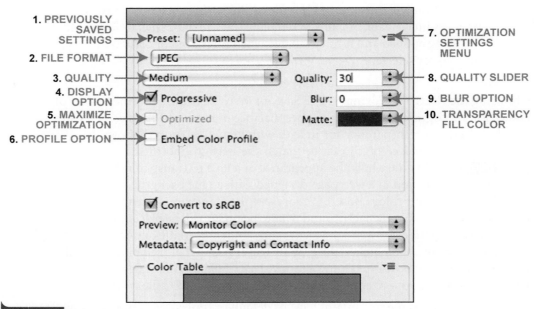

FIGURE 4-4 Options available when saving as a JPEG.

4. This option works like the Interlaced option of the GIF file format: it will progressively display a large image, with it gradually appearing in layers of visibility.

5. This option will provide the maximum optimization, based on your selection. For this checkbox to become active, you must first choose an option from the Preset pop-up menu of previously saved settings.

6. Select this option to attach the ICC profile of the image to the optimized version.

7. This pop-up menu allows you to save custom settings for use with future JPEG files.

8. The quality slider allows you to override preset optimization settings (e.g., Low and Medium) to further customize an amount to apply.

9. The Blur option will slightly blur the image quality; however, in doing so, it will also help reduce the file size. It defaults to not applying any blur.

10. This option allows you to set the color to use for the faux transparency appearance. Although it has a pop-up menu, you can click directly on the rectangle to display a color picker to enter your web equivalent values.

Choosing the PNG-8 File Format   As you can see in **FIGURE 4-5**, the options are the same as the GIF format, except that it does not include the Lossy option to discard image data. So what is the value of using it over a GIF? The true value of the PNG file format is in its PNG-24 file format.

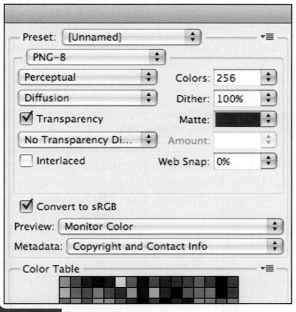

FIGURE 4-5 Options available when saving as a PNG-8.

1. LOGO WITH TRANSPARENT BACKGROUND
TO ALLOW PAGE BACKGROUND
PHOTOGRAPH TO SHOW THROUGH
USING GIF FORMAT

2. TRANSPARENT LOGO
WITH MATTE BACKGROUND
IN JPEG FILE FORMAT

3. LOGO WITH TRANSPARENT BACKGROUND
TO ALLOW PAGE BACKGROUND
PHOTOGRAPH TO SHOW THROUGH
USING PNG-8 FILE FORMAT

4. LOGO WITH TRANSPARENT BACKGROUND
TO ALLOW PAGE BACKGROUND PHOTOGRAPH
TO SHOW THROUGH TRUE TRANSPARENT
FADE USING PNG-24 FILE FORMAT

FIGURE 4-6 Save for Web transparency options.

Choosing the PNG-24 File Format   As mentioned, the JPEG file format is best for continuous tone images because of its ability to retain quality while significantly reducing the file size through the optimization process. Its only drawback is if you need the image to fade to true transparency, instead of a faux transparent background, when you have drop shadows, vignettes, etc., applied to the photo. The PNG-24 file format option is the only one that will provide true, natural full-color fading to create this appearance, as shown in **FIGURE 4-6**.

In samples one and three, the GIF and PNG-8 file formats create a pixilated edge by choosing colors at a 50% show/no show option. Sample two is the JPEG version, which will fade beautifully, but must fade to a background filled with a chosen matte color. The fourth sample is the true transparent blending of the PNG-24 option. The only major compromise when choosing this format is file size. The true transparency vs. the faux transparency comes with a price: significant increase in the size of the file. The other issue is compatibility with older browsers, which will become a non-issue in time; in knowing your audience, you will know if this will be an issue at all. However, when faux transparency is not an option, PNG-24 comes to the rescue. You can use the PNG-24 format if you want your web page to have a photograph behind the content of the page and want some of the content on the page to have

HEADLINE GRAPHIC
HAS DROP SHADOWS

WEB PAGE IS DESIGNED
FOR BACKGROUND
PHOTOGRAPH TO
SHOW THROUGH

FIGURE 4-7 Headline with PNG-24 transparency placed over photo background on web page.

effects applied to it, such as drop shadows, to seamlessly fade into the background, as shown in **FIGURE 4-7**.

In this example, you can see that the headline has drop shadows applied to it. Yet, as a PNG-24 graphic, its edges fade perfectly to reveal the photograph below it, when one is used as the background of the web page.

Another unique advantage of the PNG-24 transparency capabilities is its ability to save a graphic with less than 100% opacity, designed to allow a background image to show through the graphic on a web page. **FIGURE 4-8** exemplifies just one idea out of a world of ideas. You, as a designer, may find yourself wanting to use this option in some of your own web designs. In this example, you can see through the headline graphic, with its colored background set at 50% opacity, then saved as a PNG-24 optimized web graphic.

Fewer selections are available when the PNG-24 option is chosen in the Save for Web dialog box, as shown in **FIGURE 4-9**.

1. This pop-up menu contains a list of default optimization settings as well as any custom settings you have previously created and saved.

2. This option allows you to choose the PNG-24 file format.

FIGURE 4-8 Example of a PNG-24 with 50% opacity.

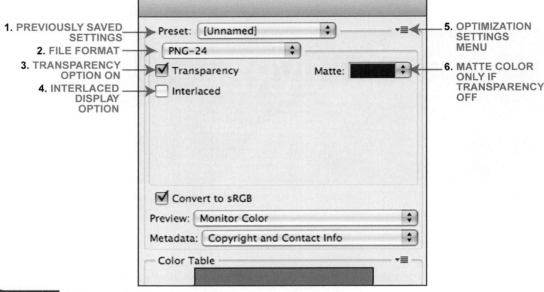

1. PREVIOUSLY SAVED SETTINGS
2. FILE FORMAT
3. TRANSPARENCY OPTION ON
4. INTERLACED DISPLAY OPTION

5. OPTIMIZATION SETTINGS MENU
6. MATTE COLOR ONLY IF TRANSPARENCY OFF

FIGURE 4-9 Options available when saving as a PNG-24.

3. By default, the option for transparency is checked. Clearing the checkbox would render the image like a JPEG with a matte background, but at a larger file size than its JPEG counterpart.

4. The Interlaced option allows the image to gradually appear as it loads, just as it does in the GIF file format.

5. This pop-up menu allows you to save custom settings for use with future JPEG files.

6. If you have cleared the Transparency checkbox, this box will become active to allow you to choose a faux background matte color, just as the same option does in the JPEG file format.

◼ 4.2.3 Dithering

When using a limited palette in either the GIF or PNG-8 file format, applying dithering can make the image appear to have more colors in it than it actually has. In **FIGURE 4-10**, the leaves on the right appear less posterized because mixing the shades of green together makes it appear as though a wider variety of shades of green were available than the limited palette of only 16 colors. Although the JPEG file format has been recommended for continuous tone images, if your work contains an image that requires one of these other formats, dithering is an option. While this may improve the look of the image, it will also slightly increase the file size: as you can

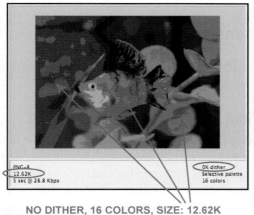 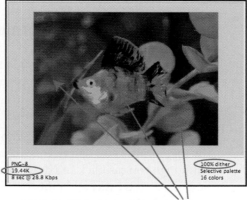

NO DITHER, 16 COLORS, SIZE: 12.62K   100% DITHER, 16 COLORS, SIZE: 19.44K

FIGURE 4-10 Dither sample.

see, the file size increase was insignificant, compared to the improvement in the quality of the image.

There are three types of dithering available for application: diffusion, pattern, and noise. While both the diffusion and the noise options use an arbitrary method of distributing the colors, pattern dithering creates a systematic placement of the colors in a grid fashion. Which one should you use? Depending on the image, test each type in the Save for Web dialog box one at a time to decide which one works the best on it.

Dithering for Banding   As a graphic artist, you may be familiar with the term *banding*, when gradients are not smoothly rendered, but instead appear as bands or stripes of color. When saving for the Web, applying dithering can significantly help address this issue with web graphics saved in the GIF or PNG-8 file formats. **FIGURE 4-11** illustrates how, at an optimization setting of 32 colors, applying dithering to the graphic minimized the banding with only a minimal increase in file size.

GIF FORMAT, NO DITHER

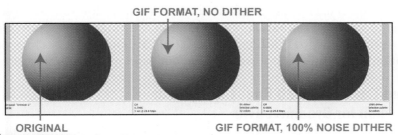

ORIGINAL   GIF FORMAT, 100% NOISE DITHER

FIGURE 4-11 Dithering for gradients.

4.3   Slicing Photographs and Web Pages

The slice feature of Photoshop is a handy and powerful option that serves two important functions: slicing graphics and slicing pages.

4.3.1 Slicing Large Graphics When Size and Quality Are a Must

If you have a large graphic, using Photoshop to slice the image into several smaller files by the number you determine will allow the image to download faster on the Web. Although you can click and drag with the Slice tool to manually create slices of any size and shape, it is easier and more predictable to divide your image into logical divisions with guides first (e.g., an 8 × 8 inch photograph with guides at 2" horizontal increments and 4" vertical increments, noting the total width of 576 pixels). If you have done that, when you choose the Slice tool, the Slices from Guides option to create slices will appear in its Options bar. When you choose this option, slices are created automatically and numbered sequentially from upper left to lower right; the option to hide or remove slices is available under the View menu. **FIGURE 4-12** illustrates this function.

Before entering the Save for Web dialog box for this feature, or any time you are saving for the Web, it is important to know that you do not have to save the Photoshop file first. If you keep the file open but not saved (and you have an ample supply of RAM), when you create or alter an image and immediately insert it into Dreamweaver only to realize it still needs tweaking, you can immediately return to the open Photoshop file, back up in the History palette if applicable, make your changes, and repeat the process.

When you enter the Save for Web dialog box for an image that has been sliced, the slices can now be individually saved as shown in **FIGURE 4-13**.

Notice how the detail of the apple is preserved when this large image with its original size of 972.0 K is sliced into eight pieces, allowing the file size of the selected slice to be only 3.182 K. This technique can be carried even further by optimizing each slice individually: solid areas of an image can be saved as a .gif file when applicable, with continuous tone sections of an image saved as a .jpg file. When you click the Save button at this point, another dialog box is displayed that will not only allow you to choose where you want to save the slices, but allow you to save all of them or selected ones, as well as to save the Images Only, HTML and Images, or HTML Only. Saving as Images Only is the option we will use, because we will build our pages using Dreamweaver.

4.3.2 Slicing Complete Web Pages Created in Photoshop for Dreamweaver

Not only can an image be sliced to improve its download time, another very valuable feature of slicing in Photoshop is the ability to create a complete web page,

SLICE TOOL   SLICES FROM GUIDES OPTION

SLICES ARE CREATED FROM GUIDES ADDED FIRST AND
ARE NUMBERED SEQUENTIALLY FROM UPPER LEFT TO
LOWER RIGHT

FIGURE 4-12 Sliced photograph.

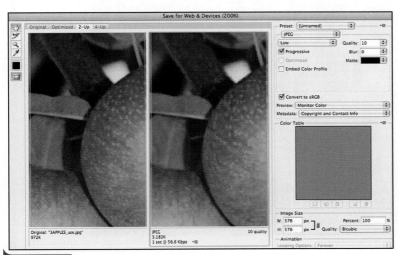

FIGURE 4-13 Saving a sliced image for the Web.

including its navigation (we will cover more extensive, astute methods of creating navigation later). To complete this process, time should be taken to plan your slices before creating them, such as determining where your headline will end, width of your navigation, and recording these dimensions on a printed copy of the page. After guides have been brought in according to your plan, and you have selected the Slice tool, choose the Slices from Guides option from the Options bar to create the slices. Because slices were created at every guide intersection of your layout, inevitably you will have some slices that you won't want, or will need to reconfigure. Choose the Slice Select tool (nested under the Slice tool) to click and delete the slices you don't want, and click and drag the handles to extend the slices of the ones you do want. For example, in **FIGURE 4-14**, the red lines indicate where slices were deleted and extended so that the entire headline became one slice instead of two (#01), the left slice remained its initial shape (#02), the top half of the building became one slice instead of six (#03), the bottom half of the image below the main navigation became one slice instead of two (#09), and the footer navigation became slice #10. The main navigation remained as individual slices numbered #04 through #08.

In the Save for Web dialog box, choose your matte color, set your optimization, and click the Save button. By selecting All Slices under the Slices options, a folder

FIGURE 4-14 Sliced page.

titled *images* will automatically be generated, in the folder you designate, with all of these slices placed in it. Later, by choosing the Selected Slices option instead, you can choose to replace ones you need to change without having to replace all of the slices in this *images* folder.

When saving for the Web, after you have told Photoshop where you want your files to be saved, whether they are slices or simply optimized images, each time you choose the Save option in the Save for Web dialog box, the same folder will be selected by default. Sweet!

Creating Navigation Graphics: Maximizing the Potential of the Save for Web Feature of Photoshop

Using images to generate multi-state navigation can be created easily using the Photoshop Layers palette combined with its Save for Web dialog box.

4.4.1 Creating Image Rollovers

Image rollovers are those cool graphics on a web page that, when you roll over them, change to something else and offer an opportunity to link to another page. Creating image rollovers is one of the ways to maximize the potential of the Save for Web feature of Photoshop. We have discussed the importance of knowing your final size for graphics before you create them. Starting with a blank document at 72 ppi in Photoshop set to those pixel dimensions is the easiest way to start to create an image rollover.

Create your rollover with its up and over states on individual layers within the same file. You can duplicate a text layer to change its color for the rollover state for example and add the image change for it on yet another layer of the same file. When it is time to save for the Web, simply turn off the layers you don't need when saving the specific state of your rollover navigation. **FIGURE 4-15** exemplifies how this process is done using student Natalie Traber's final website.

1. This is a screen shot of the completed web page, with the over state for her metal rollover graphic.
2. Here in the Layers palette, the up and over states are all in one graphic, with the up state of the text turned off.
3. With this layer turned off, when entering the Save for Web dialog box, only visible layers are displayed here, providing the ability to save just the over state as an individual web graphic.

This allows you to create a file with multiple matching sizes, font placements, etc., by simply turning on and off the layers you need visible, and then saving each specific navigation state through the Save for Web dialog box.

FIGURE 4-15 Rollover graphics. (Courtesy of Natalie Traber, student, Milford, NH.)

We have all visited a site that has a navigation graphic that shifts right or left, or becomes slightly larger/smaller accidentally when you roll over it. Using this method for creating and saving navigation graphics will prevent that problem from happening in your sites. We will take a closer look at rollover errors in Chapter 11 when learning how to insert navigation graphics in Dreamweaver.

4.4.2 Creating Navigation Bar Graphics

Although it has been removed from CS5, both the CS3 and the CS4 versions of Dreamweaver include a feature called Navigation Bar that allows you to add vertical or horizontal navigation to a web page with up to four possible navigational states: up, over, down, and over while down. (CS5 users: Don't worry! We will be learning to create cool Spry menus that slide out with additional navigation options later in this text, as well as learning how you can use image rollovers to create the same visual appearance as a navigation bar, except without as many possible states.)

FIGURE 4-16 Navigation bar for DS Dezign. (Courtesy of David Schmidt, student, Mount Vernon, NH.)

For CS3 and CS4 users, understanding why there can be up to four states and how to add them to a web page will be discussed in Chapter 11. At this time, we will discuss how to make them, using the same basic concept used to create rollover images, by maximizing the potential of the Layers palette in Photoshop combined with its Save for Web command. Before learning to create one, let's take a look at student David Schmidt's navigation for his graphic design website in **FIGURE 4-16**.

The visitor enjoys a soft blue glow that compliments its black background when in the over state of this navigation, which is sleek and professional in its appearance. After studying Natalie's rollover graphics in Figure 4-15, can you figure out how a single multi-layered Photoshop file could create David's navigation effects?

4.4.3 Creating Multiple State Navigation Graphics

If you are working in CS5 and are only interested in learning how to create the sliding Spry Menu Bar we will use in the Fishluvrz site, you can skip this section. For everyone else, let's learn how to create multiple state navigation graphics.

We have discussed the importance of planning. It is critical here to take the time to decide not only whether your navigation area will be horizontal or vertical, but also how many navigation buttons you will need and how large they will be. For example, if your web page will be 750 pixels wide and you want six navigation buttons evenly spaced horizontally across the page, the width of each button should be 125 pixels: ($6 \times 125 = 750$). What about the height? That is up to you and your design needs. The critical issue here is the width if you are creating horizontal navigation. When creating a vertical navigation bar, height will be the most critical dimension to assure that your navigation addresses the principle of the fold.

After you have determined the height and width that your navigation graphic will need to be to work in your document, create a Photoshop document with the dimensions of the single navigation button.

Always start your design using the *longest* word in your navigation bar! It is common to start with the *home* button, only to realize when creating the *services* button (for example) that your font is too large and does not work. Time is money.

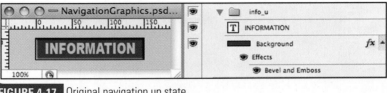

FIGURE 4-17 Original navigation up state.

After completing the up state of your longest word, make a group out of the layers you needed to create it (you can multi-select them and choose that option from the Layers palette's options menu), as shown in **FIGURE 4-17**.

Title the group by what it is, e.g., *info_u* for the up state of the Information button. Duplicate this group, change the name of the group to the next up navigation, such as *home*, open the group folder, and make the text changes to reflect the new navigation. Repeat this process for the rest of your up states. At this point, you should start to organize your navigation. Create a group titled *All Ups* and drag all of these individual groups inside it.

Your navigation scheme should now show all of your up states, with each one in its own folder (group), with all of those up states within a master folder (group), as shown in **FIGURE 4-18**.

Following this process, create the rest of your states. Begin by copying one of your up state groups, for example, your *info_u* state. Change the colors as desired, and save it as *info_o*. Now, you can repeat the process to create the rest of your over state buttons, then place them in an *All Overs* master group folder, and then repeat these steps for the rest of the states of your buttons. *Be sure to follow the same sequential order for each state when creating them* (e.g., Information, Products, Home, FAQ, and Contact Us, as shown in Figure 4-18). This will help you stay organized now, and later in the Save for Web dialog box.

We have learned that only visible layers show in the Save for Web dialog box, so let's learn how to save all of these individual states of navigation. To do this, just as in learning to create an image rollover, turn on only the layers that pertain to a particular state of a particular button of your navigation, for example, the up state of Information. When you choose Save for Web, only that state with its features will show up, as shown in **FIGURE 4-19**.

When you click the Save button in the Save for Web dialog box, it will be handy to continue to title your navigation states consistently for easy import into Dreamweaver later. For example, in the Navigation sample shown in Figure 4-19, this would be titled *info_u* (for up). Its counterparts would be *info_o* (over), *info_d* (down), and *info_owd* (over while down), remembering *not* to have a space between the word and the letter indicating the specific navigation state. Creating a checklist similar to **FIGURE 4-20** will help you keep track when saving multiple states for a navigation bar.

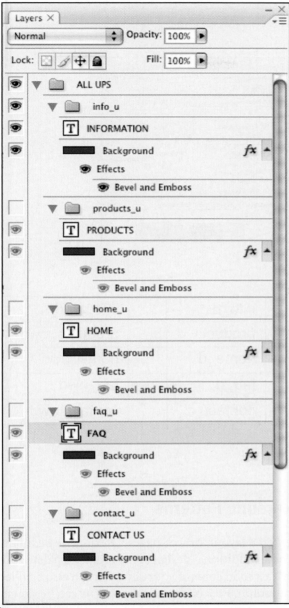

FIGURE 4-18 Sample group of all up navigation states.

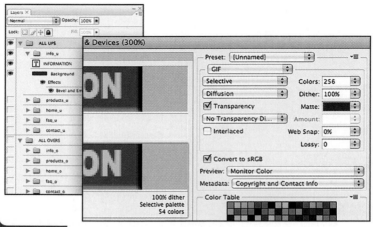

FIGURE 4-19 Navigation Save for Web.

	info_u		info_o		info_d		info_owd
	products_u		products_o		products_d		products_owd
	home_u		home_o		home_d		home_owd
	faq_u		faq_o		faq_d		faq_owd
	contact_u		contact_o		contact_d		contact_owd

FIGURE 4-20 Navigation checklist.

 ## 4.5 Web Page Background Patterns

We have discussed the use of a centered layout for web pages, offering the flexibility of utilizing the background area as an additional design area or "artist's palette" for your page. While it can be filled with a solid color of your choice, it can also be filled in with a pattern, border, or photograph. Free background patterns can be downloaded from a variety of companies, categorized by color. Just search for "download free web page background patterns" and you'll be amazed at all that are available. Be careful in your search; even though they say "free," not all of the companies that will come up in your search will be absolutely free, with no strings attached. But there are some out there, and they are a great source for a quick, easy background addition to a page. In Dreamweaver, you will be able to choose this pattern with the options to repeat it both vertically and horizontally, to repeat it only vertically or horizontally, or to not repeat it at all, which we will learn how to do in Chapter 9.

FIGURE 4-21 Background pattern.

Another option is to create your own pattern to use as a complete background or as a border. All you need to know is the height and width in pixels that you want the design to be before it repeats and build it at that size with 72 ppi as the resolution. **FIGURE 4-21** is an example of a border created to repeat vertically across the top of a page. For now, any border or pattern you create can be tested in Photoshop. With the layer selected, press Alt/Option and drag the image in a sample page to keep duplicating it so that you can see how it lines up. When we add a background pattern in Dreamweaver, it will do all the work for you! Are you getting excited?

This pattern was designed to be viewed at the top of the web page, as shown through a browser in **FIGURE 4-22**.

In **FIGURE 4-23**, you will notice that it is a left-aligned page. However, it contains a border as part of its background pattern that will continue on the right side of the page for the remaining width available in the viewer's monitor. Notice also the use of a graphic with a clear background placed on top of the border for extra pizzazz. It's another great design idea for your idea book!

What's next? We've learned about web color, type, navigation, principles of design, and now graphics preparation. We're ready to move on to Part 2 of the text and learn how to apply them all in Dreamweaver!

FIGURE 4-22 Lupine Restaurant home page with border pattern.

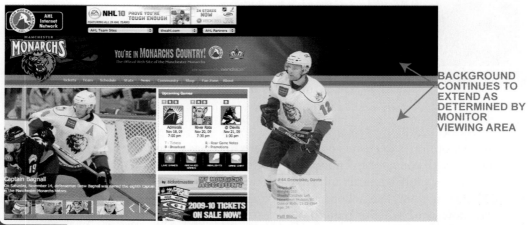

FIGURE 4-23 Monarchs' home page border extends to the right. (Courtesy of the Manchester Monarchs, http://www.manchestermonarchs.com.)

4.6 What We Have Learned

In this chapter, we learned the available options for photograph acquisition, how to crop them using the fixed ratio crop method in pixels, then complete the optimization process through the Save for Web dialog box in Photoshop. Our Save for Web discussion focused on the unique characteristics of each file format, enabling you to make educated decisions for your web graphics and the appropriate file format each one will need, depending on its characteristics and future usage. We also discussed the sequential steps required for saving web navigation graphics with multiple states and how careful planning and organization will yield professional navigation in Dreamweaver, with easy updates later if needed.

4.7 Reinforcing Your Knowledge

Before you start: Launch the CD that came with your textbook and copy the entire *Textbook Practice Files* folder to your desktop, making its files easy to access to complete the projects throughout the remaining chapters of this text.

Project 1

1. Use Photoshop to open *lupine_restaurant_page.psd*, located in the *Chapter_4PracticeFiles* folder. Notice that this file has multiple layers, and guides have been placed to divide the page. Be sure you have guides turned on in Photoshop, slice the page using the Slices from Guides feature, then delete and extend the remaining slices to match Figure 4-14.

2. Choose the Save for Web feature, set a Matte color of black (#000000), choose the JPEG file format with a quality that does not compromise the text, add the Progressive option, set Blur to 0, no ICC Profile, and click Save.

3. Choose a location on your hard drive where you will be able to locate this file later. Title the folder *sliced_page*. We will use this file when learning about AP Divs in Dreamweaver.

4. Choose Images Only, Default Settings, and All Slices. You will see that the images are placed by default within their own folders inside the folder you created.

Project 2

1. In the *Chapter_4PracticeFiles* folder, you will find a folder titled *Fish Photos* containing four images. Using the fixed ratio crop method in Photoshop, crop each of them to 275 × 100 pixels at 72 ppi. Crop the image as desired, using your artist's eye.

2. Use the Save for Web feature, set a Matte color of #FFFFFF, choose the JPEG file format with a quality that retains the integrity of the image, and click Save.

3. Create a folder on your desktop titled *Fishluvrz Project*. Create two folders inside it: one titled *original fishluvrz graphics* and one titled *FishluvrzRoot*. Inside the *FishluvrzRoot* folder, create a folder titled *images* and save these cropped images inside it. Then, save a copy of the original fish photos at their full size (or simply drag a copy of the *Fish Photos* folder in the practice files folder) into the *original fishluvrz graphics* folder. In future chapters, we will learn why these folders were created in this fashion, and how we will use them.

Project 3

Create a repeating background pattern and apply it to one of your mock layouts. It can be as simple as a gradient, as shown in the Fezzari Performance Bicycles site (Figure 3-6) or a small repeating image. Set your pixel dimensions small enough to make your pattern subtle but attractive, not large and overpowering. Using Alt/Option drag, create the appearance of the repeating vertical, horizontal, or all over pattern for the background area of the mock layout.

Project 4

Open the *fish_montage.psd* file located in the *Chapter_4PracticeFiles* folder. Slice the page using the Slices from Guides feature. In the Save for Web dialog box, choose *JPEG* for the file format, with a matte color of #FFFFFF, and an appropriate optimization for the slices. Save them into the Fishluvrz site *images* folder you created in Project 2 of this chapter, choosing *Images Only, Default Slices*, and *All Slices* for your Save for Web options. After you have done this, quit Photoshop and locate the *images* folder of slices you just created. You will see that it was created as an image folder inside your *images* folder. Rename this inner folder *images_montage* to indentify these images for use later in the text. Then, save a copy of the *original fish_montage.psd* file (or simply drag a copy of the original *fish_montage.psd* file from the *Chapter_4PracticeFiles* folder) in the *original fishluvrz graphics* folder.

4.8 Building Your Own Website

1. If you are working in either CS3 or CS4, feel free to create a multi-state navigation bar with up to four states. (By the way, if you later upgrade to CS5, your navigation bar will upgrade with you, you will just not be able to edit its states.) However, as previously mentioned, we will also be learning how to insert a Spry Menu Bar that will slide out to provide menu options. If you would like to view one now to decide if it is the look you want for your site, feel free to visit http://www.saddlebackmaine.com and click any of the home page's main navigation buttons.

   If you are working in CS5, you can still create a navigation bar instead of the slide out style navigation, if desired, by using two states for each navigation button created in the same manner as the navigation bar graphics detailed in this chapter. If you prefer that look, design your buttons with an up and over state for each (you will learn in Chapter 11 how they can be inserted as successive image rollovers, creating the same final visual and interactive effect as a navigation bar).

   If you decide to plan your navigation using either a navigation bar of up to four states or a navigation system created with two state rollovers, use one of your mock layouts from Chapter 3 that is 750 pixels wide and divide the total number of navigational links you will need in the bar into that width to determine a size for each individual navigation graphic. Then, determine an appropriate corresponding vertical height based on your mock layout, or determine their width and height if you will be creating a vertical navigation system instead of a horizontal one. After you know what size each will need to be, create a new .psd file, designing one button by the size you have determined, then follow the steps you have learned in this chapter to create the rest of the buttons and their states, and save them all for the Web. How many states do you need? You really only need two, an up and over state, which is why you can create this same look, even if you are working in CS5 and do not have the Navigation Bar feature. Creating a checklist, as shown in Figure 4-20, will help you stay organized when using the Save for Web dialog box, especially if you are creating four navigation states. Save each state in an *images* folder titled *originalFiles_MySite* inside another folder on your desktop.

If planning to insert a Spry slide-out menu instead, determine the height and width you will need, either vertical or horizontal, and add a colored area to your mock layout to design the rest of your page around it.

2. We will be learning two distinct methods of adding the rest of your page content to a web page in Dreamweaver. You will prepare some images both ways for now, so you will be able to use the method that best fits your design and learning needs later. In this chapter, you have learned how to crop, optimize, and save your images for the Web. With the final mock layout you created in Chapter 3, you now know what size your graphics need to be for your home page, and can save them accordingly. Open the final mock layout of your home page. Add any photographs or graphics you have created and cropped to the size you need for the page. Add a colored area the size your navigation will be *for design positioning only*. Complete the rest of your entire web page here in Photoshop, excluding body text (we will add that in future chapters), as shown in Figure 4-14.

3. Add guides to divide the headline from the body, and separate the navigation, the footer area, and any other divisions you will need to alter individually.

4. Choose the Slice tool, choose Slices from Guides, and then use the Slice Select tool to adjust them as necessary, deleting the excess slices.

5. Choose the Save for Web option and save all the slices *except your positioning only navigation area*. Save each slice individually in a folder titled *sliced_index* within the *images* folder of the *originalFiles_MySite* folder you created in Step 1. Remember to also save this page in its native .psd format with all of its layers in this folder as well.

6. Return to the original file. Choose View>Clear Slices, then choose View>Slices, and uncheck Slices. This should remove all of the slices and return your page to its original look, with just your guides showing. Now, sequentially turn off backgrounds, other images, etc., and optimize each

image individually using the Save for Web feature, titling each one accordingly so that you can identify it later. Save each of these in the same optimized *images* folder you created in the *originalFiles_MySite* folder in step 1.

7. You will now have the flexibility to use the entire page, or only its images, when building a web page later in Dreamweaver. After you have learned both techniques in Dreamweaver, the choice will be yours!

Building Your Site in Dreamweaver

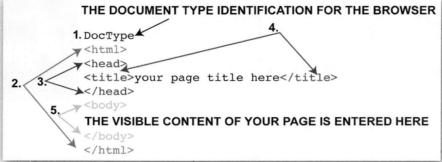

Part 2

THE DOCUMENT TYPE IDENTIFICATION FOR THE BROWSER

```
1. DocType
   <html>
   <head>
   <title>your page title here</title>
   </head>
   <body>
```
2. 3. 4. 5.

THE VISIBLE CONTENT OF YOUR PAGE IS ENTERED HERE
```
   </body>
   </html>
```

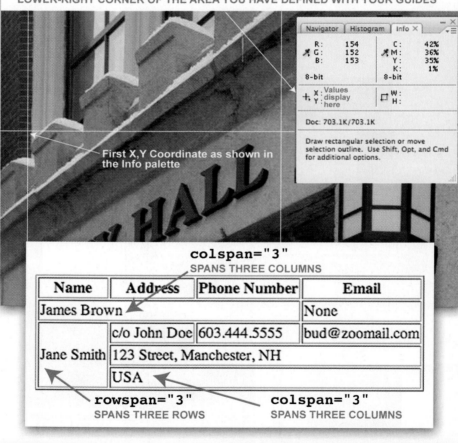

COORDINATES OF THE UPPER-LEFT CORNER, FOLLOWED BY THE ONES FOR THE LOWER-RIGHT CORNER OF THE AREA YOU HAVE DEFINED WITH YOUR GUIDES

First X,Y Coordinate as shown in the Info palette

colspan="3"
SPANS THREE COLUMNS

Name	Address	Phone Number	Email
James Brown			None
Jane Smith	c/o John Doe	603.444.5555	bud@zoomail.com
	123 Street, Manchester, NH		
	USA		

rowspan="3"
SPANS THREE ROWS

colspan="3"
SPANS THREE COLUMNS

Introduction to HTML

5

In this optional chapter, you are introduced to writing HTML code, and the terminology associated with it. After an overview of the history of the Web and a general introduction to the terms and processes, writing code for individual web page features, such as tables, forms, and CSS rules for text, is explored and practiced.

5.1   History of the Web

The World Wide Web (WWW) was the brainchild of a computer mastermind named Tim Berners-Lee. He envisioned the potential of the Web while writing a software program titled *Enquire* in 1980. By the end of 1990, he had written the code for Hypertext Transfer Protocol (HTTP), Hypertext Markup Language (HTML), and the first web server. With the assistance of a colleague named Robert Cailliau, Berners-Lee strove to convince his associates at CERN, the European Organization for Nuclear Research, in Geneva, Switzerland, of the global possibilities of his dream. As the World Wide Web (the name he coined for his worldwide communication concept) gained popularity, browsers began to be written to access it, with the first major one in 1993 named Mosaic. The following year, MIT and CERN jointly initiated the World Wide Web Consortium (W3C). Commercial browsers began to emerge, with Microsoft introducing its own browser, Internet Explorer® into its Microsoft® Windows® 95 operating system. After browsers allowed easy, no-cost home computer access to the Web, its popularity and use exploded into what it is today: truly a world wide web of resources of information, products, and services.[1]

5.2   Understanding the Jargon

Although the focus of this textbook is artistic web designs created through Dreamweaver, having a basic understanding of Hypertext Markup Language (HTML) or Extensible Hypertext Markup Language (XHTML) terminology and writing/editing will help you resolve layout and formatting issues that may present themselves as you build your sites later in Dreamweaver because it allows you to build pages in three views:

- **code view:** working strictly in HTML.
- **design view:** a strictly visual what you see is what you get (WYSIWYG) display of the page in which Dreamweaver writes the code for you; this textbook focuses on this view.
- **split view:** a combination view that allows you to see (and author if needed) the code in your page while still being able to simultaneously create and edit in the visual design view of the page.

If your learning needs or interests do not require this chapter, you may skip it and move on to Chapter 6. Even if you decide to bypass this chapter for now, you can always return to it at any time to explore or further understand the basics of HTML. In future chapters, after we are working in Dreamweaver to create pages, the HTML writing fundamentals learned here will be cited in the related projects. They will be re-examined, using the split view combination of code and its visual counterpart, to increase both your awareness of and your ability to edit the HTML code used to create the effect learned in the respective chapter.

5.2.1 General Web Terminology

Before learning the terms associated specifically with HTML, it is important to become familiar with a few general terms associated with the World Wide Web:

- **browser (a.k.a. web browser):** This is a software program used to display web pages.
- **domain name:** To understand this term, think of your own personal *domain* or residence. This is your unique name that must be different from every other website in the world because it is your personal domain on the Internet. The identifiers at the end of the domain name are part of the actual name, such as the *.com* of *mysite.com.* Your domain name is also part of the full URL, as in *http://www.mysite.com.*
- **Extensible Hypertext Markup Language (XHTML):** This is another markup language that is very similar to HTML, but it is a little fussier and less forgiving (for example, if capitalization discrepancies exist in the code written in it). However, this same fussy quality also helps it display more predictably across browsers. New pages created in Dreamweaver default to XHTML.
- **external link:** A link on a page in a website that, when clicked, displays a location in a different website on the World Wide Web.
- **file transfer protocol (FTP):** *Protocol*, meaning procedure, is the part of the name that will help you understand and remember the definition of this term. FTP is a procedure or method of transferring files over the Internet, typically used for uploading and downloading web pages to a server. We will use this method in Dreamweaver when learning how to upload websites.
- **hypertext:** This term refers to text used in a web page to link from one page to another page within the same website or to another site on the World Wide Web.
- **Hypertext Markup Language (HTML):** In this term, *language* is the key to understanding its meaning. This is the coding language used to create documents that are readable on the World Wide Web.
- **Hypertext Transfer Protocol (HTTP):** When you type an address you want to go to on the Internet, you usually type *http://* followed by the specific web address desired. Again, it will be helpful to think of the definition of the word *protocol* as meaning procedure. HTTP is a procedure or method of transferring the request to view a web page from the user to the corresponding server containing the requested page, which results in the page being displayed on the user's computer screen.
- **internal link:** A link on a page in a website that, when clicked, displays another location within the same website.

- **Internet:** If you break this name down to its parts, it will be easy to understand and remember. Think of *inter*, as in *international* or *interconnected*, and *net* as in *network*. The Internet is the network connecting all sites of the World Wide Web.
- **Uniform Resource Locator (URL):** If you think of the word *locator*, it will help you understand and remember this term. This is the term given to an official individual identification, address, or location on the Web. *http://www.yourcompanyhere.com/contact.html* is a fictitious example of the URL to the contact page of yourcompanyhere.com.
- **web host:** This is the term given to the provider of the server that stores your website on it and enables its presence on the World Wide Web.
- **web server:** A computer used to host a website.
- **World Wide Web (WWW):** Web pages, worldwide, that are accessed through the Internet.

5.2.2 General HTML Terminology

It is important to have a basic familiarity with the names and functions of the tools that create web pages before learning how to use them to build your first web page using HTML:

- **attribute:** The meaning of this word as it relates to HTML is best understood by thinking of the word *attribute* in its traditional usage as a characteristic or feature of something. Attributes define the characteristics or specific features of the directions written in an element. They are not the directions. For example, when creating a paragraph, the alignment of the paragraph would be an attribute. The actual creation of the paragraph would be the HTML directions. When inserting an attribute, it must be entered in the opening tag of the element.
- **closing tag:** Text that indicates that the element is closed or ends here. It is identified by a less than symbol (to be referred to as a left angle bracket for the remainder of this textbook), a forward slash, followed usually by the same name as that used in the opening tag, and ends with the greater than symbol (referred to as a right angle bracket for the remainder of this textbook).
- **element:** Defines what you want to happen on the page at the specified location. An element includes the following three ingredients: the opening tag (the directions), attributes if applicable (the additional features), and the closing tag to end the particular directions included in the element.
- **opening tag:** Text that indicates that the element is opened or starts here. It begins with a left angle bracket, followed by directions, and ends with a right angle bracket.
- **tag:** Text that identifies and delineates elements. HTML uses an opening tag at the beginning of the element and a closing tag at the end of the element.

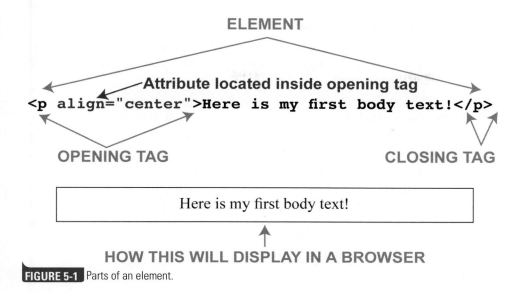

FIGURE 5-1 Parts of an element.

FIGURE 5-1 illustrates how these HTML code writing tools combine together to create the visual appearance desired when viewed in a browser.

5.2.3 HTML vs. XHTML

As mentioned previously in the XHTML definition, XHTML is fussier than HTML. Because Dreamweaver uses XHTML, when learning the basics of HTML, our work will incorporate the additional restrictions of XHTML. The restrictions are basically ones that lend themselves to best practice in web work:

- Use all lowercase text in the tags. Do not mix in any capitalization when creating elements.
- End all elements with the closing tag that corresponds to the element's opening tag.
- If an element is created inside another element, its opening and closing tags must surround it inside the outer element's opening and closing tags.
- The page must be completely contained within the opening and closing HTML element.

5.3 HTML Basics

Before learning to create a page using HTML code, it is important to understand the structure of an HTML page and what type of software is needed to build one.

5.3.1 Parts of an HTML Page

All pages must contain the following essential components that define the structure of the page, as shown in **FIGURE 5-2**. As detailed in this illustration, elements are often located inside other elements.

1. As the name implies, DocType identifies the type of document for the browser, so that the browser will be able to read it. It must be the very first thing that the browser sees, which is the reason it is located at the top of the page.

2. The HTML element, which must always be located right below the DocType, declares that everything between its opening and closing tags will be an HTML file. Its opening tag `<html>` starts the page and its corresponding closing tag, `</html>`, ends the page; as the last closing tag of the page, it defines the end of the file. *Inside* the boundaries of the HTML element are the head element and the body element.

3. The head, a critical "behind the scenes" section of the page, includes style sheets, search engine identification information, the page title, etc. Notice that it starts with the opening `<head>` tag and ends with the `</head>` closing tag.

4. As shown in Figure 5-2, the title element is located *inside* the head element. (Notice that the opening and closing tags of the title element are both contained inside the head element before its closing tag, `</head>`.) This mandatory element's function is just as it sounds: this is where you enter the title of your page. The title you enter here will display at the top of the page when viewed in a browser.

5. The body is the section of the page where you enter the page's visible content: its text, graphics, etc. Notice that it starts and ends with the

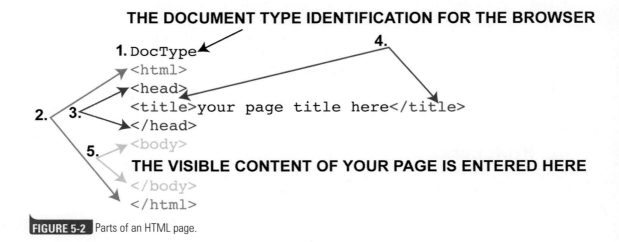

FIGURE 5-2 Parts of an HTML page.

DOCTYPE	**This section's single role is to define the HTML version of the page to a browser so that it can be read and displayed properly.**
HEAD	**This section of the page includes the location to enter the title of the page as it will be viewed in a browser. It is also the area where the operational components of the page are entered, such as its style sheets, search engine keywords, etc.**
BODY	**This is where the visual content of the page is entered, such as body text, images, etc.**

FIGURE 5-3 Three main sections of every HTML page.

body tags: `<body>` begins the page content and `</body>` ends it. This is followed by the closing `</html>` tag, which finishes the HTML element, completing the page.

These five critical HTML components are located within three general categories or sections of every HTML page, as illustrated in **FIGURE 5-3**.

Remembering this basic breakdown of the type of information entered and located in each of these three main areas will help you understand the process as we begin to build web pages using HTML.

5.3.2 HTML Writing Environment

All that is needed to create HTML pages is a basic text editing program that allows you to save the text with UTF-8 encoding; both Mac and Windows systems come with one preinstalled. The option to select the encoding is located in the Save As dialog box of the text editing program. When selecting the encoding, there may be other Unicode options in addition to UTF-8 listed in its drop-down menu. A great way to help you remember which one to choose is to think of the letters as representing *Universal Text Format*. The letters UTF actually stand for *Unicode Transformation Format*, with the *8* representing *8 bit*.

Using TextEdit for Mac   If working on a Mac, TextEdit will be located in the *Applications* folder of the hard drive. If, when launched, it opens with the editing features of a basic word processing program, such as tabs, alignment, etc., you will need to choose Format>Make Plain Text. After you are in Plain Text mode, when you enter the Save As dialog box, the UTF-8 Encoding option will be preselected for you. You also have the option to change the preference for the type of document that opens by default when choosing File>New. If you will be working extensively in Plain Text

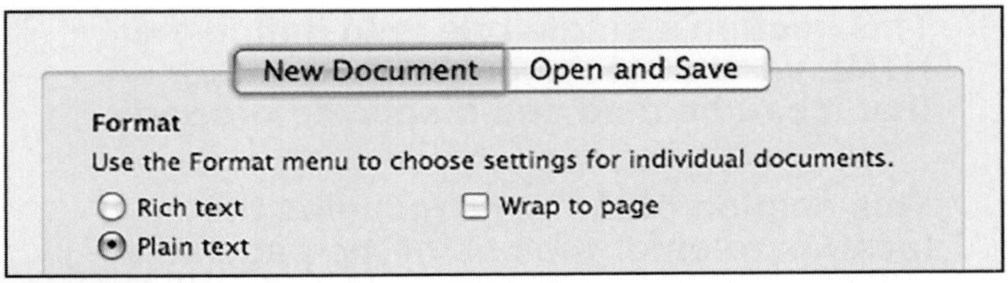

New Document | Open and Save

Format
Use the Format menu to choose settings for individual documents.
○ Rich text   ☐ Wrap to page
● Plain text

FIGURE 5-4 Plain text option on a Mac.

mode to build HTML pages, under TextEdit>Preferences>New Document, select the Plain text option under the Format category as shown in **FIGURE 5-4**.

If you change this preference, but do not always need to use this program for HTML, you can create a new document, then choose Format>Make Rich Text to convert it back to the word processing mode for the open document, leaving the program preference set for plain text.

Using Notepad for Windows   Windows comes with a preinstalled text editing software called Notepad, located under *Accessories*. After you open Notepad, in the Save As dialog box, you can choose UTF-8 from the Encoding options.

5.4 Creating a Web Page

> **Note:** *Throughout the remainder of this chapter, many of the textbook examples will incorporate images. If you wish to complete the exercises yourself as you read them, locate the* Chapter_5PracticeFiles *folder in the* Textbook Practice Files *folder that you copied to your desktop in Chapter 4. Remember, when a path to a file is written in various samples provided in this chapter as* /Users/vellenwolper/Desktop/ Chapter_5PracticeFiles/ *your code must reflect your computer's specific path to your Chapter 5 practice files folder on your desktop.*

In **FIGURE 5-5**, you will see the title *My First Page!* that displays in the title area of the browser, and a single sentence on the web page.

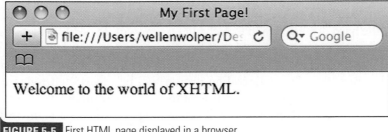

FIGURE 5-5 First HTML page displayed in a browser.

If you are building this page as its code is introduced, in a text editing program, use the following HTML:

```
<!DOCTYPE html PUBLIC "-//W3C//DTD XHTML 1.0 Transi-
tional//EN" "http://www.w3.org/TR/xhtml1/DTD/xhtml1-
transitional.dtd">

<html xmlns="http://www.w3.org/1999/xhtml">
<head>
<title>My First Page!
</title>
</head>
<body>Welcome to the world of XHTML.
</body>
</html>
```

Save the page as *sample.html*, and preview it in a browser. It is important not to get overwhelmed when you see *all* that code for virtually two visible sentences in the browser: the title of the page that shows up in the title area of the browser and the single sentence in the page area. Let's examine it closer. As learned, the first section, the *DOCTYPE* section, is simply the required information for the browser to be able to read the page. As previously mentioned, Dreamweaver uses the DocType *XHTML 1.0 Transitional*. The first part of the page code is just the standard description, worded exactly as it needs to be to complete that process. The second section, `<html xmlns="http://www.w3.org/1999/xhtml">`, is simply the `<html>` opening tag we learned about, with a required attribute that also relates to the interpretation of the document for the browser (notice the equals sign and quotes that indicate an attribute and that it is located *inside* the opening HTML tag).

Save the opening DOCTYPE informational text and the opening `<html>` information together as a separate regular word processing document (not an .html document that we will be creating from here on in). Because it will be the same for every document you create, you will then be able to simply copy and paste it into the beginning of every new .html document you start after it. That way, you only have to write this code once!

This is followed by the opening head tag to begin the head element, the opening title tag *inside* of it, followed by the title *My First Page!*, ending with the closing title tag, which is also followed by the closing head tag.

The body opening tag is next, followed by a whooping single sentence page that states: *Welcome to the world of XHTML*. As learned, because that is the end of the page content, it is followed by a closing body tag and ends the entire document with the closing HTML tag. After saving the document again and previewing it in a browser, this really *is* the time to say, "Welcome to the world of XHTML!"

```
<!DOCTYPE html PUBLIC "-//W3C//DTD XHTML 1.0
Transitional//EN"
"http://www.w3.org/TR/xhtml1/DTD/xhtml1-
transitional.dtd">

<html xmlns="http://www.w3.org/1999/xhtml">
<head>
<title>My First Page!
</title>
</head>
<body>Welcome to the world of XHTML.
</body>
</html>
```

FIGURE 5-6 Saving error occurred.

If you tried this on your own, but when you previewed your page in a browser, all you saw was another page of code, as shown in **FIGURE 5-6** (with "sample" at the top instead "My First Page!"), open your original file and return to the Save As dialog box.

The most common mistakes are not choosing the UTF-8 encoding and, more commonly, not adding the .html extension after the name when saving, instead of the default extension .txt.

Did you know that you can study the HTML code for almost any page on the Web? With your *sample.html* file still open in a browser, under the View menu, you will see an option to view the code of the page. The command's exact wording is browser specific—look for a command such as View>Source, View>Page Source, or View>Page—it's a great way to help you learn code!

■ 5.4.1 Basic Text Formatting

Now that we have learned to enter text into the body element of an HTML page, let's learn how to apply some basic formatting to it.

Headings   In the previous sample, *Welcome to the world of XHTML.* is the only sentence in the <body> element, the part that becomes the *visible* area of the XHTML page. First, we will learn how to jazz up this title as a heading. Headings are defined in HTML as an <h1> tag to apply the largest heading size, with <h6>

being the smallest heading. These will display your text in the font and size according to the default preferences of the browser. To assign the largest display size to the title, the body section must be written as:

```
<body>
<h1>Welcome to the world of XHTML.</h1>
</body>
```

(Remember that all of the code must be written in lowercase. The *W* of the word *Welcome* is not part of the element code; it is the text *inserted into* the element.)

You can add another heading, such as a subhead of secondary importance. For example, to add *The language of Dreamweaver* below this main heading, after the closing `</h1>` and before the closing of the `</body>` element, add the following code: `<h2>The language of Dreamweaver</h2>`. The `<h2>` element you add defines the text included in it as a subhead and, therefore, automatically displays it smaller and below the first heading.

When applicable in the rest of this chapter, to help delineate when an area of code requires a specific value typed into it, the value area will be defined in red. The color is for explanatory purposes and is not part of the code writing.

Alignment The `align="alignment typed here"` attribute sets the alignment of the header. By adding the alignment attribute to the opening heading tag, the heading becomes centered on the page, as shown in the following example:

```
<h1 align="center">Welcome to the world of XHTML.</h1>
```

If applied to both Heading 1 and Heading 2, the page will look as shown in **FIGURE 5-7**.

It is important to note that you must type a space between the number one of the opening `<h1>` tag and the word `align` that follows it for the sentence to display correctly when tested in a browser. Watch carefully for spaces (if any), quotation marks, equals signs, etc., needed in the exact locations and sequences given in this text in order for the specific effect to display properly when it is viewed in a browser.

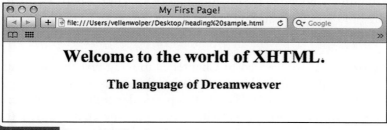

FIGURE 5-7 Centered headings in a browser.

Creating Paragraph Text   When you are ready to insert paragraph text, it is entered using the `<p>` element. Each new paragraph that you want to create must start with the `<p>` opening tag and end with the `</p>` closing tag.

Basic Text Styling   In addition to adding headings to your text, you can style your text by making it bold using the `<strong>` opening tag and the `</strong>` closing tag, or italic by adding the `<em>` (short for *emphasis*, not to be confused with the em unit of measurement) opening tag and the `</em>` closing tag around the word(s) you want to style. Note the paragraph delineations and styling added to the following sample text:

```
<p>This is the <strong>FIRST</strong> paragraph of
text, with the bold style applied to the word first.</p>

<p>This is the <em>second</em> paragraph of text with
the italic style applied to the word second.</p>

<p>This third paragraph has the last word with
both the bold and italic options applied to
<em><strong>it!</strong></em></p>
```

Although this sample begins with the paragraph element opening tag, remember that this text *must* be between the opening and closing body tags as we have already learned, which must be contained within the `<html>` element.

Before we preview it in a browser, setting the alignment for a paragraph follows the same process as adding it to a heading—insert it into the opening tag of the paragraph you want to style. To change paragraph text to be center aligned, the opening element will be `<p align="center">` instead of the original `<p>` opening tag.

Can you copy and paste any code you want to use again within the same paragraph or the same page? Yes! However, be sure it is clean and free of errors the first time by testing it in a browser. Then, copy it, place your insertion point where you want to add it, and choose Paste. Also, when building a page in a text editor, save your page every time you make any changes to it. You can keep the browser open while you are working on your HTML page and periodically check the changes in the browser by clicking the browser's Refresh button.

With center alignment added to the opening tags of each of the body elements, in addition to the bold and italic styling added to the paragraphs, the page now previews in a browser, as shown in **FIGURE 5-8**.

Creating Soft Returns   As we learned in Chapter 2, moving text to a new line without creating a new paragraph (known in print design as a soft return) is known as a *line break* in web design. In HTML, this particular code stands alone: it does not have an opening and closing part to it, you simply type `<br />` where the soft return is desired within the paragraph of text you are typing.

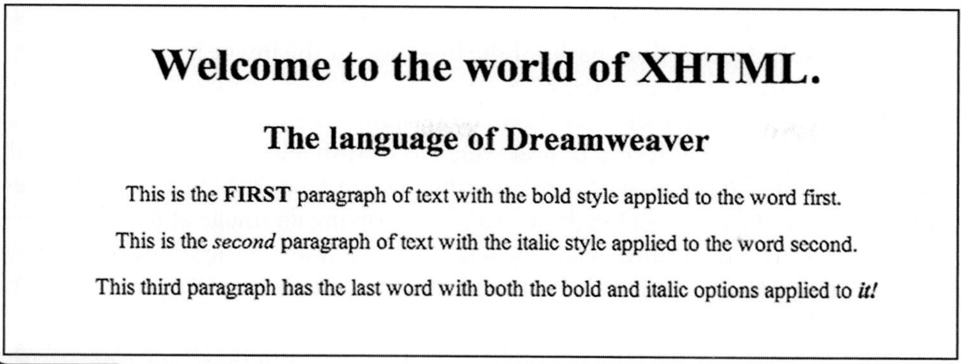

Welcome to the world of XHTML.

The language of Dreamweaver

This is the **FIRST** paragraph of text with the bold style applied to the word first.

This is the *second* paragraph of text with the italic style applied to the word second.

This third paragraph has the last word with both the bold and italic options applied to *it!*

FIGURE 5-8 Styled paragraphs displayed in a browser.

Adding Space Between Paragraphs   When writing HTML, if you try to create additional space between paragraphs by using the Return/Enter key, when you preview it in a browser, you will see that the returns added into the code have no effect on the final appearance of the text. Type   to create a space between paragraphs in HTML; unlike the rest of the code we have learned to write, it should not be enclosed with angle brackets. This code, which stands for *non-breaking space*, should be placed after the closing paragraph tag of the line you want to leave a space below and before adding the next paragraph, as shown in **FIGURE 5-9**.

5.4.2 Inserting Images

Inserting images requires the image element; however, this element differs from the ones learned thus far. Unlike the previous ones learned, it starts as `<img src`, but does not end with `</img src>`; it merely ends with `/>`. However, it still requires the equals sign, followed by the path to the file defined between quotation marks.

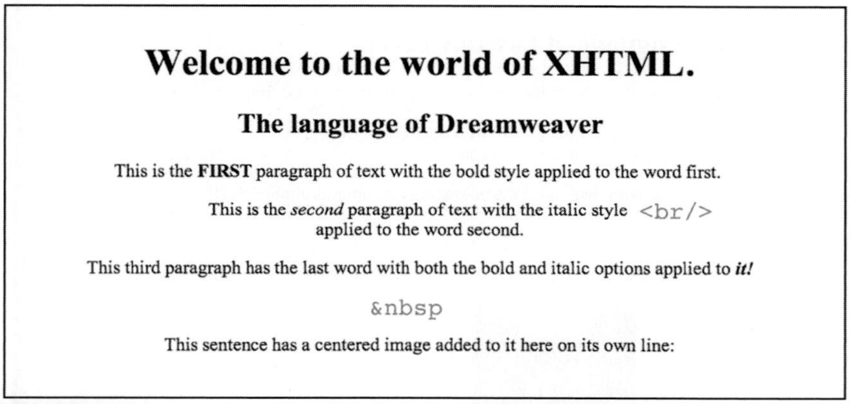

Welcome to the world of XHTML.

The language of Dreamweaver

This is the **FIRST** paragraph of text with the bold style applied to the word first.

This is the *second* paragraph of text with the italic style `<br/>` applied to the word second.

This third paragraph has the last word with both the bold and italic options applied to *it!*

This sentence has a centered image added to it here on its own line:

FIGURE 5-9 Line breaks and spacing. The codes are not shown in the browser. They are displayed here in red only to indicate where the codes were placed when the file was created.

If a specific size is desired that differs from the size of the original source image, follow the closing quotation marks of the insertion of the image by `width="the width typed here" height="the height typed here"` with the element then closed with `/>`. You could change the dimensions of the image in Photoshop before entering it; however, this option allows you to do it directly through the code at the time you are bringing in the image. Although it is not necessary to enter the width and height if you are importing an image at its full original size, *always* entering the dimensions will not negatively affect the code and will help to assure that when you need to enter a specific size, you will remember how to type that request.

To add another centered paragraph to the previous sample stating *This sentence has a centered image added to it here on its own line:* followed by a centered image below the text using the *fish.jpg* image located in the *Chapter_5PracticeFiles* folder scaled down to a width of 200 × 133 pixels. Insert the additional code as follows:

```
<p align="center">This sentence has a centered image
added to it here on its own line:</p>
```

```
<p align="center"><img src="/Users/vellenwolper/
Desktop/Chapter_5PracticeFiles/fish.jpg" width="200"
height="133"/></p>
```

The resulting page, when viewed in a browser, looks like **FIGURE 5-10**.

5.4.3 Creating Links

Links can be either relative or absolute. These differences will be discussed in detail in Chapter 11, when inserting a variety of types of links in Dreamweaver. For now, let's learn to create text, image, and image map links using HTML code.

Welcome to the world of XHTML.

The language of Dreamweaver

This is the **FIRST** paragraph of text with the bold style applied to the word first.

This is the *second* paragraph of text with the italic style
applied to the word second.

This third paragraph has the last word with both the bold and italic options applied to ***it!***

This sentence has a centered image added to it here on its own line:

FIGURE 5-10   Page with imported image displayed in a browser.

Text and Image Links   When adding a text or image link, you indicate first where you are going by typing `<a href="page_to_go_to.html">` followed by how you are going to get there (for example, using a text link or an image) followed by a closing tag of `</a>` (notice that it does *not* close with `</a href>`). The following example uses the same paragraph and fish image from the previous example, with the addition of turning the image into a link to another page named *link_sample.html*. (If you have been following along by building this first page in a text editing program and would also like to create a destination page to practice linking, change the title in the title area, change a little of the text entered, delete the image, then choose File>Save As, title it *link_sample.html*, and save it in the same location on your desktop as you saved the *sample.html* page.) Returning to the page *sample.html*, its link code has been highlighted in red simply to make it easily distinguishable from the rest of the paragraph, but the color is not a requirement when typing the code:

```
<p align="center"><a href="link_sample.
html"><img src="/Users/vellenwolper/Desktop/
Chapter_5PracticeFiles/fish.jpg" width="200"
height="133"/></a></p>
```

To link instead to the home page of a different website instead of linking locally to *link_sample.html*, you would type the full URL of the desired destination such as: `http://www.anotherwebsite.com` after the equals sign and inside the quotation marks of the `<a href=` link code.

   To use text as a link, the link must still begin with the `<a href="page_to_go_to.html">`followed by the text you want to use as the link`</a>` (ending with the closing link tag).

Using a Section of an Image as a Link   You have already used an image map link when surfing the Web; you just may not have known the official name for it. An *image map* is a section of a graphic, not the entire graphic, which is used as a link. After you understand the sequential steps required in the HTML code for it to occur, creating the code will be easier and more logical for you to remember and to generate. It is essentially a two-part process:

- Define an area of a graphic as the *clickable* area and the destination of the link.
- Assign this *mapped* area to the specified graphic.

These two steps together create the clickable link area of an image. However, as long as these two pieces of code exist within the same document, the steps defined here do not have to be in sequential order within the body element of the document for the image map to work.

Defining the Clickable Area   Figuring out how to define the clickable area is the only part of creating an image map that can be a little tricky until you understand the process. When a specific location is required in HTML code, it is defined by its X and Y coordinates. For an image map to work, the specific X and Y coordinates

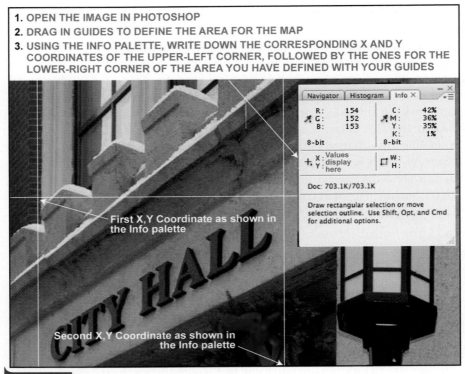

1. OPEN THE IMAGE IN PHOTOSHOP
2. DRAG IN GUIDES TO DEFINE THE AREA FOR THE MAP
3. USING THE INFO PALETTE, WRITE DOWN THE CORRESPONDING X AND Y COORDINATES OF THE UPPER-LEFT CORNER, FOLLOWED BY THE ONES FOR THE LOWER-RIGHT CORNER OF THE AREA YOU HAVE DEFINED WITH YOUR GUIDES

First X,Y Coordinate as shown in the Info palette

Second X,Y Coordinate as shown in the Info palette

FIGURE 5-11 Determining X, Y coordinates.

of the upper-left corner and lower-right corner of the desired area must be entered into the HTML code. The example shown in **FIGURE 5-11** illustrates how to determine those coordinates, if the City Hall building name area of this image was going to be used as an image map. This is part one of the process of using part of an image as a link. (A copy of the image is included in the *Chapter_5PracticeFiles* folder if you would like to try this yourself. You can add this image map to your *link_sample.html* page if you have created one.)

1. Open the image in Photoshop with the pixel dimensions of the image set to its final size.

2. With the rulers visible, draw guides to define the area that will be the *map* or *active* area of the image (to assist you when learning this process, guides have already been added to the sample image provided).

3. Open the Info palette. Move your mouse to the upper-left corner of the intersection of the guides and record the X, Y coordinates displayed in the Info palette for the point at which the vertical and horizontal guides intersect (X,Y), followed by those of the lower-right corner (X,Y), writing them down in X, Y sequence with commas between the values of each one, and in each case with the X value first, followed by the Y value.

After you have those values, the following code determines that you are defining a map:

`<map name="`name you give the map`"` followed by a space `id="`same name`">` followed by `<area shape="rect" coords="`X,Y,X,Y`"` followed by `href="`link_address.html`"` followed by the closing tag of `</map>`.

For an image size of 600×400 pixels to contain the map area, as shown in Figure 5-11, the code would be as follows if the link destination was the page *sample.html*:

```
<map name="lamp" id="lamp"><area shape="rect"
coords="37,171,366,396" href="sample.html"</map>
```

In part two of the process, you will assign this map to an image as a link. After inserting the graphic, and before listing its dimensions, type a space, then the code `usemap="#`the name you gave the map`"` followed by another space, then the rest of the code required when importing an image as shown in the following example:

```
<img src="/Users/vellenwolper/Desktop/
Chapter_5PracticeFiles/lamp.jpg" usemap="#lamp"
width="600" height="400"/>
```

 Did you test the page in a browser? Is the clickable area not covering the entire image? Great! Remember that when the coordinates were defined, they were only recorded for the lower-left area of the image, as shown in Figure 5-11, not the entire image. Remember that you specify the exact limited area you want to use for a link when creating an image map.

5.5 Adding a Table to a Page

The original inclusion of tables in HTML pages began as a method of organizing tabular data, echoing that of a spreadsheet, and is often still used in that context today. However, as you will learn in Chapter 10, in current practice, they are often also used to create entire artistic web page layouts. Because this chapter is a basic overview of HTML, tables will be introduced here only as a data organization tool, not as a page layout design tool.

5.5.1 Parts of a Table

Tables are comprised of cells, divided into rows and columns, with data entered into them. Let's learn to write the HTML code to create a table and customize its cells according to the formatting requirements of the data to be entered, beginning with an overview of its HTML structure.

PARTS OF A TABLE

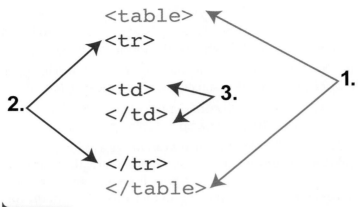

FIGURE 5-12 Table structure.

Table Structure   Tables are defined in HTML by their three basic parts: the table itself, its rows, and its cells. The diagram shown in **FIGURE 5-12** illustrates the components of a table.

1. The starting <table> and ending </table> tags define the parameters of the table, where it will begin (open) and end (close).

2. The starting <tr> and ending </tr> tags (*tr* for *table row*) define the beginning and ending points of a row within a table.

3. The starting <td> and ending </td> tags (*td* for *table data*) define the beginning and ending area for a cell's data within a row of a table.

Inserting Table Headers   If used in their traditional application, tables will often have a descriptive category known as a *header* above the columns of the table. The opening and closing tags are logically defined as <th> and </th> (*th* for *table header*). When used, they are entered between the <tr> and </tr> tags, not the <td> and </td> tags, because they replace the <td> and </td> tags in the row where they are added. When viewed in a browser, type entered as a table header will automatically be centered and bold.

Adding a Table Border   By default, a table created in HTML will not have a border applied to it. If a border is desired around the table, its width is entered within the opening table tag. For example, to add a 1 pixel border around a table, the opening tag will be <table border="1">. If sequential cells of information are required within the same row, each cell of information must be individually contained within the <td> and </td> tags within the <tr> and </tr> tags of the row displaying the data. The following code is an example of how these tags are used

Name	Address
Jane Doe	ABC Street, AnyTown, NH
John Smith	Box 1, CityName, MA

FIGURE 5-13 First table.

to define a basic table of names and addresses, with a header defining the categories and with each new cell of information being contained within the `<tr>` and `</tr>` tags that define that row. Remember that this code must be contained within the `<body>` and `</body>` elements of the page:

```
<table border="1">
<tr>
<th>Name</th><th>Address</th>
</tr>
<tr>
<td>Jane Doe</td><td>ABC Street, AnyTown, NH</td></tr>
<tr><td>John Smith</td><td>Box 1, CityName, MA</td></tr>
</table>
```

The resulting table will display as shown in FIGURE 5-13.

5.5.2 Additional Table Styling

In the table created, data was entered which defaulted to left alignment, with the table cells expanding as needed to accommodate the content requirements of the data. To reconfigure and/or apply styling to tables or individual cells, the formatting code is added to the respective opening tag.

Alignment To center the entire table on the page, following the pattern you have seen thus far, you can probably guess by now how that would be done: inside the opening table tag, after the border attribute, simply add `align="center"` to center the table in the width of the browser page. If the table has a 1 pixel border as well as being centered, the opening tag would read `<table border="1" align="center">` with a space inserted between the two attributes.

To center content within an entire row, enter the same attribute inside the opening `<tr>` tag, as shown: `<tr align="center">`.

Following the same format, to center content within a cell instead of the entire row, add the same attribute within the opening tag of the specific cell: `<td align="center">`.

Width   By default, a table's width will appear in a browser based on the maximum width needed to properly display the longest content in the table. The width can be defined, however, for the entire table, columns, or specific cells:

- To set the width of the table: `<table width="`add pixel width here`">`
- To apply width to the opening header tag for all cells in that column: `<th width="`add pixel width here`">`
- To apply width in the opening cell tag of the cell within the defined width of the table: `<td width="`add pixel width here`">`

Color   A color may be applied to the background of a specific cell, a specific header, an entire row, or the entire table. In the respective opening tag, add the following attribute: `bgcolor=` `"`the color you want to apply`"`. For example, to apply a red background to an entire table, the attribute would be added in the opening table tag as: `<table bgcolor="#FF0000">`.

Changing Table Cell Configurations   When building tables, many times cells or columns need to be combined in order to properly display the data they include. The attributes used to achieve those configurations are the `colspan="`type number here`"` to merge the number of columns in the row of the table and `rowspan="`type number here`"` to merge the cell across a specified number of rows. The attribute is added into the opening `<td>` tag before the information it will be applied to. In the following example, note that after an amount is entered in a rowspan, its `<td>` and content are not entered again in the successive rows it applies to:

```
<table border="1">
<tr>
<th>Name</th><th>Address</th><th>Phone
Number</th><th>Email</th>
</tr>
<tr>
<td colspan="3">James Brown</td><td>None</td></tr>
<tr><td rowspan="3">Jane Smith</td><td>c/o John Doe</td>
<td>603.444.5555</td><td>bud@zoomail.com</td></tr>
<tr><td colspan="3">123 Street, Manchester, NH</td></tr>
<tr><td colspan="3">USA</td></tr>
</table>
```

When this table is viewed in a browser, it will appear as shown in **FIGURE 5-14**.

Adding Tables Inside Tables   Sometimes, design work requires a table within another table, as you will see in Chapter 10. To add one, the new opening `<table>` tag is simply inserted into an existing table cell. Inside an existing `<td>` element,

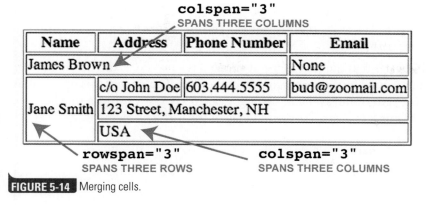

FIGURE 5-14 Merging cells.

the opening `<table>` tag is added, followed by the new table content and ending with its closing `</table>` tag, followed by closing the `</td>` cell content element where it was inserted.

5.6 Form Basics

Forms allow users to submit information to the company whose website they are visiting. In order for that information to be processed when the Submit button is clicked, forms must have special assignments, which will be discussed in Chapter 15. The focus of this chapter is to introduce the code required to create some of the most common form data entry fields used in a typical web page form. If you create a form incorporating the form fields covered in this chapter, the Reset button will work to clear the form; the Submit button will *appear* to work, but in reality, it must be tied to the server processing the data to actually send the data anywhere.

As you can probably guess by now based on the HTML code we have covered thus far, a form must be created inside a form element. The opening tag is `<form>` and the closing tag is `</form>`.

5.6.1 Common Form Elements

Form elements included within the opening and closing tags of the `<form>` element are called *controls*; they are the tools used to input the data to be submitted, such as the user's name, selections, etc. The format for all of them is relatively the same, with specific additions depending on the type of data to be collected. Most form element control types begin with an `<input>` opening tag, which includes the attributes of the form element, and end with `/>` tag. Because the uses of each form element will be explained in more detail in Chapter 15, only the names of the elements and their respective code will be covered in this chapter.

Text Field Elements

```
<input type="text" name="name reference"
size="number"/>
```

This code indicates that the type of input element is a text field, and the *name refer-ence* is the name used by the server to collect the data. The *size* entry is optional for defining the length of the available typing area. To say "Enter your name here" on the form, add this text *before* the opening tag of the text field element.

Radio Button Elements

```
<input type="radio" name="category of buttons"
value="user choice"/>User Choice
```

The element type is *radio*; the *category* is a reference name for the group of buttons, with the *value* being the option for the user to select. To include multiple radio but-tons within the same group, each one must have the same name.

Checkbox Elements

```
<input type="checkbox" name="category of options"
value="User Choice"/>
```

This element type is *checkbox*; the *category* is a reference name for the group of choices, with the *value* being the option for the user to select. Just as the radio buttons within the same group must have the same name, all checkbox elements within the same selections must have the same name as well. To say "Check your favorites" on the form, add this text *before* the opening tag of the checkbox element.

Text Area Field Elements

```
<textarea name="reference name" rows="4" cols="50">
</textarea>
```

This element differs from the previous ones you have learned because it does not begin with `<input type=>`. Instead, the element's *name* is defined in the open-ing tag, followed by the name referenced by the server. The *size* of the area for data entry is defined by rows and columns, with this element having a closing tag of `</textarea>`. Once again, to display a prefix such as "Enter your comments here" on the form, add the text before the opening tag of the text area field element.

Submit/Reset Button Elements

```
<input type="submit" name="submit" value="Submit your
request NOW"/>
```

and

```
<input type="reset" name="reset" value="Reset Form"/>
```

Both of these buttons follow the same basic format. The *type* would be either *submit* or *reset*, depending on its usage. The *name* is the reference for the server; the *value* is the words you want the button to display on it.

5.6.2 Creating a Form

The following code sample exemplifies the implementation of these form elements:

```
<form>
<p>Name:<input type="text" name="name" size="40"/><br/>
Address:<input type="text" name="address" size="40"/><br/>
City:<input type="text" name="city" size="40" /><br/>
State, Zip:<input type="text" name="sz" size="40" /></p>
<p>Residence:<br/>
<input type="radio" name="residence" value="own"/>Own
Home<br/>
<input type="radio" name="residence" value="rent"/>I
Rent</p><p>Hobbies: Check all that apply<br/>
Ski<input type="checkbox" name="hobbies"
value="ski"/><br/>
Hike<input type="checkbox" name="hobbies"
value="hike"/><br/>
Golf<input type="checkbox" name="hobbies"
value="golf"/><br/>
Horseback Riding<input type="checkbox" name="hobbies"
value="riding"/></p>
<p>How can we help you?<br/>
<textarea name="help" rows="4" cols="50"></textarea></p>
<p>Thanks for submitting your request!<input
type="submit" name="submit" value="Submit your request
NOW"/><br/>
Reset form:<input type="reset" name="reset"
value="Reset Form"/></p>
</form>
```

A sample of how this form will display in a browser is shown in **FIGURE 5-15**. The red callouts were added solely to identify the code used to create the form input area they identify.

5.6.3 Combining Tables and Forms

Often, a table is inserted into a form element to organize its data entry layout. If used, the `<table>` opening element is added *inside* and directly after the opening `<form>` tag. Each line of the form is then inserted between a data tag `<td>`, which is inserted between a row tag `<tr>`. Each line ends with the closing `</td>` tag, followed by

TEXT FIELD Name: [   ] ←——— `<input type="text" name="name" size="40"/>`
Address: [   ]
City: [   ]
State, Zip: [   ]

Residence:
RADIO BUTTON ○ Own Home ←——————— `<input type="radio" name="residence" value="own">Own Home`
○ I Rent

Hobbies: Check all that apply
CHECKBOX Ski ☐ ←————————————— `<input type="checkbox" name="hobbies" value="ski"/>`
Hike ☐
Golf ☐
Horseback Riding ☐

How can we help you? ——— `<textarea name="help" rows="4" cols="50"></textarea>`
TEXT AREA [   ]

                                    `<input type="submit" name="submit"`
                                    `    value="Submit your request NOW"/>`
SUBMIT BUTTON Thanks for submitting your request! [Submit your request NOW]
RESET BUTTON Reset form: [Reset Form] ←——— `<input type="reset" name="reset" value="Reset Form"/>`

FIGURE 5-15 Form sample.

the closing `</tr>` tag. Using this format eliminates the need to add the `<br/>` tag to move form information to a new line. The following code illustrates the same form created with the form elements enclosed within a table for layout purposes:

```
<form>
<table align="center">
<tr><td>Name:<input type="text" name="name"
size="40"/></td></tr>
<tr><td>Address:<input type="text" name="address"
size="40"/></td></tr>
<tr><td>City:<input type="text" name="city" size="40"
/></td></tr>
<tr><td>State, Zip:<input type="text" name="sz"
size="40"/></td></tr>
<tr><td>Residence:</td></tr>
<tr><td><input type="radio" name="residence"
value="own"/>Own Home</td></tr>
<tr><td><input type="radio" name="residence"
value="rent"/>I Rent</td></tr><tr><td>Hobbies: Check
all that apply</td></tr>
<tr><td>Ski<input type="checkbox" name="hobbies"
value="ski"/></td></tr>
<tr><td>Hike<input type="checkbox" name="hobbies"
value="hike"/></td></tr>
<tr><td>Golf<input type="checkbox" name="hobbies"
```

```
value="golf"/>
</td></tr>
<tr><td>Horseback Riding<input type="checkbox"
name="hobbies" value="riding"/>
</td></tr>
<tr><td>How can we help you?</td></tr>
<tr><td><textarea name="help" rows="4" cols="50">
</textarea></td></tr>
<tr><td>Thanks for submitting your request!<input
type="submit" name="submit" value="Submit your request
NOW"/></td></tr>
<tr><td>Reset form:<input type="reset" name="reset"
value="Reset Form"/></td></tr>
</table>
</form>
```

5.7 CSS Basics

Applying Cascading Style Sheets (CSS) to text is covered in Chapter 14. Because it will be covered in detail using Dreamweaver, only a basic overview of how the code differs from the rest of the HTML code learned thus far will be noted here. Because style sheets are a "behind the scenes" feature of HTML, they begin with an opening tag of `<style="text/css">` when they apply strictly to the current page, which is the type of styles that will be covered in this chapter, and close with `</style>` and are added between the opening `<head>` and closing `</head>` tags of the page.

5.7.1 Parts of a CSS Rule

Style sheets apply formatting properties to an HTML page through rules. A rule has the following parts, which are shown in FIGURE 5-16 :

1. *Selector* is the item that will be affected by the rule.
2. After adding a space, the *declaration* begins and ends with curly brackets ({ }). The specific features you want to apply to the selector item are added inside these brackets.

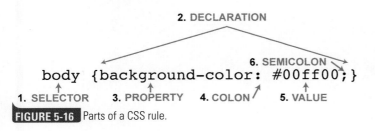

FIGURE 5-16 Parts of a CSS rule.

3. The *property* is the type of formatting you want to affect.

4. The property must be immediately followed by a colon.

5. After a space, the *value* determines how you want to affect the property selected under the property section of the declaration.

6. This value must end with a semicolon.

5.7.2 Adding Properties to a Declaration

Before the closing curly bracket of the declaration, multiple properties and values can be entered the same way, placing them sequentially each time after the previous semicolon. To change the background color of the page, plus the font, size, and color used in the form created in the previous section, the following style is added to the head element of the page:

```
<style type="text/css">
body {background-color: #ffcc33; font-family: Arial,
Helvetica, sans-serif; font-size: 16px; color:
#0000ff;}</style>
```

After this rule is applied to the form, it displays in a browser as shown in **FIGURE 5-17**. Note that this new example shows the inclusion of the form elements in a centered table.

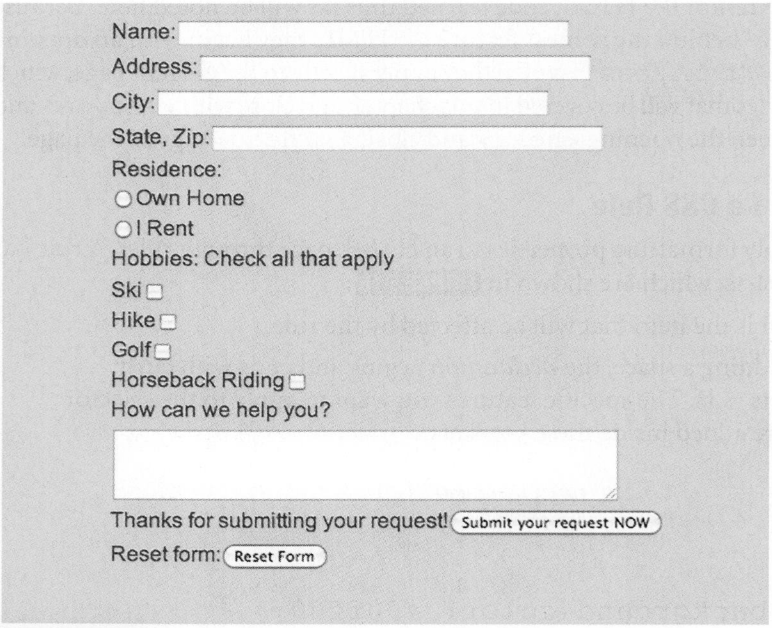

FIGURE 5-17 Form with style.

As an artist, if you began this chapter with apprehension about learning HTML, it is time to take a deep breath, pat yourself on the back, and get ready to have Dreamweaver write it for you from now on!

5.8 What We Have Learned

In this chapter, we learned the parts of a web page and where specific features are entered into the HTML page's code. We also learned how to create links using images, text, and image maps. Creating tables and forms were introduced, including how they can be combined to give more structure to a form. Lastly, we learned how to define CSS rules; its required placement within the `<head>` area of the existing HTML document when it applies to just the document containing it and how it differs from the rest of the HTML code for the page to function properly and reflect the properties of the CSS rule.

5.9 Reinforcing Your Knowledge

Project

FIGURE 5-18 provides an example of the Reinforcing Your Knowledge project for this chapter.

Use the following general steps to complete this project, but feel free to return to sections of the text as needed to complete this exercise. Oh, and remember, have fun!

1. Open a text editor.
2. Enter the standard information required for a browser to read your page. If you saved it as a regular word processing document, open that document, copy it, close it, and paste it into your new project page.
3. Add the page title: *Fall Festival!*
4. Add the following CSS to the page:
   Background color: *#FF9900*
   Font family: *Arial, Helvetica, sans-serif*
   Font size: *16px*
   Color: *#000000*

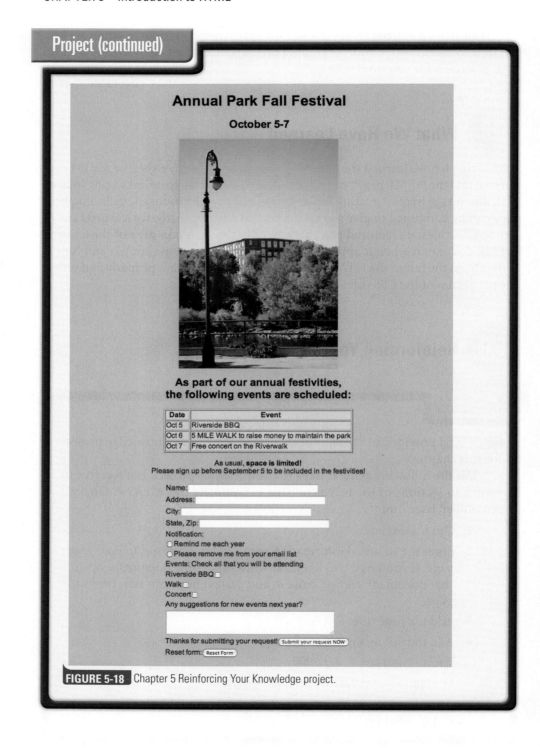

FIGURE 5-18 Chapter 5 Reinforcing Your Knowledge project.

Project (continued)

5. Add a Heading 1, center aligned, that states: *Annual Park Fall Festival*

6. Add a subhead, Heading 2, center aligned, that states: *October 5–7*

7. Locate your copy of the *Chapter_5PracticeFiles* folder and save this document as *fall_festivities.html* inside it using UTF-8 encoding.

Save and test your page as you complete each section of the project. This will enable you to catch code writing errors before you repeat them! It will be much easier than completing the entire project, then having to troubleshoot line by line.

8. Create a new paragraph with center alignment and insert the *park.jpg* image onto your page with the following dimensions:

   Width: *350*

   Height: *527*

9. Add a new subhead, Heading 2, center aligned, that states: *As part of our annual festivities, the following events are scheduled:*

10. Add a line break to this text after the comma following the word *festivities.*

11. Create a center-aligned table:

    Border: *1*

    Background color: *#FFCC33*

12. Add two headers to the table:

    Header 1 name: *Date*

    Header 1 width: *50*

    Header 2 name: *Event*

    Header 2 width: no width defined

13. Enter the following information in each cell of each row of the table as shown in the example and then close/end the table:

    Row 1 Cell 1: *Oct 5*

    Row 1 Cell 2: *Riverside BBQ*

    Row 2 Cell 1: *Oct 6*

    Row 2 Cell 2: *5 MILE WALK to raise money to maintain the park*

    Row 3 Cell 1: *Oct 7*

    Row 3 Cell 2: *Free concert on the Riverwalk*

Project (continued)

14. Add a new center-aligned paragraph that states: *As usual, space is limited! Please sign up before September 5 to be included in the festivities!*

    Add the `<strong>` tag to the words: *space is limited!*

    Insert a line break before the word: *Please*

15. Create a form and then insert the form elements inside a centered table.

16. Enter the following text fields:

    Name: use a name of *name* and size of *40*

    Address: use a name of *address* and size of *40*

    City: use a name of *city* and size of *40*

    State, Zip: use a name of *sz* and size of *40*

17. Add a category titled: *Notification:*

18. Create two radio buttons with the name: *notice*

    Button 1 value: *remind*

    Button 1 message: *Remind me each year*

    Button 2 value: *remove*

    Button 2 message: *Please remove me from your email list*

19. Add a category titled: *Events: Check all that you will be attending*

20. Add a checkbox element with the following three choices, using *events* for the name of the checkbox:

    Choice 1: *Riverside BBQ*

    Choice 1 value: *bbq*

    Choice 2: *Walk*

    Choice 2 value: *walk*

    Choice 3: *Concert*

    Choice 3 value: *concert*

21. Add a category titled: *Any suggestions for new events next year?*

22. Insert an area text field:

    Name: *suggestions*

    Rows: *4*

    Column width: *50*

23. Add a category titled: *Thanks for submitting your request!*

24. Add a submit button:

    Button name: *submit*

    Button message: *Submit your request NOW*

25. Add a category titled: *Reset form:*

26. Add a reset button:

    Button name: *reset*

    Button message: *Reset Form*

27. Sequentially close the table, the form, the body, and end with the closing `</html>` tag for the page. Save again and test your page in a browser.

5.10 Endnote

1. Berners-Lee, Tim and Mark Fischetti. 2000. *Weaving the Web: The Original Design and Ultimate Destiny of the World Wide Web.* New York, NY: HarperCollins Publishers, Inc.

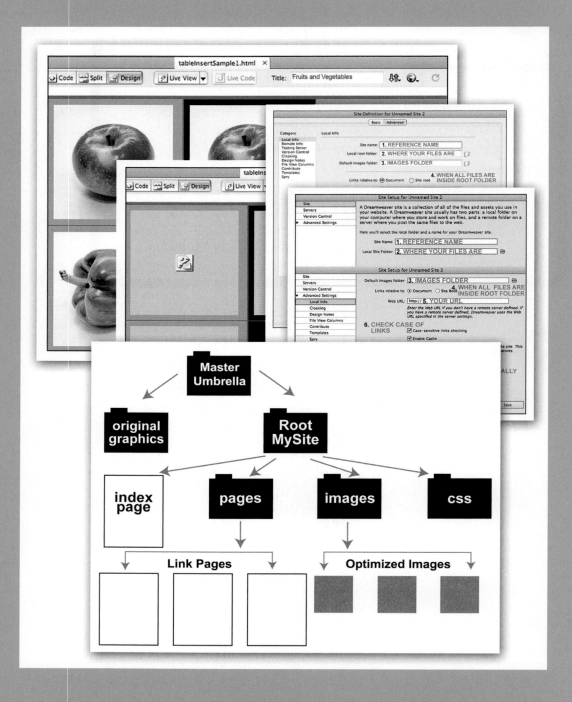

Site Definition and Management

6

After an overview of the root folder organizational system of web design, we will learn how to define a site. We will learn to create a site using the Site Definition dialog box of CS3/CS4 and its changes in CS5, followed by learning to update a site later with additions/deletions as needed while a site is being built. We will also be introduced to linking problems, with the primary goal of understanding the process, which will help you diagnose problems that may develop with your files when working on your own.

6.1   The Root Folder: The Foundation of Your Site

The *root folder* is the "life blood" of your site: the foundation of your site. All of the files that your site needs in order to function properly must be located in this folder for Dreamweaver to "manage" them for you. Acquiring an in-depth understanding of the root folder's function, components, and how to organize one is the critical first step to effectual site management.

6.1.1 Understanding the Problem

As a graphic designer, perhaps at some point you (or worse, your service provider) opened one of your files containing linked images that were missing. Depending on the graphics program used to create the file, a low-resolution image may have been automatically substituted for it, or worse yet, an empty space was displayed when the file was opened. Let's review why that happened. You created the file. Your images were linked. However, when you moved the file to an external drive, perhaps to bring it to a service provider for printing, you forgot to also move the linked files … the problem presented itself when you or the service provider later opened the file and the graphics program could not locate the missing linked images. Ouch! If that has ever happened to you, it probably had to happen only once to learn how critical it is to keep your materials together. Now, you probably have the pages of the document, a separate folder with all the linked images, and a folder containing a copy of all the fonts used (if applicable) all located within a master folder (usually titled with the name of the project) that you keep together for yourself, or prepare for a service provider if the file will be sent out for printing.

Although the folder and file needs are different in web design, the same basic concept applies. Dreamweaver will try to help you avoid these issues with various warning messages that we will discuss in this chapter. However, the fundamentals of successful web design require the basic understanding of the process and the critical organization of your website's components.

6.1.2 Functions of the Root Folder

The root folder houses all of the files you use in a website. It contains all the pages of the site, all of its images, CSS files, and any other applicable files the site will need to function properly. Dreamweaver uses this folder to manage your site as you build and update it, as well as to define its remote connection when it is time to publish your site on the Web. Following a few guidelines when creating and working with your root folder will minimize future missing link issues and add to your enjoyment of building your first site for the Web.

6.2 Organizing Your Files Before You Launch Dreamweaver

Organizing and categorizing your website files and original graphics files before you launch Dreamweaver will help to minimize problems later. The first step in this process is to define the location of these files for Dreamweaver to be able to find and manage them as needed.

Always take a few minutes to think about where you will be working on your site as you build it. What might sound like a ridiculous suggestion is really an important tip to consider before you start. If you will be building your entire site from one computer, simply choose a convenient spot on it, such as its desktop. However, if you will need to work on your site on more than one computer, for example, between your desktop computer and your laptop, or between home and work, perhaps you will want to build it on a portable external drive that you will transport and work from in both locations. After the site is complete and you are ready to publish it, move it to the hard drive of the computer that you will use to upload, maintain, and manage the site. However, until then, define the site in Dreamweaver on both computers with the same name and same site location (external drive, for example), so Dreamweaver will always know where to find your files and be able to manage them for you as you move back and forth between the computers during the construction process. One section of this chapter will be dedicated exclusively to what happens if Dreamweaver cannot find your files. However, at this time in the development process, if you take time to determine where your computer access will be as you build your site and plan accordingly, it will help you avoid many site management problems later.

6.2.1 Umbrella Folder

In actuality, all Dreamweaver needs to create a site for you is a root folder. However, learning good site management and good site organization, which is more important at this stage of the design process, will streamline the addition or editing of image files, if needed, as you continue to construct a website. Starting with an umbrella folder is a great tool to facilitate this organization. We began this process in Chapter 4 when saving images and navigation graphics, but you will now understand why we did what we did and learn to follow good practice for all future site development. The umbrella folder that we named *Fishluvrz Project* is not the root folder. It is a master folder that houses two folders inside it: one is the site root folder that we named *FishluvrzRoot*, and the other is the *original fishluvrz graphics* folder, which contains all your images in their original graphic formats that you have already created and will continue to create for this site. All site root folders should contain additional

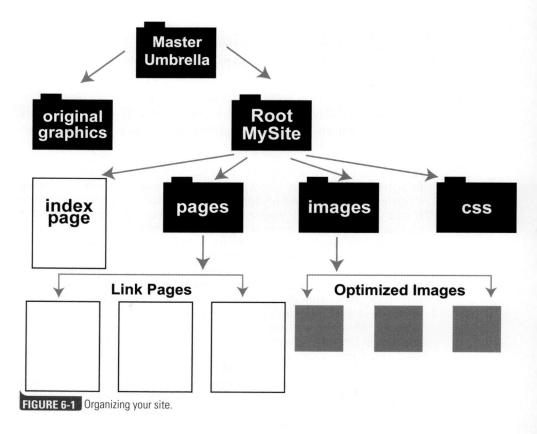

FIGURE 6-1 Organizing your site.

folders that are used to further organize a site. The diagram shown in **FIGURE 6-1** illustrates an organized, logical website project folder structure. We will discuss each element individually.

6.2.2 Original Graphics Folder

As you have learned, this folder will be used to house all of your native layered original .psd versions of the images for your website, plus any other native graphics, such as Illustrator or Flash files. Following this process each time you create a new site will maintain consistency and file organization. Ideally, all native and optimized graphics to be used in a particular site should be created before you begin to build it and should be saved in two separate folders: one for the original native files and one for the Save for Web optimized versions, as covered in Chapter 4. As you saw, after you have defined the locations to save them, Photoshop keeps track of whether the image you are saving each time is the optimized version or the native .psd version and automatically opens the respective folder you designated during the first round of saving. The native files folder, which contains the images with all their layers and full editing capabilities, should be stored in the umbrella folder, but not in the root folder; only their optimized "Save for Web" versions should be located there.

Accidentally attempting to upload native files saved in a root folder is a common mistake that can cause problems when it is time to make your site "live" on the Web. When building a site, especially if you are working on multiple sites at the same time, if all the originals pertaining to a specific website have been moved to an accessible easy-to-find location relative to that particular site, missing file or incorrectly placed file issues will be eliminated. Although it is best practice to start your site with all graphics made ahead of time for it, as a designer you know that with any graphics project, changes, additions, and deletions are usually an inevitable part of the execution process. Locating them here, not actually "in" the root folder but "with" the site's root folder, will streamline your productivity when revisions, deletions, and additions to your graphics are needed as your website develops: it's another aspect of the management process of web design.

6.2.3 Parts of the Root Folder

Inside this folder, you should organize your future site by creating three more folders: *pages*, *images*, and *css* (all written in lowercase). Although additional folders can be created at any time after a site has been defined in Dreamweaver either inside existing folders or in addition to them, creating these initial folders before you define it is a great way to learn site organization, resulting in better site management.

Index Page   This will be your site's home page. (We will discuss creating, saving, and titling the index page in Chapter 8.) This is the only component of the root folder that you cannot create at this stage of the development process, because it must be created after you have defined your site in Dreamweaver. It is important to note at this time, however, that when it is created, it must be named *index.html* or *index.htm* and must be in the root folder but not located inside any other folder. This makes it recognizable for browsers as the home page after the site has been uploaded.

Pages Folder   As shown in the diagram, this folder is designed to house all of your link pages. Although it is not mandatory to place pages inside a separate folder within the root folder for a site to function, it will aid in the organization and maintenance of the site. The folder does not have to be titled *pages*: if all your link pages are different services offered by your company, for example, title the folder *services*. If building a large site, you can create additional *pages* folders inside this folder or simply have additional folders in the root folder that have single-word lowercase titles that include the categories of the pages they contain. This breaks your links into logical collections, further streamlining your site organization.

Images Folder   This folder is the same one that you designated to save all of your optimized images during the Save for Web process in Chapter 4, when preparing images for an upcoming site. All original native graphics should be housed in an *original graphics* folder (or *original psds* folder) within the umbrella folder for the site. The *images* folder, however, containing the optimized versions of all photographs and/or drawn graphics is always placed *inside* the root folder of the site within the umbrella folder for the project.

CSS Folder   This third folder is optional, because your site may not contain custom external style sheets, and it can always be added within Dreamweaver during the construction process if needed. It is easiest, however, if it is already in place ahead of time if you decide to use CSS style sheets, and the folder can be deleted later if never used.

6.3   Defining a Website in Dreamweaver

In the Building Your Own Website section of this chapter, you will be able apply the following steps to define your site in Dreamweaver to begin its construction. For now, we will create a basic site using some preexisting optimized image files to learn the site definition process. Open the *Chapter_6PracticeFiles* folder within the *Textbook Practice Files* folder that should have been copied to your desktop in Chapter 4. Inside this folder are two image folders: *Graphics_1* and *Graphics_2*. Create an umbrella folder named *Sample Umbrella* on your desktop, with an *original graphics* folder and a root folder inside of it titled *SampleRoot*. Drag the images located in the *Graphics_2* folder into the *original graphics* folder, and then drag the *Graphics_1* folder into the root folder, changing its name to *images*. Complete this first root folder by creating both a *pages* and a *css* folder in it as well. You will use this root folder to define your first site. Although the steps for both the Basic and Advanced methods will be covered in the next section, we will define the first site using the *SampleRoot* root folder following the steps of the Advanced method.

6.3.1   Choosing to Define a New Site from the Site Menu

To begin, launch Dreamweaver. (Finally! Are you excited?) After the program is open, the first thing you will see is a familiar Adobe feature, the Welcome Screen, which we will bypass for now. We will not close it; we will just leave it open and work from its Application menu instead. If you are used to choosing the Don't Show Again option from other programs, resist the temptation for now: we will explore the Welcome Screen in Dreamweaver and its important features in the next chapter, after which you can decide if you want to keep it visible or hide it. The Welcome Screen is one of multiple ways to access the Site Definition dialog box in order to create a new site, but for now, we will use the Site menu option. From the main application menu, choose Site>New Site, as shown in **FIGURE 6-2**.

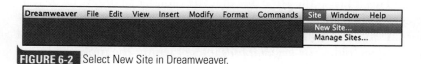

FIGURE 6-2 Select New Site in Dreamweaver.

> **Note:** *The site definition process will be covered as it pertains to CS3 and CS4 first, followed by an explanation of the applicable changes in the site definition process when using CS5. However, in order to fully understand the site definition process, CS5 users should read the following section first, for a more thorough understanding of the process and terminology of site definition.*

6.3.2 Site Definition Methods in CS3 and CS4

After you enter the Site Definition dialog box, there are two ways to define a new site: Basic and Advanced. We will cover each in detail, beginning with the Basic method.

Creating a Site Using the Basic Method   At the top of the Site Definition dialog box are two tabs: Basic and Advanced. Click the Basic tab to enter the Basic site definition mode. After you are working in the Basic definition mode, the first window has two locations to enter information. The first question asks, "What would you like to name your site?" This is any name you want to use to remember the site as you build it, one you choose simply to identify the site for yourself. It has nothing to do with the uploading process. It is part of the "in-house clerical" process of site building. It does not matter whether it is uppercase or lowercase, or if it has spaces or special characters. It is only important that it is not too long, and it is one that you can remember as specific to this site.

The second question asks for your site's HTTP address (its web address). You may enter it here if you already have it, or leave it blank for now because you can add it at any time later. **FIGURE 6-3** shows these first two steps.

After you have completed these steps, click the Next button to continue the site definition process. In the second window, the option "No, I do not want to use a server technology," which is the default selection, has correctly been chosen for you. We will always be creating regular HTML pages that do not use server technology. The server technology feature is reserved for dynamic pages, which are beyond the scope of this textbook. To continue to the next window, click the Next button.

In the first section of this third window, the default selection, "To edit your files on your machine and upload when ready," is already chosen for you and should not be changed. The second question asks, "Where on your computer do you want to store your files?" Use this data entry area to tell Dreamweaver where to find your files, which is your root folder, as shown in **FIGURE 6-4**.

Although all of the options in the site definition process are important, this one is the most critical. The easiest way to complete this section without ending up with any typographical errors when entering the exact path to the files is to click the folder icon and search your computer (or your external drive, as we discussed earlier in this chapter) to locate your root folder inside your umbrella folder. After you choose it, you will see the full path to those files identified here. For example, if your site is located on an external drive titled *My Drive*, with an umbrella folder titled *Practice Umbrella* containing a root folder titled *PracticeRoot*, the path for Dreamweaver would be */Volumes/My Drive/Practice Umbrella/PracticeRoot*.

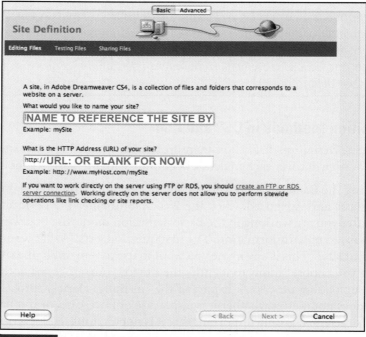

FIGURE 6-3 Basic Site Definition: first dialog box window.

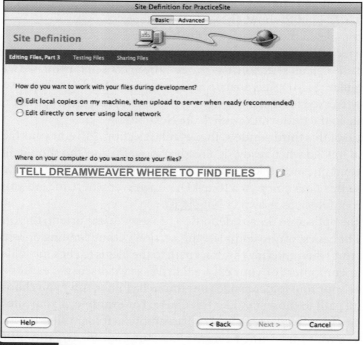

FIGURE 6-4 Where are your files?

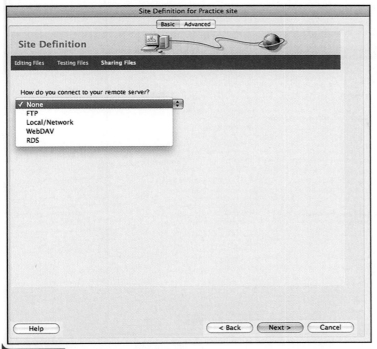

FIGURE 6-5 Connection to your remote server.

After you have completed this, click the Next button again to continue the site definition process.

In this connection window, you can choose None for now, as shown in **FIGURE 6-5**, because the option to set up your files for uploading is available in a variety of ways after you have established your site.

After you have done this, click Next for the last time. The last window is a summary window that you should always take the time to review to be sure you have filled in all of the previous windows correctly, as shown in **FIGURE 6-6**.

The nice thing about this window is that it still has an active Back button, which will allow you to go back to any stage of the definition process to make changes, if needed, before you click the Done button. However, even after the site is defined, you have the ability to make changes as needed to manage your site, and you can actually return to this dialog box at any time in the construction of your site if necessary. Notice that the last line in this dialog box says, "Your site can be further configured using the Advanced Tab." You can click the Advanced tab at any stage of the site definition process, or complete the entire definition process through the Advanced window, which is the site definition method we will explore next.

Creating a Site Using the Advanced Method After you are familiar with the site definition process, you will most likely create all of your future sites using the Advanced method instead of the Basic one. It is kind of like "one-stop shopping."

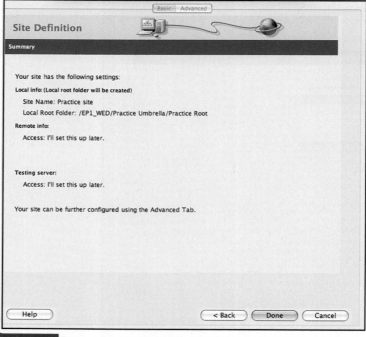

FIGURE 6-6   Summary of selections made in the Basic site definition process.

When you choose Site>New Site, and then click the Advanced tab, you will notice first of all that several categories are listed on the left side of this dialog box, and the top category (Local Info) is already chosen. The Advanced tab of the Site Definition dialog box contains many categories of site management, not just site definition. Local Info is the category that parallels the Basic tab, and allows you to define the site. This option allows you to complete the entire site definition process in just one window vs. the several windows required by the Basic site definition method. The components of this window will be discussed individually in order, as shown in **FIGURE 6-7**.

1. **Site name:** This is the same reference name that was discussed in the first window of the Basic method when defining a new site. Choose any name you want to use to reference your site, being careful to choose a unique name that differs from other sites you may be building to avoid confusion. We will title our first practice site *SampleSite* because this is simply the reference name to remember the site.

2. **Local root folder:** This is the same as the third window of the Basic method that asked you, "Where on your computer do you want to store your files?" Click the folder to search your computer to locate the full path. After it's chosen, the path to the root folder, *SampleRoot*, in this section of the Site Definition dialog box should list the path to your desktop,

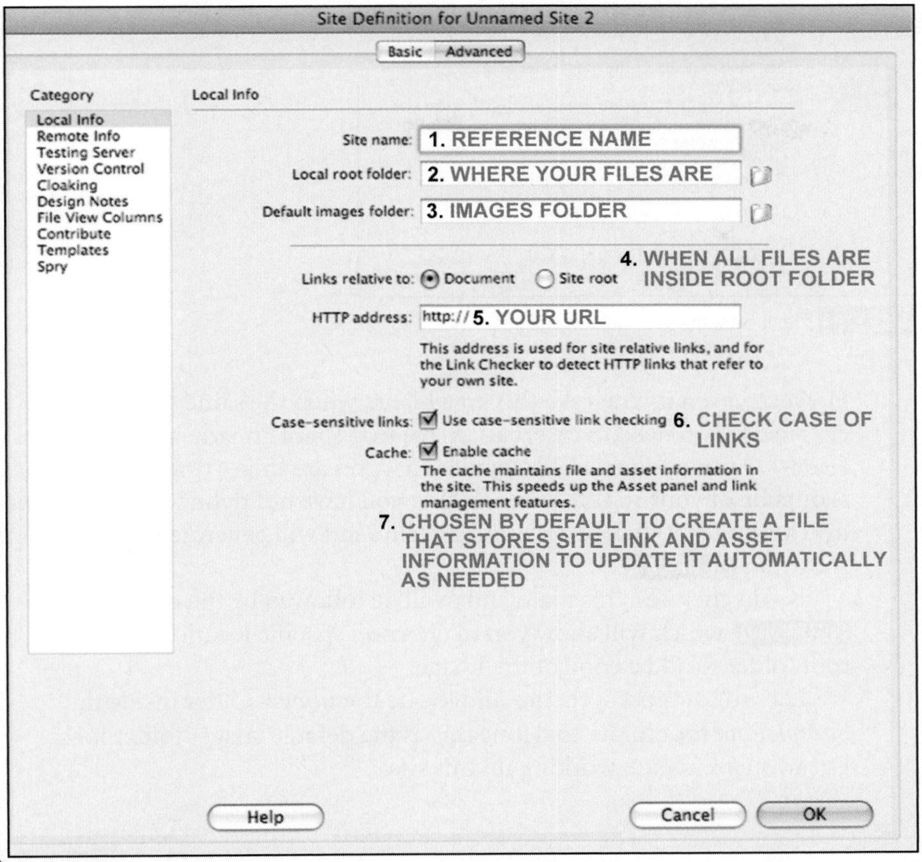

FIGURE 6-7 Local Info category in the Advanced Site Definition dialog box.

followed by a slash and the name *SampleRoot*. If you were accessing a
root folder that you created on an external drive, the first part of the path
would reflect the external drive location, followed by the umbrella folder,
and then the root folder listing—in that order—as shown in the example:
/Volumes/My Drive/Practice Umbrella/PracticeRoot. Here, the root folder
titled *PracticeRoot* was located inside an umbrella folder titled *Practice
Umbrella*, located on an external drive titled *My Drive*.

3. **Default images folder:** This option is not required, but it is recommended.
    If you have created a separate *images* folder, as shown in this chapter, this
    option allows you to tell Dreamweaver where all of your images will be
    located. After you are working in Dreamweaver, if you realize that you
    need to insert an image that is not already in your *images* folder (if this
    location has been predefined for Dreamweaver through this dialog box)
    a copy of the file will automatically be added to this *images* folder in your
    root folder when you insert the image. It's one less hassle to worry about.

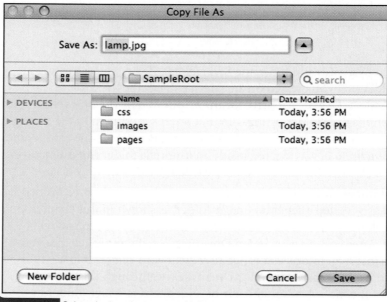

Dw

This file is outside of the root folder of site 'SampleSite',
and may not be accessible when you publish the site.

Your root folder is:
Macintosh HD:Users:vellenwolper:Desktop:SampleRoot:

Would you like to copy the file there now?

Cancel   No   Yes

FIGURE 6-8 File outside the root folder warning.

However, even if you leave this area blank, when the same scenario presents itself (you need to insert an image that is not already in your *images* folder) Dreamweaver will recognize that you are importing an image that is outside of your root folder, and that you have not defined a default *images* folder for it to copy to automatically, and will generate the dialog box shown in **FIGURE 6-8**.

If you click Yes, this dialog box will be followed by the one shown in **FIGURE 6-9**, which will allow you to choose a specific location within the root folder to add a copy of the image.

Let's follow good practice and locate the *images* folder inside the *SampleRoot* root folder to define this as the default images folder for Dreamweaver when working on this site.

Copy File As

Save As: lamp.jpg

SampleRoot   Q search

	Name	▲	Date Modified
▶ DEVICES	css		Today, 3:56 PM
▶ PLACES	images		Today, 3:56 PM
	pages		Today, 3:56 PM

New Folder   Cancel   Save

FIGURE 6-9 Select the location to store the image.

4. **Links relative to:** The default option is Document, which defines how
   the link path will be created from the page it is in, to another page within
   your site. It is the easiest to work with and preview in a browser as you
   build your site because all your files are located within your root folder,
   as we have described in this chapter.

5. **HTTP address:** This optional category allows you to enter your URL, if you
   already know it, to later assist the Link Checker feature in Dreamweaver.

6. **Case-sensitive links:** Choosing this option will ensure that when all links
   are created, the link and corresponding file names are correctly defined
   not only in name, but also in their case sensitivity. If a discrepancy exists
   when you check the links of the site later in the construction process,
   Dreamweaver will warn you of a broken link, as shown in **FIGURE 6-10**, if
   you have chosen this option ahead of time.

   Because some web servers are case-sensitive, this is a handy option to
   select to help eliminate problems later during the upload process. If you
   name all files with lowercase text as you build your site, you will not need
   to check this box; however, we all forget sometimes … so checking it will
   help prevent hassles later.

FIGURE 6-10 Case-sensitive links selected.

7. **Cache:** You may be familiar with the Image Cache option in Photoshop, which allows you to work more efficiently in the program, especially when working with large files. Although not the same, Enable Cache is a similar option, which is chosen by default in the Dreamweaver site definition dialog box, used to improve your productivity when working on your site. When you click OK, your first site will be created!

 As you can see in **FIGURE 6-11**, the same options available under the Local Info category of the Advanced tab in CS3 and CS4 are simply split into two separate categories in CS5. When you select New Site from the Site main menu, you are brought to the Site category of its site definition dialog box to assign the reference name and root folder location. By selecting Local Info from its Advanced Settings category, the rest of the options described earlier become available for assignment.

Accessing Your Files Through the Files Panel   The reference name you gave your site, *SampleSite*, will now be listed in a pop-up menu inside a panel called the Files panel. When you launch Dreamweaver the first time, the Files panel should be displayed on the right side of your work area by default. However, if it is not

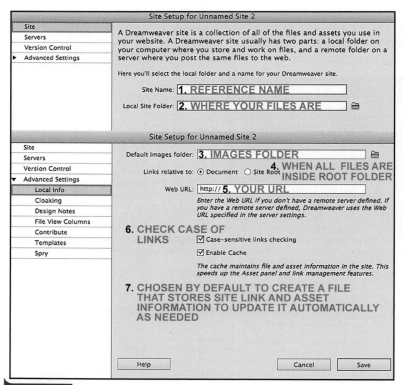

FIGURE 6-11 Site definition in CS5.

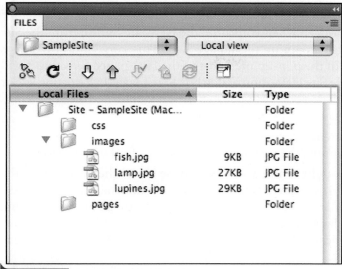

FIGURE 6-12 Use the Files panel to view your first site.

displayed, it is accessible by choosing Window>Files. This panel will now display the root folder, with the ability to click the arrow/plus sign to open it, revealing the three folders that you created inside of it before you launched Dreamweaver, as shown in **FIGURE 6-12**.

 If you decided to build your site from an external hard drive because you will work on it using two computers, be sure that you define the site in the exact same manner (same name, case, spaces, etc.) on both computers in Dreamweaver. After the site is displayed in the Files panel of the program on each computer, you can work seamlessly between them from your external drive.

Working on a Previously Defined Site   As you continue to define additional sites, they will be automatically added to the pop-up menu in the Files panel, with each new one becoming the current active site in the panel. To select a previously defined site, click and hold on its pop-up menu and scroll to select a site from the alphabetized list of all your site reference names.

 6.4 Site Management Essentials

Site management is a broad term for handling the changes/additions/deletions you will need to make as you work on a site. Some of those updates are done through the Manage Sites dialog box, while others are done through the Files panel. We will discuss them individually, and the type of changes each location allows you to make.

6.4.1 Manage Sites Dialog Box Options

You may have already noticed when you chose the New Site option from the Site menu, that there was also an option to Manage Sites. This same option is always available at the bottom of the pop-up menu list of the Files panel. Selecting it will allow you to return to the Site Definition dialog box to manage your existing site or create a new one. In the dialog box that opens, click Edit to return to the Site Definition window to make changes as needed, such as:

- changing the reference name of your site
- changing or redefining the path to your root folder for Dreamweaver

After you have been brought to this window, choose either the Basic tab or the Advanced tab in CS3/CS4, whichever one you are more comfortable using, to make the desired changes. In CS5, you are brought automatically to the needed location. After you have made a change and exited the Site Definition window, the alert box shown in **FIGURE 6-13** indicates that Dreamweaver has recognized and updated your site to reflect the changes.

This is a reassuring message! After you click OK, you can continue working on your site.

Besides editing a site's definition properties, the additional management options available in the Manage Sites dialog box are shown in **FIGURE 6-14**.

- **New:** This option provides another method of accessing the Site Definition dialog box options to create a new site.
- **Duplicate:** This option will make a copy of the site selected, and add the word "Copy" to the end of its name to differentiate it from the original.
- **Remove:** This option removes an existing site from the Files panel's pop-up menu. The Files panel does not have a trash can, a common method of deleting an item from a panel in other graphics programs. To remove a site from the Files panel, you must select the site to delete in the Manage Sites dialog box, and then click the Remove button. When you choose this option, it is a permanent removal that cannot be reversed using the History panel or Command/Control+Z. Fortunately, when you choose this option, Dreamweaver will prompt you to confirm your selection. Dreamweaver opens another dialog box that warns you,

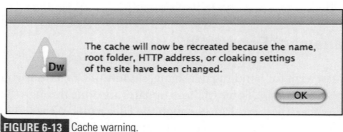

The cache will now be recreated because the name, root folder, HTTP address, or cloaking settings of the site have been changed.

OK

FIGURE 6-13 Cache warning.

FIGURE 6-14 Manage Sites dialog box.

"You cannot undo this action. Delete the selected site?" This forces you to choose Yes or No to continue.

- **Export or Import:** Dreamweaver also offers Export/Import options here to move a site from one computer to another. However, the external drive option described earlier in this chapter is a safe and familiar process that is an easy way to move and manage your sites.

6.4.2 Files Panel Options

As a graphic artist, your print experience may tempt you to highlight a file name to modify it in the root folder on your desktop (or wherever the root folder is located) and make the change if one became necessary. However, for Dreamweaver to follow your change and manage its links accordingly, all site changes, such as renaming, reorganizing, adding, or deleting files and folders, should be done internally, using its Files panel.

Creating More Folders to Further Organize Your Site's Root Files   Using the Files panel, you can add folders at any time after you have created your site: add folders to the root folder itself, or add them inside an existing folder, such as the *pages* or *images* folder of the root, to further organize your root folder. You must select the root folder first to create another folder in it, or select the specific folder within the root folder (e.g., the *images* folder) if you want the new folder created inside of it. After you have selected the folder where you want to add the new one, choose File>New Folder from the Files panel's options menu, or right-click (Windows) or Control-click (Mac) and choose the New Folder option from the context-sensitive menu. The new folder will be added in the location you selected, and it will already be highlighted, ready to be named.

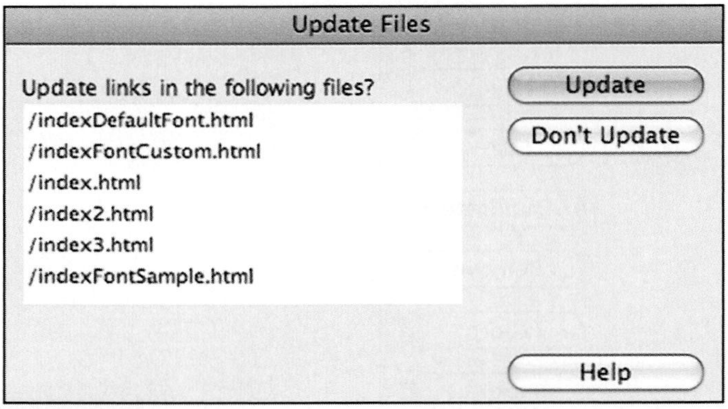

FIGURE 6-15 Updating links.

Moving and Renaming Files Within the Root Folder After you have created a new folder, it is slick and easy to move existing image or page files into it through the Files panel in Dreamweaver. Simply drag the file into the new folder. Dreamweaver will prompt you that the site will need to be updated, as shown in **FIGURE 6-15**.

If you want to rename folders or files in the Files panel, click the name then right/Control-click for the context-sensitive menu and choose Rename. The same Update Files dialog box shown in Figure 6-15 will prompt you regarding the need to update the linked files with the new name. The feature that prompts you to update your files is a default preference setting in Dreamweaver. To change this option, choose Edit>Preferences>General for Windows or Dreamweaver>Preferences>General for Mac. In the Preferences dialog box shown in **FIGURE 6-16**, two additional choices are available for handling link updates:

- **Always:** Links will be updated without asking.
- **Never:** Links will never be updated.

A Word About Links Updating links as files are moved from folder to folder in the Files panel does not only refer to "links" in the familiar sense, such as links to click for moving from page to page, moving from site to site, sending email, etc. Every time an image is placed on a page or a page is created in the Files panel, its location becomes defined in Dreamweaver, requiring an update of its "link" when it is moved.

Deleting Files When deleting a file from a root folder, there are different scenarios that will present themselves in Dreamweaver, based on the use of the file you decide to delete.

1. You want to "clean house" by deleting an extra image from your *images* folder that is not used on any page of your site. Select the file through the Files panel and choose File>Delete from the File panel's options menu, or right/Control-click and choose the Edit>Delete option from the context-sensitive menu. You will be asked to confirm that you want to

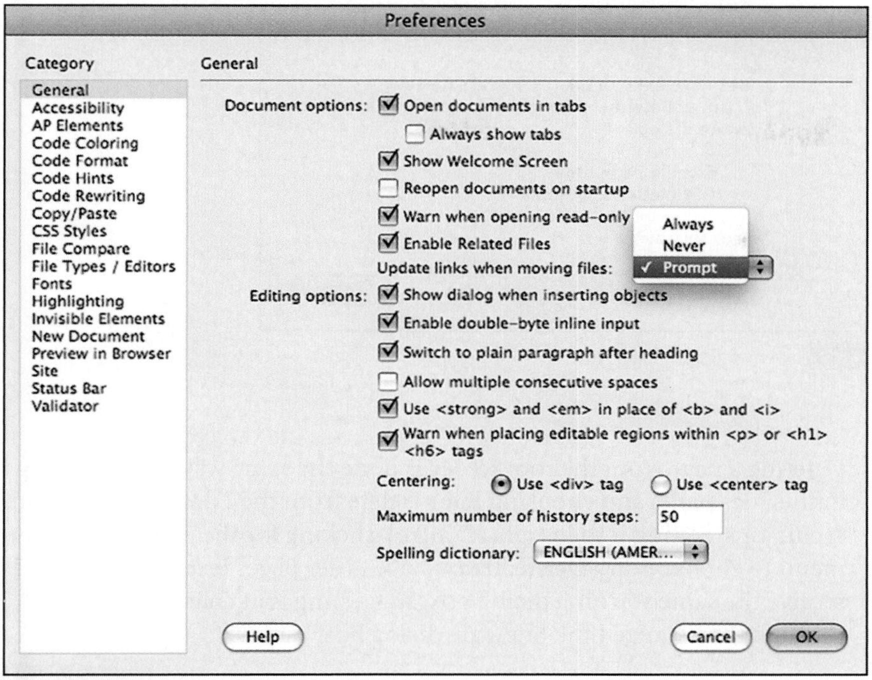

FIGURE 6-16 Link preferences.

delete the file. If you choose the Yes option, your housecleaning is done: the file is removed from your Files panel and permanently removed from the *images* folder in your root folder on your computer. It is best practice to manage all your site file changes through your Files panel. However, if you have an image that has not been used by Dreamweaver, it could also be deleted from your root folder outside of Dreamweaver by opening the root folder and dragging the image to the recycle bin/trash can on your computer. In either case, if you realize later that you deleted the image in error and you created an *original graphics* (or *original psds*) folder in your umbrella folder for the site, you can always save another web optimized version of the original file into the *images* folder of your root folder.

2. If you choose to delete an image that is actually used in a page of your site and you have chosen the preference option to be prompted for link updates, you will be warned that it has files linked to it, and asked if you want to delete it anyway, as shown in **FIGURE 6-17**.

    This handy dialog box will itemize which files will be affected to help you make your decision. It also reminds you that you can change the links to these existing pages through the Change Link Sitewide dialog box.

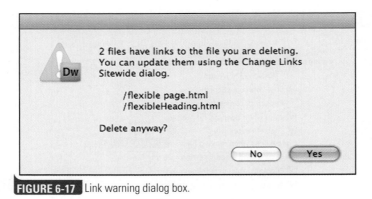

FIGURE 6-17 Link warning dialog box.

3. Deleting a page from the root folder is done the same way—by selecting it in the Files panel and choosing File>Delete from the Files panel's options menu, or selecting it then right/Control-clicking for the context-sensitive menu to choose Edit>Delete. If you have other pages linked to it, you will receive the same warning dialog box, suggesting that changes be made through the Change Link Sitewide dialog box.

6.4.3 Change Link Sitewide Dialog Box

After you are constructing a site, if you decide to delete a file and receive the previous warning message, which makes you realize that you should switch the file with another one instead of eliminating the link, you must exit this dialog box by choosing the No option. After the dialog box closes, you can choose the Change Link Sitewide menu option, which is located under the same Site drop-down menu in the Application menu you used to create your first site. Using this dialog box, you choose the new file to switch it with, as shown in **FIGURE 6-18**.

If you highlighted the file to change before entering this dialog box, it will already be listed here when you arrive. If you haven't chosen an image before you enter this dialog box, click the *Change all links to* folder icon to locate the file to change, and then click the *Into links to* folder icon to search for its replacement.

Change Link Sitewide (Site – SampleSite)	
Change all links to:	OK
/images/building.jpg	Cancel
Into links to:	
/images/bridge.jpg	Help

FIGURE 6-18 Change Link Sitewide dialog box.

FIGURE 6-19 Illustration of broken link icon.

6.4.4 Broken Links

When a broken link exists between Dreamweaver and your files, you will get the dreaded broken link icon, as illustrated in FIGURE 6-19.

The following example demonstrates a typical instance of when this will happen. The sample page, shown in FIGURE 6-20, is from a properly managed site.

After this screen shot was created, with the page still open, the name of the root folder located on the hard drive was changed by selecting it outside of Dreamweaver and editing it. The open page immediately updated to recognize that it could not find the files, as shown in FIGURE 6-21, because the root, exactly as it was originally defined with all its linked images for Dreamweaver, no longer existed.

If you accidentally do this, close the page you are working on, choose Manage Sites, select the respective site from the list, choose Edit, and change the root folder name to reflect the *new* name, or locate the root folder on your computer or external

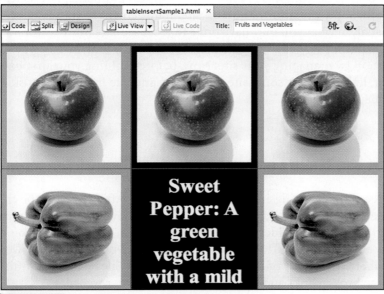

FIGURE 6-20 Page from a properly managed site.

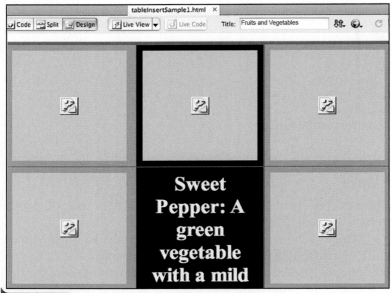

FIGURE 6-21 The name of the root folder was changed so the linked image files could not be found.

drive with its new name and change it *back* to the original name that Dreamweaver knows. When you reopen the page, your images will be back to normal. Phew! Most importantly, if you are working in Dreamweaver and do something that causes you to receive the broken link icon, it is my hope that you will not panic, but instead take a deep breath, apply the information on site management in this chapter to your situation, analyze what you may have done that caused Dreamweaver to lose its link to the file perhaps by changing its name or the path to it, and be able to rectify the situation by managing your site. Now, before building your first page in Dreamweaver, let's reinforce some site definitions and site management skills learned in this chapter.

6.5 What We Have Learned

This chapter was our first exciting entry into Dreamweaver! After covering the creation steps and defining the parts of a root folder, we learned how Dreamweaver must always be able to identify that folder for its critical operation of your site through the process of site management. After a site was defined in Dreamweaver, we were introduced to where the action of the site takes place: the Files panel, including an introduction to broken links and how to avoid them in your websites.

6.6   Reinforcing Your Knowledge

Project 1

1. If you did not build a site through the steps detailed in this chapter, define the SampleSite website now using the *SampleRoot* folder, as defined in this chapter.

2. Using the Manage Sites dialog box, duplicate your first site.

3. Select this new site. Make a folder inside the *images* folder and title it *specialimages*, choosing either File>New Folder, or right/Control-clicking the *images* folder and choosing New Folder from the context-sensitive menu.

4. Drag to move one of the images into it.

5. Delete this duplicate site.

6. Launch Photoshop ... yes, Photoshop. Locate the *winter_headline. psd* file in the *original graphics* folder of the *Sample Umbrella* folder. This will be the background of a headline for a ski shop named Vantage. Add its name in an appropriate font and include a slogan, etc., to create a realistic headline. Using the Save for Web feature, save it as a .jpg, medium quality and progressive, choosing a background matte color for it sucked up from the image itself, and save it into the *images* folder of the *SampleRoot* folder. We will use this in Chapter 10.

7. Open each of the other images located in the *original graphics* folder, and save each one, using the Save for Web feature, as a .jpg, medium quality and progressive, into the *images* folder of the *SampleRoot* folder. What about the matte color for these images? Choose a color as though each image were to be placed on a web page background that will complement the image. You do not have to choose the same color for each one: these are practice images only.

Project 2

1. Open the *FishluvrzRoot* folder on your desktop (or wherever you decided to house it) and create two more folders in lowercase type: *pages* and *css*. Your *Fishluvrz Project* umbrella folder should now have its *original fishluvrz graphics* folder, and its *FishluvrzRoot* folder, which should contain three folders: *images*, *pages*, and *css* inside of it.

2. In Dreamweaver, define the Fishluvrz site, naming it FishluvrzSite in the Site Definition dialog box.

3. Verify that you can scroll to toggle back and forth between the SampleSite website and the FishluvrzSite website in the Files panel's pop-up menu.

Project 3

Create three additional umbrella folders on your desktop. Each should include an *original graphics* folder and a root folder with its components, as you have learned, for each of the following additional companies that you were introduced to in Chapter 1:

- DistinctionRestaurant.com
- MumazYumaz.com
- Cuddluvs.com

Print a screen shot of each of the open umbrella and root folders for grading.

Project 4

1. In Dreamweaver, define sites for each of the companies you created root folders for in Project 3. When defining the sites, remember that you can give them any name you want in the Site Definition dialog box, because it is simply a name to reference the site.

2. Select the Cuddluvs.com site in the Files panel and delete the site in the Manage Sites dialog box.

3. Select the MumazYumaz.com site and duplicate it in the Manage Sites dialog box.

4. Select the DistinctionRestaurant.com site in the Files panel and add a folder inside the *images* folder named *more_images*.

Building Your Own Website

1. The native .psd files you saved from Chapter 4 should be in a folder titled *originalFiles_MySite*, which was recommended to be stored on your desktop at that stage of the design process. At that time, it contained your original .psd files and your optimized Save for Web *images* folder inside of it. Now it is time to create an umbrella folder for your site and move those folders into their appropriate locations within it.

2. Inside this umbrella folder, create your root folder and move your folder of optimized image files into it.

3. Create a *pages* folder and a *css* folder inside your root folder.

4. If you know you will have numerous pages and you want to organize them, create additional folders inside your *pages* folder, titling them as needed to reference them as you build your site. (Remember that you can add more folders or change their names later through Dreamweaver if needed.)

5. Launch Dreamweaver and define your site.

6. After the process is complete, verify that it is now listed in the Files panel as the active site. Welcome to the world of web design!

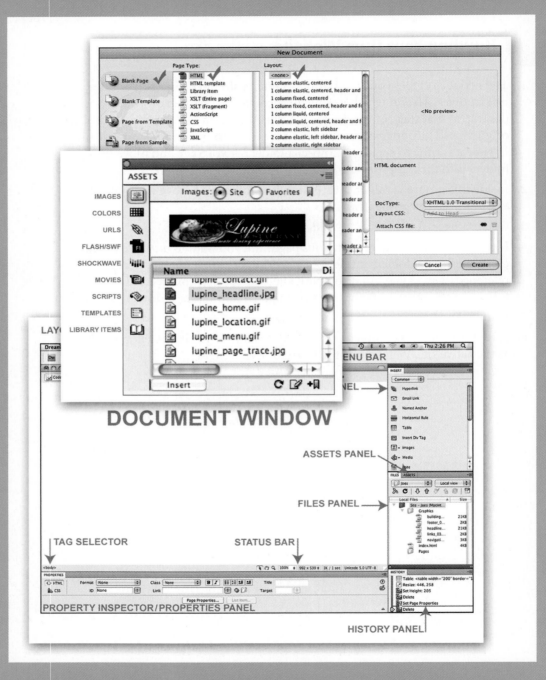

Starting a Document in Dreamweaver

7

I n this chapter, you will be introduced to the working environment of Dreamweaver. Creating a new document and the various options for building that document will be explored, while focusing on the difference between the terms work mode and workspace mode. An introductory general overview of panels and their applicable features will be the focus of this chapter.

Creating a New Document

As in other Adobe programs, after Dreamweaver is launched, you must choose a command to create a new document; one is not created automatically by default. It also echoes other Adobe programs in its ability to create one through its Welcome Screen as well as by using its File menu.

7.1.1 Examining the Welcome Screen

As we discussed in Chapter 6, there is a familiar screen for Adobe users when Dreamweaver launches: the *Welcome Screen.* The Welcome Screen serves multiple purposes, creating a new page being one of them. Let's examine it now in detail. The left column is, like in the other programs, for opening a preexisting document. If you are using Dreamweaver for the first time as you work through this text, the only item listed in this column will be a folder with the word Open. After you have been working in Dreamweaver, this column will list the last nine opened items, and the tenth item will be the folder icon with the word Open, which enables you to open a previously created item prior to the nine items listed. The middle column lists the Create New options, which includes creating a new HTML document and creating a Dreamweaver site. You have already learned to define a site using the New Site option of the Site drop-down menu: choosing this option from the Welcome Screen will bring you to the same Site Definition dialog box. Like Photoshop, after you are comfortable with Dreamweaver, you have the option to check the box in the lower-left corner of the Welcome Screen to choose not to display the Welcome Screen. If you later decide you want it to show again at startup, you may reactivate it by checking the Show Welcome Screen option under the Dreamweaver Preferences menu option accessed by selecting Dreamweaver>Preferences>General for Mac, or Edit>Preferences>General for Windows.

   To create a new document using the Welcome Screen, choose HTML from the Create New column to open a new blank HTML document.

7.1.2 Using the File Menu

Another way to create a new document is to click and hold on the File main application menu, after Dreamweaver is launched, to view some familiar graphic software menu commands that also apply to Dreamweaver:

- **New:** Another method for starting a new HTML document rather than using the Welcome Screen (Command/Control+N).
- **Open:** Another method of locating an existing item (Command/Control+O).
- **Browse in Bridge:** Locate an existing file through Adobe® Bridge®.
- **Open Recent:** Open one of the 10 most recently opened pages.

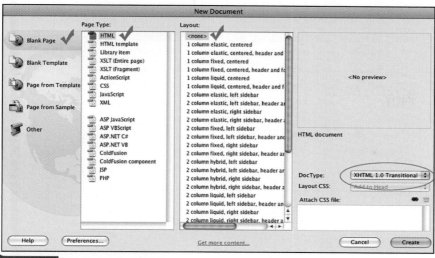

FIGURE 7-1 New Document dialog box.

When you choose to create a new page by selecting the File>New option, the New Document dialog box opens. It can be rather overwhelming, because there appear to be many options. As designers, we will focus on building a blank page from scratch for now by choosing File>New>Blank Page, Page Type>HTML, Layout>None, DocType>XHTML 1.0 Transitional (**FIGURE 7-1**).

XHTML 1.0 Transitional is the default DocType choice in Dreamweaver because of its broad application and flexibility and will always be the document type we will use to build our pages. (If you chose to complete Chapter 5, you are already familiar with the XHTML 1.0 Transitional DocType.)

7.2 An Introduction to Dreamweaver for Graphic Artists

FIGURE 7-2 introduces the working options available in Dreamweaver, identifies another way to access site management, and provides a first look at titling a page.

7.2.1 Design View vs. Split View vs. Code View

If you chose to complete Chapter 5, you have already received an introduction to these three working views of Dreamweaver. Here, we will review what they display, learn where they are located, and learn how to access them.

When a document is open, the Code, Split, and Design view tabs are located across the top of the page in an area called the *Document toolbar*. The visibility of this toolbar can be turned on or off by choosing View>Toolbars>Document. We will want this toolbar visible at all times during our design process.

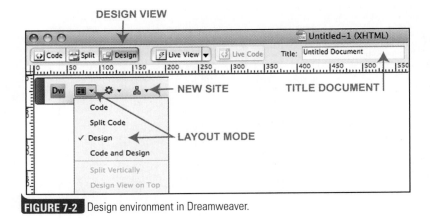

FIGURE 7-2 Design environment in Dreamweaver.

When the blank document opens, if it is not already in Design view (no code visible), click the Design tab of the view options located at the left side of the Document toolbar. This is the view we will use to build our pages because it was created for graphic artists and tagged WYSIWYG (What You See Is What You Get). However, at the end of each applicable chapter, we will also view our pages in *Split view*, which displays the Design view and the Code view at the same time (as introduced in Chapter 5) to examine the code pertaining to the features learned in that chapter. *Code view*, which allows the Dreamweaver user to work exclusively in HTML code, is not one we will cover in this textbook.

Any time that you choose the Code view or Split view and want to return to the Design view, click the Design tab again, or choose View>Design from the View menu.

Layout Menu   In CS4 and CS5, in addition to the three view tabs in the Document toolbar, nested in the Application menu area are some icons, one of which is a little square icon titled Layout that reveals a menu allowing you to also access the same three views of the Document toolbar, plus an additional view, titled *Split Code view*, for working on your document.

It is important to note here that Split Code view is not the Split view mode that we will explore at various times in this textbook. Split Code view here allows you to view two parts of a document in Code view simultaneously. The option from this particular menu that corresponds to the Split View tab in the Document toolbar is the Code and Design option. In Windows, this Layout menu is part of the main application menu. For the Mac, it is part of a movable panel that can be snapped to the top of the page, or dragged by the bar on its left side; its visibility can be toggled on or off under Window>Application Bar.

Site Menu   Another handy icon, located to the right of the Layout menu, is a "tiered pages" site icon: click it to create a new site or manage an existing one.

◼ 7.2.2 Titling a Web Page

Returning to the Document toolbar, let's explore one of the locations to title the web page. By highlighting the words *Untitled Document* in the Title area, you are able to type a title for the active page. It is important to note that this is not saving or naming the document, it is creating the title of the page as it will be viewed in a browser, written in title case (major words begin in capital letters) to clearly identify the page. Understanding more about the importance of page titles, and the difference between assigning page titles and naming and saving pages, will be discussed in depth in Chapter 8.

For CS3 Users

Although the Layout and Site management icons were new in CS4, the Design tab, Split tab, Code tab, and the title area of the Document toolbar are the same in CS3, with the ability to create and manage a site located under the Site main menu, and through the Files panel.

7.3 Exploring the Dreamweaver Workspace

FIGURE 7-3 provides an overview of the rest of the parts of the Dreamweaver workspace that we will be covering individually in more detail in this chapter. If your workspace doesn't look quite like Figure 7-3, don't worry. This chapter will include an explanation of how the CS3 workspace options and panels differ from those of CS4 and CS5.

◼ 7.3.1 Designer Workspace Options

As previously mentioned, we will build our pages using the Design view of Dreamweaver tailored for graphic artists, which refers to creating a page visually, not creating it by writing code; but, we will enter the Split view at times to examine the code that Dreamweaver has generated for us. It is important to understand the difference between Design view and the Designer workspace: one is the way the working document is displayed (Design view), the other is how the tools to create the page (the working environment) are displayed (Designer workspace). Although you can create your own custom workspace, just as you can in other Adobe programs, two workspaces were created specifically for graphic artists: *Designer workspace* and *Designer Compact workspace*, both of which echo the panel configurations of the most recent versions of other Adobe programs. This textbook will work exclusively in the Designer workspace, which is the default

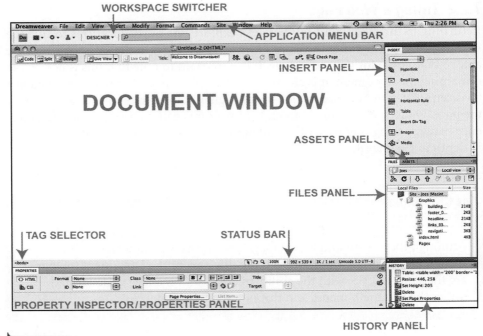

FIGURE 7-3 Dreamweaver workspace in CS4 and CS5.

option when you launch Dreamweaver CS4 or CS5, but feel free to work in the Designer Compact mode (with the panels collapsed) instead, if it is more consistent with your work habits in other programs. The workspace choices are listed in the workspace switcher pop-up menu, as shown in **FIGURE 7-4**, with the option to create your own custom workspace. These same workspace options can also be selected under Window>Workspace.

You may have already noticed that the Designer workspace option displays panels with the same collapsible features available in other Adobe programs. In this mode, the panels can be separated, redocked, collapsed, and expanded, as shown in **FIGURE 7-5**, with the option to save a current workspace either by choosing New Workspace from the same Designer pop-up menu or by choosing Window>Workspace Layout>New Workspace.

This custom workspace may be renamed or deleted at any time by choosing Manage Workspaces from either the workspace switcher pop-up menu or Window>Workspace Layout>Manage Workspaces. If, at any time, you are working in the Designer workspace and have moved and redocked or closed panels and want to return to the original Designer configuration, choose Designer>Reset 'Designer' or choose Window>Workspace>Reset 'Designer' and all panels will snap back to the original default Designer workspace locations.

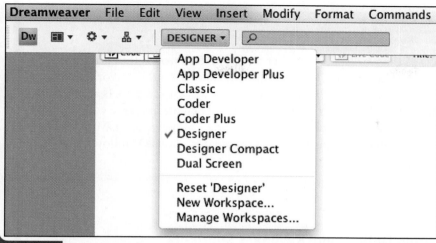

FIGURE 7-4 Workspace switcher.

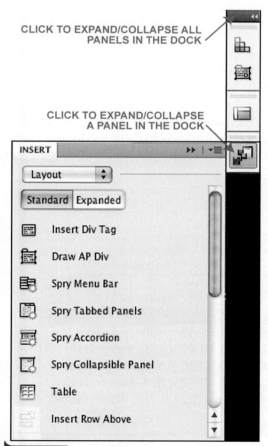

FIGURE 7-5 Accessing panels.

For CS3 Users

Don't see the workspace switcher in CS3? Don't worry, things are not very different here. The default workspace (Window>Workspace Layout>Default) is similar to the Designer workspace: panels are docked on the right side of your screen. You can still create and save your own configuration of panels by choosing Window>Workspace Layout>Save Current. To manage a custom workspace later, choose Window>Workspace Layout>Manage.

7.3.2 View Options and Keyboard Shortcuts

When you open a new page, by default the Document window will open at the 100% view. The Status bar, shown in **FIGURE 7-6**, allows you to also zoom in and out of your document page using a Zoom tool that works as it does in other graphics programs.

Click and drag with the Zoom tool to dynamically zoom into an area. Click the Zoom tool on the page to zoom in by preset increments (Option/Alt added will zoom out). Also, you can choose a preset increment or type your own percentage into the Set Magnification option in the Status bar. You can also change your view by choosing a zoom in or zoom out option under the View menu in the application main menu, or by choosing a preset magnification from the fly-out menu there as well. Whichever method you choose, you have the ability to magnify up to 6400%.

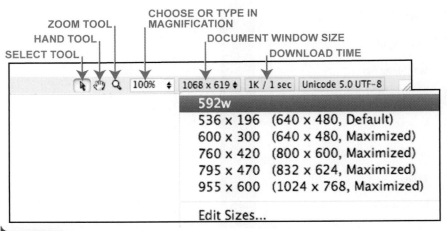

FIGURE 7-6 Status bar options.

If you have magnified in or out from the 100% view, you can double-click the Select tool as a shortcut to return to the 100% view. It is an easy transition from double-clicking the Zoom tool for the 100% view in other Adobe programs. Lastly, you may have already discovered that you can also use the Command/Control plus the +/– keys to zoom in or out of your page by the preset zoom increments, a slick Adobe shortcut that works in Dreamweaver as well.

7.3.3 Using the Status Bar to Change the Document Window Size and View Download Time

In addition to changing the magnification of your view of the page while designing it by using the Zoom tool or the magnification options previously discussed in this chapter, the Status bar also allows you to choose preset window sizes for the most common monitor screen viewing areas. In Chapter 3, we discussed screen resolution and designing according to your visitors' screen resolution settings. The Status bar allows you to choose a preset size to design your page accordingly, or set your own. In this pop-up menu, you are not choosing "page dimensions" as you would in Photoshop if you chose File>New. You are choosing a "viewing area" to help you design your pages according to your audience. Even though we will build pages at a pixel width of 750, you can expand the viewing area while working to better visualize how your chosen background (the area that will *surround* the page if the viewer's monitor setting allows) complements or overpowers your page's content area. To design a page that looks its best at a specific size, you can adjust the Document window to any of the predetermined sizes, edit those predetermined sizes, or create your own sizes. Click and hold the current Document window size and then choose a different option from its pop-up menu. When making your choice, remember that the size in parentheses refers to the monitor size. Or, you can choose the Edit Sizes option to create your own. When you choose Edit Sizes, a dialog box lets you click below the last option to type in and name your own custom size. To change or delete it later, simply return to the same dialog box, highlight your custom window size, and modify or delete it. This dialog box can also be accessed under the application preferences: Dreamweaver>Preferences>Status Bar for Mac, or Edit>Preferences>Status Bar for Windows. If all you want to do is check your page against your background, you can also grab the lower-right corner of the Document window and manually drag it to the right: you will see the dimensions change correspondingly in the Document window area of the Status bar.

Also located under the same category of the Dreamweaver preferences is the option to set the download time from the default connection speed of 56 kps. A handy page file size and an approximate download time for it is always displayed next to the window sizes in the Status bar.

Can't select a size because it is grayed out in Windows? You will need to click the maximize/de-maximize button for the document to have the sizes selectable in the Status bar, as shown in **FIGURE 7-7**.

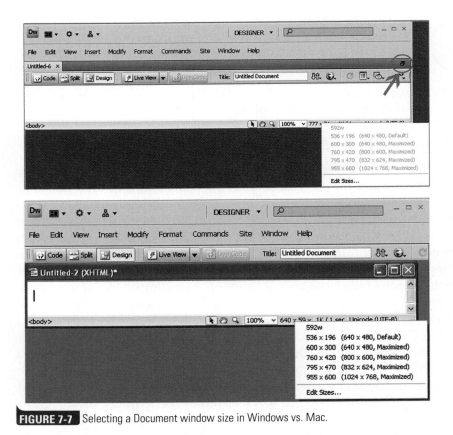

FIGURE 7-7 Selecting a Document window size in Windows vs. Mac.

When desired, if an area is magnified, there is also a Hand tool to scroll around the page that works just like it does in Photoshop.

7.3.4 Property Inspector (or Properties Panel) vs. Options Bar in Photoshop

The Property inspector (also referred to as the Properties panel) performs similar to the Options bar in Photoshop. It will constantly update to reflect the *properties* or *options* available for what is currently selected in Dreamweaver and allow you to change features of that selection. In **FIGURE 7-8**, the Property inspector reflects the features of the selected table. Notice that you must click the arrow in the lower-right area of the panel for all of the Property inspector options to be visible.

This panel will be displayed at the bottom of the Document window, but can be moved and docked with other panels if desired. If you close the panel, either intentionally or accidentally, you may display it again by choosing Window>Properties or Command/Control+F3. Or, if you are working in Designer mode, remember that

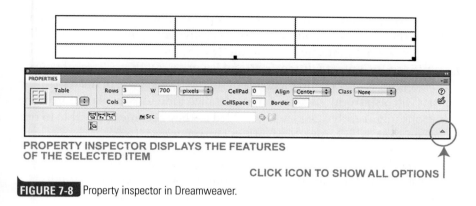

PROPERTY INSPECTOR DISPLAYS THE FEATURES
OF THE SELECTED ITEM

CLICK ICON TO SHOW ALL OPTIONS

FIGURE 7-8 Property inspector in Dreamweaver.

you can always choose Window>Workspace Layout>Reset 'Designer' to return to the default configuration of the panels.

For CS3 Users

At any time, you can grab the tab on the left side of the Property inspector to move it around the page.

7.3.5 The Dreamweaver "Toolbox": Using the Insert Panel

The Insert panel is sort of like the toolbox in other graphic programs. Although its "tools" can also be added to the page under certain main application menus, it is easier to choose from the icon buttons available under each of the eight categories of the Insert panel. To show or hide the Insert panel, choose Window>Insert or Command/Control+F2. To convert it to a horizontal bar displaying at the top of the Document window, drag the Insert tab above the Document window and release it (a blue line appears indicating you are in the right spot to release the tab). To return it to a regular panel, grab the gripper bar (on the left of the panel group), drag it back to the main panel area on the right side of the Document window, and release it. You can also choose Window>Workspace Layout>Reset 'Designer' to have Dreamweaver do it for you (much easier!) if you were originally working in the Designer workspace before you customized it. The eight "boxes of tools" of the Insert panel can be displayed as color or black and white icons, and with or without their respective names listed. You can toggle the color applied to the icons on or off by choosing Color Icons from the Insert panel's options menu, or by choosing View>Color Icons. At some point in your Dreamweaver career, you may want to choose the Hide Labels option from the Insert panel's options menu to display the icons only to minimize the need to scroll to access a particular button; however, initially, it will be easier if the name and picture of the Insert panel button are both visible until you are more familiar with the program. The eight categories of the Insert panel are: Common, Layout, Forms, Data, Spry, InContext Editing, Text, and Favorites. Of those categories, Data and InContext Editing are beyond the scope of this textbook. Each of the remaining six categories will be introduced here. A more detailed individual explanation of the various buttons under each category is provided as they become applicable to our website designing as we continue our work in Dreamweaver.

- **Common:** As the name implies, this category is used to insert the most common items you will create/import into Dreamweaver, such as links, images, and media.
- **Layout:** Although the Common category has a button to insert a table onto a page, the Layout category of the Insert panel also has the same option to add a table grouped with several other table options, plus Div tags and AP Divs, Frames, and Spry options.
- **Forms:** This category has buttons for creating all types of form elements. Although these same options are also available by choosing Insert>Form> and choosing from the fly-out menu that appears, the buttons of the Insert panel are easier to use because their icons help identify what kind of form element they are, making the selection process easier.
- **Spry:** This category allows you to add dynamic activity to your page using JavaScript™ and CSS. A variety of options are available; we will cover some that are applicable to form validation and navigation.
- **Text:** This category allows you to apply a variety of text and list formatting options.
- **Favorites:** This very handy category is one you may want to customize as you become savvy in Dreamweaver. If you right/Control-click on any button under any of the other Insert panel categories, an option to choose Customize Favorites becomes available. If selected, you enter a dialog box that allows you to scroll through all of the Insert category buttons and click to choose which one(s) you want to move a *copy* of (the original button remains in the category it is listed under) to your *Favorite objects* category by clicking the double arrows icon between the two menus. A trash can for deleting them later (remember, it is just a copy of the button!) up/down arrows to change the order in which a selected button displays, and the option to add a delineating line between your choices are also available. **FIGURE 7-9** shows items being added to the list.

It is important to understand at this time, that this is not the same as the Favorites option of the Assets panel, which allows you to save favorite assets. An introduction to the Assets panel will be included later in this chapter, and its Favorites feature is covered in Chapter 11.

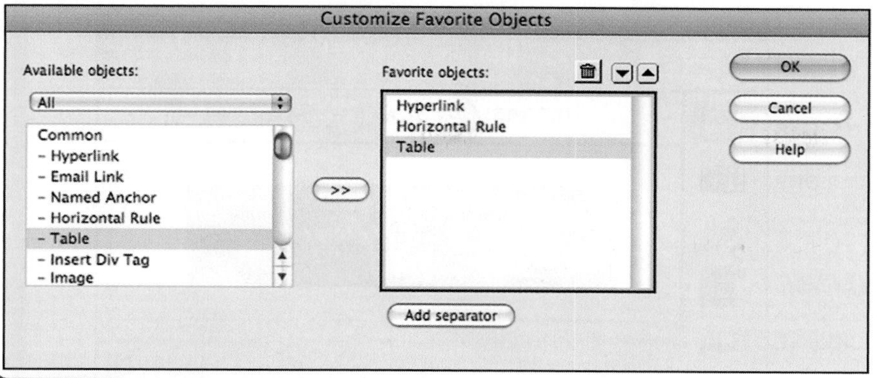

FIGURE 7-9 Customizing your favorite buttons.

For CS3 Users

Dreamweaver CS3 has seven of the eight categories found in the Insert panel of CS4 and CS5 (InContext Editing was added in CS4). It is called the Insert bar, and its categories are displayed across the top of the Document window as tabs. If you right/Control-click a tab, you can display the items of that category as a menu list. To return to the default position as tabs later, choose Show as Tabs from the pop-up menu on the left side of the selected Insert bar category. Choosing Classic as the workspace mode in CS4 or CS5 will display the insert options in this same configuration. If you are currently working in CS3, but choose to upgrade to CS5 in the future, this feature will enable you to continue to use the CS3 workspace configuration you are familiar with.

7.3.6 The Files Panel: Where the Action Is

You were introduced to the powerful Files panel in Chapter 6 and learned that it is used to access and manage all of your Dreamweaver site files for all of your sites. Because you set up the SampleSite practice website, the FishluvrzSite website, and the additional practice sites (you may also have defined your own site), those sites will be visible in the Files panel's pop-up menu . . . where the action is!

7.3.7 The Assets Panel

The Assets panel contains categories of all the ingredients of the open website—all of its images, colors, URLs, media and script files, templates, and library items—allowing you to also create a favorites collection of the items under each category that you use most frequently, as shown in **FIGURE 7-10**.

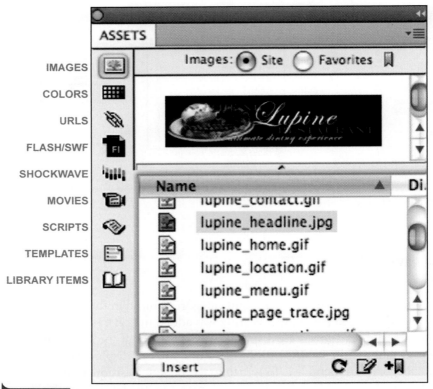

FIGURE 7-10 Assets panel in Dreamweaver.

In the Designer workspace, it is docked with the Files panel by default. This versatile panel performs many functions: it allows you to see a copy of your images so that you can preview them before inserting them, automatically stores all the colors used in your site, saves your links, and lets you copy files from one site to another, just to name a few. We will continue to reference the Assets panel and explore its many handy options as its features become relevant to our work in Dreamweaver.

7.3.8 The History Panel: Hooray for History!

Dreamweaver has multiple undos that can be accessed through Command/Control+Z. Command/Control+Y is used for the Redo command. However, to further assist you in the design process, Dreamweaver also has a History panel. Although it is not exactly like or as flexible as the one in Photoshop, it is still very handy because it is visual and lets you jump back several *steps* (not *states* as they are called in Photoshop), eliminating the need to back up one at a time through the Undo command. To display the History panel, choose Window>History. The number of default steps is set to 50, but it can be set higher based on your available RAM under Preferences>General>Maximum number of history steps.

The slider on the left is used to maneuver back in the History panel and always points to the last step. Highlighting the step itself selects the state, but will not bring you back to it. If you are not sure how far back you want to go and want to watch the steps as you go, drag the slider back up through each step and release it when you have reached the correct step. If you know exactly which step you want to back up to, click to the left of the step on the slider bar itself, or to the left of the slider bar to return directly to that step, skipping all of the steps in between. Like the Photoshop History panel in Linear mode, when you back up, the more recent steps are grayed out; you can return to one of these steps as long as you do not do something new. As soon as you back up and change something on your page, all history steps that were below that step are deleted. Unfortunately, one huge feature of this panel that differs from the Photoshop History panel is that the Dreamweaver History panel will not undo *all* of its actions; but, it is always worth checking to see if you can back up when you have done something and you want to change your mind.

An Introduction to Adding Content to a Page

In the Files panel, scroll if needed in the Files panel pop-up menu and choose the SampleSite site. If you still have a page open, it is time to add a little content to it; if not, create a new page by using the File>New command or the Welcome Screen. Title the page *Practice Only* in the title area of the Document toolbar. (Remember that titling is not saving; we will not be saving this document.) You will see that a flashing I-beam is automatically placed at the upper-left corner of the Document window area. Type the sentence: *Welcome to my first page!* Place the I-beam anywhere inside this first sentence and choose Format>Paragraph Format>Heading 1 (or Text>Paragraph Format>Heading 1 in CS3). We will learn more about headings and how to assign properties to them in Chapter 9. For now, we will let Dreamweaver format the heading when this option is chosen. After this sentence, press the Enter/ Return key to create a new paragraph and type: *Here is my first image.* Then, press the Enter/Return key one more time.

At the flashing I-beam on this last line, click the Insert panel, choose the Common category from its pop-up menu, and then select Image from its Images button. Because you selected the SampleSite site in your Files panel, you should be automatically brought to the images folder in its root folder. If not, navigate to this specific folder to locate the images provided. Choose any one of the photos in it to add to your page. Because we will not be saving this first practice page, click OK in the following dialog box regarding the file path for the image, as shown in **FIGURE 7-11**, as well as in the Image Tag Accessibility Attributes dialog box that follows. (Saving pages, file paths, and accessibility attributes will be discussed in detail in Chapter 8.)

Just as in other Adobe programs that offer multiple ways to perform a task, this is one method of inserting an image. We will continue to learn other ways to achieve the same end result, so that you can do as you have with other common graphic

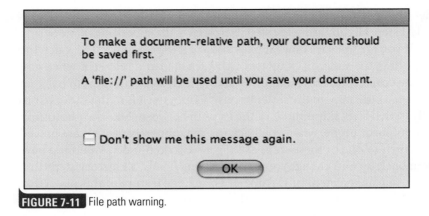

FIGURE 7-11 File path warning.

program tasks: decide which method of inserting images works best for you. After your image has been placed on the page, drag to select everything with the Select tool and choose Format>Align>Center to center your content on the page.

For CS3 Users

In CS3, the options are the same, but their access is a little different, as shown in **FIGURE 7-12**.

In CS3, click the Common tab of the Insert bar, click the Images pop-up menu, and choose Image from its available options. When applying the heading and alignment options, they are both available under the Text main menu.

Whether you are working in CS3, CS4, or CS5, the page does not look exciting yet, but it is exciting to have finally created your first page!

SELECT THE COMMON TAB,
THEN IMAGE FROM THE POP-UP MENU

PARAGRAPH FORMAT AND ALIGNMENT
OPTIONS ARE UNDER THE TEXT MENU

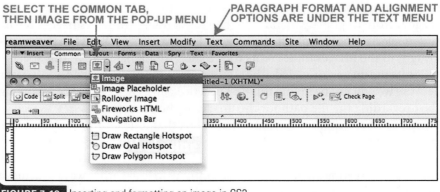

FIGURE 7-12 Inserting and formatting an image in CS3.

7.5　A Look at the Code in Split View: Basic Page Content

Does this page look familiar? We learned how to do everything here and more in Chapter 5. If you click the Split mode tab now, as shown in **FIGURE 7-13**, you will see that "behind the scenes," Dreamweaver has performed several actions.

1. Dreamweaver established the beginning code needed to have our page shown on the Web.

2. Dreamweaver placed the title of the document, *Practice Only*, in the `<head>` element.

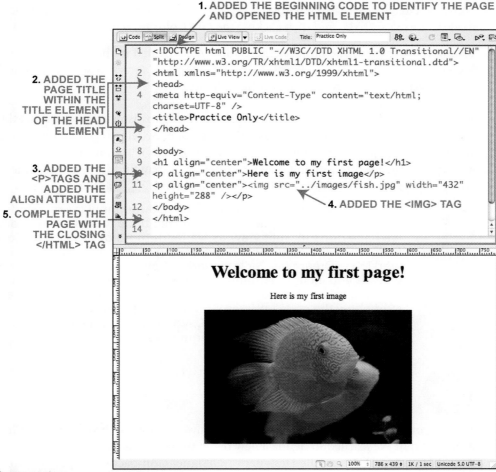

FIGURE 7-13　Split view of the first page.

3. Dreamweaver delineated the two paragraphs using the `<p>` tag contained within the opening and closing `<body>` tags and added the `align="center"` attribute to each paragraph.

4. Dreamweaver added the image with the `<img>` tag, with both the name of the file and its pixel dimensions within quotation marks.

5. Dreamweaver added the closing `</html>` tag to complete the page.

7.5.1 Code Viewing Tips

If you plan to study or write code in Dreamweaver, you can customize its display to fit your work style.

Changing the Colors of the Code   Did you notice the colors of parts of the code in the Split view? Dreamweaver assigns colors to the type of code being written, which can be very helpful. You can take a look at those and customize them if you like by choosing Dreamweaver>Preferences (for Mac) or (for Windows)>Edit>Preferences Code Coloring>HTML, and then clicking the Edit Coloring Scheme button.

Changing the Size of the Font for the Code   Also located in the Preferences dialog box is a category named Fonts. Choose Code View and then set the font and size you want the code to display in when visible.

Using the Code Inspector   An alternative to choosing to display the code using the Split view is to choose to display it as a floating panel by selecting Window>Code Inspector. This option will allow you to move the Code view around your page. As a graphic artist used to moving palettes/panels, you may find it more convenient when you want to take a look at the code, as shown in **FIGURE 7-14**.

As previously mentioned in this chapter, throughout the remainder of this text, when applicable, we will continue to look at the work we have done in Split view as we learn more of the web design features of Dreamweaver. A great thing to do from now on while working in Dreamweaver is to work in Split view instead of Design view (if you included Chapter 5 in your studies). As you add content and make changes to your pages in Dreamweaver, you can study how the code updates simultaneously! Now that you have a basic understanding of HTML, you will enhance your understanding and usage of HTML tremendously!

7.6 What We Have Learned

Adding your first content to a web page in Dreamweaver was our goal in this chapter, and we did it! We learned to define a new blank page and the basics of how to title it for a browser. Choosing the Designer or Designer Compact workspace allowed us to use the familiar Adobe expand/collapse docking features for manipulating

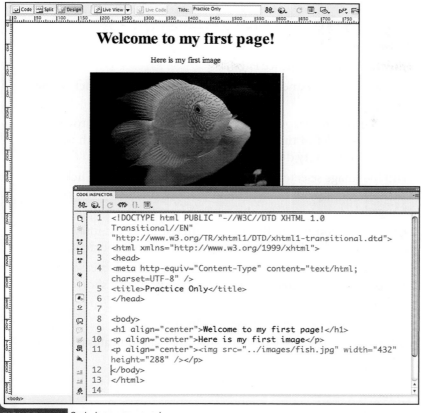

FIGURE 7-14 Code Inspector panel.

our panels. An introduction to the categories of the Insert panel, as well as an introduction to the similarities and differences of using the Dreamweaver History panel vs. that of Photoshop, helped us gain some general comfort in moving around the workface and get ready to delve deeper into Dreamweaver in Chapter 8.

7.7 Reinforcing Your Knowledge

Project

1. Launch Dreamweaver.
2. With your SampleSite active in the Files panel, create a new page.
3. When the page opens, be sure it is in the Design view and that you have chosen either the Designer or Designer Compact workspace.

Project (continued)

4. Title the page: *My Practice Page.*

5. Separate the Files panel from the dock and then add it back to the dock.

6. Insert a different image onto this page from the images provided in the *images* folder of the SampleSite, ignoring the File path warning and the accessibility dialog boxes when they open.

7. With the image selected, notice the Property inspector. Click outside the image and notice that the Property inspector has changed.

8. Dynamically zoom in to the lower-right corner of the image and then return to the 100% view using the Select tool shortcut.

9. Zoom in to 200% using the keyboard shortcut that increases your view by preset increments and then use the keyboard shortcut to zoom out to 150%.

10. Return to the 100% view and delete the image.

11. Using the History panel, return to the step that indicates the insertion of the image you chose in step 6.

12. Add a sentence of text and then change the alignment of the text to center.

13. Apply a hard return to create a new paragraph and add another sentence, keeping it left aligned; but this time, apply Heading 1 to the sentence.

14. Set the Document window size to reflect the 640 × 480 Maximized monitor view and then create your own custom window size of 1000 × 650.

15. Now, change the window dimensions to the preset window size defined as 800 × 600 Maximized monitor view. Delete the custom window size created in step 14.

16. Add a hard return (new paragraph) after your last sentence and add another image to the page.

17. Create a screen shot of this page, including the title area, for submission for grading.

18. Close and do not save this first page.

7.8 Building Your Own Website

1. Choose your own site, created in Chapter 6, from the pop-up menu in the Files panel.

2. Create a new blank page and title it *My Test Page*.

3. Insert your first photo into the page and then press the Enter/Return key.

4. Insert your second photo into the page (or your first photo again if you have only one photo for now) noting that it was placed below the first one.

5. Repeat this step to bring in the third photo (or your first photo again if you have only one).

6. Select one of your images with the Select tool and notice the image's properties reflected in the Property inspector.

7. Click the Split view option, if you would like, and notice your page title in the head area, your image names, image sizes, and how they were automatically placed with the tags as needed within the `<body>` tag.

8. Close the document and do not save the changes. We will learn how to save properly in Chapter 8.

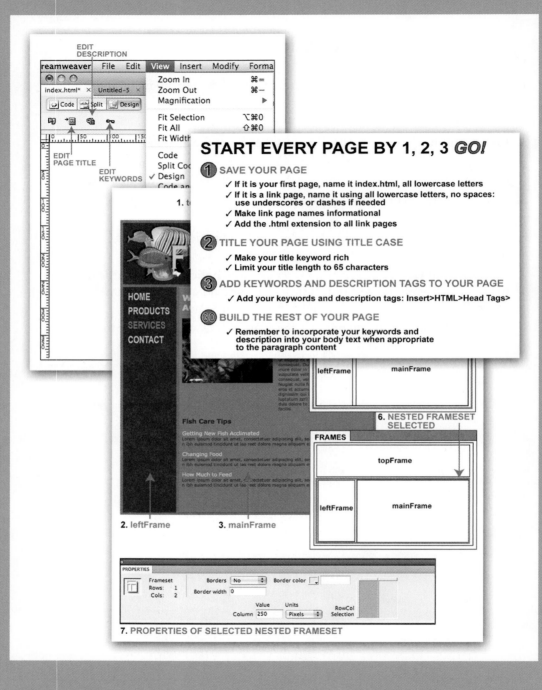

START EVERY PAGE BY 1, 2, 3 GO!

1 SAVE YOUR PAGE
- ✓ If it is your first page, name it index.html, all lowercase letters
- ✓ If it is a link page, name it using all lowercase letters, no spaces: use underscores or dashes if needed
- ✓ Make link page names informational
- ✓ Add the .html extension to all link pages

2 TITLE YOUR PAGE USING TITLE CASE
- ✓ Make your title keyword rich
- ✓ Limit your title length to 65 characters

3 ADD KEYWORDS AND DESCRIPTION TAGS TO YOUR PAGE
- ✓ Add your keywords and description tags: Insert>HTML>Head Tags>

GO BUILD THE REST OF YOUR PAGE
- ✓ Remember to incorporate your keywords and description into your body text when appropriate to the paragraph content

EDIT DESCRIPTION

EDIT PAGE TITLE

EDIT KEYWORDS

1. to

Fish Care Tips

Getting New Fish Acclimated

Changing Food

How Much to Feed

2. leftFrame   3. mainFrame

6. NESTED FRAMESET SELECTED

FRAMES

topFrame

leftFrame   mainFrame

PROPERTIES

Frameset   Borders   No   Border color
Rows: 1   Border width   0
Cols: 2

          Value   Units
Column   250   Pixels   RowCol Selection

7. PROPERTIES OF SELECTED NESTED FRAMESET

Naming, Titling, and Adding Accessibility to Traditional vs. Frame-Based Website Pages

8

In This Chapter

- Learn to properly name and title web pages
- Add keywords and description text for search engines
- Add accessibility attributes
- Understand the basics of creating a frame-based website

In this chapter, we will learn the critical differences between naming a page and titling it. We will also learn to define keywords and description text and how to add them to a web page in Dreamweaver. Our focus when learning these features will be on what you, as a designer, can do to increase your site's search engine ranking through your choice of words and body text. Lastly, we will be introduced to a frame-based website, learning how it differs from a traditionally designed site, and the basics of creating one.

8.1 Starting a Website Focused on Search Engine Optimization (SEO)

In Chapter 7, we learned to create a page and add a little content to it. However, for visitors to find them, successful websites incorporate more than simply text and images on a page. Let's learn how to begin a website that is designed to be found on the Web when potential visitors search for our products or services.

8.1.1 Naming the Index Page

Starting a web page can be divided into three important steps. The first step is naming the page. When creating a website, start with the home page, which you learned in Chapter 6 should be named *index.html* or *index.htm*. By naming the file "index," it becomes the page that browsers recognize as your home page, and the one to be displayed when a visitor arrives at your site. This is achieved by the critical naming of the page as *index.html* or *index.htm*. Although both the .html and .htm extensions are acceptable practice, the .html extension will be used throughout the remainder of this text. In Chapter 6, we learned to create a root folder and add folders inside of it for pages, images, and css; but, we said that the index page cannot be created until you are in Dreamweaver. Now is the time! If it is not already open, launch Dreamweaver. In the Files panel, scroll through its pop-up menu to locate your SampleSite. When you have located it, click the arrow next to the site name in the Files panel. If the site's folders are not visible (*pages*, etc.), choose the Manage Sites option at the bottom of this pop-up menu and locate your root folder. When Dreamweaver can locate it, the supplementary files will display, as shown in **FIGURE 8-1**.

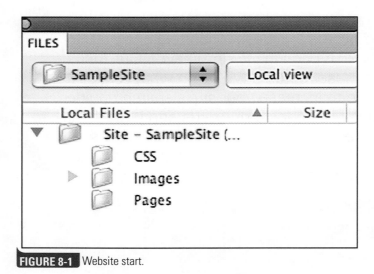

FIGURE 8-1 Website start.

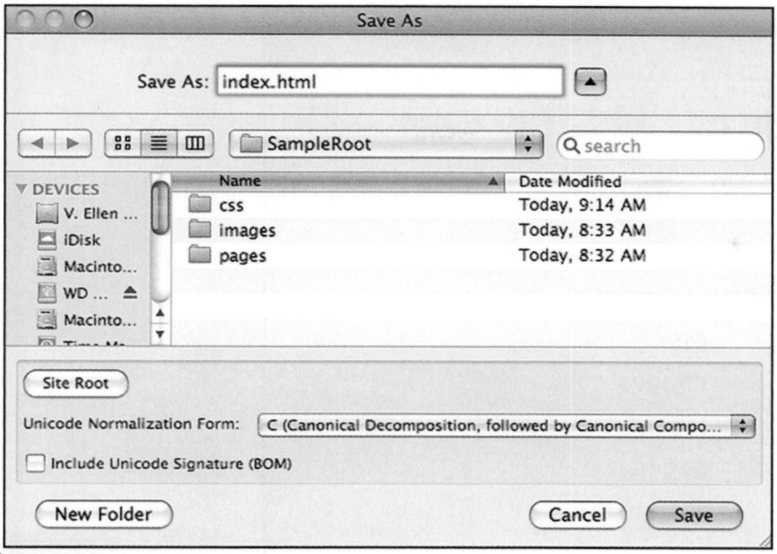

FIGURE 8-2 Save As dialog box.

Use File>New, Command/Control+N or the Welcome Screen to create a blank default page. Choose File>Save As. When the Save As dialog box appears, because your SampleSite is the active one in the Files panel, you should automatically be brought to your defined root folder: *SampleRoot* of your SampleSite first website, as shown in **FIGURE 8-2**.

After you are here, name the page *index.html* (all lowercase, including the extension). The index page, we learned in Chapter 6, belongs in the root folder, but not in the *pages* folder. After you have named the index page, it will automatically display in your Files panel, as shown in **FIGURE 8-3**.

8.1.2 Titling the Index Page

You may or may not have noticed that throughout the saving process for the index page, it was always referred to as *naming* not *titling*. That was intentional, to avoid confusion with the second critical step in the page creation process: the titling of the page. You received an initial introduction to the titling process in Chapter 7; you learned where the option was located and how to highlight it and change the default name of *Untitled Document*. Now, it is time to learn more about titling pages and how well-written titles can help increase your search engine ranking. As the popularity and use of the Web has exploded over the years, *Search Engine Optimization*, referred to as SEO, has become an ever more important consideration in the web design process. How can you be found? There are services you can purchase, but there are also things you can do for free that will help. Careful consideration when defining your page titles is one of them. Unlike a page name, a page title can have spaces, commas, etc., in it. The title is what the visitor sees at the top of the open window

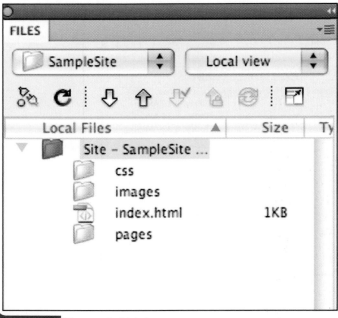

FIGURE 8-3 Files panel with index page.

when he/she visits your page. The area to type the title in Dreamweaver appears small, but as you type, you will be able to scroll over to continue your typing. Even though your full title may not be visible in the entry area of Dreamweaver, the full sentence you type will display when viewed in a browser, as shown in **FIGURE 8-4**.

As mentioned in Chapter 7, the title should be written in title case, and its length should be limited to 65 characters (letters and spaces) to accommodate the leading search engines without having part of the title cut off in the search engine listing. Search engines use your page title as one way of finding and listing you. Because of that, consider the difference in the two page titles created for a fish aquarium products home page: *Fishluvrz* vs. *Fishluvrz Wholesale and Retail Aquarium Products and Services*. The first title may be the name of the company, but what kind of company is it? A fish fan club? A restaurant? The second title includes words carefully chosen to help define the site's market. We now know that this company sells aquarium products, and that its sales cater to both the wholesale and retail markets.

8.1.3 Adding Keywords and Description Head Tags

The third stage of the page creation process is to add keywords and description text to your page to further aid in search engine recognition.

Defining Keywords   *Keywords* are the words that visitors will type into their search engines when looking for a website like yours. Brainstorming can help you

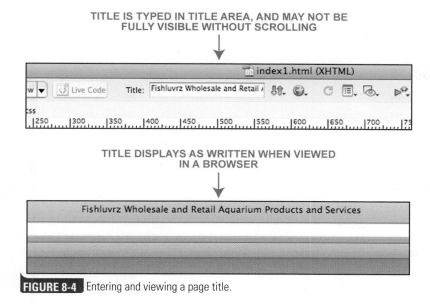

FIGURE 8-4 Entering and viewing a page title.

think of some keywords, but a great way to find keywords is to search your competition. To do this, visit their pages and view their HTML code as you learned to do in Chapter 5, and study the keywords they used. Keywords and description text will be displayed in the `<head>` section of the code, near the top of the page.

Defining Description Text   The *description text* is a sentence or two that describes the web page. It is often an introductory sentence or two taken directly from the body text of the page. The following code is from the `<head>` section of the Grace Limousine site home page that we looked at in Chapter 2, Figure 2-21 (some of the type has been changed to red strictly for identification purposes and does not reflect its color in the code).

```
<meta name="keywords" content="NH Limousine Service,
grace limo, grace limousine, NH Limo Service, NH
Airport Service, New Hampshire Limousine, NH Wedding
Limousine, Limousine Rates, NH Limousine Service, NH
Bus & Charter Service, NH Limo Rental, Boston Limou-
sine Service, nh limo">
```

```
<meta name="description" content="Serving New Hamp-
shire, the Merrimack Valley and Boston North, Grace
Limousine is a full service ground transportation pro-
vider operating the newest, most diverse fleet in New
England.">
```

NH Limo: New Hampshire Limousine Company, Grace **Limo**, Is Your One ...
Serving **New Hampshire**, the Merrimack Valley and Boston North, Grace **Limousine** is a full
service ground transportation provider operating the newest, ...
Contact Us - Airport Service - Wedding Service - Boston Service
www.gracelimo.com/ - Cached - Similar

FIGURE 8-5 Search engine results sample.

In this example, the description text echoes the introductory paragraph of the Grace Limousine home page. The keywords represent typical search words a visitor would type when searching for limousine services in New Hampshire. Note the importance of adding the words *New Hampshire* to narrow the search for limousine companies to the locale of the person(s) searching for this type of service. Unlike a company selling a product that could be sold worldwide, such as aquarium products, this company's services are area specific. Adding that relevance in its keywords dramatically increases its search engine ranking when a visitor types in a request for a limousine company in its listed service area. Notice also the additional keywords listing the state's name written out as well as its abbreviation in both uppercase and lowercase, and the inclusion of "limo," the abbreviated name for limousine. These keywords are well thought out, comprehensive, and effective: a quick Google™ search of "limousine service in nh" brings them up on its first page as shown in **FIGURE 8-5**.

Adding Keywords and Description Text   The head section of the HTML page is where these critical "behind the scenes" bits of text are added. If you chose to include Chapter 5 in your studies, you learned that the head element includes a variety of "behind the scenes" data and how to add content into it. But now, we're in Dreamweaver! Let's learn how Dreamweaver will do the code writing of these important SEO head tags for us!

With your index page still open, choose Insert>HTML>Head Tags>Keywords, as shown in **FIGURE 8-6**, or choose Keywords from the Head icon pop-up menu located under the Common category of the Insert panel.

In the dialog box that follows, type some keywords, separated by commas. **FIGURE 8-7** shows the fictitious Fishluvrz site example with some applicable keywords to aid in its search engine visibility.

Later, when you begin to add body text to the page, it will enhance your SEO to incorporate some of your defined keywords into it as well, when applicable.

As you can see in Figure 8-6, the Insert main menu and the Head icon pop-up menu of the Common category of the Insert panel both bring you to the option to add description text. The dialog box will look the same as the Keywords dialog box; however, here you will type a sentence or two about your company.

Editing Keywords and Description Text   To add or delete existing keywords or description text after they have been entered is a two-step process. **FIGURE 8-8** illustrates the first step in the editing process. The head content must be visible in

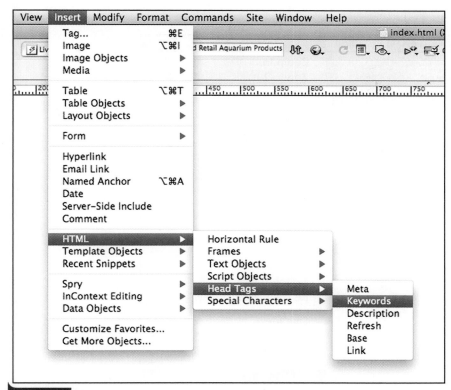

FIGURE 8-6 Adding head tags.

order to be able to edit it. If it is not currently showing, select Head Content from the View main menu and then drag the Document window down by grabbing the top edge (if needed) to reveal the head icons. After you have done that, the corresponding icons for any meta tags that have been added to the document will be displayed above the Document window, but below the Document toolbar.

The second step is to click and highlight the one you want to edit, which will activate it in the Property inspector where the text can be edited, as shown in **FIGURE 8-9**.

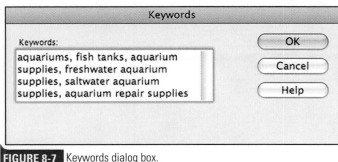

FIGURE 8-7 Keywords dialog box.

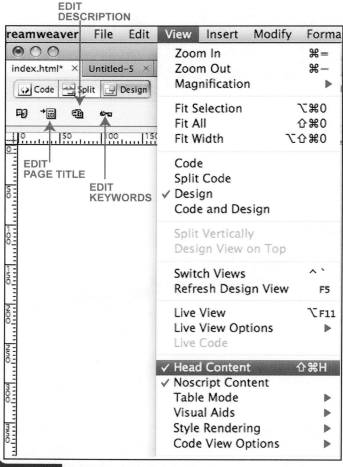

FIGURE 8-8 Viewing head content.

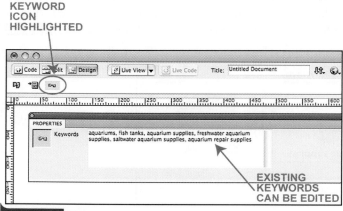

FIGURE 8-9 Editing head content.

Notice that the page title is one of the head tag icons that can be clicked and edited in the Property inspector. You can also drag across it in the title area to change the wording of your page title at any time.

8.1.4 Naming the Rest of the Pages of Your Site

We have discussed the critical first three steps you should complete when creating your home/index page. It is important to realize, however, that these critical first steps should be followed when creating *all* the link pages of a site as well. Remember, that while page titles can have capitals, spaces, exclamation points, etc., page names cannot. Like the home page of *index.html*, all link page names should be typed in all lowercase, no spaces, using only hyphens or underscores if delineations between words in the name are required, followed by the .html extension. Link page names should reflect what the page is about (generally, not specifically): a page name of *repair_services.html* would be more effective than your own reference name of *repserv.html*.

If you have created a *pages* folder, choose Save As, locate the *pages* folder, and save the additional link pages inside of it. As you learned in Chapter 6, instead of a folder named *pages*, your site may be better organized with individual folders, with one named *services*, for example, if you have several types of services that will be detailed on individual pages in your site. When the visitor arrives at that page, the address will reflect the domain name followed by the folder name (if it is inside of one), ending with the name you have given the page. If the page was called repair_services and was located in the *services* folder of the root folder, the web address would be *http://www.mycompanyname.com/services/repair_services.html*. Notice that the server recognizes that the address of the page requested identifies that it is located inside the *services* folder of the root folder.

8.1.5 The 1, 2, 3 Go Checklist

These three critically important steps in the web page creation process have been presented in this manner to help you remember to incorporate them into your work, and to avoid forgetting to include them later in the page development process. It is easy to be so excited to finally start building a page that you forget to title it, or forget keywords and description tags to help your page be found later on the Web. Although we will also learn how to do a final check for these types of errors before uploading, it's embarrassing to view your site on the Web, or worse, send friends or potential visitors to it and have them arrive at a page with a title that says *Untitled Document*. Ouch! Or a few weeks after your site is live and you are anxiously waiting for it to be available in a search, that you realize you never added keywords to enhance your visibility! To help prevent these problems from happening to you, use the steps detailed in the following checklist, shown in **FIGURE 8-10** (a printable copy is included in the *Chapter_8PracticeFiles* folder for your convenience) to start each new page until it becomes automatic.

START EVERY PAGE BY 1, 2, 3 *GO!*

① **SAVE YOUR PAGE**

- ✓ If it is your first page, name it index.html, all lowercase letters
- ✓ If it is a link page, name it using all lowercase letters, no spaces: use underscores or dashes if needed
- ✓ Make link page names informational
- ✓ Add the .html extension to all link pages

② **TITLE YOUR PAGE USING TITLE CASE**

- ✓ Make your title keyword rich
- ✓ Limit your title length to 65 characters

③ **ADD KEYWORDS AND DESCRIPTION TAGS TO YOUR PAGE**

- ✓ Add your keywords and description tags: Insert>HTML>Head Tags>

GO **BUILD THE REST OF YOUR PAGE**

- ✓ Remember to incorporate your keywords and description into your body text when appropriate to the paragraph content

FIGURE 8-10 1, 2, 3 Go Checklist.

8.2 Applying the Benefits of Web Accessibility to All Your Images

The World Wide Web Consortium has recognized the need for web accessibility for users with disabilities through their Web Accessibility Initiative. You can visit their website for a thorough understanding of the standards at http://www.w3.org/WAI/intro/accessibility.php.

Here, we will discuss a feature of Dreamweaver that is easy to include in your web page designs that will increase their accessibility. The *alt text* option (short for alternate text) allows visitors who use screen readers to learn about an image identified with the alt text option, if they are unable to see it. In addition to employing this feature as best practice, it is also one more feature of your site that will add to its professionalism and aid in its search engine strength. To be sure you remember to add it each time you insert an image, a preference can be chosen for Dreamweaver to prompt you to add alt text when you are inserting an image; a dialog box opens automatically to enter the alt text. To do that, let's first check the preferences for the accessibility attributes. Open the Dreamweaver Preferences by selecting Dreamweaver>Preferences for Mac or Edit>Preferences for Windows. After you are in the Preferences dialog box, the second preference category in the menu on the left is Accessibility. When you click on this category, the options to "Show attributes when inserting: Form objects, Frames, Media, and Images" should all be chosen by default. Great! Leave them all checked and click OK to leave the Preferences dialog box.

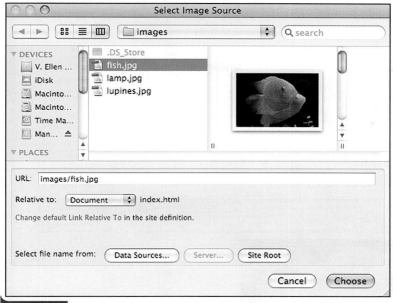

In Chapter 7, we practiced adding an image to a page, but ignored the Accessibility Attributes dialog box at that time. From now on, every time you add an image to a page, be sure to assign accessibility attributes to it when prompted. Because the accessibility preferences have all been activated, Dreamweaver reminds you every time you insert an image. The benefits are twofold: professionalism and one more action you can do to help your search engine ranking.

If it is not currently open, double-click the index page in the Files panel to open it. In Chapter 7, we learned to insert an image using the Common category of the Insert panel, choosing the Images icon, and then selecting Image from its pop-up menu. Let's learn a second way to insert an image and apply some alt text to it this time. By default, this blank page will have a flashing I-beam in the upper-left corner of the page. From the main application menu, choose Insert>Image. Because your SampleSite is the active site in the Files panel, the dialog box that follows will bring you immediately to this site's root folder. Inside the *images* folder, choose any photo from the available images, as shown in **FIGURE 8-11**.

After you have chosen an image, you will immediately be brought to the Image Tag Accessibility Attributes dialog box, as shown in **FIGURE 8-12**. In the Alternate text input area, type a description of the image (with spaces, etc.) as if you were describing it to someone over the phone, being careful to limit your characters to 50 or less. Usually, this description will be adequate. However, if a more detailed description is required, you can type a longer description in a text editor, save it as an .html file into your root folder, and then link to this longer description by typing the link address in the Long description input area in this same dialog box.

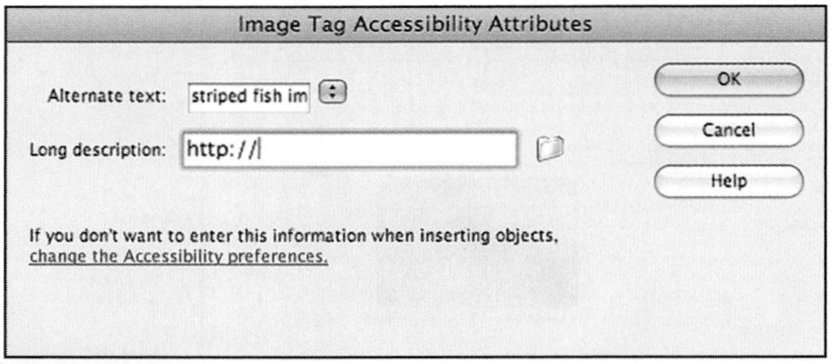

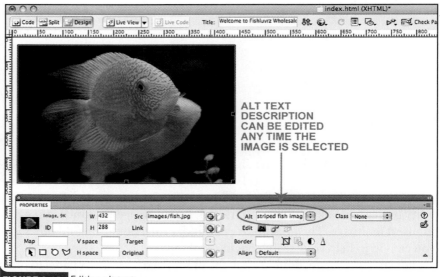

FIGURE 8-12 Image Tag Accessibility Attributes dialog box.

FIGURE 8-13 Editing alt text.

After you click OK, the alt text is applied to your image. When the image is selected, the Property inspector will display the alt text that you added, allowing you to edit it at any time, as shown in **FIGURE 8-13**, or add it later if you forgot to add it when inserting it!

8.3 An Introduction to Frame-Based Websites

Creating a website using frames can sometimes cause search engine difficulties. Because of this, frames remain a controversial method of website creation. However, they are an easy-to-learn method of website construction; therefore, a general coverage of the process will be included in this chapter.

One of their unique and very positive features is the ability to have the company headline and navigation constantly visible and still scroll through content on a page. Depending on the type of site being designed, this feature alone could be the deciding factor when you consider building a site using frames. After you understand how frames work and can recognize their usage on the Web, you will be able to search your competition and your audience to decide if frames are right for you.

8.3.1 The Basic Concept of a Frame-Based Website

In a frame-based website, the site is contained within a *frameset*. This can be thought of as a window frame, with individual "window panes" inside it, or basically a master web page with multiple individual .html web pages contained within it. Because the frameset is comprised of multiple individual web pages within it, each one is controlled individually: this is how a site's headline and navigation can remain in place and constantly visible, for example, while another area (a separate page within the frameset) can be scrolled if needed. **FIGURE 8-14** illustrates this concept.

1. This sample of a frameset displays the home page with its applicable body content information. The body content area does not require scrolling to read all of its information. However, if it did require scrolling, it would contain a scroll bar for this section of the frameset page only.

2. As the visitor selects a link page from the site's navigation, the headline and navigation remain in place, but the body content area changes to reflect the link page chosen.

3. When the visitor chooses to scroll down to read information located farther down in this part of the services link page, because it is a separate "page within a master page," other main page content, such as its headline and navigation, remain visible and do not scroll with it.

8.3.2 Creating a Frame-Based Website

Now that you understand the concept of a frame-based website, let's learn the basics of creating one.

Choosing the Option to Create a Frameset Page   There are a variety of ways to begin a frameset page. The easiest way is to choose the option when in the File>New dialog box. When we have used this dialog box thus far, we have always chosen a blank HTML document. As **FIGURE 8-15** illustrates, by choosing the Page from Sample>Frameset>Sample Page option, a variety of premade framesets become available as a starting point. As you click the Sample Page name, a diagram of its layout displays on the right, including a more detailed description of the layout option you have selected. The sample shown in Figure 8-14 was built using the Fixed Top, Nested Left option.

Alternatives to starting the document in this manner are available after any blank page is open by choosing Insert>HTML>Frames and then choosing the frameset;

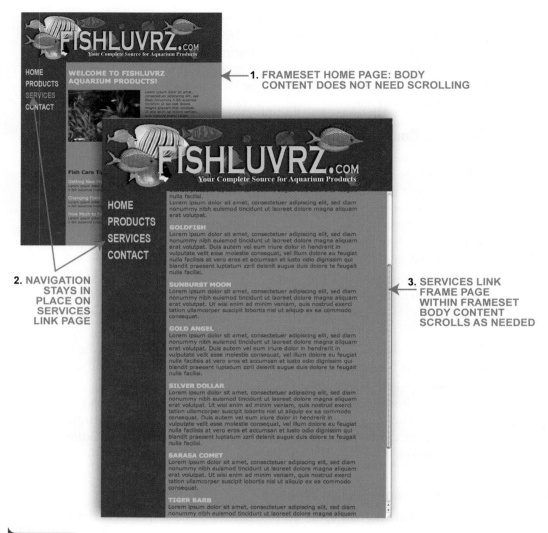

1. **FRAMESET HOME PAGE: BODY CONTENT DOES NOT NEED SCROLLING**

2. **NAVIGATION STAYS IN PLACE ON SERVICES LINK PAGE**

3. **SERVICES LINK FRAME PAGE WITHIN FRAMESET BODY CONTENT SCROLLS AS NEEDED**

FIGURE 8-14 Frameset sample.

or using the Layout tab of the Insert panel, choosing Frames and then choosing the desired frameset template from its pop-up menu.

Adding Accessibility Attributes to Frames   After you have chosen a frameset, if you checked to include frames in the accessibility options of the accessibility preferences, you will be immediately brought to the Frame Tag Accessibility Attributes dialog box, as shown in **FIGURE 8-16**. Here, you can choose the frame titles that Dreamweaver has given to each frame (or page) within the frameset (or master page), or you can change them to your own, more accessibility-friendly titles, such as *Fishluvrz Aquarium Products and Services* (instead of *topFrame*), *Fishluvrz*

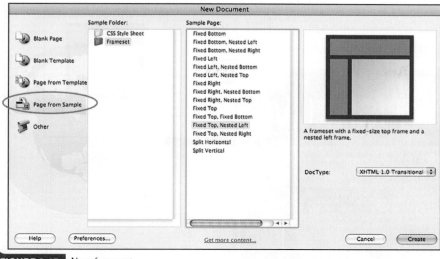

FIGURE 8-15 New frameset.

website navigation (instead of *leftFrame*), and *Fishluvrz page content* (instead of *mainFrame*).

Selecting Frames   After you have completed the Frame Tag Accessibility Attributes dialog box, the frameset layout you selected will display. The chosen layout should be visible with solid or dotted borders around the frames. If the borders are not visible after clicking on the page to get a flashing I-beam, select the option View>Visual Aids and check Frame Borders to define the edges of the frames. After the edges are visible, clicking the edge of a frame will activate a double arrow,

Frame Tag Accessibility Attributes

For eac   topFrame
          leftFrame
Frame: ✓ mainFrame

OK

Cancel

Title: Fishluvrz page content

Help

If you don't want to enter this
information when inserting objects,
change the Accessibility preferences.

FIGURE 8-16 Frame attributes assigned.

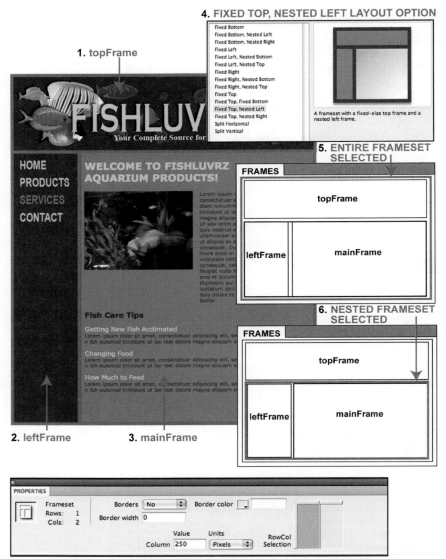

FIGURE 8-17 Selecting frames.

allowing you to manually drag and reshape the frame as desired. When selecting a frame, you will notice differences in the Property inspector content depending on your selection. **FIGURE 8-17** details the selection options for frames.

1. This first frame will be named *topFrame* in the Property inspector, but can be changed if you want to give it a different one containing no spaces. The names topFrame, leftFrame, and mainFrame are different from the accessibility attributes titles; these names are code name identifications

that also need to be identifiable by you and are not seen by a visitor to the site. To change one, select the frame in the Frames panel (visible by choosing Window>Frames), then type a new name in the Frame name area of the Property inspector.

2. This frame would typically house the navigation when used in this type of configuration. The name of the frame could be changed in the Property inspector to *navigation* if desired. Also, remember to first activate the desired frame in the Frames panel, and be sure that the new name contains no spaces.

3. This frame would typically be used for the changing body content of the site. Its name could also be changed in the Property inspector. Again, remember to first activate the desired frame in the Frames panel, and be sure that the new name contains no spaces.

4. This screen shot displays the chosen frameset layout.

5. The Frames panel (Window>Frames) allows you to select the individual frames of the frameset or the entire frameset. The selected frameset becomes outlined in black in the Frames panel (detailed here in red for visibility purposes).

6. The lower nested frameset is selected in the Frames panel.

7. When a frameset is selected, properties for the frameset can be chosen in the Property inspector, such as setting a specific column width, rather than dragging the border to redefine the frame width. If the I-beam is inside a frame instead of selecting it in the Frames panel, the Property inspector will change to reflect content features of the page instead of its frame features.

Saving a Frameset and its Frame Pages   The hardest concepts to understand and remember when creating a frame site are how to save the site initially and keeping track to save the right page within the master frameset page later in the process. The first time you save the document, you must choose File>Save Frameset As. Click the outer edge of the entire frameset in the Frames panel first to get the black border surrounding it, as shown in item 5 in Figure 8-17. Remember what you are saving—the page your visitor will be brought to must be named *index.html*. After you have named it, click inside each individual frame and choose Save Frame As for each of these frames, remembering the rules for naming pages learned earlier in this chapter. In the sample shown in Figure 8-17, a total of four pages were saved: the main frameset, and the three pages contained within it. After all of the pages have been named, the easiest way to be sure you are saving what you want is to choose the option File>Save All every time you save, no matter which page you have modified.

Adding Content to Frames   Content can be built directly within a frame, which is the easiest way to build the headline and navigation pages. However, the page

FIGURE 8-18 Targeting frames.

content for the body area, and the additional link pages that will be housed in it when inserted, are easiest to build outside of the frameset first and then imported into it. We have learned only basic page construction so far; more sophisticated methods of creating pages will be covered in future chapters. For now, we will simply cover the insertion process, as if a page had already been created. To insert content into a frame, click inside the frame you want to import it into, choose File>Open in Frame, and then locate a page you have created (built to fit within the dimensions of the frame area provided), which should be located in the website's root folder.

Targeting Frames   In Figure 8-14, the larger illustration displays a link page in its body content area. We will cover links for traditional website construction in detail in Chapter 11. For frames, the important thing to understand is how to define where you want the link page to display because, as you have learned, you will want the content to be entered into the main "container" page of the frameset. To link navigation to display its corresponding link page in the chosen body content area of the frameset page, select the desired navigation in the navigation frame, then scroll from the pop-up Target menu in the Property inspector to select the name of the main frame page area of the frameset, as shown in **FIGURE 8-18**.

Setting the Scroll Option   Setting the option for the page to scroll, if necessary based on its content, requires you to select the frame properties, not the page properties. When a frame is selected using the Frames panel, the Scroll option will display in the Property inspector, as shown in **FIGURE 8-19**.

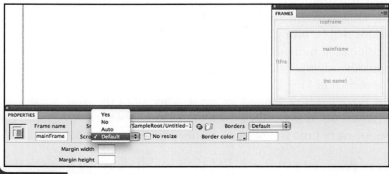

FIGURE 8-19 Scroll options.

Choosing Auto is great: a scroll bar will be added automatically if the imported content requires it.

A Look at the Code in Split View: Adding Titles, Keywords, and Description Text

FIGURE 8-20 details the head content information learned in this chapter and its code identified in the Dreamweaver Split view.

1. The title of the page has been typed in the Design view.

2. The title code has been entered by Dreamweaver: notice its location between the `<title>` opening and `</title>` closing tags, contained within the `<head>` element.

3. The keywords typed in Design mode are displayed between quotations, and after the equals sign contained in a meta tag within the `<head>` element.

4. Description text typed in Design mode is displayed between quotations and after the equals sign contained in a meta tag within the `<head>` element.

5. The title icon is displayed in Design view, indicating that a page title has been added to the page, entered into its `<head>` section.

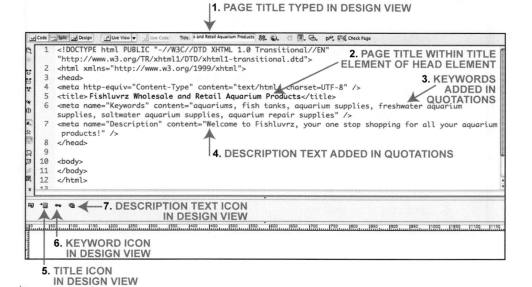

FIGURE 8-20 Head content in Split view.

6. The Keyword icon is displayed in Design view, indicating that keywords have been added to the page, entered into its `<head>` section.

7. The Description text icon is displayed in Design view, indicating that description text has been added to the page, entered into its `<head>` section.

8.5   What We Have Learned

Starting a web page can be as simple as "1, 2, 3" if you know the steps. In this chapter, we learned those three steps and why they are so important. We also learned how to add accessibility attributes to enhance the professionalism of our pages and broaden our audience to include visitors using screen readers.

Our discussion also covered a basic introduction to the use of frames for web design. We began by learning first what makes a frame website different from a traditionally created website, followed by a general overview of how one is constructed.

8.6   Reinforcing Your Knowledge

Project 1

1. For this exercise, we will pretend, for now, that the SampleSite is a website for a ski shop named Vantage. Make the SampleSite the active site in the Files panel.

2. Create an index page for the website if you have not already done so.

3. To bring future visitors to our site, choose an appropriate title for the home page.

4. Add search-engine-rich keywords about the store and the products it would offer.

5. Add a keyword-rich sentence of description text.

6. Save and close the page.

Project 2

1. Using the sites you created in Chapter 6, make each site the active site in the Files panel one at a time and create the index page for it.

   - DistinctionRestaurant.com
   - MumazYumaz.com

2. To bring future visitors to each site, choose an appropriate title for each of the home pages.

3. Add search-engine-rich keywords to each business's home page addressing the products/services it would offer.

4. Add a keyword-rich sentence or two of description text to each home page.

5. Save and close the index page of each site.

8.6.1 Creating the Fishluvrz Site

Project 3

Much of the remaining chapters of this text will be dedicated to real world learning by continuing to build a website for the fictitious company named Fishluvrz, and applying our learning by developing it through the Reinforcing Your Knowledge section of each chapter.

In Chapter 4, you created the necessary folders for this site and started adding images to the site's *images* folder. At that time, you should have created a master umbrella folder on your desktop titled *Fishluvrz Project*. Inside it, you should have a folder titled *original fishluvrz graphics* and a folder titled *FishluvrzRoot*, with another folder inside of it titled *images*, which should contain your cropped fish photos. We will continue to add more images to its *images* folder and to the *original fishluvrz graphics* folder as our site develops in future chapters.

In Chapter 6, we created the rest of the folders to complete its root folder, and defined the site for the Fishluvrz project.

1. Let's begin the page construction phase of the site building process now by adding its *index.html* page. With the FishluvrzSite active in the Files panel, create its index page, being sure after you have named and saved it that it displays within the site's root folder, but outside of any of its existing folders.

Project 3 (continued)

2. Title the index page *Fishluvrz Wholesale and Retail Aquarium Products.*

3. Add the following keywords to the index page:
   aquariums, fish tanks, aquarium supplies, freshwater aquarium supplies, saltwater aquarium supplies, aquarium repair supplies.

4. Add the following description text:
   We offer a full line of aquarium products and services specializing in answers to your fish health and aquarium water quality problems.

5. View your existing keyword head tags and add the following words to them: fish health problems, regulating aquarium PH levels.

6. Edit the title to read:
   Fishluvrz Wholesale and Retail Aquarium Products and Services.

7. Save and close the index page.

8.7 Building Your Own Website

1. The time has come to create your personal website's home page! Locate your site in the Files panel and make it the active website.

2. Create your index page. Save it in your root folder and check to verify that it shows up in the Files panel within your site folder.

3. Title the index page, thinking carefully about how you can add keywords to your title to increase its SEO.

4. Add some powerful, carefully thought out keywords to your page.

5. Add a sentence or two of description text.

6. Save your index page.

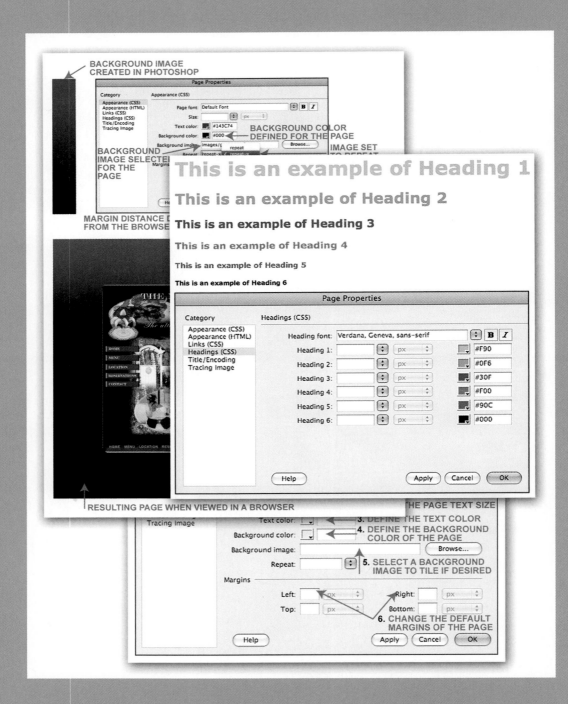

BACKGROUND IMAGE
CREATED IN PHOTOSHOP

BACKGROUND COLOR
DEFINED FOR THE PAGE

BACKGROUND
IMAGE SELECTED
FOR THE
PAGE

IMAGE SET
TO REPEAT

MARGIN DISTANCE
FROM THE BROWSER

This is an example of Heading 1

This is an example of Heading 2

This is an example of Heading 3

This is an example of Heading 4

This is an example of Heading 5

This is an example of Heading 6

RESULTING PAGE WHEN VIEWED IN A BROWSER

THE PAGE TEXT SIZE

3. DEFINE THE TEXT COLOR

4. DEFINE THE BACKGROUND
COLOR OF THE PAGE

5. SELECT A BACKGROUND
IMAGE TO TILE IF DESIRED

6. CHANGE THE DEFAULT
MARGINS OF THE PAGE

Defining Page Properties in Dreamweaver and Previewing a Page in a Browser

9

This chapter introduces changing the default page properties preassigned by Dreamweaver (such as font, font color, text link font, and link state colors) and customizing headings used to delineate content through its Page Properties dialog box. We will also learn how to apply a custom background color, image, or both to a page and learn how to preview the properties we have assigned in a browser. Lastly, we will cover the default encoding settings in Dreamweaver and how the use of a tracing image as a template can be used to help lay out the contents of a web page.

An Introduction to Page Properties from a Graphic Designer's Perspective

Typically, when you choose File>New in a graphics program, you will be entered into a dialog box to set some basic properties for the page you plan to build. Depending on the specific program's features, you may also be able to bring up a dialog box to change those properties later in your design work. Although the particulars in Dreamweaver are different, the concept of setting general page properties, and modifying those settings later, is the same as it is in other graphics programs. In Dreamweaver, however, these properties are defined after the page has been created, using its Page Properties dialog box.

 ## Defining and Modifying General Page Properties in Dreamweaver

The Page Properties dialog box contains categories for defining the page's font, background and link properties, assigning its title and encoding, and selecting an image to use as a template for tracing. Let's examine its categories in detail, learning what features are available under each general category and how to assign and modify them.

9.2.1 Defining Page Properties

After a page has been created in Dreamweaver, basic formatting properties for the page can be changed in the Page Properties dialog box by either choosing Modify>Page Properties or clicking the Page Properties button in the Property inspector. Changes might be needed because basic formatting will be preassigned in Dreamweaver by default. Those preassigned features include: a font and size for paragraph text and headings, as determined in the Dreamweaver Preferences dialog box; a default font color of black; a default background color of white; and margins, even though when you arrive in the dialog box, no values are listed in its Margins category.

Understanding the CSS vs. HTML Tabs of the Page Properties Dialog Box
Before we begin to explore the individual features of this multi-category dialog box, let's compare the available features of the Appearance (CSS) tab with the Appearance (HTML) tab of the Page Properties dialog box, shown in **FIGURE 9-1**.

As shown in Figure 9-1, there are some confusing similarities. Best practice is to define all applicable page appearances using CSS. Choosing to assign these properties under the CSS tab vs. the HTML tab will provide more options and flexibility now and later when changes are desired. Chapter 14 is devoted to working with text in Dreamweaver, including customizing its formatting through CSS for individual pages and assigning global formatting properties to an entire website.

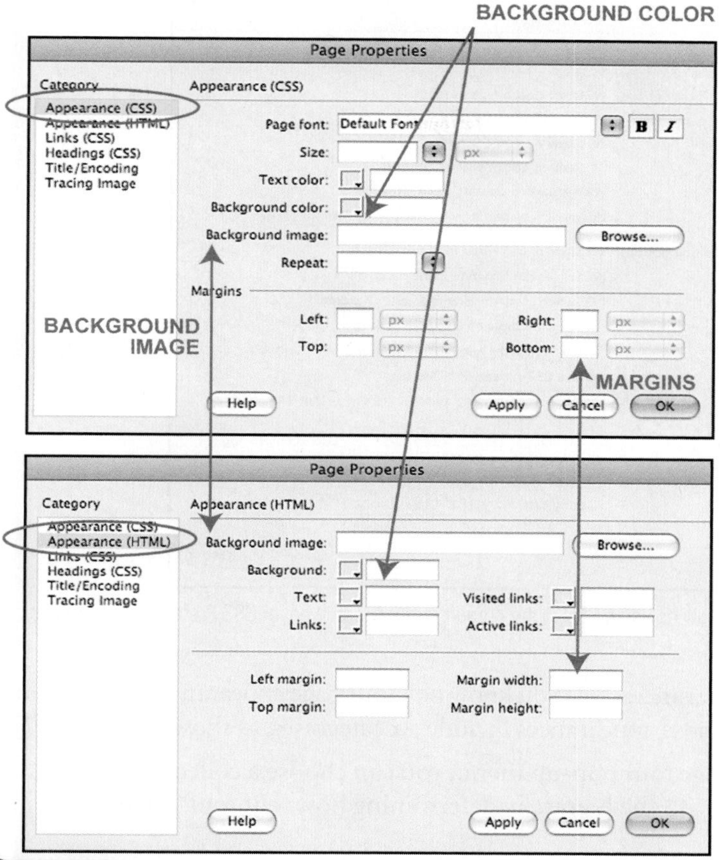

BACKGROUND COLOR

Page Properties

Category   Appearance (CSS)
~~Appearance (CSS)~~
~~Appearance (HTML)~~   Page font: Default Font   ⬍ **B** *I*
Links (CSS)
Headings (CSS)   Size: px   ⬍
Title/Encoding
Tracing Image   Text color: ⬜

                      Background color: ⬜

                      Background image: Browse...

                            Repeat: ⬍

                          Margins

                              Left: px   ⬍   Right: px   ⬍
BACKGROUND
    IMAGE   Top: px   ⬍   Bottom: px   ⬍

                                                                         MARGINS
                     Help   Apply   Cancel   OK

Page Properties

Category   Appearance (HTML)
~~Appearance (CSS)~~
Appearance (HTML)   Background image: Browse...
~~Links (CSS)~~
Headings (CSS)   Background: ⬜
Title/Encoding
Tracing Image   Text: ⬜   Visited links: ⬜

                                 Links: ⬜   Active links: ⬜

                           Left margin: Margin width:

                            Top margin: Margin height:

                     Help   Apply   Cancel   OK

FIGURE 9-1 Appearance (CSS) vs. Appearance (HTML) in the Page Properties dialog box.

In preparation for that, always assign appearance properties using the Appearance (CSS) category.

For CS3 Users

If you are working in CS3, don't be concerned that your dialog box doesn't contain the Appearance (HTML) tab shown in Figure 9-1. In CS3, appearances are prechosen by default to be formatted using CSS. As shown in **FIGURE 9-2**, all of your appearance options in the Page Properties dialog box will already be CSS options unless you uncheck the preselected *Use CSS instead of HTML tags* default option under the General category of the Dreamweaver preferences.

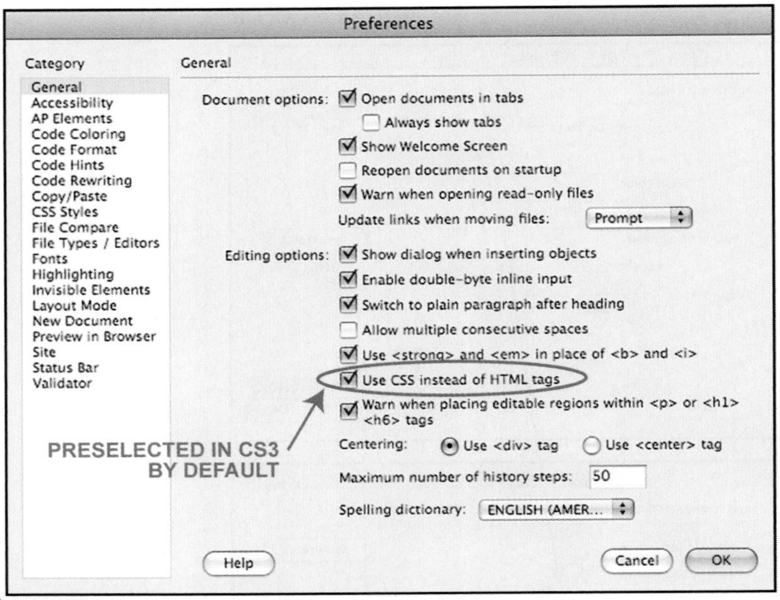

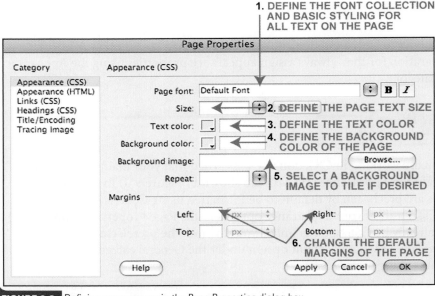

FIGURE 9-2 Page appearances using CSS is the default in the Dreamweaver CS3 Preferences dialog box.

Assigning Page Appearances   As you know now, our page appearances will always be defined using CSS. Those appearances include six categories, as shown in **FIGURE 9-3**.

1. Using the Page font pop-up menu, you can choose a collection of fonts to be used (with the hierarchy determining how that font will be chosen,

FIGURE 9-3 Defining appearances in the Page Properties dialog box.

based on the fonts available on the user's computer, as you learned in Chapter 2). You can add optional basic styling of bold and italic to your chosen font as well. If you leave the Default Font setting, all text you add to the page will be displayed in the visitor's browser using its default assigned font—something you would most likely never want to happen.

2. The Size option sets the size of the page's text in your choice of a variety of size formats, most commonly pixels or ems. As we also learned in Chapter 2, we will use pixels when defining font size.

3. If you do not want the default font color to be black, click the icon to choose one of the 216 web safe colors from the palette provided, or type in a custom hexadecimal web equivalent, being sure to add the hash symbol (#) before the value. Another color selection option that echoes other graphic programs is the ability to select the eyedropper here, drag it out onto the page, stop on an area of an image, for example, and sample the color to use from there. Dreamweaver will convert the selected color into its hexadecimal equivalent.

4. The Background color option defines the background color of your page if you want to change the default color of white. To change it, click the icon and choose one of the 216 web safe colors from the palette provided; type in a custom hexadecimal web equivalent, once again being sure to add the hash symbol (#) before the value; or use the eyedropper and sample a color from an existing image on the page.

5. We learned the use of a background image or pattern and how to create one in Chapters 3 and 4. Here is where you can insert one you have made or downloaded. To add one, browse to locate the image or pattern to add as a background in place of, or in addition to, a background color. When choosing an image in the Appearance (CSS) category of the Page Properties dialog box, you can also choose whether you want the background image to repeat or *tile* and how you want it to do that. Additional CSS positioning options for background images will be explored in Chapter 14.

6. By default, the content of your page (not its background) will be indented a few pixels from the edges of the browser window, with the pixel distance varying slightly among browsers, even if there is no margin value defined here. If desired, this can be prevented by typing in a value of zero for each of the four margin options to force the page to be flush with the top of the browser window, or enhanced by setting a specific distance that you want the page content to display away from one or more of the page's edges. **FIGURE 9-4** exemplifies the implementation of a background color, a repeated image used as a border, and setting a margin to bring the page content away from the top of the browser window.

As shown in this illustration, the 66 × 396 px graphic to be used as a background border pattern was created in Photoshop, then saved for the Web into the *images* folder of the website. However, because this pattern is designed to be used only as a

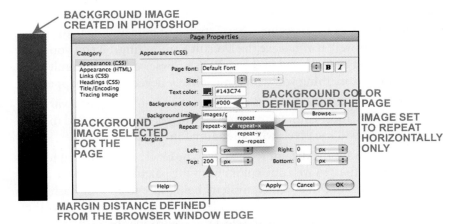

BACKGROUND IMAGE
CREATED IN PHOTOSHOP

BACKGROUND COLOR
DEFINED FOR THE PAGE

BACKGROUND
IMAGE SELECTED
FOR THE
PAGE

IMAGE SET
TO REPEAT
HORIZONTALLY
ONLY

MARGIN DISTANCE DEFINED
FROM THE BROWSER WINDOW EDGE

RESULTING PAGE WHEN VIEWED IN A BROWSER

FIGURE 9-4 Background options.

border, a background color of black (#000000) has also been selected for the page. In the Background image section of the Appearance (CSS) category of the Page Properties dialog box, the image created for the border has been selected from the *images* folder using the Browse option, then set to repeat using its X coordinate only (horizontally) so that it will span the remaining width across the top of the visitor's monitor viewing area. As shown in Figure 9-4, additional repeat options include repeating its Y coordinate only (vertically), repeat (the default choice, which fills the entire background by repeatedly placing the image as needed), and an option to have the inserted background image not repeat at all.

What width do you need to create for a border image, pattern, or gradient? The width of an image or pattern will be determined by its content. However, for a gradient, this sample was created large enough to understand the process for demonstration purposes only. In reality, because you assign a gradient to repeat in Dreamweaver, one as narrow as a single pixel width will work. I recommend creating it with a width of 5–10 pixels. That width is narrow enough to keep the file small, yet is large enough to work on easily and be able to visually confirm that it has been created as desired before applying it in Dreamweaver.

Lastly, a top margin was set to 200 px to allow the page to appear to be vertically centered on the background and to intentionally overlap the background image for design effect, as shown in the browser sample of the resulting page.

Setting Text Link Properties Using CSS   CS4 and CS5 users may have noticed that the Appearance (HTML) category of the Page Properties dialog box also contains basic text link color options, as shown in Figure 9-1. However, there is a separate category in the Page Properties dialog box titled Links (CSS), which will once again offer more options and flexibility, and therefore, will be the category of the Page Properties dialog box that we will learn to use for assigning text link properties. CS3 folks, you're already working in CSS by default, so no problem!

Applying text links will be covered in Chapter 11. At this time, we will learn how to define their properties in the Links (CSS) category of the Page Properties dialog box. As shown in **FIGURE 9-5**, when you select the Links (CSS) category of the Page Properties dialog box, the font, font style, and size for the links will have been predetermined by the properties you defined for the page under the Appearance (CSS) category, but can be overridden and customized here. The rest of the link options define the various states for the link (such as its over and visited indicative colors) and whether the link will be identified on the page by underlining. When

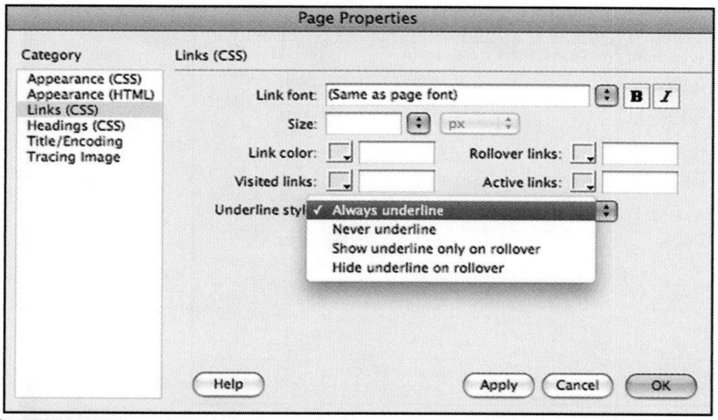

FIGURE 9-5   Text link properties set in the Page Properties dialog box.

choosing link state colors, just as the text and background colors are selected under the Appearance (CSS) category, you may choose one of the 216 web safe colors from the supplied palette; type in a hexadecimal web equivalent, being sure to add the hash symbol (#) before the value, or suck up a color from an image on the page. If you customize some of the link color states, but not others, the ones you do not specify will have the default colors applied to them.

Assigning Headings   The Headings (CSS) category of the Page Properties dialog box allows you to format a page in a way that is similar to assigning headings and subheads in a page layout program. As you saw in Chapter 7, by default, headings will be styled bold, with their sizes and colors assigned relative to the font chosen in the Appearance (CSS) category, which can be customized, with Heading 1 being the largest and Heading 6 being the smallest. As shown in **FIGURE 9-6**, colors can be assigned individually to each heading.

Headings are paragraph specific: placing the I-beam anywhere inside a paragraph and changing its heading will assign that heading to the entire paragraph. After you hit the Return/Enter key, your next paragraph will no longer have the previous heading applied to it. There is more than one way to assign headings to text after

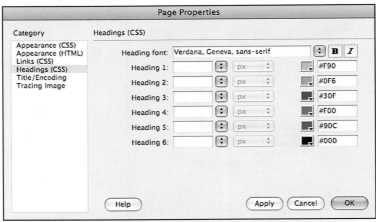

FIGURE 9-6 Heading samples.

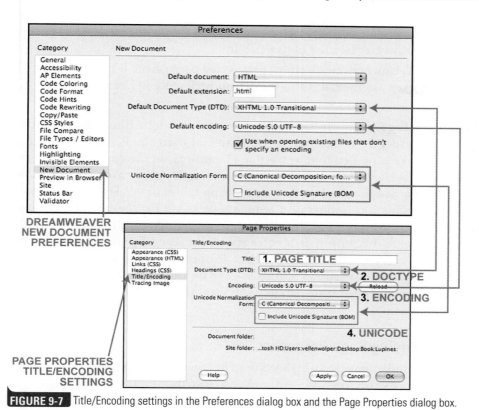

DREAMWEAVER
NEW DOCUMENT
PREFERENCES

PAGE PROPERTIES
TITLE/ENCODING
SETTINGS

FIGURE 9-7   Title/Encoding settings in the Preferences dialog box and the Page Properties dialog box.

they have been created; the other methods will be covered in Chapter 14. For now, we will assign them through the Format>Paragraph Format> in CS4 and CS5, and Text>Paragraph Format>in CS3 as we learned in Chapter 7. To remove a heading later, choose the None option in the same location the heading was chosen from.

Title/Encoding Settings   When you choose this category of the Page Properties dialog box, the options available should be already set and do not require any changes. You will have already titled your page as part of the 1, 2, 3 Go Checklist, as shown in **FIGURE 9-7**, and the rest of the options will already be properly selected because they are default preferences options of Dreamweaver.

1. This is another location to title the page, in addition to the two input areas you have already learned: the Document toolbar and the Property inspector (when the Head Content is visible and the title icon is selected).

2. By default, the Dreamweaver preferences for a new document assign the XHTML 1.0 Transitional document type. It will be preselected in the Title/Encoding category of the Page Properties dialog box, because we learned when creating a new page to retain its preselection in the New Document dialog box.

3. The encoding is also preselected as UTF-8, the default preference in Dreamweaver because of its flexibility.

4. The C Unicode option is also preselected because the UTF-8 encoding has been assigned; it is also the default preference in Dreamweaver.

Using a Tracing Image   If you have experience in Adobe Illustrator, you most likely have imported a sketch as a template and used the Pen tool to trace it. Although there is no Pen tool to trace in Dreamweaver, the concept of importing a design as a template for tracing is similar. In Dreamweaver, tracing allows you, as a web designer, to lay out a page using tables or AP Divs, for example, using the design you import as a template or guide for the layout. Although its actual application will be demonstrated in Chapter 12, the concept will be introduced here, because it is a category of the Page Properties dialog box. After the category is selected in the Page Properties dialog box, the resulting Tracing Image window allows you to browse to locate the design you want to trace and set a degree of transparency you want the design to display while you are tracing it.

9.2.2 Modifying Page Properties

If you have familiarity with style sheets used in other graphics programs, you know that after they have been defined and applied to text, their beauty lies in the ability to change a style and have it immediately update all uses of that particular style. Such is the case with the page properties you define for the specific page you are working on in Dreamweaver. In Chapter 14, we will learn how to make global text changes that affect your entire website through CSS; but for now, the changes you make, for example, font or color, will immediately affect all text that has the specific property assigned to it on your active page only. To make a change, simply return to the Page Properties dialog box either by choosing Modify>Page Properties or by clicking the Page Properties button in the Property inspector.

9.3 Previewing a Page on the Web

At any stage of the design process, you can preview your page in a browser. This is an extremely valuable feature that you should take advantage of frequently.

9.3.1 Creating a Page and Viewing It in a Browser

Let's create a page, assign some page appearances to it, add a little content, and then preview it in a browser. With the SampleSite active in the Files panel, create a new page and save it as *preview_page.html* into its *pages* folder. Assign the following page properties, as shown in **FIGURE 9-8**.

Page Properties

Category	Appearance (CSS)

Category
Appearance (CSS)
Appearance (HTML)
Links (CSS)
Headings (CSS)
Title/Encoding
Tracing Image

Page font: Arial, Helvetica, sans-serif   **B** *I*

Size: 14   px

Text color: #FFFFFF

Background color: #000099

Background image: Browse...

Repeat:

Margins

Left: px   Right: px

Top: px   Bottom: px

Help   Apply   Cancel   OK

FIGURE 9-8 Appearance (CSS) properties for *preview_page.html*.

Now, let's insert content. Following the example in **FIGURE 9-9**, add any text you would like, creating each line as its own paragraph. Assign Headings 1 and 2 as shown, followed by the insertion of the *lamp.jpg* image, and then select all of your content on the page and choose Format>Align>Center.

By the way, after inserting this content, have you seen a "ship's wheel" sometimes appear on the page when working in CS4 or CS5? It went away as you clicked with

Type a sentence here and apply Heading 1

Create another sentence and apply Heading 2

Enter an image after this sentence

FIGURE 9-9 Preview page in browser.

your mouse, but you may have wondered what its purpose was. That icon is called the Code Navigator indicator, a feature of CS4 and CS5. Just ignore it for now. We will understand its purpose, and how to turn off its visibility if it is not applicable to your working style, in Chapter 14.

To test a page in a browser, it must have already been saved. If you have not saved it and choose the command to preview it, you will be prompted to save it first. If you have not saved the page since you added its content, save it now. Let's preview the page by choosing File>Preview in Browser and select the specific browser you want to use to preview your page if you have more than one installed on your computer. Dreamweaver will be prompted to launch the browser for you and display the page. Note that you can choose here to edit the browser list, which will automatically reroute you to the Preview in Browser category of the Dreamweaver Preferences dialog box to add or delete browsers from your Preview in Browser list. However, to be accessible for previewing, they must be already installed on your computer.

Did your page, when viewed in a browser, not look like Figure 9-9? If your background is white and/or your text is black on your *preview_page.html* page when previewed in a browser, remember that all hexadecimal values must include the *hash symbol (#)* before the number. Even though the page will appear to apply the color(s) in Dreamweaver, it will not display properly in a browser without the prefix of the hash symbol.

Another option is to use the Preview/Debug in Browser icon (picture of a globe) in the Document toolbar, as shown in **FIGURE 9-10**.

It is important to test your page in as many different browsers as you have installed on your computer to be sure the look you want displays properly across multiple browsers.

FIGURE 9-10 Preview icon with its options displayed.

9.3.2 Previewing Your Page Across Platforms

As you build your pages, you should also occasionally preview them on the opposite operating system than the one you are using, if possible. Even the same browser may display a page differently on a Mac vs. viewing it in Windows. The good part about this is that the second computer does not need to have Dreamweaver installed on it to preview your page. Simply launch the browser(s) installed on the computer, choose File>Open, and then locate the page you want to preview. If you have link pages, you can open your *index.html* file and be able to see not only how the index page looks, but you can click the links in the index page to view any linked pages.

9.3.3 Using the Live View Feature

Located in the Document toolbar is a button titled Live View, available in CS4 and CS5, which you can click at any stage of the design process. This feature will allow you to get a general idea of how your page will preview in a browser. However, because it is not browser-specific it cannot be totally accurate. While it has the advantage of not having to save your page before previewing changes you made, you also do not get the reliability of actually seeing your page truly live that you get when you choose the Preview in Browser option instead.

CS5 brings some enhancements to the Live View feature. One of the enhancements is the ability to test the page's links. In CS4, when Live View is selected, the result looks like you took a screen shot of the web page in a browser: it displays a static sample of the page. In CS5, the Live View feature provides more options. While the static option is the default, a special Address window below the Document toolbar area displays the address of the active page, and a pop-up menu to the right of it provides additional Live View features. One of its options is Follow Links Continuously. This option allows the Live View page to become dynamic, providing the ability to test all the links it contains: Live View forwards you to the chosen link page(s) and returns to the page you opened in Live View and/or links to any other page, even to an external one, just as if the site really is live.

9.3.4 BrowserLab for CS4 and CS5

As previously mentioned, your pages should be tested in as many different browsers on both the Windows and Mac platforms as possible. To help address the need of designers to achieve consistency in the appearance of their pages across browsers, Adobe provides an online BrowserLab component of its CS Live services, which allows CS4 and CS5 users to accurately preview their pages in multiple browsers before uploading. Although not free, there is a free trial period upon signup. Available for CS4 by downloading required operational components, it was built into CS5, with access through its own panel. Key features are its ability to display the same page in two different browsers side-by-side, and even place a copy of a page in one browser on top of one displayed in a different browser like tracing paper, with the ability to preview possible layout discrepancies in the display of its content between them. If you lack the ability to test your pages in a variety of browsers on your own system, this service may be of interest to you. If it is, when you sign up for this service with Adobe, its site provides an intuitive interactive tutorial of its operation.

 A Look at the Code in Split View: CSS Page Properties

FIGURE 9-11 includes a small screen shot of the completed page as viewed in a browser; notice that it displays the home link in the rollover state. Now let's take a closer look at the code written to create the page properties shown in this sample.

1. Because the appearances were defined using CSS, they appear in the `<head>` section of the page, within the `<style>`element.
2. After the body selector, the declaration is included within curly brackets. A colon is placed after each property and a semicolon is placed after each value.
3. The headings are listed using the h1, h2, and h3 tags, with the color property followed by a colon, and the assigned color value followed by a semicolon.
4. The properties assigned in the Appearance (CSS) category are defined here, displayed as a CSS rule.
5. The link properties are listed individually for each state, as defined under the Links (CSS) category of the Page Properties dialog box.
6. After it is defined, when a heading is applied, the corresponding tag is reflected in the body element of the page.

 What We Have Learned

If page properties are not defined, a web page will have a default background color of white, a default text color of black, and a font determined by the default setting of Dreamweaver when designing; but, when viewed by a visitor, the web page is displayed with his/her browser default font. We learned how to change those properties, as well as assign link and heading properties using the CSS categories of the Page Properties dialog box, and then modify those settings later in the design process, culminating in a sneak peak at our first pages in multiple browsers. We also examined the default selections of the Title/Encoding category of the Page Properties dialog box and learned how a tracing image can be used as a template to help lay out a page.

```
3  <head>
4  <meta http-equiv="Content-Type" content="text/html; charset=UTF-8" />
5  <title>Practice only</title>
6  <style type="text/css">        ◄───────────── 1. STYLE CSS IN HEAD SECTION OF PAGE
7  <!--
8  body {
9      background-color: #6b267d;     ◄──────── 2. BACKGROUND COLOR
10     background-image: url(images/gradientReverse.gif);    BACKGROUND IMAGE SOURCE
11     background-repeat: repeat-x;             BACKGROUND REPEAT HORIZONTAL AXIS
12 }
13 h1 {
14     color: #FFF;
15 }
16 h2 {
17     color: #FFF;                ◄───────────── 3. DEFINED HEADING PROPERTIES
18 }
19 h3 {
20     color: #FFF;
21 }
22 body,td,th {
23     font-family: Georgia, Times New Roman, Times, serif;  ◄── 4. APPEARANCE PROPERTIES
24     color: #F9F;
25 }
26 a:link {
27     color: #FFF;
28     text-decoration: none;
29 }
30 a:visited {
31     color: #000;
32     text-decoration: none;
33 }
34 a:hover {
35     color: #F96;
36     text-decoration: none;             ◄── 5. LINK PROPERTIES
37 }
38 a:active {
39     color: #C69;
40     text-decoration: none;
41 }
42 a {
43     font-weight: bold;
44     font-family: Verdana, Geneva, sans-serif;
45 }
46 -->
47 </style></head>
48
49 <body>                          ◄───────────── 6. HEADINGS APPLIED TO BODY
50 <h1 align="center"><img src="images/new black Lupine/Lupine-Black_01.jpg" width="750" height="200" /></h1>
51 <h2 align="center">Welcome to New Hampshire's famous</h2>
52 <h1 align="center">Lupine Restaurant</h1>
```

FIGURE 9-11 Split view: page properties.

9.6   Reinforcing Your Knowledge

Project 1

1. Make the SampleSite the active site in the Files panel and open its *index.html* page.
2. Choose a font collection, size, and color that will complement the winter_headline background color you chose when optimizing that graphic in Chapter 6 in the Page Properties dialog box under its Appearance (CSS) category.
3. Assign the same background color to the page that you chose when you optimized the ski shop's headline graphic.
4. Choose a link font collection, size, and colors for each of its states to complement the font color you chose for the page using the Links (CSS) category of the Page Properties dialog box and choose to show the link as underlined only on rollover.
5. Choose a font collection, colors, and sizes for Headings 1, 2, and 3 only to complement the rest of your chosen font colors.
6. Save and preview its background color in a browser.

Project 2

1. Be sure your FishluvrzSite website is the active site in the Files panel.
2. Open the site *index.html* page you created in Chapter 8.
3. Using the Appearance (CSS) category of the Page Properties dialog box, choose the page font collection *Arial, Helvetica, sans-serif.* Set the size to *14 px,* and set the color to *#000066.*
4. Set the page background color to *#000066.*
   Enter *zero* for all four of its margins.
5. Set the link properties using CSS.
   Define the link font as: *Same as page font*
6. Define the following link state colors and underline option:
   Link color: *#336600*
   Rollover links: *#333300*

Project 2 (continued)

Visited links: *#FF0000*
Active links: *#333300*
Underline style: *Never Underline*

7. Select the Headings (CSS) category and choose the font collection *Georgia, Times New Roman, Times, serif.*

8. For both Heading 1 and Heading 2, define the color as *#000066.*
   Heading 1: *24px*
   Heading 2: *18 px*
   Headings 3–6: *No custom colors or sizes*

9. Select the Title/Encoding category and double-check that your proper index page title displays as you defined it in Chapter 8 by reviewing it in the Title area of the dialog box.

10. Click OK to apply your page properties. Your index page should have the appearance color applied to its background. Save and preview your page in a browser. At this point, you will only see the page background color of #000066. However, we have begun to customize the home page of Fishluvrz! We are ready to learn to add content to our page through the structure and organization of tables in Chapter 10.

9.7 Building Your Own Website

1. Through your layout designs, you have decided on a specific background color that you want for the home page of your site. Locate your site in the Files panel and make it the active site.

2. Open your index page.

3. Use the Page Properties dialog box to set your page font collection, its color, and its size. If you are not exactly sure what you want, type a sentence or two first, then apply the settings. Return to the Appearance (CSS) category of the Page Properties dialog box as many times as you need until you have the perfect combination of these three font characteristics. As you have learned, you will not need to select the text; it will automatically update each time you make a change to the options in the Page Properties dialog box.

4. Apply your chosen page background color. If you also have created a background image or border to use as well or instead of the background color, browse to locate it and set the Repeat option according to your design layout.

5. Define your link properties using CSS.

6. Define page heading properties, from Heading 1 to Heading 6, as your page needs require.

7. Click the Title/Encoding category. Be sure you titled your page properly in title case with no spelling errors!

8. Click OK to see your page with your chosen background color applied to it. Your home page is starting to take shape!

9. Save and preview your index page in a browser.

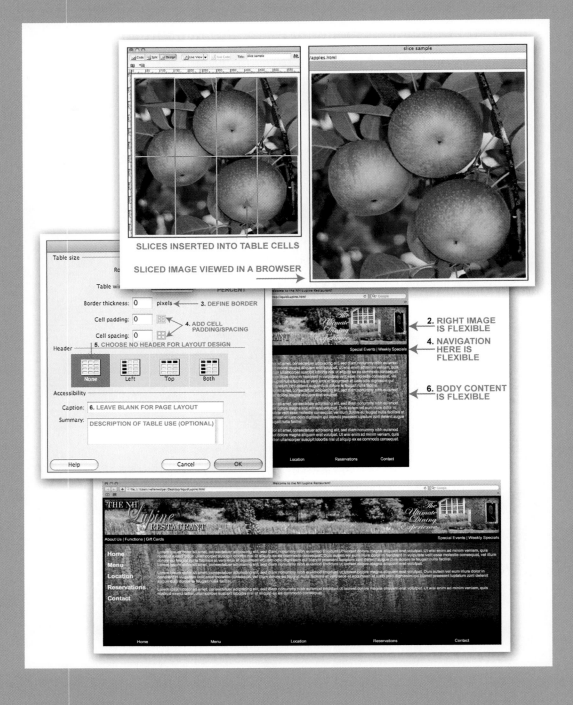

SLICES INSERTED INTO TABLE CELLS

SLICED IMAGE VIEWED IN A BROWSER

Table size

Ro

Table wi   PERCENT

Border thickness: 0   pixels   → 3. DEFINE BORDER

Cell padding: 0   ⊞   ⎫
                         ⎬ → 4. ADD CELL
Cell spacing: 0   ⊞   ⎭   PADDING/SPACING

Header   5. CHOOSE NO HEADER FOR LAYOUT DESIGN

None   Left   Top   Both

Accessibility

Caption: 6. LEAVE BLANK FOR PAGE LAYOUT

Summary: DESCRIPTION OF TABLE USE (OPTIONAL)

Help   Cancel   OK

2. RIGHT IMAGE IS FLEXIBLE

4. NAVIGATION HERE IS FLEXIBLE

6. BODY CONTENT IS FLEXIBLE

Creating a Web Page Using Tables

10

I n this chapter, we will build our first structured pages. Tables provide a great introduction to web design because they are an easy-to-learn method of page layout and organization, with dependability across platforms and browsers. This chapter will provide multiple options for table layouts, exemplifying their versatility and usability for creating both fixed and liquid layouts.

Designing a Web Page Using Tables

Although formatting web pages using CSS is often described as the *avant-garde* direction of web page development, creating a page using tables remains a feasible, predictable method of web page design that has stood the test of time. For graphic artists exploring the medium of web design for the first time, tables create organized, structured, successful page layouts within a workable, manageable learning curve. The basics of CSS will be introduced in Chapter 14 for formatting text, images, and basic page structure, paving the way for you to explore further applications of CSS for additional formatting and layout on your own after that. The goal of this textbook is the introduction of artistic website creation that focuses on adapting the graphic skills, which you, as an artist, have already mastered in other programs, to the medium of web design. Using tables is one method of bringing your original web page design concepts from Chapter 3 into reality. Let's learn how to use them!

10.1.1 Understanding the Design Problem First

We have added type to a web page and applied a couple of methods of importing images. As you have learned, when a new page is created, an I-beam flashes in the upper-left area of the page, indicating where any text or images will be entered. However, if you have already tried on your own to create an artistic web layout this way, after the content has been centered on the page, any additional artistry you tried to add probably left you frustrated and disappointed. Here is where the application of tables to web page layout can offer you, the artist, more design creativity. Artists who came before you recognized the potential that tables could offer by providing the additional design flexibility needed for creative web page layout. You may have used tables in other software programs for tabular data. Their original inclusion in web design was to serve the same organizational purpose, and they remain a typical method of listing tabular data on web pages. However, by thinking outside the box over the years, artists have discovered innovative ways to build entire web pages using tables for predictable layouts with more creative appeal. After you understand the basics of table layout, you will be able to tap into your own creativity to design sophisticated web pages using this page layout method.

 The Design Possibilities of Tables

To understand the potential of tables, you must first learn how to create them, how to modify and reconfigure them, and examine some of their typical design applications.

10.2.1 Creating a Basic Table

Let's start by learning how to insert a basic table. Launch Dreamweaver, make your SampleSite the active site in the Files panel, and then create a new blank page. (You may notice that the colors and font features you applied to its home page are not carried over to this new page. We will learn why and how to have them carry over to new pages in Chapter 14. For now, let's focus on learning tables.)

During this practice, it will not be necessary to add a title, keywords, and description text to this page. However, remember that you must start each page of a real site with these critical steps. Because the new page defaults to displaying a flashing I-beam in the upper-left area of the page, it is ready to insert a table with that location as the upper-left corner of the table when created. Choose any one of the following methods to insert a table onto the page:

1. From the main application menu, choose Insert>Table.
2. With the Common category of the Insert panel active, click the Table icon illustrated in **FIGURE 10-1**.
3. We also learned in Chapter 7 that the Layout category of the Insert panel has several options. One is the option to insert a table by choosing the same Table icon shown in Figure 10-1 from its list of layout icons.

Whether you click the Table icon from either the Common or the Layout category of the Insert panel, or choose the Table option from the Insert menu, the Table dialog box appears, as shown in **FIGURE 10-2**.

As a Photoshop user, you know that settings applied in its dialog boxes become the new default settings. Before discussing each option individually, it is helpful to know that, yes, any selections you set for any of the Table dialog box options in Dreamweaver will also become its new defaults: the next time you enter the Table dialog box, your previous selections will already be chosen for you.

1. Define the number of rows and columns in your table. The default table has 3 rows and 3 columns. Although you define the number of rows and columns you want for your table here, you have the ability to change its configuration at any time as needed for your layout. For now, let's keep the default row and column configuration settings.

FIGURE 10-1 Illustration of Table icon.

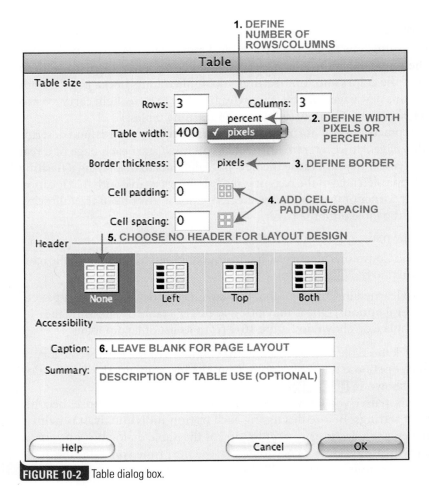

FIGURE 10-2 Table dialog box.

2. Identify the table width in pixels or percent. Defining a table's width
   in pixels restricts the table to displaying at that width—regardless of
   the viewer's screen resolution—and it's the default measurement
   setting the first time you enter this dialog box. Setting a percentage
   for the table's width will display the table at the chosen percentage on
   the viewer's monitor. (Setting 100% will fill the width of your visitor's
   screen, or fill the width of the table if it is nested inside another table.)
   We have learned about liquid layouts: later in this chapter, we will
   learn how the table width option controls a layout's flexibility. You may
   have noticed that there is no table height option: the height of a table
   is calculated automatically by the content added to it. Let's set a width
   of 400 pixels for now.

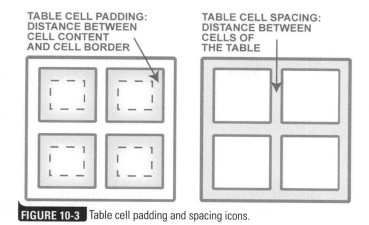

TABLE CELL PADDING: DISTANCE BETWEEN CELL CONTENT AND CELL BORDER

TABLE CELL SPACING: DISTANCE BETWEEN CELLS OF THE TABLE

FIGURE 10-3 Table cell padding and spacing icons.

3. The border thickness is just as the description implies; the table and cells will have a border around them based on the thickness typed in here. When using tables to lay out a page, this option should be set to zero, not left blank.

4. *Cell padding* refers to the distance, or padding, added between the content of a table cell and the outer edge of the cell. *Cell spacing* refers to defining a distance between the cells of a table. **FIGURE 10-3** shows an enlargement of the padding and spacing icons displayed in the Table dialog box located to the right of each option, with the cyan color representing the effect of the corresponding option. The red dotted lines have been added to further illustrate the padding area of the cell sample. Learning to identify these early can be very helpful because choosing which one you want to use by name can sometimes be confusing.

   When using tables to lay out a page, both of these options should also be set to zero, not left blank. Setting padding or spacing for individual nested tables (tables inside other main tables), however, can often be used to enhance a web page design, and it will be discussed in further detail later in this chapter.

5. Although the Header option is valuable when using tables for tabular data with screen readers for accessibility, when using tables for page layout this option should be set to None.

6. Both of these additional accessibility features should definitely be assigned when using a table for tabular data designed to be displayed as rows and columns. However, when using a table for page layout, the caption section should be left blank because it is visible in a browser when added; the Summary section is optional because it will not display in browsers, but it will be read by screen readers for accessibility. If you

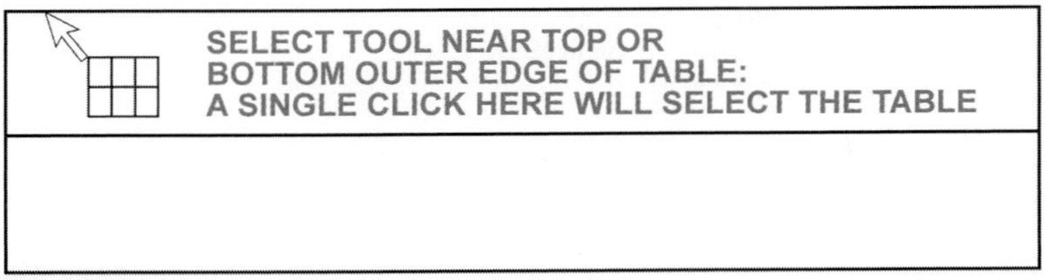

SELECT TOOL NEAR TOP OR
BOTTOM OUTER EDGE OF TABLE:
A SINGLE CLICK HERE WILL SELECT THE TABLE

FIGURE 10-4 Table grid icon.

decide to add text to the Summary category based on your audience, you may want to use a description such as, "Table applied for page structure."

You are now ready to click OK to insert the table onto the page. Note that it appears at the upper-left corner where the I-beam was located at the time the Table icon was chosen. By default, the table will be displayed with its perimeter and cell borders indicated by dotted lines. If they are not visible, choose View>Visual Aids>Table Borders to view the edges: these are for design purposes only and do not display when the page is viewed in a browser. If you prefer, under the same main menu, you can also choose View>Visual Aids>Table Widths to display green measurements below the table cells indicating their width. As we learn more about tables, you may find this visual aid of particular value. In Chapter 7, we learned about the Document toolbar. Located in it, is an icon with an eye on it. When you click this pop-up menu, all the visual aids are listed, with the option to toggle the table aids on and off from here as well.

Modifying Table Properties   When a table is added to a page, it is automatically preselected, with options for it visible in the Property inspector. If you accidentally click away from the table, you can reselect it by clicking near the top or bottom edge of the table using the Select tool. When you are near the edge, the Select tool will turn white and the table grid icon will appear letting you know that when you click you will reselect the table, as illustrated in **FIGURE 10-4**.

Another easy way to select it that echoes other Adobe programs is to drag the Select tool from the page area outside of the table to anywhere inside the table: the table will immediately be selected as soon as it is touched.

When the table displays selection handles, the same properties that were chosen when inserting the original table can be changed in the Property inspector, and you have the ability to set the alignment of the table on the page. In Chapter 3, we discussed a centered page design to accommodate varying monitor screen resolutions. This is where that option is chosen when creating a fixed width page using tables by choosing Align>Center in the Property inspector. There are also quick click icons here for clearing the column widths and row heights and for changing the current width or unit of measurement applied to the table, as shown in **FIGURE 10-5**.

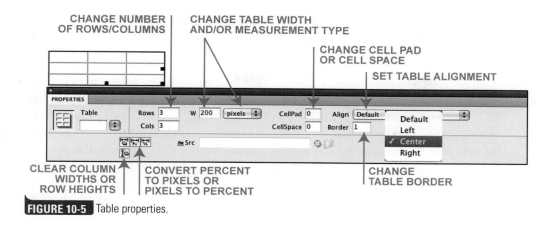

FIGURE 10-5 Table properties.

In addition to changing the width of a table using the Property inspector, a table can also be manually resized by selecting the edge of the table with the Select tool and dragging it to adjust the table as needed. Drag the right-center handle to change the width, the bottom-center handle to change the height, or drag the corner handle diagonally to adjust both dimensions to make the table larger or smaller as needed. It is important to note, however, that reducing the size of a table is restricted to the limitations determined by any content already existing in the table.

Modifying Cell Properties   When you do not have the selection handles activated, but are still selecting the table, changes will affect the cells of the table, instead of the table itself. When you select one or more cells of a table, the information displayed in the Property inspector will change to reflect properties specific to cells vs. properties relative to the entire table, such as the alignment of the content within a selected cell or cells.

In addition to changing the number of rows and columns in the Property inspector, rows and columns can be added to an existing table if a cell or cells are selected by using insert icons, which become active under the Layout tab of the Insert panel, or by choosing Modify>Table, or by right/Control-clicking the table and choosing the desired option from the Table category of the context-sensitive menu. In addition to selecting a single cell, clicking on the *outside left* of a row or the *top* of a column of the table will allow you to select all the cells in that row/column. When you position the Select tool on the outer edge, a small arrow will appear as well as a red outline around the respective cells to indicate that when you click, they will be selected. When selected, their borders will become bold to verify that they are selected. If you prefer to select only one or more cells in a row or column without selecting all of them, place the I-beam inside an individual cell, or place the I-beam inside one cell and drag across the cells you want to select.

Adding Content to Tables   Now that we have examined the basic structure of a table, let's learn how this structure can be used to help you lay out page content from an artist's perspective.

Adding Text and a Background Color to a Cell   Although we will learn to customize text features using CSS in Chapter 14, we learned in Chapter 9 how to set the page font, size, style, and color in the Page Properties dialog box. The font properties assigned in the Page Properties dialog box will apply to text added to a table inserted on that page by default. To add text to a table, simply click an insertion point in the table cell where you want to add the text and start typing. In most cases, you will want to leave the *No wrap* default option unchecked in the Property inspector, which will force your text to wrap and flow down within the defined width of the cell where you are typing. (If *No wrap* is selected, your cell will expand its width automatically as needed to accommodate the text added to it.) To change the horizontal and vertical alignment of the text within the cell, with the I-beam clicked inside the cell, choose the Horz and Vert options in the lower-left section of the Property inspector, rather than the alignment icons at the top right of it. To assign a background color to a cell, with the I-beam inside of it, click the Bg icon and choose one of the 216 web safe colors from the palette provided, type in a custom hexadecimal web equivalent, or use the Eyedropper tool to suck up a color from an image on the page.

For CS3 Users

When working in CS3, be sure you choose the Bg color option in the Property inspector for a cell background color, not the Brdr option to add a border color located to the right of it, or the Bg for background image (with the folder icon next to it) located directly above it.

Adding an Image Using Drag and Drop: Files Panel and Assets Panel   You can use one of the two methods we have already learned for adding images onto a page to insert an image into an empty cell, or to combine it with text already added to a cell if the I-beam is flashing inside a cell of a table. Another method of adding images to a page is the drag-and-drop feature you are familiar with from other graphic programs. To add an image to a page or into a table cell, simply drag and drop an image from the Files panel or the Images tab of the Assets panel into the page or table. If you would like to try this method, save this page as *table_page.html* in the *pages* folder of your SampleSite. After you have saved it, place the I-beam inside the cell you want to add the image to and locate the *fish.jpg* image in the SampleSite *images* folder in the Files panel (we made SampleSite the active site in the Files panel earlier in this chapter) and simply drag and drop the image into the cell you want to add it to. Alternatively, click the Images icon in the upper-left area of the Assets panel (select Window>Assets if it is not showing) and click and drag the image into the desired cell from there. The nice thing about using the Assets panel is that you may have noticed that when you click an image in it, the image is displayed at the top of the panel, just in case you are not sure of its name. This is a great feature for visual artists like you!

Alternatively, you can click the desired image in the Images category of the Assets panel and then click the Insert button at the lower-left of its panel to add it to your page. As soon as you have selected an image to insert, no matter which method you used, you will be prompted to add an appropriate alt text description, after which your chosen image will be added to the cell you selected in the table. As you can see, if the cell is not large enough for the image, the table will automatically adjust in size to accommodate it. If a cell contains only an image, and the I-beam is inside the cell containing the image (instead of selection handles on the image), the same Horz and Vert options used for text are used to position the image within the cell. If it is combined with text, more positioning can be added by selecting the image with the Select tool to activate selection handles and then choosing the Align option in the lower-right area of the Property inspector to align the selected image with the line of text it was added into according to the option selected (such as Baseline or Top).

When an image is added to a cell, spacing can also be applied to give "breathing room" around the graphic, or further customize its location in a cell beyond the Horz and Vert placement options. If combined with text in a cell, it can create an effect similar to text wrap in other Adobe graphic programs. This is not cell padding or spacing for the table, it is specific to the imported image and therefore will become active in the Property inspector only when the image has selection handles and is assigned by using the V Space and H Space options for vertical and horizontal breathing space, respectively, located in the lower-left area of the Property inspector. **FIGURE 10-6** illustrates the available options when adding text and/or an image to a table cell.

Adding a Background Image to a Cell or Table   We have learned how to add text, a background color, an image, and text and an image together to a table, with the text wrapped around the image. What if, as a designer, you would like an image as a background for a cell with text added on top of it, or want an image behind an entire table? After we have learned CSS, you can define a rule for this, but for now, it can be added using the Tag inspector. Select a cell or the entire table and then choose Window>Tag Inspector. After the panel is open, choose the Attributes tab and the A/Z icon to show the list view, as shown in **FIGURE 10-7**.

When you click to the right of the background option, a folder will appear to browse and locate the image you want to use as a background. After the image is inserted, you will be able to place an I-beam on top of the image in the respective cell and type. However, be aware that until we learn to assign background properties

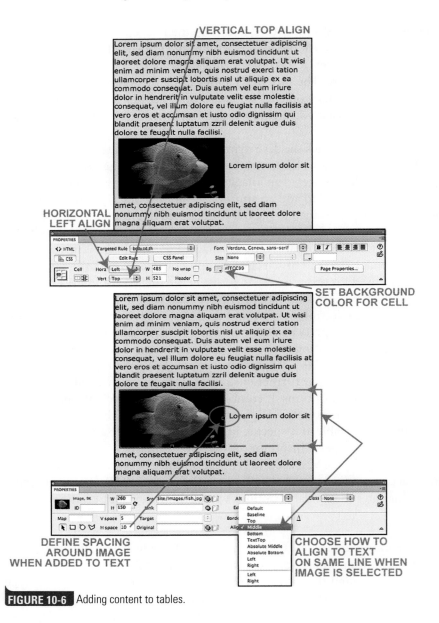

FIGURE 10-6 Adding content to tables.

using CSS in Chapter 14, background images placed in cells will automatically tile to fill the cell space provided, and you should plan the size of the background image relative to the cell it will be inserted into accordingly.

Adding a Sliced Image to a Table   In Chapter 4, we learned how to slice images and pages created in Photoshop. When an image is sliced, it is important to note its pixel dimensions and the number of slices used for the image. Then in Dreamweaver,

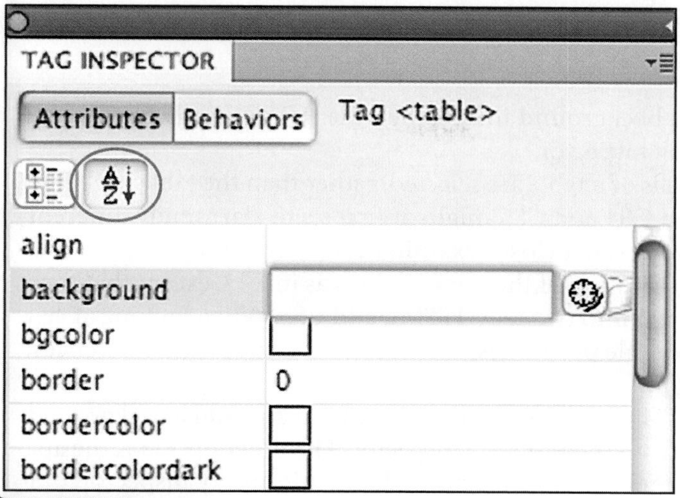

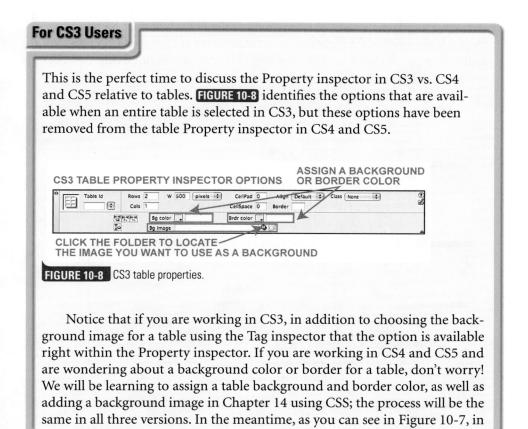

FIGURE 10-7 Tag inspector.

For CS3 Users

This is the perfect time to discuss the Property inspector in CS3 vs. CS4 and CS5 relative to tables. **FIGURE 10-8** identifies the options that are available when an entire table is selected in CS3, but these options have been removed from the table Property inspector in CS4 and CS5.

FIGURE 10-8 CS3 table properties.

Notice that if you are working in CS3, in addition to choosing the background image for a table using the Tag inspector that the option is available right within the Property inspector. If you are working in CS4 and CS5 and are wondering about a background color or border for a table, don't worry! We will be learning to assign a table background and border color, as well as adding a background image in Chapter 14 using CSS; the process will be the same in all three versions. In the meantime, as you can see in Figure 10-7, in

For CS3 Users (continued)

addition to adding a background image, the other two options can also be assigned using the Tag inspector.

When a cell or cells of a table are selected, rather than the table itself, the Property inspector in CS4 and CS5 might at first seem alarmingly different than that of CS3. However, a closer examination of it will reveal that it is basically just a reorganization of the same options as in CS3, except that they have been broken down into two tabs: HTML and CSS. When looking at cell properties instead of table properties, there are only a couple of differences, as shown in **FIGURE 10-9**.

As you can see, if you are working in CS3 you can also add a background image to a cell right from the Property inspector. The other option is the application of a border color to a cell right in the CS3 Property inspector, but not in CS4 and CS5, which we will also learn to apply through CSS, but can be achieved using the Tag inspector until then. The major difference between the CS3 Property inspector vs. the two tabs—HTML and CSS of the CS4 and CS5 Property inspector—lies in its text features. In CS4 and CS5, as you can see, when a cell is selected, whether you have the HTML or the CSS tab active, the table properties are identical. So why separate HTML and CSS tabs? We will take a much closer look at why and how they are divided into two tabs for text in Chapter 14.

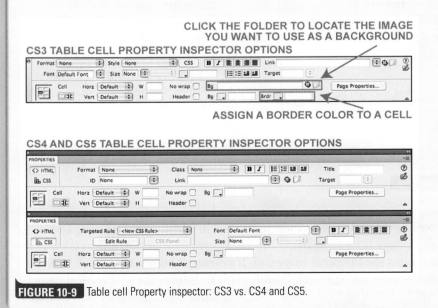

FIGURE 10-9   Table cell Property inspector: CS3 vs. CS4 and CS5.

SLICES INSERTED INTO TABLE CELLS

SLICED IMAGE VIEWED IN A BROWSER

FIGURE 10-10 Sliced image in a browser.

if a table is created with the same outer pixel dimensions and same number of cells, with zero set for the cell padding, cell spacing, and border options of the table (remember not to leave them blank), you will be able to simply insert the slices into the table for a perfect fit. They will be prenumbered. For example, they will be numbered 1–8 if you sliced the image into eight pieces. When you insert them into the table, one at a time, from the upper-left position to the lower-right position, the image will appear seamless when viewed in a browser. Remember the image of apples that was sliced in Photoshop in Chapter 4? **FIGURE 10-10** is that same sliced image, placed into a table and then viewed in a browser.

Reconfiguring the Cells of an Existing Table for Page Layout Purposes   Except as shown in the previous example of inserting a sliced image onto a page, rarely will you want a table's configuration to remain exactly as you defined it, when using one to structure a page layout.

Modifying Table Cells   If you place the Select tool over the border between the cells of a table, a double arrow appears to offer you the opportunity to drag and reshape the rows and columns of the table. While this can be very handy, usually just adjusting the height and width of rows and columns will not provide enough layout flexibility for your page content. When using a table for page layout, you may begin to lay out a page and find that you have enough cells in one row but not enough cells in the next row. And what about a row that you don't want broken up by *any* cells? The next option is to reconfigure the table by merging, splitting, adding, and deleting some of its cells. In addition to changing the number of rows and columns of the

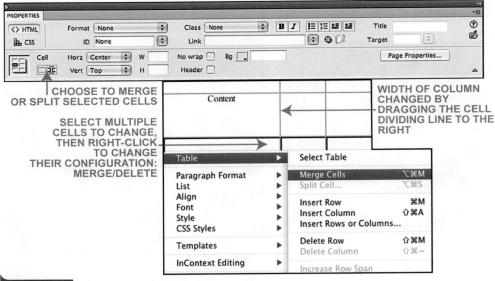

FIGURE 10-11 Ways to reconfigure a table.

table structure when the table is selected, when a cell is selected or multiple cells are selected, all of these reconfiguration options become available to add even more design flexibility to the table. These options can be chosen under the Modify main application menu by choosing Modify>Table, the layout category of the Insert panel, or by right/Control-clicking the cell(s) and selecting the desired effect from the Table option of the context-sensitive menu. The ability to merge or split a cell or cells can also be conveniently applied using the icons in the lower-left area of the Property inspector. **FIGURE 10-11** illustrates a variety of these reconfiguration options applied to a table.

Nesting Tables   Carrying this design concept further, in addition to combining cells and adjusting row and column heights manually, another table can be added inside the cell of an existing table, referred to as *nested*. Sometimes, just reconfiguring a table may not give you enough design flexibility. When you drag to change the width of a column or the height of a row, you are changing the width of the column in all of the rows, or the height for all the columns in a row. Adding a nested table will solve this problem. **FIGURE 10-12** illustrates merging and splitting cells in a table and nesting another one inside it for more design flexibility.

In addition to giving you more design freedom, a nested table also adds more flexibility in how the content inside the cells will display. Earlier in this chapter, cell spacing and cell padding were defined. Let's explore the relevance of these attributes when laying out an actual page. If cell padding and/or spacing are applied to a table, they are automatically applied to all cells of the table and cannot be selectively added or deleted. One of the advantages of nesting an additional

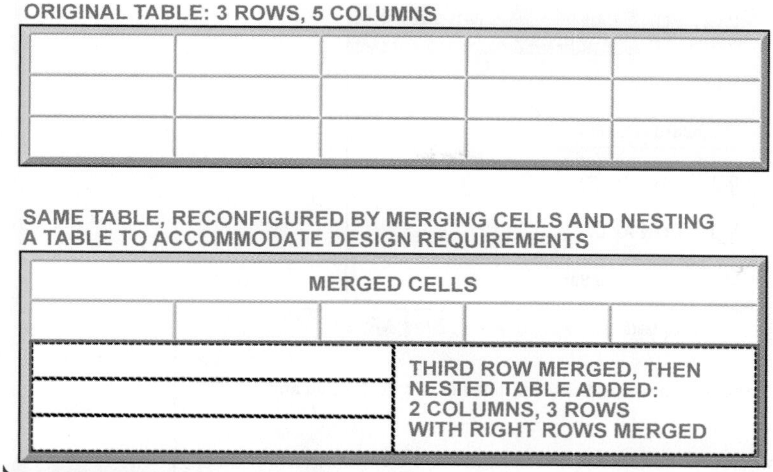

ORIGINAL TABLE: 3 ROWS, 5 COLUMNS

SAME TABLE, RECONFIGURED BY MERGING CELLS AND NESTING
A TABLE TO ACCOMMODATE DESIGN REQUIREMENTS

MERGED CELLS

THIRD ROW MERGED, THEN
NESTED TABLE ADDED:
2 COLUMNS, 3 ROWS
WITH RIGHT ROWS MERGED

FIGURE 10-12 Table reconfiguration with nested table.

separate table inside a cell is the ability to apply padding and/or spacing to part
of your design without affecting the entire design by assigning spacing and/or
padding properties to the nested table only, leaving the rest of the content in the
main table cells unaffected.

When nesting a new table inside a cell, be sure to set the
vertical alignment of the cell that will contain the nested table
to Top.

Viewing and Selecting Tables   If you have been practicing on your own thus far, you
may have experienced difficulty at times selecting a nested table or a table cell's edge
to manipulate it in some manner. To handle this problem, Dreamweaver has two features that will help. One is called the *tag selector* (not the Tag inspector we have already
learned about), located in the lower-left area of the Document window, which will
identify all the elements on the page and allow you to click the one you want to select.
The other selection aid, which is specific to tables, is called Expanded Tables mode.
This mode can be accessed by choosing View>Table Mode>Expanded Tables Mode; by
selecting a table first and then right/Control-clicking to choose Table>Expanded
Tables Mode from the context-sensitive menu; or by clicking the Expanded option in
the Layout tab of the Insert panel, as shown in **FIGURE 10-13**.

   Although this will be a handy option at times, do not be alarmed the first time
when it seems to throw off your entire layout! Expanded Tables mode temporarily
thickens the borders of the cells to make the selection task easier when working
with tables. Figure 10-13 also includes the dialog box you will see the first time you
choose the mode that explains what the mode does, and warns you *not* to change

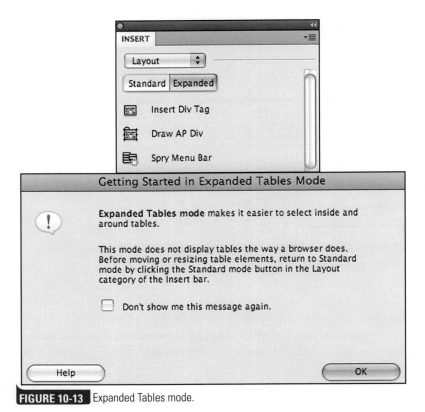

FIGURE 10-13 Expanded Tables mode.

your layout based on what you see in Expanded Tables mode. Notice that you can also choose here to tell Dreamweaver, "Don't show me this message again." This is always a handy option in any graphics program after you understand what the feature does. After you click OK, you will enter the Expanded Tables mode the first time. To exit this mode and return to the regular viewing/working mode, which is referred to as Standard mode, you can choose the Standard mode option in all the same locations that you chose to enter the Expanded Tables mode; however, while you are in Expanded Tables mode, you can also choose Exit at the top of the Document window, which will return the table's view back into Standard mode, as shown in **FIGURE 10-14**. After you have made your selection in Expanded Tables mode, you should return to Standard mode as soon as possible to continue work

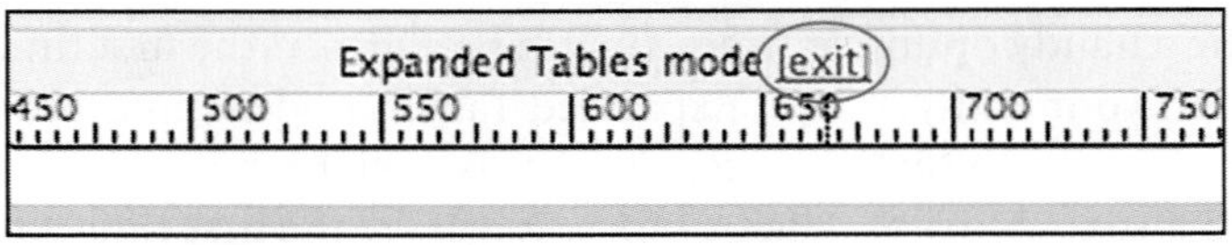

Expanded Tables mode [exit]

FIGURE 10-14 Exiting Expanded Tables mode.

on your layout because, as you have just learned, Expanded Tables mode does not display your layout accurately.

10.2.2 Planning and Organizing a Table Structure Before Implementing It

Now that you have an understanding of how table layout works and a little introduction into the use of tables, you probably realize the importance of planning a layout strategy ahead of time, before trying to use them to structure a page in Dreamweaver. Remember, time is money. Taking a little time to plan the initial table(s) you should start with (number of rows and columns) and how you will configure those cells and table(s) in Dreamweaver will maximize your productivity when you start building the page. This plan does not have to be fancy (just a scribbled sketch will do), but it will allow you to organize your thoughts before you begin to construct the page.

The page layout shown in **FIGURE 10-15** illustrates how the reconfigured table shown in Figure 10-12 was used to add the page content to the reconfigured cells. Note the orange lines indicate the cell divisions of the original table, and the yellow lines indicate the nested table.

FIGURE 10-15 Reconfigured table with content added.

10.3 Ways to Use Tables to Create Pages

There are basically four methods of using tables to create a web page, each of which will be explored in this section. After you understand how the process works, you will most likely choose a favorite method that works best for you or, through your own artistic creativity, be able to think outside the box and arrive at your own combination of methods that best suit your specific design needs.

10.3.1 Building a Layout Using a Main Table

To create a layout using this table layout method, begin with a main table that has the initial number of rows and columns you will need, as determined by the sketch you drew as your guide. Choose a width of 750 pixels for the table if you are planning a fixed centered layout as introduced in Chapter 3. Set the table border, cell padding, and cell spacing to zero, and then select center alignment in the Property inspector after the table has been created. After the table has been aligned to the center, you are ready to reconfigure its cells or nest additional tables inside it as your design dictates.

10.3.2 Building a Layout Using Individual Stacked Tables

In this method, a page is built by stacking multiple individual tables on top of each other, instead of beginning a layout with one main table. For a fixed page layout, again, set the width of the first table to 750 pixels in the Table dialog box. Choose a value of zero for all of the following: the border thickness, the cell padding, and the cell spacing. Choose the number of rows/columns you want for this first table. For example, perhaps choose one row and one column if the table will be used to insert your headline graphic. When the table appears on the page with selection handles, align the table to the center. While the table still has selection handles, click the right arrow of your keyboard to automatically place an I-beam at the end of the table (you will be able to see it flashing). Do *not* hit the Enter/Return key now. Instead, go directly to the Table dialog box to create the second table that will display below your first one. By inserting the new table in this manner, it will be automatically snapped right to the bottom of the previous table with no space between the two tables. It is important that you do not place the I-beam below the table when adding the next table to ensure a seamless appearance when the page is viewed in a browser. Repeat this process for all major tables needed for your design, each time matching the table's width and alignment that you assigned for the first one. You can still add nested tables within any of these individual tables as your design dictates.

10.3.3 Beginning a Layout with a Master Umbrella Table

Another method of building a page using tables begins with a master umbrella table. This table is defined with a width of 750 pixels (if designing a fixed centered layout), with one row, one column, and a value of zero for its cell padding, spacing, and border. When the table is inserted into the page, choose center alignment in the Property inspector. Before adding any content to this table, click above the top of the table to activate the small arrow, indicating that you are selecting its one column, and choose a vertical alignment of Top in the Property inspector. This will ensure that all content added inside will snap to the top of this umbrella table. After you have done this, click inside this table and nest the table(s) you will use to import your page content. However, all tables added inside an umbrella table should have their widths set to 100% percent, not pixels. This will ensure that they will fill the master table completely, keeping your layout centered and 750 pixels wide as you continue to insert your page content. If you forget to assign this property in the Table dialog box, remember that you can change the width of any table selected at any time in the Property inspector. Using the concept of an umbrella table will work with any number of tables stacked within it, each set to a width of 100%.

10.3.4 Creating a Flexible Liquid Layout Using Tables

In the table layout methods introduced thus far, each one created a fixed centered layout. As we learned in Chapter 3, another option to tailor your website to your audience is to design a liquid page layout that adjusts automatically to the width provided by your visitor's monitor settings. The secret to creating a liquid layout is first setting the table's width to 100%, vs. a specific width in pixels, such as the width of 750 pixels we have used to create fixed centered designs thus far. The second consideration is designing the flexibility of the table's cell content. Perhaps you have some items on your page that need to remain stationary, while others can slide and adjust according to the room provided. To accommodate this, flexible tables are set to 100% (remember: select percent, not pixels, for its width), with some cells assigned fixed widths defined in pixels and others allowed to stretch, filling the remaining table width without restriction. After you have created a table set to 100%, select a column of the table (usually one at the left, right, or left and right if you have three columns) and set a specific width for it in the W category of the Property inspector. It will default to add the value in pixels, which is what you want: do not add the percent sign to the value and leave the width of the remaining column(s) blank. In a layout based on percentages, blank columns signify to Dreamweaver that they can stretch as needed. As your table is expanded, it will expand in the column(s) with an undefined width and reposition the text or image located in the cells as needed, keeping the fixed pixel width column(s) from stretching.

Let's take a look at another design for the New Hampshire Lupine Restaurant. This liquid layout was created using multiple stacked tables, each with a width of 100%. Shown in two contrasting monitor viewing scenarios, **FIGURE 10-16** illustrates this concept in more detail.

1. The cell containing the headline is defined with a fixed width of 400 pixels.
2. This cell has no width defined (blank, not zero), allowing it to flex according to the visitor's monitor screen viewing width.

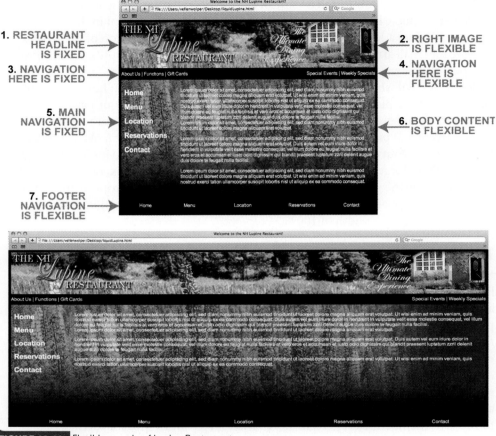

FIGURE 10-16 Flexible sample of Lupine Restaurant.

3. This table's navigation cell has a fixed width of 250 pixels.

4. This navigation cell has no width defined, allowing it to flex according to the visitor's monitor screen viewing width.

5. This table's cell has a fixed width of 175 pixels for the web page's main navigation.

6. This body content cell has no width defined, allowing it to flex according the visitor's monitor screen viewing width.

7. This table of five columns has a width of 100%. Each cell has an individual width percentage, with all five totaling 100%.

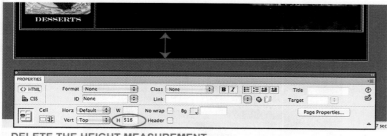

DELETE THE HEIGHT MEASUREMENT

FIGURE 10-17 Table adjustments.

Sometimes, when content is added to a cell, your layout seems to suddenly "explode" with table cells expanding and throwing off your entire layout. Usually, grabbing the edge of a table or cell and dragging will bounce it back into shape. Sometimes, however, you may be trying to tighten up a table, and dragging the selection handle just doesn't seem to work. If you have a nested table with the I-beam inside the cell the table has been inserted into, first check that you do not have a flashing I-beam below the table in that cell. If you don't, check the height option for the cell, as shown in **FIGURE 10-17**. A value may have been added that is restricting your ability to tighten the table. After you delete the value (do not type zero) that appears in this box, your table(s) should snap back for you.

A Look at the Code in Split View: Examining Tables, Rows, Columns, Cells, and Nested Tables

10.4

FIGURE 10-18 details the code Dreamweaver wrote for the sample shown, with its tables and cells color coded by Dreamweaver, in Figure 10-15. The only difference in this sample is that the body text has been shortened so that this example can focus on the page's HTML code.

1. `<table width=` is the opening tag of the main table element with its attributes (size, border of none, center aligned, etc.).
2. `colspan="5"` indicates that the five cells of the original table have been merged.
3. `<td>`indicates the opening tag of the table cell (table data) containing the "contact" graphic located inside its corresponding `<tr>` tag.
4. `</td>` indicates the closing tag of the same cell.

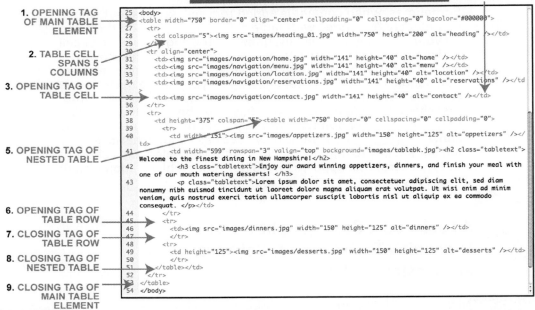

1. OPENING TAG OF MAIN TABLE ELEMENT

2. TABLE CELL SPANS 5 COLUMNS

3. OPENING TAG OF TABLE CELL

4. CLOSING TAG OF TABLE CELL

5. OPENING TAG OF NESTED TABLE

6. OPENING TAG OF TABLE ROW

7. CLOSING TAG OF TABLE ROW

8. CLOSING TAG OF NESTED TABLE

9. CLOSING TAG OF MAIN TABLE ELEMENT

```
25  <body>
26  <table width="750" border="0" align="center" cellpadding="0" cellspacing="0" bgcolor="#000000">
27    <tr>
28      <td colspan="5"><img src="images/heading_01.jpg" width="750" height="200" alt="heading" /></td>
29    </tr>
30    <tr align="center">
31      <td><img src="images/navigation/home.jpg" width="141" height="40" alt="home" /></td>
32      <td><img src="images/navigation/menu.jpg" width="141" height="40" alt="menu" /></td>
33      <td><img src="images/navigation/location.jpg" width="141" height="40" alt="location" /></td>
34      <td><img src="images/navigation/reservations.jpg" width="141" height="40" alt="reservations" /></td>
35      <td><img src="images/navigation/contact.jpg" width="141" height="40" alt="contact" /></td>
36    </tr>
37    <tr>
38      <td height="375" colspan="5"><table width="750" border="0" cellspacing="0" cellpadding="0">
39        <tr>
40          <td width="151"><img src="images/appetizers.jpg" width="150" height="125" alt="appetizers" /></td>
41          <td width="599" rowspan="3" valign="top" background="images/tablebk.jpg"><h2 class="tabletext">
                Welcome to the finest dining in New Hampshire! </h2>
42            <h3 class="tabletext">Enjoy our award winning appetizers, dinners, and finish your meal with
                one of our mouth watering desserts! </h3>
43            <p class="tabletext">Lorem ipsum dolor sit amet, consectetuer adipiscing elit, sed diam
                nonummy nibh euismod tincidunt ut laoreet dolore magna aliquam erat volutpat. Ut wisi enim ad minim
                veniam, quis nostrud exerci tation ullamcorper suscipit lobortis nisl ut aliquip ex ea commodo
                consequat. </p></td>
44        </tr>
45        <tr>
46          <td><img src="images/dinners.jpg" width="150" height="125" alt="dinners" /></td>
47        </tr>
48        <tr>
49          <td height="125"><img src="images/desserts.jpg" width="150" height="125" alt="desserts" /></td>
50        </tr>
51      </table></td>
52    </tr>
53  </table>
54  </body>
```

FIGURE 10-18 Split view of table page.

5. This is the opening tag of the table element nested within the main table.

6. `<tr>` is the opening tag indicating every time a new row is created in the table.

7. `</tr>` is the closing tag for the row cited in item number six.

8. `</table>` indicates the closing tag of the nested table element.

9. `</table>` indicates the closing tag of the main original table element.

10.5 What We Have Learned

Tables can offer artistic freedom and creativity that we have not been able to experience before now. We learned how to create a table, customize its configuration, and add content to it. We broadened this knowledge to include multiple methods of applying tables to page layout, including the ability to create a flexible liquid layout easily by setting table widths to 100%, offering the possibility to tailor our pages even further to accommodate our audience demands.

10.6 Reinforcing Your Knowledge

Project 1

1. With the SampleSite active in the Files panel, open its *index.html* page.
2. Insert a table with 4 rows, 1 column, a width of 750 pixels, and zero for its cell padding, spacing, and border.
3. After the table is inserted into the page, choose to center it. Select all of its rows and choose Top in the Vert field of the Property inspector.
4. Insert the *winter_headline.jpg* into its top row. Add *Vantage headline* as its alternate text.
5. Save and preview this page in a browser.
6. Close this *index.html* page.

Project 2

1. Make your FishluvrzSite the active site in your Files panel.
2. Open the site *index.html* page you worked on in Chapter 9. At that time, we set page properties for it. We will now begin to structure the page using tables.
3. Begin the page with a 1 row, 1 column umbrella table with a width of 750 pixels and zero assigned to its cell padding, spacing, and border options. (When inserting tables while building the FishluvrzSite, add accessibility summary comments if desired.) Assign its alignment

Project 2 (continued)

to center and set a vertical alignment of Top for its single cell to be sure our page will be centered in our visitor's viewing area and our content will snap to the top of this umbrella table.

4. Add a nested table inside of it with a width of 100% with 5 rows, 3 columns, and zero for its cell padding, spacing, and border options. Select all of the cells of the table and set their vertical alignment to Top.

5. Merge all the cells in the first row because this row will be used to add the page headline.

6. Merge all the cells in the second row because we will add the navigation into this row in Chapter 11.

7. Merge all the cells of the third row because this row will hold our main body text.

8. With this nested table selected with its selection handles (you may want to enter Expanded Tables mode to help select it, or try using the tag selector), press the right arrow of your keyboard to add a flashing I-beam to the right of this nested table. **FIGURE 10-19** exemplifies this alternate table selection method.

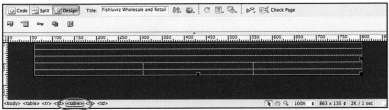

TABLE SELECTED BY CHOOSING IT FROM THE TAG SELECTOR

FIGURE 10-19 Table selected using the tag selector.

9. Insert another table below it that has 1 row, 6 columns, a width of 100%, and zero for its cell spacing and border options. Set 10 pixels for its cell padding for "breather" space because this will be used for our footer navigation.

At this point, your index page should resemble **FIGURE 10-20** when viewed in Expanded Tables mode.

10. You have learned that when you insert an image that is not already in the *images* folder of the active site's root folder, Dreamweaver will add it for you when prompted. Alternatively, you can add images

Project 2 (continued)

UMBRELLA TABLE: 1 ROW, 1 COLUMN

NESTED TABLE: 5 ROWS, 3 COLUMNS

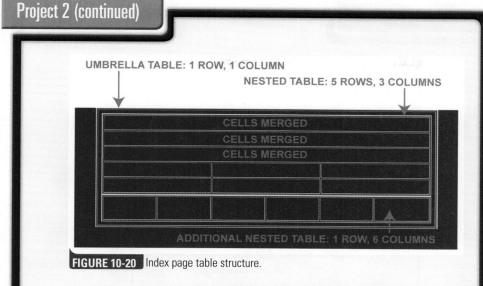

CELLS MERGED
CELLS MERGED
CELLS MERGED

ADDITIONAL NESTED TABLE: 1 ROW, 6 COLUMNS

FIGURE 10-20 Index page table structure.

to a root folder outside of Dreamweaver if needed. Locate your *FishluvrzRoot* folder and add the *fishlurz_static_headline.jpg* located in the *Chapter_10PracticeFiles* folder to its *images* folder. When you return to Dreamweaver your FishluvrzSite should now look like **FIGURE 10-21** in the Files panel.

11. Add the *fishluvrz_static_headline.jpg* to the first row of the top nested table and add *Fishluvrz headline* for its alt text. Now that we have added a photo headline, let's remove the automatic margin created at the top of the page by typing zero in all four margin categories of the Page Properties dialog box.

12. Select the second row and set the background color to #336600. Then, select the third and fourth rows and set the background color of both rows to #FFFFFF.

13. Select all the cells in the fifth row and apply #336600 for a background color. Double-check that the cells are vertically aligned to Top.

14. Select the second nested table designed for the footer navigation. Assign a background color to the table (selected with selection handles to assign it to the entire table) of #FFFFFF. Add the following word in all caps to each cell from left to right: HOME, PRODUCTS, INFORMATION, FAQ, CONTACT US, and SITE MAP.

15. Select the cells and set the horizontal alignment to Center. The vertical alignment, as you have seen, defaults to Middle, which is what we want to keep it at this time. Set the width of the cells to the

Project 2 (continued)

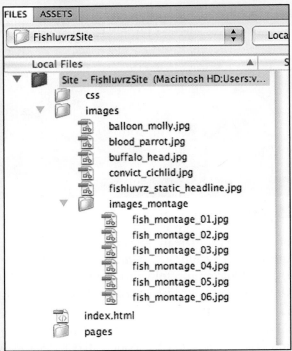

FIGURE 10-21   Fishluvrz Files panel with *fishluvrz_static_headline.jpg* added to the images folder.

following percentages because the different widths of the contents require custom settings. To do this, place the I-beam inside the respective cell and type the provided width in the W area of the Property inspector for each cell.

HOME: 13%, PRODUCTS: 19%, INFORMATION: 20%, FAQ: 12%, CONTACT US: 19%, SITE MAP: 17%.

16. Save and preview the page in one or more browsers. We have added our first content to the FishluvrzSite home page! Your page should now resemble **FIGURE 10-22**.

This concludes our work on the FishluvrzSite for this chapter. We will continue to build the index page, as well as our other four main pages of the site, in subsequent chapters.

FIGURE 10-22 Current index page for FishluvrzSite.

10.7 Building Your Own Website

In the supplementary assignment in Chapter 3, you created mock layouts for your first site. In Chapter 4, you prepared for your index page by using two distinct methods of graphics preparation: one sliced the entire mock layout page, the other involved optimizing and saving each individual image into the *images* folder of your site root folder. We will learn how your slices can be used to create an entire web page in Chapter 12. At this time, you can begin to build your index page using one of the table methods in this chapter and implementing the graphics you optimized in Chapter 4.

1. Now that you understand how tables work, sketch a table structure for your index page, including merged cells, split cells, and nested tables as needed. Be sure that your layout includes where your main navigation and footer navigation will be inserted in Chapter 11. When designing for the main navigation, only one cell is required for its insertion.

2. Launch Dreamweaver and select your site in the Files panel. Open your *index.html* page.

3. Click to insert a table onto your page. The table layout structure you have sketched out will determine the number of rows and columns you will need to choose here, and whether you want your table width to be set at a fixed width created at 750 pixels or a flexible liquid layout created at 100%.

4. Add your headline graphic into your table. If your final layout design resulted in a liquid layout, it may require you to return to Photoshop first to split it into two graphics, as shown in Figure 10-16, to have part of its design expand naturally from 800 pixels to 1024 pixels or higher, with other areas remaining fixed.

5. Add your footer navigation. As we did in step 15 of the Reinforcing Your Knowledge Fishluvrz project, type percentages for your various footer navigation words so that they appear equal across the page if using a fixed width for a main table. If you are building the page as a liquid layout, the entire footer table can be set at 100% to flex as needed following the sample shown in Figure 10-16.

6. If your design dictates any background colors or images in any of its cells or entire tables, add those at this time.

7. Following the example in Figure 10-6, if your design has text and images together in some of its cells, try adding them now. If you want space added between lines, use a regular return instead of a soft return: you will want to experiment and test the look in a browser. Add as much content as you feel comfortable with, knowing that we will be learning how to add margins, etc., for further content structure in future chapters. Don't be discouraged because your page doesn't look like much yet. Dreamweaver is huge: that's why you are learning it in digestible building blocks! We'll get there!

8. When you have added all the content you are comfortable with adding at this stage of the learning process, stop for now, save your page, and preview it in one or more browsers. In the next chapter you will learn not only how to add your navigation, but also how this first page can be used as a template for the beginning layouts of the rest of the pages of your site.

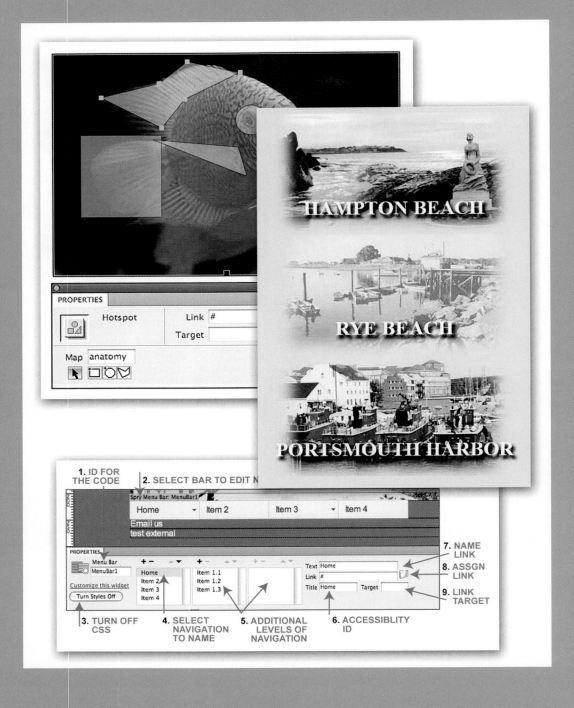

PROPERTIES

Hotspot   Link #

                Target

Map anatomy

HAMPTON BEACH

RYE BEACH

PORTSMOUTH HARBOR

1. ID FOR THE CODE

2. SELECT BAR TO EDIT N

Spry Menu Bar: MenuBar1

| Home | ▾ | Item 2 | Item 3 | ▾ | Item 4 |

Email us
test external

PROPERTIES

Menu Bar
MenuBar1

Customize this widget

Turn Styles Off

+ − ▲ ▾

| Home |
| Item 2 |
| Item 3 |
| Item 4 |

+ − ▲ ▾

| Item 1.1 |
| Item 1.2 |
| Item 1.3 |

+ − ▲ ▾

Text Home

Link #

Title Home   Target

7. NAME LINK

8. ASSGN LINK

9. LINK TARGET

3. TURN OFF CSS

4. SELECT NAVIGATION TO NAME

5. ADDITIONAL LEVELS OF NAVIGATION

6. ACCESSIBLITY ID

Adding Links, Adding Link Pages, and Inserting Media

11

I t is time to learn how to provide our visitors with the tools they need to maneuver through our sites. After learning the differences between internal and external page links, we will explore inserting a variety of navigation methods onto a page. Carrying this concept further, we will learn how a page with navigation applied to it can be used as a prototype to build other pages to expedite the web development process. To add even more professionalism and interest to our pages, we will learn how to insert Flash movies and videos into Dreamweaver and assign browser visibility and operational properties to them.

Understanding Links

We have learned to create a site, add pages to the site, and add backgrounds, text, and images to those pages. However, so far, our pages have been static. It is time, at last, to learn how to add interactivity to our pages by creating links. In this chapter, we will learn how to apply various types of links: text links, anchors, email links, image links, image maps, rollovers, navigation bars (in CS3 and CS4), and Spry navigation menus.

Before we learn how to create each of those types of links, it is important to understand the difference between the two main types of links: relative links and absolute links.

11.1.1 Relative Links: Site Root and Document

A *relative link* is an in-site, internal link—one that connects from one page to another page within the same site. There are two types of relative links: site root relative links and document relative links. Site root relative links are typically used for large websites that require multiple servers. When learning to define a website in Chapter 6, we learned that the option of document relative links is the default, and it will be the type of relative links we will focus on in this textbook. Document relative links do not require the full URL path to the page because the new page is *relative*, located within the same site as the page containing the link.

11.1.2 Absolute Links

An *absolute link* is one that is used to link from the page it is located on to a page in a different, or *external*, site. In order to do that, an absolute link requires the full URL path. For example, to link from the *index.html* page of our SampleSite to a page called *guidance.html* located inside a *services* folder of the fictitious Stable Rock Investments site, the absolute link would be *http://www.stablerockinvestments.com/services/guidance.html*. Notice that the link path begins with the website domain name, is followed by the folder the page is located in (if contained inside a folder in the root folder of the site), and ends with the page that you want to link to inside that folder.

11.1.3 Targeting Links

Before we begin to learn how to create links, let's learn what *targeting* refers to. We learned a little about targeting in Chapter 8 when introduced to frames. At that time, we learned that when frame pages were linked, you could define where the linked page would be displayed, such as having it replace the existing content of a body frame page by assigning its target location in the Property inspector.

When referring to links in traditional web pages, the concept remains basically the same. Here, you really only need to select one alternative option. If you do not select a target destination, the default target (_Self) will replace the existing page in the viewer's browser with the linked page, which is the most common application of links. When creating internal links, that is great. However, if you are creating an external link to someone else's site, you probably do not want your site to be replaced in the browser window by the new site the visitor was sent to by the link. That is why having the external link open in a separate browser window (_Blank) is so important. In this scenario, when the visitor clicks to close that site window, your site is still open underneath it. Yes! Another chance to re-engage your visitor!

11.2 Adding Links to a Page

Now that you have learned the difference between relative and absolute links and how to assign the proper target option depending on which kind you will add to a page, it is time to learn about the most common linking methods used on the Web and how to create them.

11.2.1 Assigning Text Links

In Chapter 9, we learned how to define link properties using the Links (CSS) category of the Page Properties dialog box by setting their font, style, size, the colors to be used for their various link states, and whether you wanted the link text to be identified by underlining or not. In order to learn how to assign them now, start by making your SampleSite the active site in the Files panel. Create a new page named *link_page.html* and save it inside the *pages* folder. (During this practice, it will not be necessary to add a title, keywords, and description text to this page. However, remember that you must start each page of a real site with these critical steps.) In this *link_page.html*, choose Modify>Page Properties or click the Page Properties tab in the Property inspector to enter the Page Properties dialog box. Notice that the link properties you assigned for the SampleSite's index page have not been carried over to this page. Let's practice assigning properties again by defining the link properties for the *link_page.html*. Set the following properties as shown in **FIGURE 11-1**. (If you are working in CS3, select the font collection Verdana, Arial, Helvetica, sans-serif.)

 Have you noticed if working in either CS4 or CS5 that when you select a color from the web safe 216 color palette, it is listed in the Page Properties dialog box as only three letters/integers? Because web safe and web smart colors contain duplicate letters or numbers in their definitions, Dreamweaver needs to list the duplicated letter or number only once. The full name of our visited link color listed as #60F is actually #6600FF. However, because any time you want to use a color that is not web safe or web smart, you need to type all six letters/numbers plus add the hash symbol (#) in front of its hexadecimal value. It's an excellent habit to do it every time for all colors when assigning hexadecimal values.

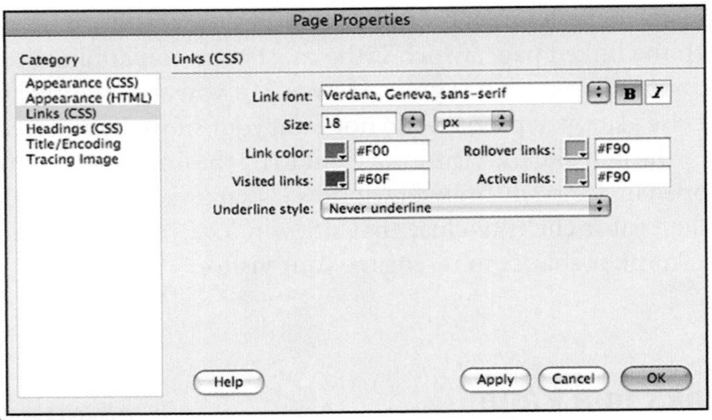

FIGURE 11-1 Text link properties.

Now that we have created a page to link to, let's add some text to use as the link to it. Return to the *index.html* page and type *Go to link page* inside one of the cells below the headline of the table you created in Chapter 10. Drag across just the words *link page* to highlight them. With the text highlighted, we are ready to assign the link. The link can be assigned multiple ways; the easiest is the Point to File method. When the text is highlighted, go to the HTML tab of the Property inspector and click the icon next to the link option, as shown in **FIGURE 11-2**, and drag the Point to File icon to assign the link (this circular icon will resemble a piece of string as you click and drag it onto the file you want to link to) to the *link_page.html* (in CS3, the link option is located in the upper-right area of the Property inspector). Done! You will know that you have created a link because your text will automatically change to reflect the defined link color and font properties, and the link page will be listed in the link area of the Property inspector when you select the text. When you save and test this page in a browser, it will forward you to the new link page.

The link you applied reflected the link properties you previously assigned to the *index.html* page in Chapter 9. We will need to create a link from the *link_page.html*

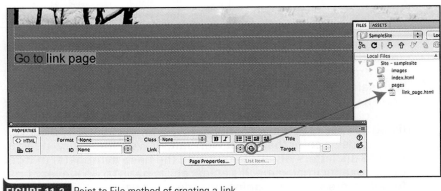

FIGURE 11-2 Point to File method of creating a link.

page back to the *index.html* page to see its properties applied. On the *link_page.html* page, add a table with the following characteristics: 750 pixels wide, 2 rows, 1 column, with zero for its border, cell padding, and spacing. Center it on the page. In its top row, type *Return to home page*, highlight the text, and drag the string to highlight the *index.html* page in the Files panel. Save and test the page in a browser.

As another alternative, you may have noticed the folder icon next to the Point to File icon in the Property inspector. By clicking on this folder, you can browse to locate the page you want to link to. You can also choose Modify>Make Link or right/Control-click and choose Make Link from the context-sensitive menu to browse to locate the page to link to. You can also choose Insert>Hyperlink for a dialog box to assign the link page. Lastly, you can click the Hyperlink icon (chain) in the Common tab of the Insert panel to enter the same dialog box to assign the link. After you have created a link using any one of the methods you have just learned, you will need to save the page to preview it in a browser to test the link.

Adding a Tooltip to a Text Link (CS4 and CS5 Only)   Before previewing the page in a browser, when you have created a text link, another category will come to life in the Property inspector called *Title* in the upper-right area. Adding a description here will aid in accessibility and provide a cool visible *tooltip* when the words are rolled over in a browser. Try adding one, then enjoy not only testing your newly created text link, but also seeing the tooltip before you click to go to the linked page!

 When you tested your page in a browser, did any of your link states display in colors different than what you assigned? Just as you learned in Chapter 9 when applying background and font properties, when assigning any hexadecimal values to links, you must always add the hash symbol (#) before the value for it to display properly in a browser. Remember: don't be fooled if it appears to display properly in the Dreamweaver Design view!

To reassign a link to a different page, simply highlight the text and point to the page you want to link to instead, use one of the other methods you have learned, or right/Control-click and choose Change Link from the context-sensitive menu.

To remove a link altogether, simply highlight the link in the Property inspector, delete it, highlight it, and choose Modify>Remove Link, or highlight it and right/Control-click and choose Remove Link from the context-sensitive menu.

Designating the Target   Located next to the link option in the Property inspector, located in the dialog box if you chose to add the link using the Insert>Hyperlink, or in the same dialog box accessed in the Common tab of the Insert panel by a chain link icon, is the option to assign the target. As we have learned, if you do not assign one, the option to load the linked page in place of your current page in the visitor's browser will be chosen by default. If you have assigned one, and later want to change it, you can reassign it in the Property inspector, or select the link and choose Modify>Link Target.

■ 11.2.2 Using Images as Links vs. Image Map Hotspots for Links

Before learning to create these two kinds of links it is important that you understand the difference between them. If you chose to add Chapter 5 to your learning about web design, you already understand the concept of an image map. However, to clarify it for all readers, it will be further explained here.

Using an image as a link is just as it sounds. An entire image is selected and link properties are assigned to it, so that when the visitor clicks anywhere on it, he/she is forwarded to the new location. In contrast to using an entire image as a link, an *image map* uses a *hotspot* to define a specific area of an image, rather than the entire image, to create a link to the respective link page—allowing multiple different links to be created from one image if desired.

Using an Image as a Link   Now that you understand the process of creating text links, converting an existing image on a page to a link follows the same concept. To learn how to do this, open the *link_page.html* page that you created earlier and drag any one of the images (*except* the *fish.jpg*) from the *images* folder into the second row of its table, or browse to locate an image. After it's inserted into the table, select the image with the Select tool to activate its selection handles, and notice that the link option appears in the Property inspector. Use the Point to File method, or click the folder icon to browse to assign the link to go to the *index.html* page. Save the *link_page.html* page and test its link in a browser.

Creating Image Map Hotspots for Links   When an imported image is activated with selection handles, you will see icons appear at the left of the Property inspector: a selection tool referred to as the Pointer Hotspot tool and three drawing tools that are similar to those in other Adobe programs. These tools allow you to "draw" the area you want to define as the link, rather than use the entire image. Right above these icons is an entry box to assign a name that identifies the image to be used for the map, because you can use more than one image for map hotspots on the same page if desired. To understand this concept and learn how to create one, on the *link_page.html* page, delete the image you chose to add into its table and replace it with the *fish.jpg* image. With the image selected with selection handles, title the map *anatomy* in the map identification area of the Property inspector. Right below this area, select the Rectangle Hotspot tool and draw a small rectangle over the mouth of the fish. As soon as you do, you will be prompted to add alt text for the hotspot in the Property inspector: add *mouth* for the alt text description. The screened cyan color that automatically defines the map area is displayed for identification and working purposes only and will not be visible when the page is viewed in a browser. Continue to create additional hotspots by using the Circle Hotspot tool to trace the eye, the Rectangle Hotspot tool to trace the tail fin, and the Polygon Hotspot tool to click points to trace the dorsal fin on the top of the fish and the pectoral fin on its side, and add appropriate alt text each time when prompted. Drawing a hotspot with the Polygon Hotspot tool will work similar to drawing a selection using

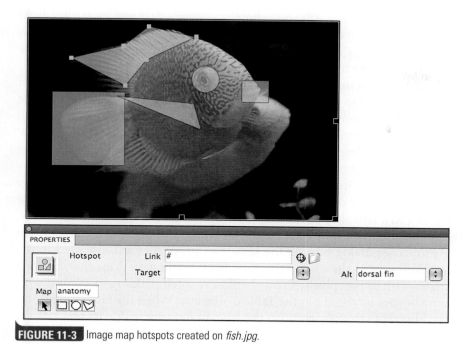

FIGURE 11-3 Image map hotspots created on *fish.jpg*.

the Polygonal Lasso tool in Photoshop. The Pointer Hotspot tool (a selection tool to the left of the rest of the hotspot tools) will allow you to move or delete your created hotspots, as well as tweak the shape of your polygon hotspots by selecting points and moving them. When you have added your hotspots, your fish should resemble **FIGURE 11-3**.

Notice the link area of the Property inspector when one of these hotspots is selected. Until you assign a specific page destination to the link, Dreamweaver will automatically add the hash symbol (#), meaning that the link is created but does not currently go anywhere. What is great about this feature is that it allows you to test the links in a browser, even if you have not assigned a page for the link. Let's test the image map with a link applied to one of the hotspots. Choose any one of them and link it back to the *index.html* page, then save and test the *link_page.html* page in a browser. You should see the hand only when you roll over the location of each hotspot; when you click the hotspot you linked to the *index.html* page, you should be forwarded to it. That's all there is to it! If you added the necessary coordinates to create the hotspots in the image map sample in Chapter 5, you'll love creating them here and having Dreamweaver make all those decisions for you!

11.2.3 Adding Anchor Links

First of all let's understand what an anchor is when referring to links. When you visited a web page that had topics or selections at the top of the page, you chose one of them and the page "jumped" to that content located somewhere else on the same page instead of taking you to a whole new page. That was an anchor link! To create an anchor link in Dreamweaver, the anchor or destination location is defined first, followed by assigning the link to the anchor. To learn how to create one, we will need some text to link to as the destination. Open the *specials.doc* Microsoft® Word® document located in the *Chapter_11PracticeFiles* folder. (If you do not have access to Microsoft Word, the *specials.rtf* [Rich Text Format] file is also available in the same folder. It can be opened in any text editor, and it will work with some formatting adjustments.) Highlight all the text, copy it to the Clipboard, and then close the word processing program. (Copying and Pasting will allow you to bring text into Dreamweaver from an outside source at any time.) Now, return to Dreamweaver and create a new page named *anchor_page .html* in the *pages* folder of your SampleSite. (During this practice, it will not be necessary to add a title, keywords, and description text to this page. However, remember that you must start each page of a real site with these critical steps.) In the Page Properties dialog box, set the same link properties as those used in the *link_page.html* page, as shown in Figure 11-1. After you have done that, create a table with a width of 500 pixels, 1 row, 1 column, a cell padding of 10, and with spacing and border set to zero in the Table dialog box. When the table appears on your page, align it to the center. With the I-beam flashing inside its one cell, set the vertical alignment to Top, then choose Edit>Paste Special. Choose *Text with structure plus full formatting (bold, italic, styles)* from the dialog box that follows, as shown in **FIGURE 11-4**.

If you used a text editor other than Microsoft Word and only have the first two options available, choose the second option, *Text with structure (paragraphs, lists, tables, etc.)* and then apply the paragraph returns as shown in **FIGURE 11-5**.

 Paste vs. Paste Special? If you know that you always want to import text with the option just chosen, you can define the preference for pasting text, allowing you thereafter to simply choose Paste, instead of Paste Special. To do that, open the Dreamweaver Preferences (or go directly to it from the Paste Special dialog box by clicking the Paste Preferences button) and choose the Copy/Paste category from the Preferences menu. After you arrive at this

---

Paste Special

Paste as:

  ○ Text only
  ○ Text with structure (paragraphs, lists, tables, etc.)
  ○ Text with structure plus basic formatting (bold, italic)
  ● Text with structure plus full formatting (bold, italic, styles)

  ☑ Retain line breaks
  ☐ Clean up Word paragraph spacing

  [Paste Preferences...]

[OK]   [Cancel]   [Help]

FIGURE 11-4   Paste Special dialog box.

SECTION OF
ANCHOR
PAGE IN
DREAMWEAVER

SECTION OF ANCHOR
PAGE IN BROWSER

SPECIALS OF THE WEEK

Shrimp Supreme

Prime Rib

Haddock Florentine

Lupine Veal ◄——————— ROLLED OVER LINK

Lamb Lambrusco ◄—————— VISITED LINK

SHRIMP SUPREME

Lorem ipsum dolor sit amet, consetetur sadipscing elitr, sed diam nonumy
eirmod tempor invidunt ut labore et dolore magna aliquyam erat, sed diam
voluptua. At vero eos et accusam et justo duo dolores et ea rebum. Stet
clita kasd gubergren, no sea takimata sanctus est Lorem ipsum dolor sit
amet.

Lorem ipsum dolor sit amet, consetetur sadipscing elitr, sed diam nonumy
eirmod tempor invidunt ut labore et dolore magna aliquyam erat, sed diam
voluptua. At vero eos et accusam et justo duo dolores et ea rebum. Stet
clita kasd gubergren, no sea takimata sanctus est Lorem ipsum dolor sit
amet.Lorem ipsum dolor sit amet, consetetur sadipscing elitr, sed diam
nonumy eirmod tempor invidunt ut labore et dolore magna aliquyam erat,
sed diam voluptua. At vero eos et accusam et justo duo dolores et ea
rebum. Stet clita kasd gubergren, no sea takimata sanctus est Lorem ipsum
dolor sit amet.

Lorem ipsum dolor sit amet, consetetur sadipscing elitr, sed diam nonumy
eirmod tempor invidunt ut labore et dolore magna aliquyam erat, sed diam
voluptua. At vero eos et accusam et justo duo dolores et ea rebum. Stet
clita kasd gubergren, no sea takimata sanctus est Lorem ipsum dolor sit
amet.

Back to Top

PRIME RIB

Lorem ipsum dolor sit amet, consetetur sadipscing elitr, sed diam nonumy
eirmod tempor invidunt ut labore et dolore magna aliquyam erat, sed diam
voluptua. At vero eos et accusam et justo duo dolores et ea rebum. Stet
clita kasd gubergren, no sea takimata sanctus est Lorem ipsum dolor sit

SPECIALS OF TH

Shrimp Supreme

Prime Rib

Haddock Florentine

Lupine Veal

Lamb Lambrusco

SHRIMP SUPREME

Lorem ipsum dolor sit amet, conse
eirmod tempor invidunt ut labore e
voluptua. At vero eos et accusam d
kasd gubergren, no sea takimata sa
Lorem ipsum dolor sit amet, conse
eirmod tempor invidunt ut labore e
voluptua. At vero eos et accusam d
kasd gubergren, no sea takimata sa
ipsum dolor sit amet, consetetur sa
tempor invidunt ut labore et dolore
vero eos et accusam et justo duo d
gubergren, no sea takimata sanctus
Lorem ipsum dolor sit amet, conse
eirmod tempor invidunt ut labore e
voluptua. At vero eos et accusam d
kasd gubergren, no sea takimata sa

Back to Top

PRIME RIB

Lorem ipsum dolor sit amet, conse
eirmod tempor invidunt ut labore e
voluptua. At vero eos et accusam d
kasd gubergren, no sea takimata s

FIGURE 11-5 Anchor sample.

category, you will see that it echoes the Paste Special dialog box
shown in Figure 11-4, except that here it allows you to declare the
default option. Thereafter, you can choose Paste Special only when
you want to use an alternative format other than what you have
previously defined as your default option.

With the text now added to the table, we can define the anchors. Before we
do that, however, it is important to note that it was not required to create a table
in order to paste text. It has been added here simply to give us a more organized

structure to work in. (By the way, did you notice how adding cell padding to the table created a margin around the text?)

Adding an anchor to a page is a two-part process. The first step is to place an I-beam first where you want the link to take the visitor. In our sample, place the I-beam to the left of SHRIMP SUPREME at the beginning of the first paragraph below the list of menu items. With the I-beam flashing, choose to add an anchor either by clicking on the anchor icon in the Common tab of the Insert panel, or by choosing Insert>Named Anchor. Using either method, you will be brought to a dialog box to define the name of the anchor. We will call this one *shrimp*. An anchor name cannot have spaces and should be lowercase. After you click OK, the anchor icon is inserted onto the page (it will not display in a browser).

Don't see the anchor icon? Be sure Invisible Elements is checked under View>Visual Aids, or under the Visual Aids pop-up menu we have learned about (located in the Document toolbar).

Let's add four more named anchors the same way, placing each one before the words to link to in the successive paragraphs: PRIME RIB, HADDOCK FLOREN-TINE, LUPINE VEAL, and LAMB LAMBRUSCO. Assign a corresponding one-word identifier in the Named Anchor dialog box each time you add an anchor.

The second step in the process is to assign a link to the named anchor. Highlight the words *Shrimp Supreme* located just below the SPECIALS OF THE WEEK heading. Using the Point to File icon in the Property inspector, drag the string to the anchor you added to the left of the words SHRIMP SUPREME, being sure to drag it directly on top of the anchor icon. After you have done that, the Property inspector should show *#shrimp* in the link option. Remember the hash symbol (#) when a link was created but didn't go anywhere? When creating an anchor, it indicates that the link's destination of *shrimp* is within the same page as its link. Dreamweaver adds it automatically for you when creating a link using an anchor. If you would like, reinforce your learning by adding the necessary links to the rest of the named anchors and then save and test the page in a browser.

To refine the application of anchors on a page and allow your visitors to conveniently return to your master list at the top, you may want to also add a *Back to Top* link from each section of information back to the top of the page. To do this in our sample, insert just one more anchor icon before the *S* in the *SPECIALS OF THE WEEK* line. In the sample shown, a soft return (line break) was applied at the end of each section before the words *Back to Top* were typed for appearance purposes. Once created, you can highlight each *Back to Top* and link them all to the same anchor at the top of the page. If you have completed this exercise, your page in Dreamweaver and then saved and viewed in a browser should resemble Figure 11-5.

If you are working in a text editor other than Microsoft Word and have only two active options in the Paste Special dialog box, choose the second option for the imported text, add a soft return after each paragraph about the menu item, and apply

Heading 2 to the *SPECIALS OF THE WEEK* title. After you do that, when previewed in a browser, your final page should now more closely resemble the sample shown in Figure 11-5.

11.2.4 Adding Email Links

Creating an email link uses the words *mailto:* (written as shown) added at the beginning of the email address in the link area of the Property inspector to uniquely identify it as such. To create one, open your *index.html* page of the SampleSite and add the words *Email us*, or any text that you would like to use, into one of its empty cells. Highlight the text and click the Email icon in the Common tab of the Insert panel (picture of an envelope), or choose Insert>Email Link. In either case, you will immediately enter a dialog box where you can type in the email address for the link, as well as change the link text if desired. To test the process, type your own email address for the destination of the link. After you have done that, the Property inspector lists the link in the link area with the *mailto:* prefix already added to it.

If desired, instead of using one of the two methods described to create an email link, you can highlight the text on the page that you want to use as the link, then simply type the desired destination email address directly into the link area of the Property inspector (in this practice exercise, that would be your own email address) as long as the *mailto:* prefix is added to it first. When you save the page and test it by previewing it in a browser, it will immediately launch your own email program to prompt you to write an email to yourself!

11.2.5 Adding Absolute/External Links

As we have learned, absolute links are external links: they will take the visitor to a page within another site, not another page within the same site. Because of that, when creating one, the full URL address must be used for the site for the browser to know where to locate the requested external page on the Web. To create one, text is highlighted, or an image or hotspot is selected to activate the link area of the Property inspector. After it's activated, the full URL is typed in, including the http:// prefix before the www.companyname.com is added. To try this, type some more text on your *index.html* page of the SampleSite, select its headline image, or create a hotspot on an area of its headline image, perhaps around its name, *Vantage*. After you have done that, with your selection active, type in the full address of your favorite website in the link area of the Property inspector, followed by the selection of *_Blank* for its target. Save the page and preview it in a browser. When you click the external link you created, the browser will bring you to your favorite site! It is important to remember, however, that even a single accidental space added when typing the URL will make it unidentifiable by a browser. To be safe, go first to the site you want to link to, highlight and copy its URL, return to Dreamweaver, and paste it into the link area of the Property inspector. By doing it this way, you will be assured that it is entered correctly.

■ 11.2.6 Reusing Links and Other Elements Through the Assets Panel

Speaking of favorites, this is the perfect time to cover the Assets panel in more depth. One of its very handy features is its URL option. Addresses added once to a page can easily be accessed and used on any additional pages of the site at any time thereafter through the Assets panel. Let's take a closer look at this panel in FIGURE 11-6.

Before discussing the URL features of the Assets panel specifically, it is important to note that the general options available when the URL category is selected are the same as they are for all the categories of the Assets panel. The Assets panel was first introduced to you in Chapter 7 and was used as a method of applying images to a page in Chapter 10. Here we will learn the rest of the main features of this powerful, useful panel.

1. When a color, image, URL, etc., is used in a site, a copy is automatically added to the Assets panel under its appropriate category. Therefore, any address, either an email or an external link that is typed on a page once, has a copy of the address added automatically to the URLs category of the Assets panel for the entire site.

2. Click the Favorites button to access any saved favorites—all URLs, images, etc.—that have been added to the Favorites category of the Assets panel.

3. In addition to providing another location to choose to insert a selected Asset onto a page, edit it, or add it to the Favorites category,

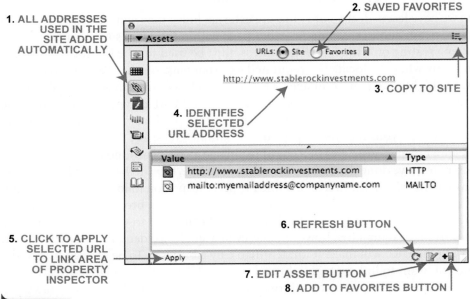

FIGURE 11-6 Understanding assets.

there is a handy option under the Assets panel's options menu to *Copy to Site*, which will allow you to move a copy of the selected Asset to any other site listed under your Files panel's pop-up menu list of previously defined sites.

4. When an item under any Assets category has been selected from the list of items in the lower half of the panel, the item is identified in the upper half of it. Because all of your colors selected for your *index.html* page of the SampleSite were automatically added behind the scenes to the Assets panel, click its color icon and then click any of your site colors to see your selected color displayed in the upper half of the panel.

5. Reuse any URL or email address listed in the Assets panel by selecting where you want to add it first, then selecting the link in the panel and clicking the Apply button to automatically add it to the link area of the Property inspector.

6. When anything new has been added to a page, you may need to click the Refresh button before you are able to see it listed under its applicable category of the Assets panel. If you select the URL icon in the Assets panel now, you may not see your recent external link or your email address that you added to the *index.html* page of the SampleSite listed yet. Clicking its Refresh button will "wake it up" so to speak, causing it to automatically update itself to display any new assets with all of the existing site assets.

7. Select an item under a category of the Assets panel (except colors and URLs) and then click the Edit Asset button to edit the item: if Dreamweaver can locate the necessary editor, it will launch the application and open the file in it. Editors can be defined under the File Types/Editors category of the Preferences dialog box. (We will learn more about assigning file editors in Chapter 13.) To test this feature if you have assigned Photoshop as your .jpg editor, click the *lamp.jpg* image under the Images category of the Assets panel and then click this icon. It should automatically launch Photoshop and display the image in it.

8. Select any item under any category of the Assets panel and then click this button to add a copy of it to the Favorites category. To edit colors, external URLs, and email addresses listed in the Assets panel, add them first to the Favorites category, then select the item and click the Edit Asset button.

11.2.7 Linking Directly to PDF Files

You may want a link to go directly to a separate .pdf file, rather than link to another page of your site or someone else's site. In order to do this, the .pdf should be saved for the Web first. To save the file for the Web using the dialog box of the program you created the .pdf file in, there will be just a few important options to choose. The

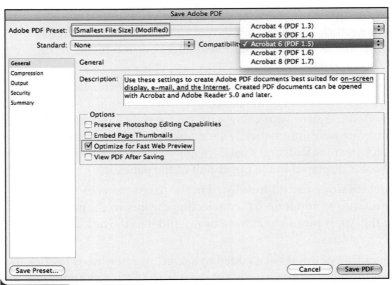

FIGURE 11-7   Settings for saving a .pdf file in Photoshop.

dialog box shown in **FIGURE 11-7** illustrates those options chosen in Photoshop. When you choose the Save Adobe PDF option in the Save As dialog box of Photoshop, select *Smallest File Size* from the Preset pop-up menu. The description area of the dialog box will confirm your selection by stating that this setting is best for the Internet. In the Compatibility pop-up menu, choose a version based on your audience needs. Any time you select the *Smallest File Size* option, *Optimize for Fast Web Preview* is chosen by default.

Before you arrived in the dialog box shown in Figure 11-7, you would have already told Photoshop where to save the file. This file should be saved into your *images* folder of the site you want to use it in, and saved as a copy if the original file has multiple layers.

After the file is in the *images* folder of your site, simply link to it using one of the methods you have learned. When tested in a browser, the link should launch Adobe® Reader® and open the .pdf file in it. Although Adobe Reader is a standard application available on most computers, if desired, you can add the link to the Adobe website to your page as a convenience to your visitors if your research indicates that some of your viewers may not already have it, or may need an upgrade. That link is http://get.adobe.com/reader/.

If you would like to practice viewing a .pdf file added to a site now, move a copy of the *organizing.pdf* file located in the *Chapter_11PracticeFiles* folder to the *images* folder of your SampleSite root folder. With the SampleSite *index.html* file open, type some text in one of its cells to use as a link, then use the Point to File method to link to the *organizing.pdf* file in its *images* folder. After the Property inspector link area confirms your assigned link, save and test the page.

11.3 Creating Links Using Image Objects and Spry Menu Bars

Adding links that use images that change when the visitor mouses over or clicks them, or menus that slide out to provide more links to select from, add more visual interest and sophistication to the navigational system of a website.

11.3.1 Inserting Image Rollovers

When a visitor's mouse rolls over an image rollover, a new image appears, which provides the link action. We learned how to create image rollover graphics in Chapter 4: here we will learn how to insert them into Dreamweaver. In Chapter 4, we learned how the stages of the rollover image should all be layers of the same Photoshop file to assure that the transition in the rollover is seamless. In addition to learning how to insert them into Dreamweaver, we will also examine when the images are *not* the same and the ramifications of this scenario.

If you would like to practice this as it is explained, you will need to add the six images—*hampton_dn.jpg, hampton_up.jpg, portsmouth_dn.jpg, portsmouth_up.jpg, rye_dn.jpg,* and *rye_up.jpg*—located in the *rollover_images* folder in the *Chapter_11PracticeFiles* folder to the *images* folder of the SampleSite. (Do not add the *error_sample.jpg* for now.) Now, add three new pages to the *pages* folder of this site, with the following names: *hampton_page.html, portsmouth_page.html,* and *rye_page.html.* Save and close each one after creating it. Lastly, create one more page named *rollover_page.html.* Assign a background color of #BBD5E8 to it, save this page, and keep it open because the rollover images will be added to this page. (During this practice, it will not be necessary to add a title, keywords, and description text to these pages. However, remember that you must start each page of a real site with these critical steps.)

Add a table with 3 rows, 2 columns, a width of 750 pixels, and zero for its cell padding, spacing, and border in the Table dialog box. Center the table after it is inserted onto the page. Drag to select all three rows in the left column of the table and change their widths to 300 pixels, because this is the width of each of the rollover images that will be added to these cells. Although this can be done at any time, it is easiest to assign the width if it is known before adding the images. (The corresponding three rows on the right would typically hold applicable body content. However, we will not be adding any body content in this exercise.) Both stages of a rollover are added at the same time through a special Insert Rollover Image dialog box. Click to place the I-beam inside the cell you want to add the rollover into first, then access the Insert Rollover Image dialog box either by choosing Insert>Image Objects>Rollover Image, or by choosing Rollover Image from the Images pop-up menu of the Common tab of the Insert panel. After you are in the dialog box, the options are as shown in **FIGURE 11-8**.

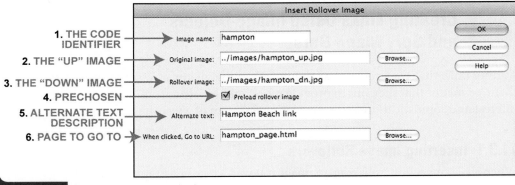

1. THE CODE IDENTIFIER
2. THE "UP" IMAGE
3. THE "DOWN" IMAGE
4. PRECHOSEN
5. ALTERNATE TEXT DESCRIPTION
6. PAGE TO GO TO

FIGURE 11-8 Insert Rollover Image dialog box.

1. This is an identifier for the rollover code, a word with no special characters added.
2. This is the initial up state of the rollover that the visitor will see upon arriving at the page.
3. This is the image that you want to appear when the visitor rolls over the up state.
4. This option is prechosen by default, and assures that the rollover navigation will display quickly in the visitor's browser because it is preloaded.
5. This is the identifying accessibility alternate text for the rollover.
6. Browse to locate the page you want the rollover navigation to take your visitor to when clicked.

After you have assigned the properties shown in Figure 11-8 to the hampton rollover, you can repeat the steps for the rye and portsmouth rollovers, respectively, in the second and third rows of the left column, and then save the page. You may want to try using the opposite access method for the Insert Rollover Image dialog box when inserting the rye rollover to decide which method works best for you. The final look should echo **FIGURE 11-9** when viewed in a browser with the Rye Beach image in the rollover state.

So, what about the image in the folder called *error_sample.jpg*? Delete the *hampton.jpg* graphic from the table on the *rollover_page.html*. You will notice that when you do that, both the up and over states are automatically deleted. Reinsert the rollover using the *hampton_up.jpg* for the original image, but substitute the *error_sample.jpg* for its rollover image (browse to locate it inside the *Chapter_11PracticeFiles* folder). Save and preview the page. Ouch! Instead of the seamless transition that the other two rollovers have, the image "jumps" because *error_sample.jpg* was purposely created a few pixels different in size from the original state, and it is forced to adjust to the allotted space defined by the up state when viewed in a browser. By building the rollovers on separate layers of the same file as you learned in Chapter 4, you will prevent this error from happening to you.

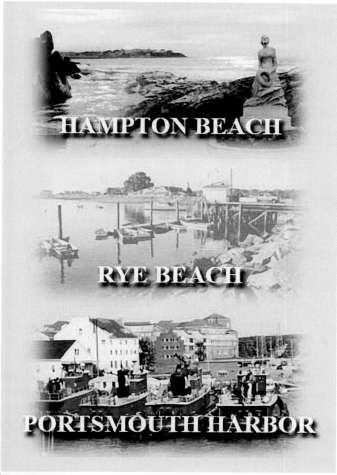

FIGURE 11-9 Rollover sample.

11.3.2 Inserting a Navigation Bar in CS3 and CS4

As introduced in Chapter 4, navigation bars allow you to use graphics to insert up to four states of interactivity for each button included in a horizontal or vertical navigational scheme. Now it's time to learn how a multi-state navigation bar is added to a page.

When adding a navigation bar to a page, it is easiest to place it inside a cell of a table designed to accommodate the navigation bar's vertical and horizontal final space requirements based on size. With the I-beam flashing inside the chosen cell, the options to insert a navigation bar are in the same locations as the options for adding image rollovers: either by using Insert>Image Objects>Navigation Bar, or by choosing Navigation Bar from the Images pop-up menu of the Common tab of the

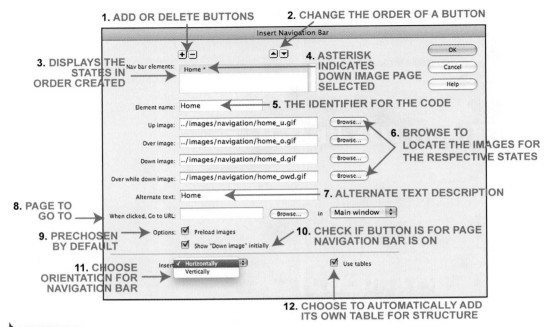

FIGURE 11-10 Insert Navigation Bar dialog box.

Insert panel. From either location you will be brought to the Insert Navigation Bar dialog box. Because navigation bars allow up to four states of interactivity for each navigation link you have designed for your site, the dialog box is more complex than the Insert Rollover Image dialog box. However, after you have used it a few times, it is substantially easier than it initially appears. **FIGURE 11-10** details the options when inserting a navigation bar onto a page.

1. After creating the first button, click the plus icon to add each button to your navigation bar, or with one selected, click the minus icon to remove it.

2. These arrows allow you to select an existing button in the *Nav bar elements* area to adjust its order within the bar (top to bottom, or left to right).

3. Each time you add another button to the navigation bar, its name is displayed here.

4. When you check the *Show "Down Image" initially* option (#10) for a link, the asterisk identifies the assigned page.

5. This is the identifier for the particular button you are creating: after it's typed here, it automatically displays in the *Nav bar elements* option (#3).

6. Click the browse button each time to locate the image to assign to the respective button.

7. Assign alternate text for the button here.

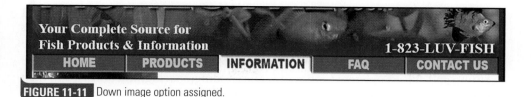

FIGURE 11-11 Down image option assigned.

8. Browse to locate the link page destination for the button.

9. Just as with rollover images, this option is prechosen by default and assures that the navigation bar will display quickly in the visitor's browser because it will have been preloaded.

10. This is an important feature that can be confusing. A navigation bar must be inserted on each page of the site, with the links assigned on each page as well. If the *Show "Down image" initially* option has been checked, the down state will display automatically when a visitor arrives at that page to identify it. This option must be assigned uniquely using this dialog box for every page, but only when you are selecting the options for the specific page on which you are currently creating the navigation bar. **FIGURE 11-11** shows the effect when this information page is viewed in a browser. Notice that the blue on white "down" state of the navigation button indicates that this is the active open page.

11. Set the orientation of the navigation bar here.

12. If you would like the buttons to be automatically placed in individual cells of the navigation's own nested table, select the *Use tables* option.

Do you need all four states for a navigation bar to work? The answer to that question is no. Obviously an up and over is needed, so that your visitors know they can access another location using that navigation. However, as a minimum, you could create a navigation bar using just those two by assigning the *over* state also to the *down* and *over while down* states. You would need to assign the *When clicked go to URL*, and may want to assign the *Show "Down image" initially* option, but the navigation would work with just those two. That is why CS5 users can create almost the same final browser look by inserting multiple consecutive image rollovers if desired. When viewing Figure 11-11, if the user rolled over the information page's identifying *down* state, the *over while down* state would appear as shown in **FIGURE 11-12**.

FIGURE 11-12 Over while down state.

If you are working in either CS3 or CS4, the images used to create the navigation bars shown in Figures 11-11 and 11-12 are included in the *Chapter11_PracticeFiles* folder in a folder named *Navigation*. Feel free to create a new page in the sample site named *information_page.html*. Create a table that is 750 pixels wide, with one column and at least one row, with zero for its padding, spacing, and border, and then center the table after it has been inserted. Practice adding and testing the navigation buttons when you roll over them. You can even choose to assign some of the buttons to link to other pages we have created thus far in the SampleSite if desired. Be sure to assign the *Show "Down image" initially* when inserting the information button to take advantage of its slick feature. You may even want to try adding the navigation bar once with and once without the *Use tables* option selected.

Modifying an Existing Navigation Bar   After a navigation bar has been inserted on a page, it can be modified and updated at any time by choosing Modify>Navigation Bar. In the dialog box that follows, changes can be made to any of its original options, except its orientation and whether it was built with or without the use of a table.

Inserting a Spry Menu Bar   As you searched the Web, you probably visited websites that had navigation that expanded dynamically when you rolled over it, sliding out either vertically or horizontally to provide more link page selections. As websites have continued to provide more information to their visitors, the need for easy access to more and more pages within a site has become critical. These slide out style of menus have become an extremely popular solution to this demand.

FIGURE 11-13 exemplifies the typical implementation of this type of navigation. When you hover over any of the main navigation items across the top of the page, a variety of additional links become available for selection.

FIGURE 11-13   Saddleback Ski Area. (Courtesy of Saddleback Ski Area, http://www.saddlebackmaine.com.)

Styled and activated using CSS and JavaScript, the Dreamweaver Spry Menu Bar feature makes it easy for you to create this type of navigation by writing the JavaScript code for you and preassigning CSS formatting for the menu's initial sizes, colors, and font properties, allowing it to be customized by you, the designer, as needed. Here we will learn how to insert one. Later, after we have learned CSS, we will learn how to tailor the menu to the unique design needs of the site where it is inserted.

Let's add a Spry Menu Bar to the index page of the SampleSite website. With SampleSite active in the Files panel, open its *index.html* page. On this page, which contains a table with four rows, delete any content in its second row, directly below the winter headline graphic. With the I-Beam flashing within the table cell, choose to insert a Spry Menu Bar by any of the following methods: Insert>Layout Objects>Spry Menu Bar, choose Spry Menu Bar from the Layout category of the Insert Panel, or choose Spry Menu Bar from the Spry category of the Insert Panel. After it is inserted, you will enter the Spry Menu Bar dialog box to choose whether you want to insert either a vertical or horizontal navigation bar. In our case, we will choose to insert a horizontal navigation bar.

The navigation bar is inserted into the area provided with a cyan tab above it in the upper-left area identifying the menu bar. As you can see, the navigation bar by default contains four tabs prenamed *Item 1*, *Item 2*, *Item 3*, and *Item 4*. When you click on the cyan tab, its properties can be customized in the Property inspector, as shown in **FIGURE 11-14**.

1. Here, Dreamweaver will preassign a changeable identifying name for the code.

2. Any time your mouse rolls over the menu bar, this cyan tab will become visible. When it has been selected, link properties for the menu bar become active in the Property inspector for assigning and editing.

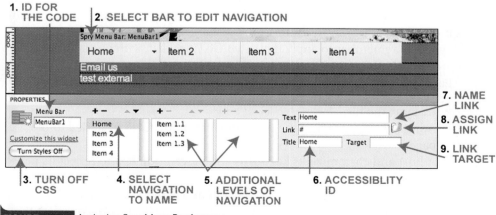

FIGURE 11-14 Assigning Spry Menu Bar features.

3. Spry menus are actually just sophisticated lists. If you click this button, the navigation will remain as designed when viewed in a browser; however, you will be able to see and edit its list hierarchy.

4. When you select an item, you are able to rename it. The plus and minus icons allow you to add and delete navigation as needed. The up and down arrows allow you to change the order in which the navigation will display in the bar.

5. Two additional levels of navigation are available, which follow the same format for adding, deleting, and changing the order of the links.

6. An identifying name here provides an accessibility tooltip when viewed in a browser.

7. When one of the items is selected, the link name for it can be customized.

8. Here, you can browse to locate the destination page for the selected link.

9. If left blank, the link target will be assigned the default (_Self).

Feel free to assign various pages of the SampleSite to link to, including adding one more menu item to the list, so that there are five main menu items, with each one containing as many submenu items as you would like to add. Then, test the navigation in a browser. When you save, you will be informed that dependent files are required for uploading. We will learn all about dependent files in Chapter 16.

Don't like the gray background, font, etc., of the bar? Its color, along with the font properties of the bar and its width, are all customized using CSS …, just a few chapters to go before we learn how!

 Building Additional Pages from an Existing Page

At any phase of the construction of an index page, you can also begin to build the site's link pages from it by using the Save As command, renaming the pages, and saving them into the appropriate *pages* folder of the site. Creating link pages using this method is a great way to continue to build a site, as long as after the page is created, you still remember to apply the 1, 2, 3 Go Checklist, with one additional step required: navigation modification.

Each link page created using the Save As command will need to be modified:

- Rename the file.
- Adjust its title to reflect the new information that will be added to the page.
- Adjust and customize its keywords and description text to reflect its new content.
- Adjust its navigation to reflect the links and active page. Use the Modify> Navigation Bar command if you created one in CS3 or CS4, or select the

Spry Menu Bar's cyan tab to activate its items in the Property inspector to assign/modify the links as needed.

After you have completed these steps, you can begin to customize each link page to reflect its unique content.

 Inserting Media

We have added some interactivity to our pages thus far by learning to create rollovers, navigation bars, and Spry Menu Bars. Shockwave® Flash® (SWF) files have become very popular as a way to add yet another dimension of activity to a web page. SWF files require the Adobe® Flash® Player in order for them to be viewed in a browser. However, if an SWF file has been added to a page in Dreamweaver, and a visitor's browser does not have the needed player, the visitor will be prompted to download the update, with a link to the Adobe site automatically provided by Dreamweaver.

11.5.1 Inserting SWF Files

To insert an SWF file onto a page with the I-beam flashing, choose Insert>Media>SWF (or Insert>Media>Flash when using CS3), or choose the SWF option from the Media pop-up menu of the Common tab of the Insert panel. Using either method, if the file is not already in the root folder, you will be prompted to locate it and asked if you want to add it to your active site root folder. If it was already in your root folder, you could also simply drag it to the page from the Files panel, or if using the Assets panel, click the SWF/Flash icon first, then select the file and click the Assets' Insert button, or simply drag it to the page. When the accessibility dialog box opens, you will notice that it is different from what we have seen thus far. The name *Title* here assigns an accessibility name for the media object, just as alt text does when inserting other types of images. After the SWF has been inserted, it's just a gray box! No, not really, that's just how it looks until it is previewed.

Assigning SWF Properties   Let's add an SWF file to a page to learn how to assign properties to it. Open the *hampton_page.html* page of your SampleSite and click to place the I-beam on the page. Insert the *flash_sample.swf* file located in the *Chapter_11PracticeFiles* folder. After it is inserted, with the selection handles activated, you will notice that the Property inspector reflects some familiar features, and some options specific to SWF files, as shown in **FIGURE 11-15**.

1. If you created an SWF file for a site yourself, you would have created it at the final required size. If not, you can use these entry fields to adjust its size. An icon appears when you change these dimensions, allowing you to click it to return to the original imported dimensions. (The arrow to return to the original size is available only in CS4 and CS5; however, the process can be reversed using History in CS3, or simply reinserted if needed.)

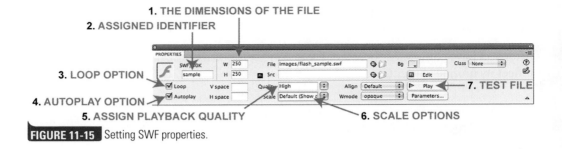

FIGURE 11-15 Setting SWF properties.

2 Just as a code identifier was used for rollovers, an identifier is required for SWF files as well. Assign an appropriate name to this sample movie as shown.

3. Here, you can set whether you want the animation to continue to keep looping and playing, or play once and stop. The default option is to loop. However, depending on your animation and its future viewers, it may be more effective to play only once.

4. Unless changed, this default option will begin the animation automatically after the page has loaded in the visitor's browser.

5. The quality will default to high, relating to the processing speed settings that define the appearance of the movie when viewed.

6. If you have designed your own SWF, you can leave this at the default *Show all* setting. The other two options reflect how you want it to display if forced to fit into a smaller area that is not proportional to the dimensions of the file.

7. When you imported the SWF file, you probably noticed, to your dismay, that it does not show/play automatically in Dreamweaver. You can click the Play button to test its appearance on the page before previewing it in a browser.

As you already know, pages cannot be viewed in a browser until they are saved. The first time you save a page containing an SWF file on it, a dialog box will warn you about dependent files. Simply click OK for now. As previously mentioned, we will learn about dependent files when learning to upload a website in Chapter 16.

To Loop or Not to Loop   The decision about looping must be based on the movie, your audience, and your page design requirements. Let's look at a couple of sites that exemplify the application of variations of this option. The Xtreme Toyz website homepage shown in **FIGURE 11-16** has an "X" in "Xtreme Toyz" that continues to pulsate as you view this and all pages of the site, drawing attention to its headline graphic and the bikes displayed in it.

The Stowe Mountain Resort website in **FIGURE 11-17** incorporates an SWF movie with a different twist. On its home page only, when the page opens, a small tag is

FIGURE 11-16 Xtreme Toyz home page. (Courtesy of Xtreme Toyz, http://www.xtreme-toyz.com.)

visible on the right side of the page, which expands to the left to display additional information while the visitor is watching. This movie does not loop; after it has expanded, it remains stationary. However, if the visitor links back to the home page from a link page, the home page displays a different background photograph, but the same SWF movie will slide out again from the right side of the page and remain stationary after it is fully extended.

 Be careful if you are creating your own SWF files in Adobe Flash: native Flash files use the extension .fla. Dreamweaver will be able to import an .swf copy of the movie; it does not recognize native .fla files. If you create them before defining the site, always be sure to keep the .fla files in the master umbrella folder with your original graphics for editing purposes, but do not add them to the root folder of the site.

FIGURE 11-17 Stowe Mountain Resort home page. (Courtesy of Stowe Mountain Resort, http://www.stowe.com.)

11.5.2 Inserting Video Files

Just as an SWF file requires the Adobe Flash Player to display, video files also require plug-ins to display in a browser. Video formats that can be inserted into Dreamweaver include: Windows Media®, RealMedia®, QuickTime®, and Flash video (FLV). Because the FLV format requires the same Adobe Flash Player as an SWF file and most visitors already have the necessary plug-in to view them, it has become a popular choice

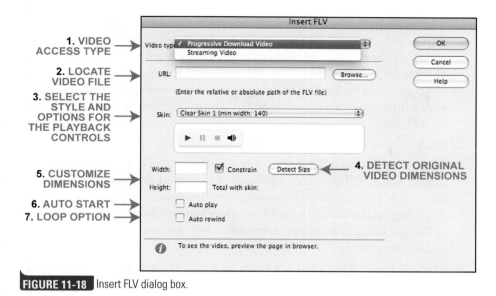

FIGURE 11-18 Insert FLV dialog box.

for web designers, and the one we will focus on when learning to import video in this chapter.

Video files can be saved simply as SWF files and imported, with the ability to assign the same property options as you learned in the SWF section of this chapter. However, the FLV format contains more sophisticated viewing options, providing a more professional appearance to the movie and offering your visitors more control over its playback. Let's compare the two formats and learn how to assign properties to the FLV format using your SampleSite.

With your SampleSite active in the Files panel, let's create a new page, saving it as *video_sample.html* in the *pages* folder of the site. Although we won't add keywords and description text to it, let's practice titling it as *The Difference Between SWF and FLV*. After you have titled the page, with the I-beam flashing, choose Insert>Media>SWF (or Insert>Media>Flash in CS3), or choose the SWF option from the Media pop-up menu of the Common tab of the Insert panel. Add the *fish_video.swf*, file located in the *Chapter_11PracticeFiles* folder, to the page. After it is inserted, we will leave the default options in the Property inspector for this movie. Now, add a hard return to create a new paragraph, and choose Insert>Media>FLV (or Insert>Media>Flash Video in CS3), or choose it from the Media pop-up menu of the Common tab of the Insert panel, and locate the *fish_video.flv* video also located in the *Chapter_11PracticeFiles* folder. Before the video is inserted, the Insert FLV dialog box opens to assign the initial properties to the video, as shown in **FIGURE 11-18**, that we will follow to insert the *fish_video.flv*.

1. This pop-up menu allows you to choose the download method for the movie. Progressive Download is the default option, which literally progressively downloads the video onto the visitor's computer, allowing the video to begin while the balance of the movie finishes downloading. It offers quick downloading of quality video without the additional server requirements of the Streaming Video option. Therefore, it will be the one we will use.

2. Click to browse to locate the FLV file you want to import.

3. These skins are cool playback control options, offering various degrees of user control of the video playback. A variety of designs are available from its pop-up menu, with a sample of the chosen style displayed. Applying each one individually and then testing the page in a browser will allow you to decide which option is best for your movie and audience needs.

4. Click this button to have Dreamweaver detect the original dimensions of the video.

5. After the dimensions have been recognized by clicking the Detect Size button, if Constrain has been checked, when you type in one new dimension here, the other one will be calculated and listed automatically. With both the Detect Size Constrain and options selected, let's test that by typing in 300 pixels for the new width and noticing that the corresponding height changes to 225 pixels.

6. If checked, the video will begin to play automatically when the visitor arrives at the page containing it; let's select it.

7. Just as you can choose whether you want an SWF file to loop, here you can determine that option when importing an FLV file as well. To loop or not to loop? You decide!

After it is inserted, but before learning to edit it, save and preview the page in a browser. You will immediately recognize the advantages provided by inserting the file as an FLV vs. an SWF file due to its visitor interactivity flexibility.

Editing Inserted FLV Files   After the FLV file is inserted onto the page, when selected by the Select tool, almost all of the same options assigned in the Insert FLV dialog box can be changed as needed in the Property inspector, with only a couple of differences. After the video access type has been chosen (e.g., Progressive Download), it cannot be changed without reinserting the video. The only other differences are in the Property inspector: the need for an identifier for the code just as an SWF file requires, and the option to assign a CSS class, which we will learn to do in Chapter 14.

To delete an FLV file from a page, select it on the page, and click the Delete/Backspace key.

For CS3 Users

There are two minor differences regarding the insertion and deletion of FLV files in CS3 vs. CS4 and CS5. When inserting an FLV file into CS3, the Insert Flash Video dialog box has one extra section at the bottom of it, as shown in FIGURE 11-19.

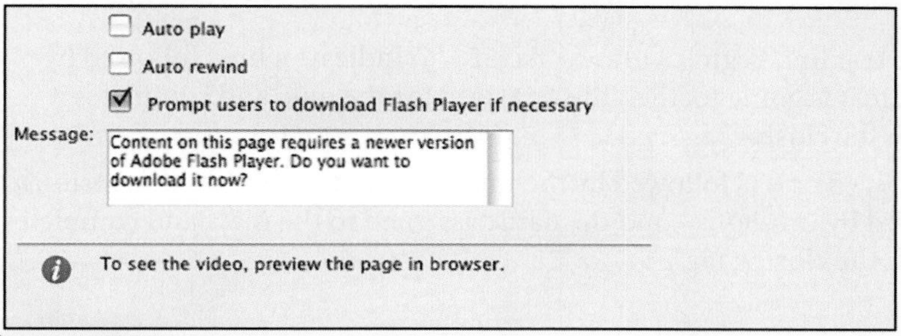

FIGURE 11-19 Inserting an FLV in CS3.

Although the rest of the dialog box is the same, just below the *Auto rewind* checkbox is another checkbox to prompt your visitors to download the Flash player if needed to view the video. Although a default message displays in the Message text box, it can be highlighted and customized according to your needs. In CS4 and CS5, Dreamweaver has built the version detection feature into the insertion code for you, making this message unnecessary. In CS4 and CS5, when you delete an FLV, the code is deleted with it automatically.

However, when you delete an FLV in CS3, you must also delete the detection code that provides the prompt to your visitors. Whether it is before or after you actually delete the FLV, you must choose Commands> Remove Flash Video Detection to assure that the code is also removed from the page. This command only becomes active if you have inserted an FLV and will remain active even after the video has been deleted and the page has been saved with the changes, until you choose the command to remove the code.

11.6 A Look at the Code in Split View: Text Links, Image Links, and Image Maps

FIGURE 11-20 details the code Dreamweaver wrote for a link page similar to the SampleSite's *link_page.html* that we used to practice the image map feature, with a text link and image link added to it for code demonstration purposes. Instead of showing the entire page in split view, the illustration focuses on the part of the page that incorporates links.

1. The text link begins with <a href= to indicate a link, followed by where it is going to, then the text used for the link, and completes it with the closing tag </a>.

2. <img src= is followed by the image, its alt text, and its dimensions, followed by usemap= and the name assigned to the map, and completes it with the closing tag />.

1. DEFINES THE LINKED PAGE AND TEXT LINK

2. DEFINES SOURCE FOR MAP

3. DEFINES MAP NAME

4. COORDINATES FOR HOTSPOT AND LINK DESTINATION

5. CLOSES THE MAP

6. EMAIL TEXT LINK

7. IMAGE USED AS A LINK

```
36    <p>Go to <a href="link_page.html">link page</a>. </p>
37    <p><img src="images/fish.jpg" alt="Fish Photo" width="432" height="288" border="0" usemap=
      "#anatomy" />
38      <map name="anatomy" id="anatomy">
39        <area shape="poly" coords="241,156,235,115,125,111,240,158" href="#" alt="pectoral
      fin" />
40        <area shape="circle" coords="247,86,19" href="#" alt="eye" />
41        <area shape="rect" coords="297,87,335,119" href="link_page.html" alt="mouth" />
42        <area shape="rect" coords="35,105,136,211" href="#" alt="tail fin" />
43        <area shape="poly" coords="235,25,169,10,134,38,62,56,137,95,166,58,235,24" href="#"
      alt="dorsal fin" />
44      </map>
45    </p>
46      <a href="mailto:vellen@ugraphique.mv.com">Please email your comments to us at
      Fishluvrz.</a></p>
47      <a href="pages/link_page.html"><img src="images/lupines.jpg" alt="Lupine Photo" name=
      "lupines" width="432" height="288" border="0" id="lupines" /></a></p>
48    </body>
```

FIGURE 11-20 Split view links.

3. This identifies the map name and id opening map element.

4. This code identifies the coordinates for the hotspots of the image map. Each one begins with `<area shape=`, then lists its coordinates followed by `href=` where it links to, its assigned alt text, and its closing tag `/>`.

5. After all area shapes have been defined for the image, the element is closed with the `</map>` tag.

6. The email text link begins with `<a href=` to indicate a link, followed by where it is going to (beginning with the `mailto:` email identifier), then the text used for the link, and completes it with the closing tag `</a>`.

7. The use of an image as a link begins with `<a href=` to indicate a link, followed by where it is going to, followed by the image to be used as the link, its alt text, its dimensions, and completes it with the closing tag `</a>`.

11.7 What We Have Learned

A link provides the visitor with an interactive tool for navigation. In this chapter, we learned how to create several navigational tools: a text hyperlink, an anchor link, an email link, an image link, a hotspot link, an image rollover, a navigation bar, and a Spry Menu Bar. We also learned how to add more link pages to a site by reconfiguring an existing page rather than starting from scratch and how to update their navigation after they are created.

Our pages were brought to an even higher level of sophistication through the addition of SWF and FLV media files, including the incorporation of customized playback options relative to our future visitors.

11.8 Reinforcing Your Knowledge

Project

1. Be sure your FishluvrzSite website is the active site in the Files panel and open your *index.html* page.

2. Highlight HOME in the footer navigation and apply the hash symbol (#) for its link destination. Use this same symbol for the link destination for each of the rest of the footer navigation links, until we have created the destination pages for the links.

Project (continued)

3. Choose the Expanded Tables mode from the Layout category of the Insert panel to easily identify the cells of the tables. Place an I-beam inside the second row of the top table and choose to add a Spry Menu Bar to this page using any one of the methods you have learned. In the dialog box that follows, select Horizontal for the layout style of the menu bar. Assign the properties as shown in **FIGURE 11-21**. Note that for the products and contact navigation categories, each one must begin with the main navigation added in capital letters in the far left column first, followed by adding the submenu navigation items as shown. For the submenu Fish under the Products main menu, add *Fish* in its Text and Title categories and use *Contact* for the Text and Title categories for the Contact Us submenu under the Contact main menu.

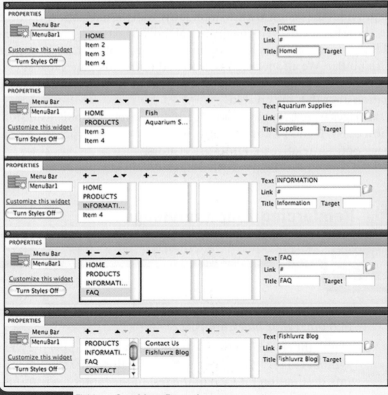

FIGURE 11-21 Fishluvrz Spry Menu Bar options.

Project (continued)

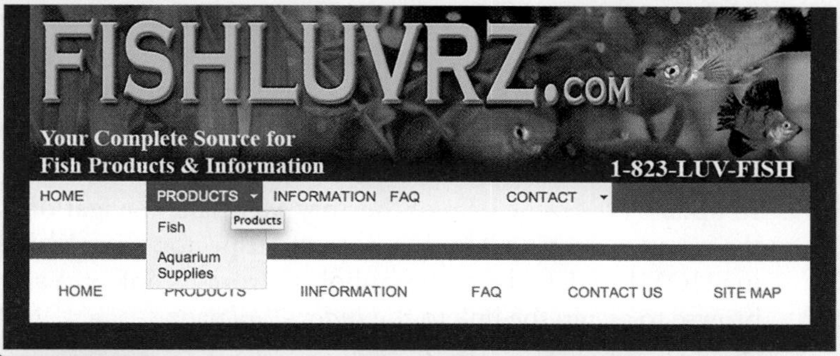

FIGURE 11-22 Spry Menu Bar navigation in browser.

4. Save and preview the page. Your navigation should display as shown in **FIGURE 11-22** (note that if the Contact option were clicked, its sub-menu options of Contact Us and Fishluvrz Blog would slide down from it, just as the Products ones do).

5. Choose Save As and rename the page *information_page.html*. Be sure that you are saving it into the *pages* folder of your FishluvrzSite website and choose to update the links when prompted.

6. Before continuing to build the *information_page.html* page, let's return to the *index.html* page and change the headline of just the index page to a moving one. We will be keeping all of the link page headlines static. Select and delete its static headline. Choose Insert>Media>SWF and locate the *fishluvrz_moving_headline.swf* file located in the *Chapter_11PracticeFiles* folder. Assign an appropriate title in the accessibility dialog box when prompted. After it's inserted, assign it to Autoplay, but uncheck the Loop option and then save the page. Remember to click OK regarding the dependent files prompt when saving; we will understand its importance in Chapter 16. It is time to test this interactivity in a browser. Enjoy!

7. Now, close the *index.html* page and open the *information_page. html*. Make the following beginning page adjustments:

   ▪ Change its title to *Fish Information Provided for You by Fishluvrz-We Know Fish!*

   ▪ Change its keywords to *fish health problems, regulating aquarium PH levels, fish facts, fish breeding, fish foods and feeding*

   ▪ Change its description text to *The fish facts you need to know provided by Fishluvrz: your complete source for fish products and information.*

Project (continued)

8. Let's add a hotspot to take our visitors back to the *index.html* page. Often, clicking the headline of a link page will return a visitor to the home page of a site. Select the headline first, then select the Rectangle Hotspot tool and trace the company name: *Fishluvrz.com*. Assign it to link back to the *index.html* page.

9. To update the Home item of the Spry Menu Bar navigation, select the menu to activate it in the Property inspector. After highlighting HOME, delete the hash symbol (#) from its link area and then browse to assign the link to the *index.html* page.

10. Use this page to choose the Save As command one more time for now, naming the new link page *contact_page.html*. Now, you can update the link to the information page by following the same steps you used in step 9 for the HOME item. What about the FAQ and products link pages? We will build the FAQ page using AP Divs in Chapter 12 and build the products page in Chapter 14 as part of our introduction to CSS. Your Files panel, at this point, should look like **FIGURE 11-23**.

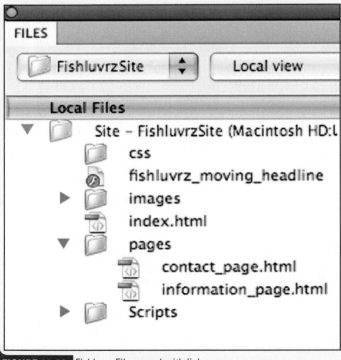

FIGURE 11-23 Fishluvrz Files panel with link pages.

Project (continued)

11. Returning to the *information_page.html*, we can also assign some of the footer navigation to its final destination now: assign the HOME link to point to the *index.html* page and assign the CONTACT US link to go to the new *contact_page.html* page.

12. Now, we will reconfigure the page's table to accommodate the unique content requirements of the information page. Be sure that you are working specifically on the *information_page.html* page to complete the following steps:

    - Delete rows three, four, and five of the top table.
    - Select this table with its remaining two rows so that its selection handles are visible, press the right arrow key to ensure that the I-beam is at the end of the table, and insert a new table below it. It will be helpful to do this in Expanded Tables mode.
    - Define the new table with 1 row, 2 columns, 100% for its width, and set its cell padding, spacing, and border to zero.

13. After it's inserted, assign the Vertical alignment to Top and set the background of both cells of this new table to white. Select the left cell only and change its width to 210 pixels.

14. Nest another table inside the left cell. Make the new table 6 rows, 1 column, 200 pixels for its width, and zero for its cell padding, spacing, and border. Assign an alignment of left to the table after it has been inserted (or leave it at the default alignment, which is left) and assign the Vertical alignment to Top for all of its cells. Insert the six *fish_montage* slices you saved into your *images* folder sequentially into its six cells from top to bottom, assigning corresponding alt text for each slice. If you remembered to have vertical alignment Top assigned to the cell that the nested table of slices has been added to and to the cells of the nested table, they should now appear seamless when viewed in a browser. We assigned the left cell a width that is 10 pixels wider than its nested content to create the appearance of a margin between the images on the left and the text that will be added to the cell on the right. In Chapter 14, we will learn to create margins by using CSS.

15. Open the *information_text.doc* file located in the *Chapter_11PracticeFiles* folder in Microsoft Word and copy it to the Clipboard. (If you do not have Microsoft Word available, a copy of the text in .rtf format is also provided.) After you have done that, exit Microsoft Word, return to the *information_page.html* page of

Project (continued)

your FishluvrzSite website, and place an I-beam in the right cell of the table you inserted below your navigation. Choose *Paste Special* and then select the third option, *Text with structure plus basic formatting* for the pasting option, followed by also checking *Clean Up Word Paragraph Spacing* located below the four pasting options. This feature assures that no additional paragraph spacing will be added automatically when the text is pasted.

After the text has been imported onto the page, use the Return/Enter key to create a new paragraph after *The fish facts you need to know* and one after *Types of foods and feeding schedules* in the same top section. Add one after each descriptive paragraph below it, except for the last paragraph. (If you used a text editor other than Microsoft Word, choose the second option in the Paste Special dialog box, then refer to Figure 11-25 to preview where you will need to apply the *B* for Bold option in the Property inspector to each topic heading and insert additional paragraph returns as needed to match the sample provided.)

16. Click inside the first line of text at the top of the page: *The fish facts you need to know*. Assign Heading 1 to the text either from the Format>Paragraph format menu or from the Format pop-up menu under the HTML tab in the Property inspector.

17. Insert an anchor icon before the word *Aquarium* in the first description paragraph below the *Types of foods and feeding schedules* line in the top section of the page. Assign an appropriate one-word identifier for the anchor and then repeat the process in front of the first word in each successive paragraph. After you have inserted all of them, highlight each topic in the top section one at a time and link it to the corresponding anchor paragraph.

18. Lastly, we will add convenience to our future visitors with a *Back to Top* option. Add the words at the end of each description paragraph, then add the anchor to the left of *The fish facts you need to know* heading, and complete the process by linking each *Back to Top* individually to the same anchor at the top of the page.

19. Before saving and previewing your page with all of its links, check to be sure that you do not have the I-beam flashing below the last paragraph, *Types of foods and feeding schedules*, so that you can tighten the distance between this table and the one below it if necessary. Your page in Dreamweaver should look like **FIGURE 11-24**.

When viewed in a browser your information page should resemble **FIGURE 11-25**.

Types of foods and feeding schedules
Lorem ipsum dolor sit amet, consetetur sadipscing elitr, sed diam
tempor invidunt ut labore et dolore magna aliquyam erat, sed diam
dolore magna aliquyam erat, sed diam voluptua. At vero eos et ac
dolores et ea rebum. Back to Top

| TS | INFORMATION | FAQ | CONTACT US |

FIGURE 11-24 Tight tables.

FIGURE 11-25 Information page for Fishluvrz site.

Building Your Own Website

1. Launch Dreamweaver and select your site in the Files panel's pop-up menu. Open your *index.html* page. Click inside the cell you created to hold your navigation to add an I-beam and then choose to insert a Spry Menu Bar or a navigation bar. If inserting a navigation bar, locate your button state images in the *images* folder of your site and insert the navigation buttons as learned, remembering that your Home button must have the *Show "Down image" initially* option checked. Remember that at this stage, you should leave the *When clicked go to URL* option blank for your other link pages until you have added them to your site. After you have created the navigation for this page and exited its dialog box, save your *index.html* page and preview it in a browser.

   If adding a Spry Menu Bar, follow the directions provided in step 3 of the Reinforcing Your Knowledge section, adding your personal number of menu items and submenus as needed.

2. After the page is saved, choose Save As, and save a copy of this page into your *pages* folder named as one of your link pages.

3. Return to your *index.html* page and choose to update its navigation to reflect the addition of the link page. If using a navigation bar, in the Modify Navigation Bar dialog box, select the link page you just created and browse to select it in the *When clicked go to URL* section. If using a Spry Menu Bar, update both the new page and the *index.html* page to reflect the specific page for the link destination.

4. Highlight your footer navigation words individually and assign a text link to their corresponding link pages. Assign the actual link address to the page you just created, but use the hash symbol (#) when creating the links to all other link pages for now.

5. Close your *index.html* page now and reopen the link page you created. Continue the 1, 2, 3 Go Checklist by changing the title of the page, adjusting the keywords as needed, changing the description text to reflect the specific content of the page, and updating its navigation.

6. Activate its footer navigation so that the page you are on is identified in the link option of the Property inspector with the hash symbol (#), but your *home* link is assigned to return visitors to your *index.html* page.

7. Add a link or hotspot link from your headline on this page to also link back to your *index.html* page.

8. Adjust/redesign your table as needed to insert the link page's unique content and then save your page. Don't worry if this page or any of the pages of your first site do not require anchor links on their pages. You know

how to create them now, so you will be able to use them when needed! Have text content that just doesn't look right on the page? Not to worry, we will learn lots of text formatting secrets in Chapter 14. You can enter the text you want on this page and learn to format it later, or enter images and hold off on the text content for now.

9. Return to your *index.html* page and choose to preview it in a browser. Test your navigation: click its link to the new link page you just created. Once there, test the link page's navigation by clicking back to your home page using your navigation bar, your footer navigation, and/or your hotspot!

This concludes the work with link pages for this chapter. We will learn to create pages using AP Divs in Chapter 12, opening additional possibilities for the construction of the remaining link pages of your site.

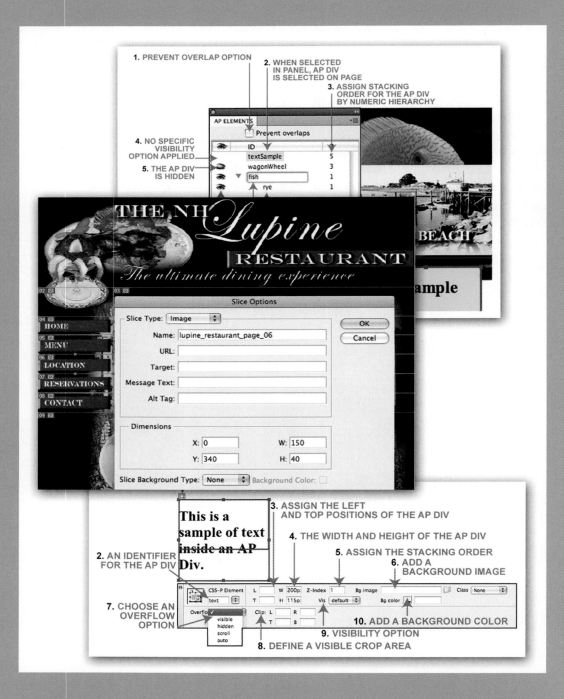

Creating a Page Using AP Divs for Layout

12

This chapter introduces another method of adding content to a web page: the use of AP Divs. While learning how to use them, we will employ familiar graphic designer tools (i.e., rulers, guides, grids, and tracing images) to assist in our layouts. Although AP Divs allow overlapping of page elements and stacking order for more design creativity, after learning how to use them in that manner, we will also learn how a page can be built using the "drawing" freedom of AP Divs, combined with the reliability of conventional tables. Lastly, CS3 users will learn how the drawing freedom experienced when using AP Divs can also be achieved through the Dreamweaver Layout mode, which was eliminated in CS4.

12.1   AP Divs for Page Layout

We have learned to create pages using tables, a tried and true web page design method that has stood the test of time because of its reliability across browsers and platforms. As a graphic designer, you may have been wondering whether there is any alternative to using tables or CSS to lay out a page—there is. To graphic artists entering web design, AP Divs offer familiar "containers" they can draw in any size or shape to insert text and images into, which can overlap with the wonderful "stacking order of creation" feature they are familiar with from other programs. This can be exciting and refreshing and, depending on your future audience, the ticket to creative layout freedom. However, audience is the issue here. Pages created using AP Divs may not render properly in older browsers; they can actually make a great visually aligned layout appear to have parts of the page overlapped when they should not, which can result in a page that no longer appears professional. So now what? This chapter will introduce the flexibility features of using AP Divs for layout purposes, then move on to a slick and steadfast method of creating a page by combining the drawing and layout freedom of AP Divs with the dependability of tables if your audience's needs demand it. After learning these skills, what happens once you know your audience? Design away! By having a clear grasp of your future audience's needs, you will have more design and layout options to add to your "graphic artist's web design toolbox" and be able to tailor your sites to the specific needs of the vast majority of your visitors.

12.1.1   The Basics of Using AP Divs

Chapter 14 will focus on utilizing CSS for text and image formatting, with an introduction to its use for positioning and page layout. However, for now, when you insert an AP Div on a page, Dreamweaver automatically generates CSS coding for the positioning of the element. The *AP* part of the name means *Absolute Position*. Another way to remember it is *Assigned Position*, because, as you will see, you can determine AP Div positions on a page by assigning values for their placement. The *Div* stands for *Division*. Thus, AP Divs create divisions (containers to insert content) with absolute or specifically assigned positions on a web page.

Creating AP Divs and Inserting Content   With your SampleSite the active site in the Files panel, create a new page and save it as *ap_sample.html* into the site's *pages* folder. (During this practice, it will not be necessary to add a title, keywords, and description text to this page. However, remember that you must start each page of a real site with these critical steps.) With this page open, let's add two AP Divs to the same page using two different methods.

Add the first one by choosing Insert>Layout Objects>AP Div. This method inserts an AP Div where the I-beam is flashing, with the default starting width of 200 pixels and height of 115 pixels, based on the Dreamweaver preferences that you can customize in the AP Elements category of the Dreamweaver Preferences dialog box. These are starting dimensions because, as you may guess, when it appears on the page, it has the familiar selection points that you can use to drag and reshape it. Keep the default size and location for now and click away to deselect it using the Select tool. Insert the second AP Div somewhere else on the page by choosing the Draw AP Div tool option in the Layout category of the Insert panel. Then, create a rectangular container by dragging the mouse from the upper-left corner of the rectangle to the lower-right corner of the rectangle.

When using the Draw AP Div option of the Layout category of the Insert panel, you can hold down the Command/Control key if consecutively drawing them to avoid having to select the tool each time. To use this handy feature, be sure to have the Command/Control key held down when you *choose* the tool, and continue to keep it held down until you are done drawing your consecutive AP Div containers.

Text content can be added to an AP Div by simply placing an I-beam inside the container and typing. In the first AP Div you created, type: *This is a sample of text inside an AP Div*. Assign Heading 1 to the text. Notice that the AP Div automatically adjusts its size to accommodate the larger text as needed; a blue line indicates its original height when the AP Div's selection points are visible.

If you are inserting an image instead of text into an AP Div, the methods you have learned for inserting images onto a page so far also work when inserting them into an AP Div. Using the Insert>Image command, selecting the Images icon of the Common category of the Insert panel, simply dragging the image from the *images* folder of the site in the Files panel, or dragging the image from the Images category of the Assets panel, insert the *fish.jpg* image into the second AP Div—the one you drew by selecting the Draw AP Div icon in the Layout category of the Insert panel. Because we assigned accessibility preferences for images, you will be prompted to assign appropriate alt text for the image before it will be added to the AP Div. After it's inserted, the AP Div will automatically enlarge if needed to accommodate the image, just as the first AP Div did when the text required more space, and it will also indicate the original dimensions with a blue line. (Notice that it enlarges right and down.) Don't see a blue line? Your original AP Div must have been large enough or larger than its content. If you do see a blue line, don't worry about it for now; we will understand its purpose when learning about the Property inspector for AP Divs.

Selecting, Moving, Aligning, and Deleting AP Divs   When the Select tool is clicked on the edge of an AP Div, its eight selection points become active with a familiar hand icon that comes to life for moving. When using the hand, you will need to drag an edge, not a selection point, to move the AP Div without changing its shape. When the AP Div is active, you will notice there is also another little rectangle sitting above the upper-left corner of the AP Div. When you click and drag this rectangular *mover* icon, you will be able to drag the AP Div and be guaranteed that you will not accidentally reshape the AP Div by dragging one of its selection points. A familiar graphic feature of moving an item using the arrow keys will work with a selected AP Div as well. Alignment, another typical graphics program option, can also be applied to AP Divs. Shift-click to select multiple AP Divs on a page and then choose Modify>Arrange to select the desired alignment from its menu options, with all the selected AP Divs aligning to the last one you highlight. Before we move on, feel free to try this with your two AP Divs on the page.

To delete an individual AP Div from a page when it has been activated with selection points, press the Backspace/Delete key. If you start structuring a page by drawing AP Div and decide you want to delete them all at once, you can choose Edit>Select All or Command/Control+A to select all of them: they will be outlined in blue without their selection points showing, but will still allow you to press the Backspace/Delete key to remove all of them.

Assigning Properties to an AP Div   **FIGURE 12-1** details the options available in the Property inspector when an AP Div is selected.

1. The mover rectangle and eight selection points indicate that the AP Div is currently selected.
2. An identifier for the AP Div is required for the code. With AP Divs, if you do not customize it, Dreamweaver will assign one automatically with the sequential names apDiv1, apDiv2, etc. Identifiers should be a word or word and number (but cannot start with the number) and avoid special characters. Identifiers can be highlighted and edited at any time in the Property inspector when the AP Div is selected.

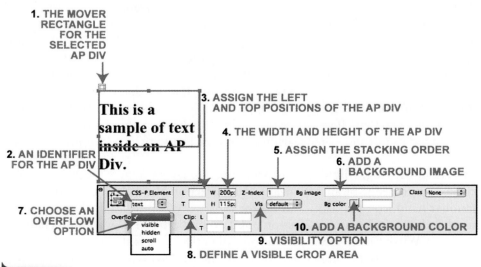

FIGURE 12-1 AP Div Property inspector.

3. The L for Left and T for Top define the absolute position of the AP Div on the page. In Figure 12-1, because the I-beam defaulted to the upper-left corner of the page, when this AP Div was inserted using the Insert>Layout Objects>AP Div command, these coordinates remained blank, reflecting the default page margin distance of Left 10 pixels and Top 15 pixels. Any pixel distances typed in the L and T options of the Property inspector will move the left and top edges of the box, respectively, to the new location. If you manually drag the AP Div, you will see these numbers dynamically update to reflect the new top and left location of the element. For precision, instead of moving an AP Div manually, or tweaking its position after it has been moved to its general location, typing in the required location coordinates here will ensure that your AP Div is exactly where you want it to be.

4. When an AP Div is selected on a page, its width and height are listed here and can be edited at any time. If you know a specific size you need, typing the pixel dimensions here is easier and more accurate than dragging the handles to define it. You can also use these data entry areas to adjust and tweak the size of an existing AP Div.

5. AP Divs can be overlapped if they are assigned as such. The stacking order of overlapping AP Divs is defined by their z-index: the higher the number, the higher the element is in the stacking order.

6. A background image can be added to an AP Div here. A default background image can also be assigned in the AP Elements category of the Dreamweaver Preferences dialog box.

7. This pop-up menu allows you to assign an overflow option. The blue line that appears in the text AP Div shown in Figure 12-1 indicates the original dimensions of the AP Div prior to adding the content, and signifies that the added content requires more room. It alerts you to define how you want Dreamweaver to handle it by choosing an overflow option here. Choosing *Auto* will assign the content to scroll if needed when viewed in a browser. Three additional options are also available:

   - **Visible:** Content will always display, no matter how much smaller the AP Div is than its content.
   - **Hidden:** Any content beyond the original dimensions of the AP Div is not displayed.
   - **Scroll:** A scroll bar is displayed when the AP Div is viewed in a browser, even if the content does not require it.

8. If you want inserted content to be only partially visible, you can define a left (L), top (T), right (R), and bottom (B) pixel dimension of visibility for the element, similar to *cropping* in other graphics programs. If you create your AP Divs to match their future content, they will not require clipping after the content is added.

9. This is not the same as the overflow option for visibility, which is used to display content that flows beyond the defined size of the AP Div. This feature will not only show or hide a selected AP Div while working on a page, it also enables AP Divs to be assigned behaviors with dynamic show/hide visibility capabilities that incorporate scripting, which are beyond the scope of this text. For our purposes, making a specific AP Div visible or hidden when working on a page will be chosen in the AP Elements panel using its eye icons.

10. A background color can be added to an AP Div here. A default background color can also be assigned in the AP Elements category of the Dreamweaver Preferences dialog box. If a default color is assigned in its preferences, it will apply to all new AP Divs; existing ones remain unaffected by the change.

Don't see the AP properties in the Property inspector when an image is selected? Be sure you are selecting the AP Div, not the image contained in it. The AP Div will still have a blue outline, but will not display its blue selection points if its content is selected instead of the actual AP Div container.

Now that we have explored the application of the Property inspector to AP Divs, let's understand the importance of the blue line when inserted content exceeds the original dimensions of an AP Div. Reselect the text AP Div you created using the Select tool to activate its selection points. In the Property inspector, choose *Auto* from the Overflow pop-up menu. The original size of the AP Div should appear to cut off the remaining text below the blue line; however, it will display with a scroll bar when viewed in a browser. **FIGURE 12-2** illustrates this option applied to both AP Divs. The second AP Div shown in this example created using the Draw AP Div option was drawn with a width of 250 pixels and a height of 150 pixels. The inserted image dimensions of the *fish.jpg* are 432 pixels for its width and 288 pixels for its height, requiring both vertical and horizontal scrolling when viewed in a browser if Auto is chosen for the overflow option.

Before continuing, feel free to experiment with the rest of these various overflow options to better understand their applications.

FIGURE 12-2 Overflow samples.

Trying to edit text content in an existing AP Div with the Scroll option applied to it? You must have Visible selected from the pop-up menu of the Overflow options in the Property inspector to have the I-beam appear for text.

Features of the AP Elements Panel   In addition to the Property inspector, AP Divs have additional control options in their own panel. If it is not currently visible, choose Window>AP Elements to display it, as shown in **FIGURE 12-3**. This panel has some similarities to the Photoshop Layers palette, with some distinct differences as well.

1. We have not explored the overlap feature yet. However, only when this box is not checked can you take advantage of the stacking order characteristic of AP Divs.

2. When an item is selected in the AP Elements panel, it is selected on the page. This can be particularly handy when trying to select an item buried in the stacking order.

3. Assign or change the stacking order of the AP elements.

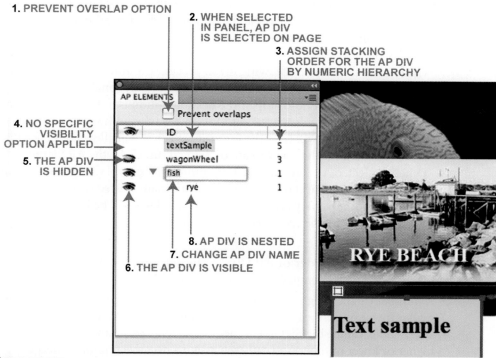

FIGURE 12-3 AP Elements panel.

4. The eye icons toggle sequentially when clicked, switching from *no eye* to *closed eye* and then to *open eye*. Contrary to Photoshop convention, when *no eye* appears next to an AP Div in the Elements panel, the AP Div is visible because it assumes the default visibility properties of the document page, which is defined as its *parent*. The *no eye* visibility selection is the default option (always visible), but this default can be changed in the AP Elements category of the Dreamweaver Preferences dialog box by selecting a different visibility from its pop-up menu: the change will be applied to all new AP Divs added after assigning the new visibility preference.

5. Choosing the *closed eye* will hide the AP Div.

6. The AP Div is visible. When applied to nested AP Divs, the AP Div that the new AP Div is nested inside of is defined as the *parent*. If the nested AP Div has the *open eye* icon, it will *override* a parent AP Div that has been set as hidden. Choosing the *open eye* icon for AP Divs that are not nested when the parent document page has been defined as visible will have no effect on it, as if the *no eye* option was chosen.

7. Just as you can change an assigned name of an AP Div in the Property inspector, you can double-click and change its name here as well.

8. Just as tables can be nested, AP Divs can be nested. This feature must already be activated in the AP Elements category of the Dreamweaver Preferences by checking *Nest when created within an AP Div*. If this option has been checked, an AP Div can be drawn inside of another one. However, any time this feature is turned on and you would like to draw an AP Div on top of an existing AP Div without nesting it, holding the Alt/Option key down when drawing it will prevent the automatic nesting. Just as the Alt/Option key can toggle the type of Polygonal Lasso tool you want to use in Photoshop, if the nesting option is not assigned in the preferences, holding down the Alt/Option key when drawing on top of an existing AP Div will have the opposite effect: it will allow the new AP Div to nest within the one you are drawing it on. Using the AP Elements panel, a selected AP Div can also be Command/Control dragged on top of another AP Div to nest one that was not originally nested when created. Regardless of how they are created, nested AP Divs will be identified as such in the AP Elements panel by indentation.

Adjusting the Stacking Order of AP Divs   The stacking order of AP Divs that overlap on a page can be changed in multiple ways:

- A number can be assigned in the z-index area of the Property inspector—the higher the number, the higher in the stacking order the AP Div will appear.
- The z-index can be highlighted in the AP Elements panel and changed to a higher or lower number. You can even assign a negative number if needed, such as −1.

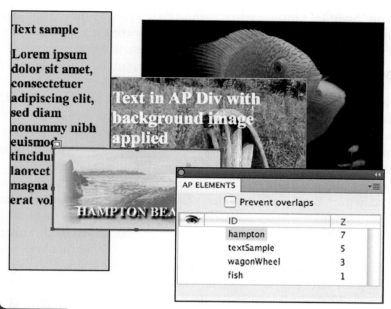

FIGURE 12-4 Stacking order of AP elements.

- Like the Photoshop Layers palette, you can grab an AP Div in the AP Elements panel and drag it to change its stacking order in the panel; the typical *black line* indicates where it will be moved when you let go. When you use this familiar method, it will assign a new stacking order number (the z-index) automatically for you. When assigning stacking order, as long as the numbers are in a hierarchal format, they do not necessarily have to be sequential, as shown in **FIGURE 12-4** .

12.2 Exploring the Various Uses of AP Divs for Page Layout

AP Divs can be used in a variety of ways to build a page in Dreamweaver. Let's examine them in detail, including how guides, grids, and tracing images can assist in the page construction process, providing you, the designer, with more tools for your web page layout toolbox based on your creative preferences and your future audience needs.

12.2.1 Building a Page from Scratch Using AP Divs

One application of AP Divs for layout is to simply draw containers on a page and insert the required content into them. Incorporating the assistance of guides or a grid and a tracing image can make the task easier and more organized.

Guides, Grids, and "Snap To" Options when Using AP Divs for Layout   Although guides, grids, and "snap to" options can be handy when creating a page using any layout method in Dreamweaver, we will discuss their use here as we learn to use AP Divs. If you have designed a page in Photoshop or on paper, you have already given thought to the locations and sizes of your page's contents.

Viewing rulers, displaying a grid, or adding guides to help you build pages are all available in Dreamweaver. The way they work is similar to the way they do in other graphics programs. Visibility can be toggled on and off from the View menu of the main application menu. As in other programs, a check mark signifies their visibility. Features such as guide and grid color, snap, and lock options can be altered, as well as the ability to change the spacing of grid lines. Also, as in other graphics programs, guides are dragged in from the top and left rulers of a page, as long as they are visible; if they are not visible, choose View>Rulers>Show. The zero point may be moved by dragging it, and it is reset to the upper-left corner of the document by choosing View>Rulers>Reset Origin or, by double-clicking in the zero point corner between the vertical and horizontal rulers, just as it is in other graphic programs.

It is best to keep the ruler measurement set to the default unit of pixels. However, it can be changed by selecting View>Rulers and choosing either Inches or Centimeters as alternative options. A slick feature is the ability to identify their exact distance from each other or the edge of the document window when you hold down the Command/Control key and move your mouse around the document window. In addition to this, you can also double-click a guide to enter a specific location for it. Both of these features are illustrated in **FIGURE 12-5**.

Using a grid offers another means of measurement, which also echoes Photoshop in its options. However, unlike Photoshop, where the grid options are set under the *Grids, Guides and Slices* preferences, the grid options in Dreamweaver are chosen from the View>Grid>Grid Settings dialog box and offer the selections shown in **FIGURE 12-6**.

Using Tracing Images   Using a tracing image can also help to lay out a page, following the basic concept of the *Template* feature of Adobe Illustrator. Any GIF,

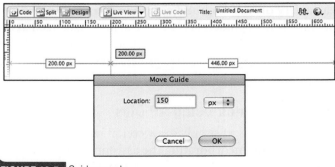

FIGURE 12-5 Guide sample.

FIGURE 12-6 Grid Settings dialog box.

JPEG, or PNG file can be used as a tracing image. The use of a tracing image was introduced in Chapter 9 when we learned that it can be assigned in the Appearances (CSS) category of the Modify>Page Properties dialog box. You can also choose to add one to a page by selecting View>Tracing Image>Load. If chosen here, after browsing to select the image you want to use for tracing, you are then still forwarded to the same Tracing Image category of the Page Properties dialog box. In either scenario, after you have chosen the image you want to use, it is in this dialog box that you drag its slider to set the degree of transparency for the tracing image. Setting a transparency of 50% allows you to see your tracing image, yet still clearly see your AP Divs as you draw and manipulate them on the page. After the image appears on the page, you can return to the Tracing Image category of the Page Properties dialog box at any time to change its transparency to a higher or lower percentage. A tracing image is only visible in Dreamweaver: it will not display when viewed in a browser. At any time, you can hide a tracing image that you are using by choosing View>Tracing Image>Show and unchecking the *Show* option. To delete a tracing image that you no longer want, return to the Tracing Image category of the Page Properties dialog box. Highlight and then delete the image from the Browse option.

The position of the tracing image on the page will be relative to the default margins of the page, which will therefore be Left 10 pixels and Top 15 pixels, unless you have customized them. Similar to a template layer in Adobe Illustrator, it is *locked* in position and cannot be dragged to move it. However, as you have learned, you can set the page margins to *zero* in the Page Properties dialog box under the Appearance CSS category to make the page flush with the edge of your document window, which will also move the tracing image. Alternatively, you can set or adjust the position of the tracing image using the View>Tracing Image>Adjust Position or Reset Position options.

After a tracing image is inserted onto a page, you can use it as a design guide to draw AP Divs, tracing its shapes to then fill the AP Divs for its matching content. Although this sounds great, you may be wondering at this point if the freedom of design that AP Divs provide is worth the possible unpredictability of your page with overlapping AP Divs in certain browsers. The option to convert a page created using AP Divs to tables offers a solution to this issue.

12.2.2 The Convert AP Divs to Table Option

The Convert AP Divs to Table option will convert a page created using AP Divs into a dependable table. However, first of all, to be able to apply this command, the AP Divs must have been created with the *Prevent overlaps* box checked in the AP Elements panel. If you intend to convert a design layout constructed using AP Divs to a table after creating it, be sure this option is chosen prior to starting to build the page. When you are ready to convert your AP Divs to a table, choose Modify>Convert>AP Divs to Table. In this dialog box, the following options are available, as shown in FIGURE 12-7.

1. Here, you can choose how you want Dreamweaver to convert the existing shapes into a standard table configuration. As you will see in the following example, you must account for empty space. The *Most accurate* option will help to retain your original appearance as closely as possible, but will create empty table cells as needed in order to achieve that look. The *Smallest* option allows you to determine how small empty cells must be before you do not want Dreamweaver to generate them. However, accuracy of content placement may be compromised when choosing this option.

2. Applying transparent GIFs will automatically add a row to the bottom of the resulting table to assure that its width will be consistent across all browsers after the conversion.

3. This is a convenience feature, which will automatically center the resulting table for you. However, if not chosen, you can select the table and center its alignment in the Property inspector after it has been created, as you have already learned how to do.

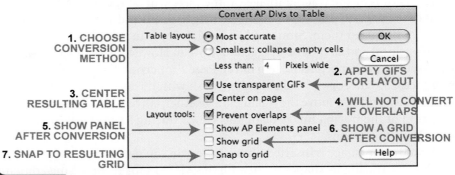

FIGURE 12-7 Convert AP Divs to Table dialog box.

4. This option has a check to *Prevent overlaps.* However, if you have any that overlap, regardless of what you plug in here, a dialog box will pop up telling you that the table cannot be created because it contains overlapping AP Divs.

5. This option will display the AP Element panel after the conversion. However, if you are converting it to a table, you will no longer need the AP Element panel to display anyway.

6. This option will add a grid to the table after it has been created using the current grid spacing settings.

7. If a grid is applied, choosing this option will snap the resulting converted table to that grid.

Working with the Resulting Table of an AP Div Converted Page The following example, **FIGURE 12-8**, shows a sample page with AP Divs and its resulting table, based on the options applied, as shown in Figure 12-7.

1. This is a screen shot of the AP Div page prior to its conversion, created with no overlaps. Notice that the wagon wheel image is used as a background so that text can be added on top of it.

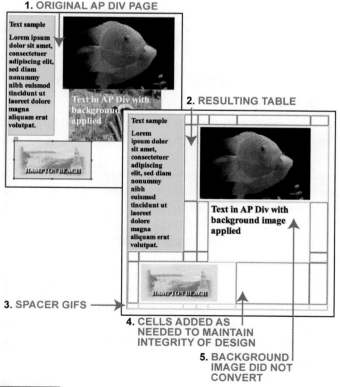

FIGURE 12-8 AP Divs page converted to a table.

2. This screen shot displays the resulting table after the conversion, with the *Most accurate* option chosen in the conversion dialog box. It actually resembles the original layout very well. (In this example, it does not appear to resemble the original layout exactly, because it is shown in Expanded Tables mode.)

3. Because the option *Use transparent Gifs* was selected, a row of cells was added below the rest of the table content for uniformity across browsers.

4. To retain the original appearance of the AP Div page, cells have automatically been added to the new table as needed to fill the space.

5. Here, you can see that the background image was not preserved in the conversion. However, it can now be reinserted as a background into the cell of the resulting table.

As you have learned, you can go through this table now to select and merge/delete excessive cells when possible, if when doing so, you are able to retain the integrity of the original look. This will help to minimize excessive code required by the empty cells. You can also nest additional tables inside any of its cells, because it now has all the properties of a table that you already learned to create in Chapter 10. You may have noticed under the same Modify>Convert menu that there was also an opposite *Convert tables to AP Divs* option, allowing you to create AP Divs from tables. When this option is selected, the selections to prevent overlaps, to show the AP Element panel, and to choose the grid become available. Then, the new AP Divs are created.

12.2.3 Using the AP Divs Layout Method to Insert a Page Created and Sliced in Photoshop

We have learned how to create a page totally using AP Divs and explored their stacking order feature. We moved on to more dependability by converting an existing page created using AP Divs to a table. However, as you can see, that will create extra cells, which create extra code unless you can eliminate some without destroying the layout. Worried that this is the best there is? Now let's explore the "slick and steadfast method of creating a page by combining the drawing and layout freedom of AP Divs with the dependability of tables" that I promised at the beginning of this chapter.

In Chapter 4, you sliced a NH Lupine Restaurant page in Project 1 of the Reinforcing Your Knowledge exercises and chose the Save for Web option for its slices. At that time, you were instructed to place the resulting folder, titled *sliced_page*, somewhere on your hard drive where you would be able to locate it for Chapter 12. Now, place that folder into the *images* folder of your SampleRoot folder. Create a new page named *slices_drawn.html* and save it into the SampleSite *pages* folder. (Once again, during this practice, it will not be necessary to add a title, keywords, and description text to this page. However, remember that you must start each page of a real site with these critical steps.)

Assign the font collection *Georgia, Times New Roman, Times, serif.* Set a background color for the page of #FFFFFF. Set all margins to zero. Set the following link colors: link #FFFFFF; visited links #996699; rollover links #6699CC; and active links #6699CC. Keep the link font setting *Same as page font.* Add the *B* for bold style option. Choose *Never Underline* for the underline style. Add the tracing image titled *lupine_page_trace.jpg* provided in the *Chapter_12PracticeFiles* folder and set a transparency of 50%. After the tracing file is inserted, if you would like the transparency higher or lower for the tracing image, you may return to the Page Properties dialog box to adjust it. This "template" will help us to visualize our layout as we insert AP Divs in the exact location and size as the slices that they will be designed to house. By doing this, when the page is converted to a table, Dreamweaver will not need to fill empty space with excessive cells because everything will fit together perfectly. To create the AP Divs exactly as needed, you must know the exact size and location requirements of each slice. In this example, I have done that for you. However, **FIGURE 12-9** illustrates how easy it is for you to get that information from any page you have sliced in Photoshop.

The displayed options are for the selected slice, which is the *location* slice, as shown by its yellow selection handles. Double-clicking on any slice will display its properties in the dialog box shown. The *X* and *Y* coordinates correspond to the *L* and *T* options in the Property inspector when an AP Div is selected. The width and height of the slice are also shown in this dialog box and can be typed directly into the *W* and *H* options of the Property inspector when an AP Div is selected.

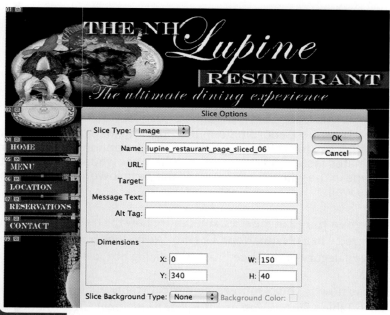

FIGURE 12-9 Slice coordinates and dimensions.

Let's build the page by drawing AP Divs and setting their coordinates to match the slices we made. First of all, be sure that *Prevent overlaps* has been checked in the AP Elements panel. Select the Draw AP Div tool and drag to create an AP Div anywhere on the page. With it selected, type the following values in the Property inspector: L=0px, T=0px, W=750px, and H=200px. Be sure to add or leave the lowercase *px* each time; Dreamweaver will not recognize the measurement if typed in uppercase letters. Using either the Property inspector or the AP Elements panel, rename the AP Div to *headline1*. When you are done, as you can see by the tracing image visible below it, you have created an AP Div exactly the final size of the content you will add to it! However, we are not going to add content yet; we will, instead, build the rest of the AP Divs containers on the page.

Be sure to begin by drawing an AP Div anywhere on the page (except on top of an existing one) or choose the Insert>Layout Objects>AP Div command, and be sure it is selected to be able to specialize its location and size in the Property inspector. When using the Insert>Layout Objects>AP Div command, each AP Div will be placed at the upper-left corner of the page, even if another AP Div is underneath it and *Prevent overlaps* has been checked. Create the remaining AP Divs using the same described method and setting their coordinates and names as follows:

shrimp1: L=0px, T=200px, W=150px, H=60px

body1: L=150px, T=200px, W=600px, H=260px

home1: L=0px, T=260px, W=150px, H=40px

menu1: L=0px, T=300px, W=150px, H=40px

location1: L=0px, T=340px, W=150px, H=40px

reservations1: L=0px, T=380px, W=150px, H=40px

contact1: L=0px, T=420px, W=150px, H=40px

body2: L=0px, T=460px, W=750px, H=271px

footer1: L=0px, T=731px, W=750px, H=19px

 You can type the L coordinate in the Property inspector and then use the Tab key to cycle through the next three options to type your coordinates faster and easier. Just remember when typing to not only type in the value; be sure to add the *px* in lowercase text each time as well.

Even though I have given you all of the sizes, you can see how the tracing image can help you stay organized when creating your AP Divs. We no longer need it now, so in the Tracing Image category of the Page Properties dialog box, delete the path to the file and click OK.

All that remains now is your "soon to be perfect" table. Choose Modify> Convert>AP Divs to Table. Choose *Most accurate*, *Use transparent GIFs*, and *Center on page*, leaving all other options unchecked. When your table is created on the page, change the background color for the page in the Page Properties dialog box to Black (#000000) and turn on *Expanded Tables mode* for the table. Your resulting table should look like **FIGURE 12-10**.

The only difference between your table and Figure 12-10 is that I have added the corresponding identification number for each of the slices, so that you will know where to add them. Alternatively, you could leave the tracing image visible to know where your slices need to go. As you can see, we have one clean, perfect table ready to insert the page slices. Let's do it! (The bottom row is the *transparent GIFs* row that Dreamweaver added for us, which we will ignore when inserting our content into the table.) Placing the I-beam into each cell, insert the corresponding *lupine_restaurant_page_01.jpg*, *lupine_restaurant_page_02.jpg*, etc., except for the *lupine_restaurant_page_10.jpg*. For this one, let's insert a nested table inside this last row for the footer navigation. Place the I-beam inside this cell, check that it has its vertical alignment set to Top, and then add a table into it the traditional way with 1 row, 6 columns, 100% width, and zero for its padding, spacing, and border. Insert *lupine_restaurant_page_10.jpg* as a background to this nested table, either by using the Property inspector if you are using CS3, or by using the Attributes A/Z tab of the Tag inspector when using CS3, CS4, or CS5. Applying the image as a background will allow you to type on top of the image to add the appropriate link text in each of its cells. After you have done that, select its row of cells and set a horizontal alignment of Center and a vertical alignment of Top. Type the following text links in uppercase text sequentially from left to right in each cell: *HOME, MENU, LOCATION, RESERVATIONS, CONTACT*, and *SITE MAP*. For practice purposes

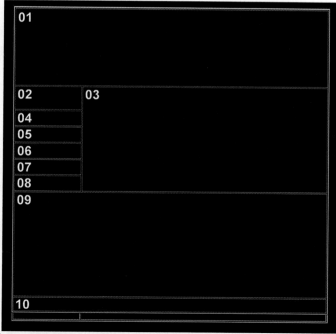

FIGURE 12-10 Lupine table from AP Divs.

FIGURE 12-11 Final Lupine Restaurant sliced page in a browser.

only, highlight each link individually and assign a link using the hash symbol
(#). Adjust the width of each cell as needed to accommodate the size of the word
inserted, either by manually dragging the cell border or by typing in a percentage,
and preview your resulting page in a browser. It should resemble the sample shown
in **FIGURE 12-11**. If a gap appears below the shrimp when previewed in a browser,
you may need to simply tighten up the table cells for the content.

That's it! A perfect page! Now, if you would like, add rollover and visited link colors
to the footer navigation of the Lupine Restaurant page, or even return to the layered
original .psd file of the page, add another layer for an over state, and change the main
navigation's text or background color to rollovers for extra practice! The more you
reinforce the tools, the easier they will become to use when building your own sites.

12.2.4 Using the AP Divs Table Conversion Method to Build a Page from Scratch

The versatility and dependability of this concept can be carried to yet another level
of sophistication. By sketching a complete layout, including the dimensions needed
for all of its future content, it can then be drawn using AP Divs and converted to a
table, making it ready to insert all the text and images you have planned for the page.
FIGURE 12-12 is a sketch of a future page with its dimensions calculated for the content.

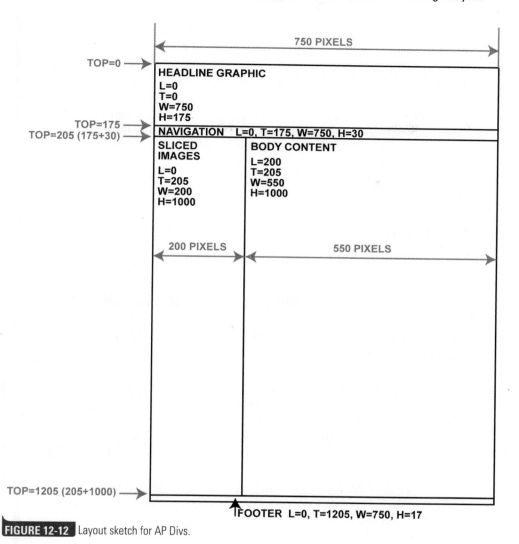

FIGURE 12-12 Layout sketch for AP Divs.

Although this one was neatly drawn in Adobe Illustrator, when using this method yourself, any quick pencil sketch will do, as long as you have accurately calculated the dimensions each section will require for its future content.

When drawing your sketch, the only dimensions you need to calculate are the ones in black: the left, top, width, and height of each area where you will be adding content. The additional notations in red were added simply to help you further understand how the dimensions were calculated. As shown, the *Top* dimension for each container below another one must begin with the height designated for the previous Top, added to the height that the new container's content requires (e.g., sliced images Top=205, representing the combined value of the navigation Top=175 plus its height=30).

After you have done this, following the same method used for the *slices_drawn.html* page, draw an AP Div for each shape, making sure the *Prevent overlaps* option is checked in the AP Elements panel before you begin. As you create each one, type in the four coordinates you have calculated for it. After drawing all of them, choose the Modify>Convert>AP Divs to Table option. Select *Most accurate*, *Use transparent GIFs*, and *Center on page*, leaving all other options unchecked. Your table will be customized to your exact specifications and ready for you to insert its content!

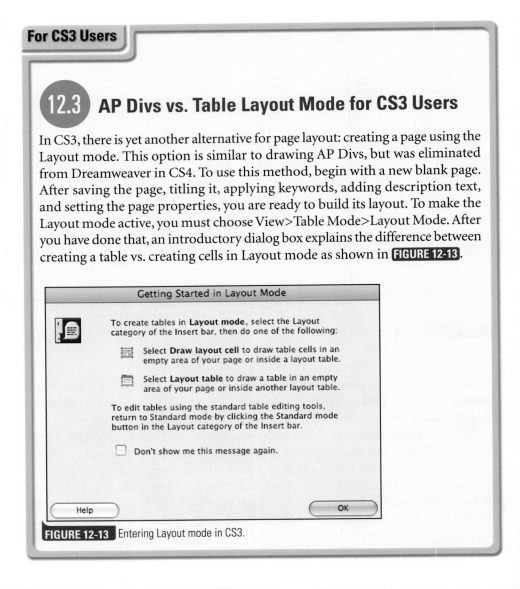

For CS3 Users

12.3 AP Divs vs. Table Layout Mode for CS3 Users

In CS3, there is yet another alternative for page layout: creating a page using the Layout mode. This option is similar to drawing AP Divs, but was eliminated from Dreamweaver in CS4. To use this method, begin with a new blank page. After saving the page, titling it, applying keywords, adding description text, and setting the page properties, you are ready to build its layout. To make the Layout mode active, you must choose View>Table Mode>Layout Mode. After you have done that, an introductory dialog box explains the difference between creating a table vs. creating cells in Layout mode as shown in **FIGURE 12-13**.

Getting Started in Layout Mode

To create tables in **Layout mode**, select the Layout category of the Insert bar, then do one of the following:

Select **Draw layout cell** to draw table cells in an empty area of your page or inside a layout table.

Select **Layout table** to draw a table in an empty area of your page or inside another layout table.

To edit tables using the standard table editing tools, return to Standard mode by clicking the Standard mode button in the Layout category of the Insert bar.

☐ Don't show me this message again.

Help   OK

FIGURE 12-13. Entering Layout mode in CS3.

The Draw Layout Cell and Layout Table icons are at the far right of the Layout tab of the Insert bar. If they are grayed out, you have forgotten to choose View>Table Mode>Layout Mode. Only then do they become active for use. If you want to create a centered table at 750 pixels, use the Layout Table icon (green left icon) first to draw the table; the centering is best done in Standard mode after you have created all cells for the table. Notice when you draw that Layout mode is identified at the top of the page and that the Property inspector allows you to set a size for the height as well as the width of the layout table when the table is selected. After it's created, when you switch to the Draw Layout Cell icon (blue right icon), you can build the design of your page with custom sized and shaped cells inside the table you drew, as long as you do not try to overlap them. Here again, the use of a tracing image can be a handy template when building your layout. Just as when using AP Divs, holding down the Command/Control key when using the Draw Layout Cell tool will keep you in the tool without having to reselect it each time if you want to draw multiple cells consecutively. Existing cells in Layout mode can be selected to get bounding box handles to reshape them within the perimeter of the table boundary. When you choose the Standard mode or Expanded Tables mode feature at any time, you will automatically exit Layout mode and will need to choose it again from the View>Table Mode menu to enter it again. After you have created all the cells of your table, if you check the page again using Expanded Tables mode, you may see that *spacer GIFs* were added if needed to square off the table. You can eliminate these by merging the cells, or by simply typing the required width of each cell in the Property inspector to assure that the combined width and height of all the cells equal the original table dimensions. After creation, you can select the table in Standard mode, center it in the Property inspector, and add your content. You can also nest additional tables inside it after you have exited Layout mode by adding them in either Standard mode or Expanded Tables mode.

One important sizing difference between building a table in Layout mode vs. a traditional table is the *Autostretch* vs. the *Fixed Width* option feature of the Property inspector. The fixed width option is chosen by default; the autostretch layout is optional and would be the same concept as choosing a table width of 100% vs. a specific fixed pixel width, creating a liquid or flexible layout to expand or shrink as needed to accommodate the viewer's browser. When you select this option, you will enter a dialog box asking you what you want Dreamweaver to do to incorporate the Autostretch option as shown in **FIGURE 12-14**.

Clicking OK, which chooses the default option to *Create a spacer image file*, will ensure that the layout will look as designed. In the Save As dialog box that follows, save it to the *images* folder of the site: it will automatically be named *spacer.gif*. If you assign the Autostretch feature to a page, it will require adjusting

For CS3 Users (continued)

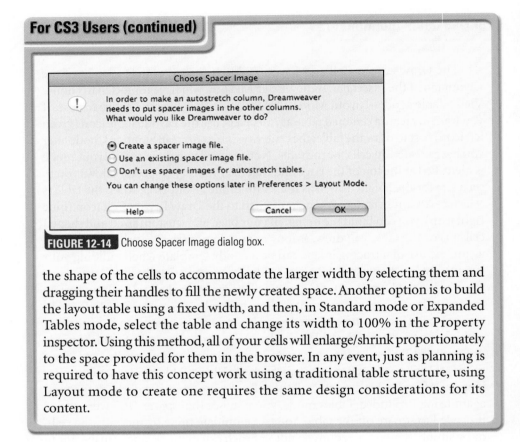

FIGURE 12-14 Choose Spacer Image dialog box.

the shape of the cells to accommodate the larger width by selecting them and dragging their handles to fill the newly created space. Another option is to build the layout table using a fixed width, and then, in Standard mode or Expanded Tables mode, select the table and change its width to 100% in the Property inspector. Using this method, all of your cells will enlarge/shrink proportionately to the space provided for them in the browser. In any event, just as planning is required to have this concept work using a traditional table structure, using Layout mode to create one requires the same design considerations for its content.

12.4 A Look at the Code in Split View: CSS for AP Div Page Positioning

FIGURE 12-15 details a section of the CSS code written by Dreamweaver for the *slices_drawn.html* page. Instead of showing the entire page in split view, this illustration focuses on the opening of the styles element and the first few CSS rules contained in the head section of the page.

1. The `<style type="text/css">` code indicates the opening of the styles element.
2. The `body` code is the selector for the page appearance CSS rule.
3. This is the CSS rule for the page appearance, including its margins and background color.
4. The left curly bracket indicates the beginning of its declaration.

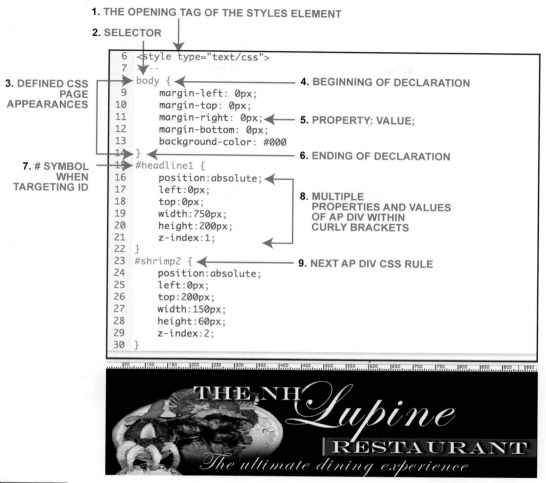

1. THE OPENING TAG OF THE STYLES ELEMENT

2. SELECTOR

3. DEFINED CSS PAGE APPEARANCES

4. BEGINNING OF DECLARATION

5. PROPERTY: VALUE;

6. ENDING OF DECLARATION

7. # SYMBOL WHEN TARGETING ID

8. MULTIPLE PROPERTIES AND VALUES OF AP DIV WITHIN CURLY BRACKETS

9. NEXT AP DIV CSS RULE

```
 6  <style type="text/css">
 7  <!--
 8  body {
 9      margin-left: 0px;
10      margin-top: 0px;
11      margin-right: 0px;
12      margin-bottom: 0px;
13      background-color: #000
14  }
15  #headline1 {
16      position:absolute;
17      left:0px;
18      top:0px;
19      width:750px;
20      height:200px;
21      z-index:1;
22  }
23  #shrimp2 {
24      position:absolute;
25      left:0px;
26      top:200px;
27      width:150px;
28      height:60px;
29      z-index:2;
30  }
```

FIGURE 12-15 Split view of AP Divs.

5. As we have learned, inside a declaration, each of its properties is followed by a colon, a space, its value, and ends with a semicolon.

6. The right curly bracket indicates the ending of the declaration of this particular CSS rule.

7. In the #headline1: code, the hash symbol (#) before the selector indicates that it is targeting an id; in this case, it indicates the AP Div used for the headline image.

8. Inside the curly brackets defining the declaration are the properties and values of the CSS rule for the #headline1 code. Note the property (position) followed by a colon, a space, and then the value

(`absolute`), followed by a semicolon. Notice that the remaining properties and values for the AP Div are listed in the same order that they are typed into the Property inspector: Left, Top, Width, Height, and Z-index, respectively.

9. The same format is followed sequentially for all remaining AP Divs on the page and any additional CSS rules applied to links, etc., before the ending of the style element would be indicated by its closing `</style>` tag (not visible in this illustration).

12.5 What We Have Learned

CSS-driven AP Divs, with their assigned positioning and overlap capabilities, offer another dimension for web page layout. Drawing containers for images and text, with the ability to assign stacking order to them, introduces artistic freedom not possible using traditional tables. We also learned how their absolute positioning characteristic, coupled with their Prevent overlap feature, can be used to create dependable complete web pages, either created and sliced originally in Photoshop or built by inserting text and images into a designed, drawn layout. The incorporation of guides, grids, and tracing images were introduced as additional tools in our toolbox to assist in executing layout designs, no matter how they will be built. We concluded this chapter with an overview of a similar "draw and build" page creation process that uses the Layout Tables mode available only for CS3 users, because it was elemininated in CS4.

12.6 Reinforcing Your Knowledge

Project

1. Copy the following files from the *Chapter_12PracticeFiles* folder into the *images* folder of your FishluvrzRoot folder: *faucet.jpg*, *plants.jpg*, *question.swf*, and *temperature.jpg*.

2. Be sure your FishluvrzSite is the active site in your Files panel and check that the files listed in step 1 have been added to its *images* folder.

3. Create a new page, choose File>Save As, name the page *faq_page .html*, and save it into the *pages* folder of the FishluvrzSite.

4. Title the new page: *Your Fish Care Questions Answered by the Experts at Fishluvrz.*

5. Add the following keywords: *aquarium water quality, aquarium water temperature, fish feeding, fish health problems, regulating aquarium PH levels.*

6. Add the following description text: *We offer a full line of aquarium products and services specializing in answers to your fish health and aquarium water quality problems. Our FAQ page is designed to help you create and maintain a healthy aquarium for your fish!*

7. Assign the following page properties:

   Appearances (CSS):
   > Page font: *Arial, Helvetica, sans-serif*
   > Size: *14px*
   > Text color: #000066
   > Background color: #000066
   > Margins: *all set to 0px*

   Links (CSS):
   > Link font: *Same as page font*
   > Link color: #336600
   > Visited links: #FF0000
   > Rollover and Active links: #333300
   > Underline style: *Never Underline*

   Headings (CSS):
   > Heading font: *Georgia, Times New Roman, Times, serif*
   > Heading 1: *24px*; Color: #000066
   > Heading 2: *18px*; Color: #000066
   > No settings for Headings 3–6

8. Add the following AP Divs, with *Prevent overlaps* checked in the AP Elements panel (they are the same dimensions as those in Figure 12-12):

   > headline1: *L=0px, T=0px, W=750px, H=175px* (Did you notice that the AP Div handles are yellow? Dreamweaver makes them yellow or blue depending on the background they are being drawn on!)
   > navigation1: *L=0px, T=175px, W=750px, H=30px*
   > images1: *L=0px, T=205px, W=200px, H=1000px*
   > body1: *L=200px, T=205px, W=550px, H=1000px*
   > footer1: *L=0px, T=1205px, W=750px, H=17px*

9. After you have added all of the AP Divs, convert them to a table choosing the following options in the Convert AP Divs to Table dialog box: *Most accurate, Use transparent GIFs,* and *Center on page*. Leave all other options unchecked. After created, remembering that

the bottom row is only for browser consistency, your table should resemble **FIGURE 12-16** when viewed in Expanded Tables mode.

10. Insert the *fishluvrz_static_headline.jpg* into the single cell of the top row of the table.

11. Open your *contact_page.html* page, select the cyan tab of the Spry Menu Bar, copy it to the Clipboard, and close the page. Place the I-beam inside the single cell of the second row of the table, assign a background color of #336600 to the cell, paste the navigation menu into it, and then update its links as needed.

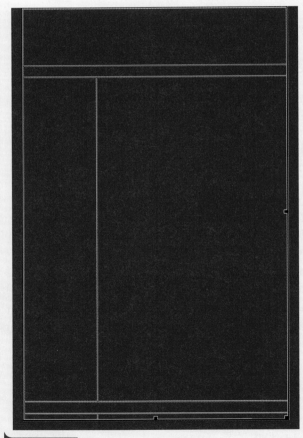

FIGURE 12-16   Table displaying layout for the *faq_page.html* web page.

12. Select the remaining three cells of the table and set a background color of #FFFFFF for all of them, being sure that you do not select the row of transparent gifs inserted by Dreamweaver.

13. Click inside the left cell below the navigation and use the Insert>Media>SWF menu option to insert *question.swf*. Do not make any changes in the Property inspector for the SWF, leaving *Loop*, *Autoplay*, and all other options at their default settings.

14. With the SWF selected with its selection handles, press the right arrow on the keyboard to place the I-beam to the right of the movie. Choose Insert>Image and add the *fish_montage_02.jpg* below the SWF. Using the same method of insertion, continue to add the *fish_montage_03.jpg*, *fish_montage_04.jpg*, and *fish_montage_05.jpg*, in that order, placing each consecutively below the previous image. (We will not use *fish_montage_01.jpg* and *fish_montage_06.jpg* on this page.)

15. Place the I-beam in the right cell of the table, below the navigation. In uppercase letters, type: *YOUR QUESTIONS ANSWERED!* Apply *Heading 1* to this paragraph.

16. Open *faq_text.doc*, located in the *Chapter_12PracticeFiles* folder. In Microsoft Word, select all of the content, copy it to the Clipboard, and then close the file. The folder also contains a copy of the text in .rtf file format for use with other text editors if needed.

17. Return to Dreamweaver. Add a hard return after *ANSWERED!* This creates a new paragraph. Choose Edit>Paste Special. In the dialog box that follows, choose the second option: *Text with structure (paragraphs, lists, tables, etc.)*. When this option is chosen, both the *Retain line breaks* and the *Clean up Word paragraph spacing* options are preselected as part of the *Copy/Paste* default settings. We do not want Dreamweaver to alter the paragraph formatting this time, so we will uncheck the *Clean up Word paragraph spacing* box.

18. After the text has been added to the page, click anywhere inside each question sentence, one at a time, and select *Heading 2* in the Property inspector under the HTML Format pop-up menu, or the Format>Paragraph Format main menu.

19. Place the I-beam at the end of the first question and insert *temperature.jpg*. When selection handles are visible on it, choose the Align>Right option in the Property inspector to move it flush to the right, below the first question.

Project (continued)

20. Place the I-beam at the end of the fourth question, insert *plants.jpg*, and assign an alignment of Right for this image as well.

21. Place the I-beam at the end of the last question, insert *faucet.jpg*, and again align it to Right in the Property inspector when its selection handles are active.

22. Add a nested table into the single cell directly below the body text and fish montage (remembering that the row of cells at the very bottom of the table were added by Dreamweaver for layout consistency and will not have any content inserted into them), with 1 row, 6 columns, a width of 100%, and zero for its spacing and border. But, once again, set a padding of 10px for breather space, as we did for the Fishluvrz index page. After it's inserted, select its cells, and assign a Horizontal alignment of Center and a Vertical alignment of Middle (default).

23. Create the following text links, typing one in each cell in the order listed, and assign the links to their respective pages as follows: *HOME*, *PRODUCTS*, *INFORMATION*, *FAQ*, *CONTACT US*, and *SITE MAP*. Use the hash symbol (#) for the links of the *PRODUCTS*, *FAQ*, and *SITE MAP* pages.

24. Adjust the width of the footer link cells in the Property inspector just as we did for the Fishluvrz index page: HOME: 13%, PRODUCTS: 19%, INFORMATION: 20%, FAQ: 12%, CONTACT US: 19%, and SITE MAP: 17%.

 Want a power user tip? Instead of steps 22, 23, and 24, alternatively, open one of your other pages that already has the footer navigation applied, copy the entire nested footer table to the Clipboard, close the page, return to *faq_page.html*, place the I-beam inside the footer cell, and paste the navigation table into it! All you will need to do now is update the links to reflect the pages that we have started thus far in the site.

25. Again, add a rectangular hotspot over the *Fishluvrz.com* name in the headline and link it to the *index.html* page, just as you did in the *information_page.html* in Chapter 11. After you have done that, your page in Dreamweaver should resemble **FIGURE 12-17**.

This concludes our work on the *faq_page.html* page for now. Save and preview the page. After learning CSS in Chapter 14, we will tweak this page with text and layout formatting adjustments, as well as finalize its navigation bar to polish its appearance.

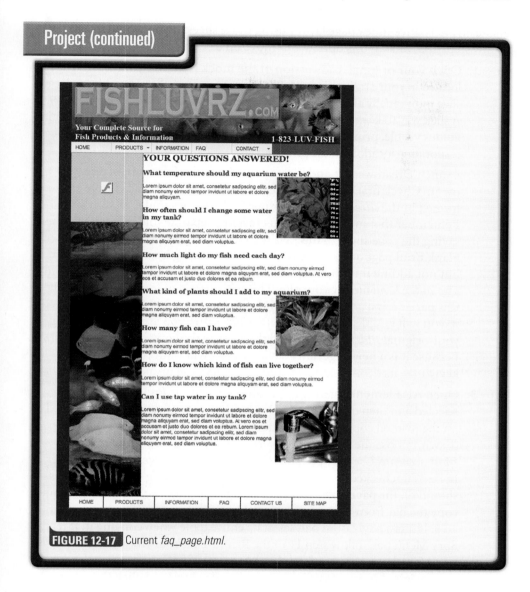

FIGURE 12-17 Current *faq_page.html*.

12.7 Building Your Own Website

As we have continued to learn more about Dreamweaver, your page layout options have also continued to grow! In Chapter 4, you sliced a copy of your mock layout for your index page. Now that you know how to import a sliced page into a table created using the *Convert AP Divs to Table* option, perhaps you would like to try to create an alternative index page layout using those slices. If you would like to try it, follow steps 1–3, or skip this option and move on to step 4.

1. Open your original .psd version of the mock layout of your index page located in your *originalFiles_MySite* folder with all its slices. Double-click each slice individually and write down its dimensions, as shown in Figure 12-9. A slick way to keep track of them is to take a screen shot of the page with its guides visible, print it, and then write each slice's dimensions on its corresponding location on the printed copy.

2. Launch Dreamweaver and locate your site in the Files panel's pop-up menu. Check first that your images created from your sliced page are located in the *sliced_index* folder inside the *images* folder of your site. Remember that in Chapter 4 you created a separate folder for them when saving the page slices in the Save for Web dialog box. Now, create a new blank.html page and save it as *index1.html*, saving it to your root folder, but not adding it to the *pages* folder. Why *index1.html*? There can be only one *index.html* file for your site. This will allow you to experiment with this page design alternative, test it in a browser, and if you decide to keep it, you will be able to rename it *index.html* after you are done, replacing your original *index.html* file, and then delete the copy named *index1.html*. Because it is a new page, after saving it, you will want to title it, add its keywords, its description text, and assign its page properties.

3. Open AP Elements panel and double-check that *Prevent overlaps* is selected and then draw your AP Divs, with the specifications you recorded on the printed copy of your mock index page. After they have all been drawn, choose the Modify>Convert>AP Divs to Table option. Select *Most accurate, Use transparent GIFs,* and *Center on page,* leaving all other options unchecked. Insert your slices into the resulting table. Your slices should fill the page except for your navigation area. For your navigation, copy the bar from your original index page and paste it into its assigned area. If it is a navigation bar, select its entire table when copying it. If it is a Spry Menu Bar, follow step 11 of the Reinforcing Your Knowledge exercise.

   After the page is previewed in a browser, if you prefer this page over your original *index.html* file, rename it *index.html* and click OK when asked if you want to replace the existing file. If you decided to use it, to keep your Files panel up to date, right/Control-click the *index1.html* file and choose Edit>Delete.

4. Perhaps you would like to keep your index page as you have created it thus far, but want to create a custom table through the Convert>AP Divs to Table option to build one or more of your link pages, instead of building them using traditionally drawn tables as you learned in Chapter 10. To do this, begin by sketching a plan for one of your link pages, determining the dimensions

you will need for all of its containers as shown in Figure 12-12. Create a new page, name it any one of your link pages other than the one you created in Chapter 11, use the 1, 2, 3 Go Checklist to begin the page, and assign its page properties. Following the method we used in the Reinforcing Your Knowledge section of this chapter, lay out the page using AP Divs according to your plan, convert them to a table, and insert your content.

Alternatively, you can return to Photoshop, build an entire link page, slice it, insert its slices into a table created using AP Divs according to your Photoshop slices, and then convert them using the Modify>Convert>AP Divs to Table option. Just be sure your layout accounts for the dimensions of your navigation system, regardless of the type you have decided to use.

In the final four chapters of the text, you will learn to edit images and media, create a favicon, be introduced to CSS, build a form, and learn to upload your site. Feel free to construct your remaining link pages now using tables, AP Divs, or AP Divs converted to tables. You can also wait until we learn how to structure a page using CSS to decide which building method works best for you. As you learned when creating the Fishluvrz *faq_page.html* page, a site can contain pages created by different methods within the same site. If one of your pages will include a form, you will want to wait and build that one through the Building Your Own Website section of Chapter 15.

For any pages you create between now and Chapter 14, no matter how you create them, remember to always begin each new page with the 1, 2, 3 Go Checklist before inserting content. We will refine the text format and image placements of our Fishluvrz pages after we have learned CSS in Chapter 14. Until then, don't be concerned if body text or images you add to your pages are not as polished in their positioning as you would like them to be. Concentrate, at this point, on simply inserting your images and navigation systems and entering your body content.

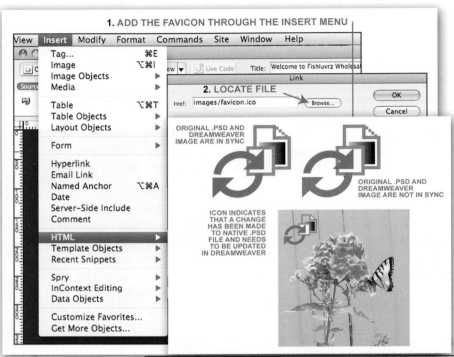

1. ADD THE FAVICON THROUGH THE INSERT MENU

2. LOCATE FILE

ORIGINAL .PSD AND
DREAMWEAVER
IMAGE ARE IN SYNC

ORIGINAL .PSD AND
DREAMWEAVER
IMAGE ARE NOT IN SYNC

ICON INDICATES
THAT A CHANGE
HAS BEEN MADE
TO NATIVE .PSD
FILE AND NEEDS
TO BE UPDATED
IN DREAMWEAVER

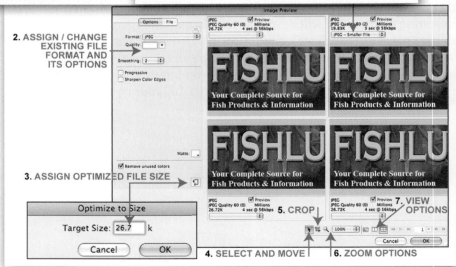

2. ASSIGN / CHANGE EXISTING FILE FORMAT AND ITS OPTIONS

3. ASSIGN OPTIMIZED FILE SIZE

4. SELECT AND MOVE

5. CROP

6. ZOOM OPTIONS

7. VIEW OPTIONS

Adding Favicons and More Options for Accessing, Importing, and Editing Image Files

13

In This Chapter

- Learn to create and insert a favicon
- Use the internal editing tools in Dreamweaver
- Copy multiple layers in Photoshop and paste them directly into Dreamweaver
- Learn how to import and edit Dreamweaver Smart Objects
- Insert files from Adobe Bridge directly into Dreamweaver

This chapter will focus on image/graphic preparation and insertion into Dreamweaver. After learning how to create and insert a favicon, we will move on to explore the basic image editing capabilities available within Dreamweaver itself.

The balance of this chapter will encompass accessing, inserting, and editing web images using Photoshop and Adobe Bridge, focusing on their integration with Dreamweaver and its internal optimization Image Preview dialog box.

13.1 Adding a Favicon

Favicons are an easy way to add a professional touch to your websites, and also provide a great tool to help encourage visitors to return.

13.1.1 What Is a Favicon?

You have seen favicons, but you may not have known what they were called or whether they even had a special name. When you go to the website of your favorite sporting goods store or fast food chain, for example, you will typically see a little copy of their logo (usually an abbreviated form of it) to the left of their URL in the address bar of your browser. As you may have already guessed by now, *favicon* is an acronym for *favorite icon*; when you review your browser's history or favorites, the favicon is located to the left of the site's name. They continue to gain in popularity, and you will want to incorporate them into your own sites because they are cool, trendy, easy to create and add, and most importantly, because they will be automatically displayed in your visitors' browser history. A favicon is another tool to re-engage your audience.

13.1.2 Creating a Favicon

Although they may not seem this small, favicons are actually only 16 x 16 pixels! That helps to clarify why many companies may not be able to add their logo in its full design and will often choose, as an alternative, to use its first letter, or its *signature* part of their name/logo and couple it with their company's identifying logo color(s). Taking a few minutes to do a quick Internet search of a few companies will help you get an idea of how they have abbreviated their logos in their favicons and will also expose you to the typical level of design intricacy of favicons, or their lack of it.

Although there are companies you can pay to create a favicon for you, as a graphic artist, you will want to create your own in Photoshop, at 72 ppi. It can be built in any larger ratio of 16 x 16 pixels (such as 32 x 32 px or 64 x 64 px); however, you will want to test it at its final size to be sure it is still readable and identifiable after it is reduced. That is why simplicity is the key to success. Adding sharpening, however, actually slightly *over* sharpening (Filter>Sharpen>Unsharp Mask) can help to retain the definition of the edges of letters and shapes after the favicon's size has been reduced to its final 16 x 16 pixels.

Save the file, as you should with all images, first in a native .psd format in an *original graphics* folder within your site's umbrella folder for future reworking purposes. While some newer browsers also support favicons saved in .png, .jpg, or .gif file formats, the safe, standard, universal file format for favicons is .ico. One mistake that is often made is to simply add the .ico extension to the graphic and expect it to work: you must actually save the file in the special .ico file format. To do that, a quick Internet search will provide you with multiple companies that will convert a .png or .jpg file to an .ico file for you, or you can download a plug-in that can be added to Photoshop that will allow you to save a file as an .ico right within the application itself. Whatever method you use to convert your favicon into the .ico file format, the file must be named specifically *favicon.ico* (for Dreamweaver to know what to do with it) and then added to the *images* folder of the site root folder.

Adding a Favicon to a Web Page   **FIGURE 13-1** details the steps needed to insert a favicon.

1. The favicon is added to a page by choosing Insert>HTML>Head Tags>Link, or by selecting Link from the Head button's pop-up menu under the Common category of the Insert panel. Notice that this command is grouped with the commands to insert keywords and description text, which we have already learned how to add to a page. Because of that, as you would expect, after it's inserted, it will be accessible for changes by clicking a Link icon when the Head area is visible in the Document window, just as keywords and description text are, by choosing View>Head Content.

2. As previously mentioned, to be able to add a favicon to a page, the *favicon.ico* must be located in the site's root folder. Click to browse and locate it in the dialog box that follows your selection of Link from the Head Tags

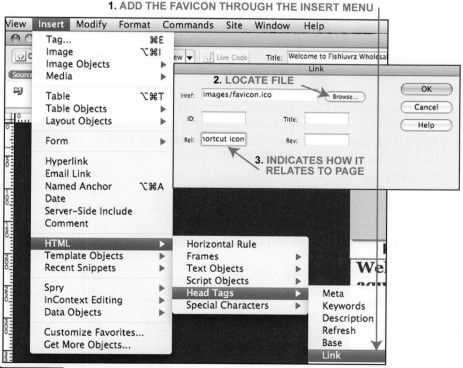

FIGURE 13-1   Adding a favicon to a page.

fly-out menu. When located, if it had not already been previously added to the root folder, choose *Yes* when prompted to add a copy of it to the root folder and select the *images* folder as the destination. After you have done that, the Href area of the Link dialog box will display the path to the file.

3. This dialog box is not used exclusively for the insertion of favicons. Therefore, the only additional part of this dialog box that must be completed to have the favicon work is the Rel section. Here you must type in *shortcut icon*. After you have done that, click OK.

Some websites have a favicon applied only to their home pages, while others display it on all pages. To apply it to additional pages of a site and have its visibility consistent across multiple browsers, it should be added individually to each page by following the same procedure for its insertion.

 Even if the favicon is not visible when you preview the page in a browser, you may have added it correctly. Some browsers will let you preview the page with the favicon on it by simply using the File>Preview in Browser command, while others require the site to be live before it will be displayed.

13.2 Editing Imported Graphics

So far, we have learned to prepare web graphics and images in Photoshop, through its Save for Web dialog box, by choosing the desired file format to optimize them and then saving them into an *images* folder within a site root folder. However, sometimes an image imported into Dreamweaver isn't perfect and needs to be revised. If you return to Photoshop, reopen the image, make the changes, and resave it with the same name back into in your same *images* folder through the Save for Web dialog box, the dialog box shown in **FIGURE 13-2** will follow.

When you click the Replace button, it will update every use of this file in Dreamweaver. To return to Photoshop to make changes to the optimized version, you can launch Photoshop while still in Dreamweaver by selecting the image to edit and then right/Control-clicking to choose Edit With>Photoshop from the context-sensitive menu that follows, or you can simply double-click the image in the Files

---

Replace Files
Some of the specified files already exist in the target location. The files marked below will be replaced:
☑ fishluvrz_static_headline.jpg
Cancel   Replace

FIGURE 13-2 Replace Files dialog box.

panel. Dreamweaver contains a few editing options within the application itself, as well as intuitive Photoshop integration features for creating and editing web images that we will explore in detail.

13.2.1 Setting Editing Preferences

Before exploring its internal editing options, preferences need to be assigned for editing purposes. In the Dreamweaver Preferences dialog box, choose the File Types/ Editors category, as shown in **FIGURE 13-3**.

In this category of the Dreamweaver Preferences dialog box, preselected file extensions are listed in the left column, with plus and minus sign icons available to add or delete file types on its list. When you select any one of them, the right column allows you to define the primary editor for the extension you have selected in the left column. If you have Adobe® Fireworks® installed on your computer, it will be listed as the primary editor by default. If your primary editor is listed as Fireworks, let's learn how to change the primary editor for a file type. Because this text focuses on the use of Photoshop with Dreamweaver, click each web design file extension (.png, .gif, and .jpg) one at a time, choose Adobe Photoshop in the right column, and click the Make Primary button. After you have done that, the word *Primary* will be added next to Photoshop for each particular extension. To add more file editors, or to add Photoshop to the list if it is not currently listed as an editor, click the plus icon above

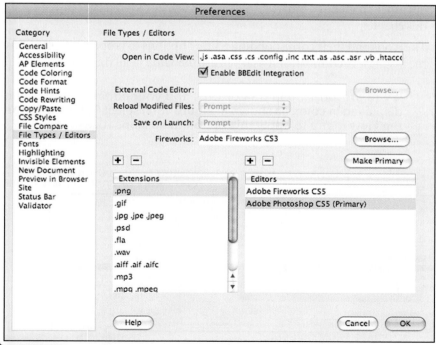

FIGURE 13-3 Set editing preferences.

the Editors column. You will be forwarded to the Applications folder of your hard drive to select the application you want to add. To delete one, click the application in the Editors column, and then click the minus icon above its column.

13.2.2 Internal Image Editing Tools in Dreamweaver

Although you will want to prepare your web graphics and images in Photoshop to take advantage of its multiple editing capabilities, sometimes you need to make minor size, color, value, or clarity adjustments after the graphic or image has been inserted. You can always return to Photoshop to make those changes as we have just discussed. However, when an image is selected on a page, Dreamweaver contains some basic editing options within the application itself that are accessible under the Modify>Image menu and in the Property inspector. **FIGURE 13-4** compares these tools in the CS3 vs. CS4/CS5 Property inspector. They are identical in the three versions, except for the name of one option and the addition of one feature added in CS4.

1. This icon will represent the primary editor you have assigned in the File Types/Editors category of the Dreamweaver Preferences dialog box.

2. The Image Preview dialog box access is represented with an optimize icon. The icon resembles a clamp in CS3 that displays the word Optimize when rolled over, and in CS4 and CS5, the icon resembles two interlocking gears that, when rolled over, display the words Edit Image Settings.

3. This feature is exclusive to CS4 and CS5 and will be active only if your document contains a Smart Object, which will be covered later in this chapter.

4. The icons and their corresponding editing options to crop, resample, adjust the brightness/contrast, and sharpen are the same in all three versions.

 If you are working in CS4 or CS5, and your editing icons are not displayed in color, as shown in Figure 13-4, select Color Icons from the View menu to apply this option to all icons if desired.

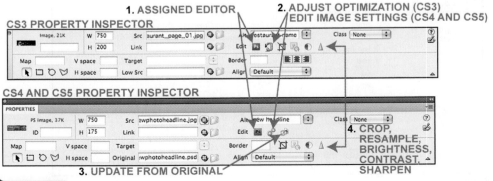

FIGURE 13-4 CS3 vs. CS4 and CS5 editing tools.

Assigned Editor After you have assigned Photoshop as your primary editor, the Photoshop icon will display next to the word *Edit* in the Property inspector when an image is selected. Clicking this icon will launch Photoshop if it is not currently open and display the image you selected ready for editing.

Adjusting the Image Settings for a Selected Graphic With an image selected, if you click the optimize icon (the clamp in CS3 or the gears in CS4 and CS5) in the Property inspector, or choose Modify>Image>Optimize or Commands>Optimize, you will enter the Image Preview dialog box where you can change the current optimization settings and file format for the image. As you can see in FIGURE 13-5, although its layout is different, many of its options echo those of the Save for Web dialog box in Photoshop.

1. Like the Save for Web dialog box in Photoshop, optimization presets can be selected from a pop-up menu in the preview panel area of this dialog box. When viewing the choices at 2-up or 4-up, your selected optimization is identified with a blue outline around it.

2. Select the desired file format from the pop-up menu (GIF, JPEG, PNG) and choose from the same options that you learned to assign using the Photoshop Save for Web dialog box in Chapter 4.

3. Click the Optimize to Size icon to type in a specific final optimization size you want in the Optimize to Size dialog box that follows.

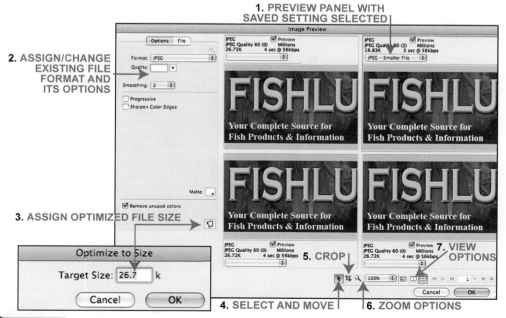

FIGURE 13-5 Image Preview dialog box in Dreamweaver.

4. Although this appears to be a selection/pointer tool, it turns into a "grabber" hand tool if part of the image is hidden when you click and drag it over one of the sample optimization windows.

5. Select this tool to add handles to the outside edges of the image, allowing you to drag the handles to crop the image manually.

6. Use either the Zoom tool or the Percentage pop-up menu to enlarge the view of your selected optimization to examine it for quality and legibility.

7. Here, you can choose to display one, two, or four views of your image to help you make your optimization decision.

Although this dialog box defaults to its Options tab because most of the optimization settings are selected under it, there is also a File tab in this dialog box for scaling the image proportionately, as shown in **FIGURE 13-6**.

You can type in a percentage, drag the slider to choose one, or type in one of the dimensions and press the Tab key to add its corresponding proportional dimension if the Constrain boxed is checked. Checking the *Export area* option will activate the Crop tool to draw a crop area, with the crop coordinates recorded in the export section of the dialog box. When cropping here, it is easiest to change one of the file dimensions first and then use the Crop tool for the other dimension. Being a Photoshop user, you may prefer the fixed ratio crop method of Photoshop to this method: this Crop tool will work in a pinch. It is just less intuitive than cropping directly in Photoshop.

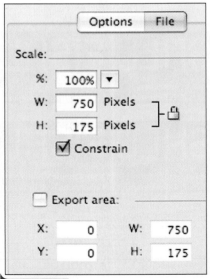

FIGURE 13-6   File tab in the Image Preview dialog box.

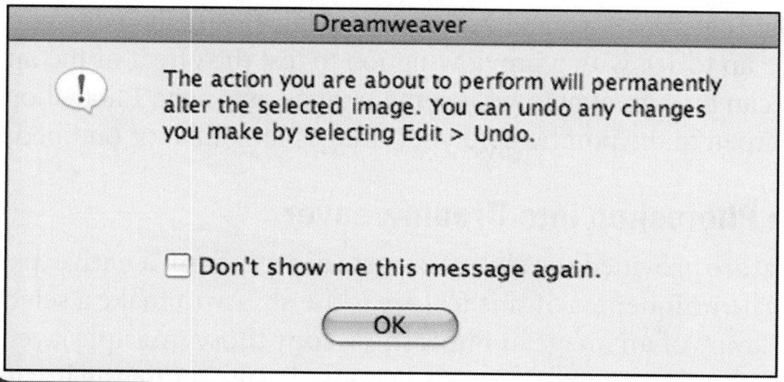

FIGURE 13-7 Image editing warning dialog box.

Exploring Internal Crop, Resample, Brightness/Contrast, and Sharpen Tools in Dreamweaver   When an image is selected on a page, these options are available by choosing Modify>Image, or by clicking their respective icons in the Property inspector. However, when chosen from either location, you enter a warning dialog box first, as shown in **FIGURE 13-7**.

This warning dialog box means that you will be able to change your mind about the settings you apply to the image through the Undo command or History panel while the document is open; however, after you close the document, the changes you make to the image will become permanent. These permanent changes will be made to the image copy you have added to your root folder. You have learned to always save a native .psd version of all your images anyway in a separate *original graphics* folder, which you could return to later if you are not satisfied with the permanent changes you made to any images while in Dreamweaver. After you are familiar with this feature, you may want to click the *Don't show me this message again* option to bypass this warning dialog box when selecting one of these tools in the future.

Crop Tool   When you choose this tool, handles are added to the image, allowing you to drag them as desired, as well as the ability to click and drag to reassign the crop area. To complete the crop, press Enter/Return, double-click inside the image, or click the Crop icon in the Property inspector.

Resample   Just as in Photoshop, resampling should be avoided if possible. Whether resampling up or down, pixel data must be either added or deleted, which can result in a lack of image detail. However, to use this feature, select the image and drag its handles to the new size first. While the image is still selected, the Resample icon will become active to click to apply the corresponding resampling in the Property inspector.

Brightness/Contrast   With the image selected, when you click this icon in the Property inspector, the dialog box that follows echoes the Adjustments>Brightness/Contrast dialog box in Photoshop.

Sharpening   This feature is similar to the sharpening options in Photoshop. After selecting an image and clicking on this icon in the Property inspector, you will enter a dialog box with a slider that allows you add sharpening (increasing the edge contrast) by entering a value up to 10, with a preview option to test the effect of the application. Although this can be a great help with some images, just as in Photoshop, be careful not to oversharpen to the point where your images look fake or outlined.

13.2.3 Pasting from Photoshop into Dreamweaver

In version CS3, a new feature provided the ability to paste directly from a native .psd file into Dreamweaver. The uniqueness of this feature is the ability to make a selection including multiple layers of an image in Photoshop, copy those multiple layers to the Clipboard, open a page in Dreamweaver, and choose Paste. Before the image is inserted into Dreamweaver, you are immediately entered into the Image Preview dialog box shown in Figure 13-5 to assign a file type and optimization, forwarded to a Save Web Image dialog box to name it and add it to the *images* folder of the site you are working in, and then brought to the Image Tag Accessibility Attributes dialog box to add appropriate alt text, completing the command by its insertion onto the page. The best part is that later, when you want to edit it or change the selection, clicking the Edit button in the Property inspector with the image selected will launch Photoshop and open the *original* .psd file again with all your layers.

Let's test this out using a variation of the *lupine_restaurant_page.psd* file you created slices from in Chapter 4 and then used to create the *slices_drawn.html* page in Chapter 12. This time, the file has been modified so that we can create a Dreamweaver page by pasting its slices directly into the page and designed for us to be able to continue to work with it in Chapter 14 when learning CSS.

1. We will begin by preparing a table to hold the parts of the page. With Dreamweaver open, make your SampleSite the active site in your Files panel. Create a new page in your *pages* folder named *paste_sample.html*. (During this practice, it will not be necessary to add a title, keywords, and description text to this page. However, remember that you must start each page of a real site with these first critical steps.) In the Page Properties dialog box, assign the font collection *Georgia, Times New Roman, Times, serif*; a font size of 14 px; text color of #000000; and background color of #FFFFFF. Also, assign Heading 1 a size of 24 px and a color of #FFFFFF. Assign Heading 2 a size of 18 px and a color of FFFFFF. Add a table with the following characteristics: 3 rows, 2 columns, 750 pixels wide, with zero for its padding, spacing, and border. As usual, after it has been added to the page, select the table and set the alignment to Center. Drag-select all its cells and set the Vertical alignment to Top. Merge the cells in the first and third rows. Select the right column of the second row and choose to split it into two rows. Before adding content using the Copy/Paste integration feature with Photoshop, check to see that in Expanded Tables mode your table resembles **FIGURE 13-8**.

2. Now let's paste some native .psd images from Photoshop directly into Dreamweaver. Launch Photoshop and open the *lupine_restaurant_paste.psd*

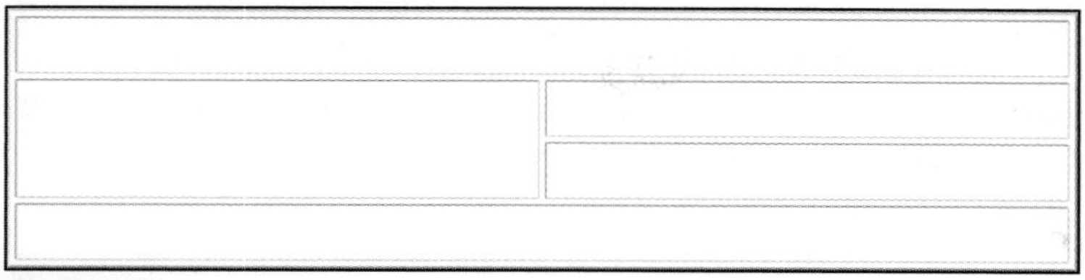

FIGURE 13-8   Table for pasted images.

file in the *Chapter_13PracticeFiles* folder. As you can see, this is a multi-layered Photoshop file. If you are familiar with activating a selection saved in a channel, choose Select>Load Selection and choose *navigation selection* in the Load Selection dialog box. A rectangular marquee selection will appear around the *home* navigation button. If you are not comfortable with channels, use the guides around the navigation button to use the Rectangle Marquee tool to draw a selection around it. After you have the selection, choose Edit>Copy Merged. Do *not* simply choose Edit>Copy. The nice thing is that you do not need to merge the .psd file; Photoshop will just automatically recognize the necessary layers based on your selection and merge them on the Clipboard for you!

Return to Dreamweaver and place the I-beam inside the left column of the second row of your table and then choose Edit>Paste. The Image Preview dialog box will open, allowing you to set the web specifications for the image. Choose *GIF – WebSnap 128* for the optimization with its default settings and click OK. (On your own, experiment with the rest of the default GIF settings to further understand their advantages and limitations.) Double-check under the File tab of this dialog box to be sure that its dimensions are 144 px wide and 30 px high. Just as you would expect, a dialog box named Save Web Image automatically opens, allowing you to navigate to the *images* folder of the SampleRoot folder to name the file *home.gif* and save the file into it. After adding the alt text *home navigation*, the image will be added to the web page. Click the cell it has been inserted into and set the width of the cell to 144 px in the Property inspector. With the image activated by selection handles, click the right arrow on the keyboard to place the insertion point to the right of the image so you are ready to add the next navigation button below it.

3. Return to Photoshop. Hold the Shift key as you drag the selection down to surround the *menu* navigation, lining the top of the selection with the guides provided (be sure you have *Snap to Guides* activated under the Photoshop View menu), then repeat the steps to optimize and insert it into Dreamweaver, naming it *menu.gif.* Continue to select the remaining three navigation buttons one at a time in the same manner and paste them into Dreamweaver, remembering each time in Photoshop to choose Edit>Copy Merged, not Edit>Copy. After all the navigation buttons have been added

in Dreamweaver, click each one individually and add the hash symbol (#) in the link category of the Property inspector to assign link action to it, even though it will not go to another page. After you assign each link, while the image is still selected, type zero in the Border category of the Property inspector to be sure your links will display uniformly, as designed, across all browsers.

4. Return to Photoshop and draw a rectangular selection across the entire headline (drag diagonally from the upper-left corner of the page down to the horizontal guide above the *home* link), choose Edit>Copy Merged, and paste it into the top cell of the table in Dreamweaver. When setting an optimization in the Image Preview dialog box, choose one that you feel allows the text to be read clearly, but keeps the file size manageable. Name the file *headline.jpg*, using the JPEG format because of its continuous tone quality.

5. Lastly, return to Photoshop and draw a rectangular selection around the building, snapping to the guides provided for accuracy. Copy it (Edit>Copy Merged), choose your optimization, name it *building.jpg*, add alt text, then paste it into the lower cell of the split cell in the second row. Viewed in Standard mode in Dreamweaver, your table should now resemble **FIGURE 13-9**.

FIGURE 13-9 Pasted images in Dreamweaver.

6. Before we move on, however, test its integration with Photoshop. Select any one of the images in the *paste_sample.html* page. Click the Edit button in the Property inspector, or right/Control-click and choose Edit Original With>Photoshop from the context-sensitive menu. You will be returned to the original layered .psd file for editing. Once there, you are able to make any changes needed, but will then need to draw a new selection. Choose the Edit>Copy Merged command again, return to Dreamweaver, delete the old file, and then paste the updated image into in its original location on the web page. Save and close the page for now.

 As you create selections to paste into Dreamweaver when working in a Photoshop file, if you think you may need to return to the file for changes and you are familiar with saving selections in channels, each selection you make can be individually saved in its own channel that you can reactivate after altering the image in Photoshop to copy/paste it back into Dreamweaver.

Although we used this feature to almost completely build a web page, it can be used any time you want to add any type of image to a page. We practiced it to build this NH Lupine Restaurant page because we will use this page again in the next chapter to add some text and practice applying CSS. Let's move on to Smart Objects.

13.2.4 Using the Dreamweaver CS4 and CS5 Smart Object Feature

If you have used Smart Objects in Photoshop, you are familiar with their characteristics, which you will find are similar to Smart Objects in Dreamweaver. In Photoshop, you can make changes to a placed Smart Object, which will not affect the original file. Also, in Photoshop, if a vector image is placed as a Smart Object, you are able to return to the original vector file, make changes, and have it update all uses of that vector file in Photoshop. Smart Objects in Dreamweaver have the same basic characteristics. Unfortunately for CS3 users, the Smart Objects feature is exclusive to CS4 and CS5. If you are working in CS3, the Copy/Paste feature works great and is similar to the Smart Object feature, with one exception. What sets the Smart Object feature apart is the ability to have the native .psd file remain *linked* to the Dreamweaver file, so that when changes are made to it, they are reflected throughout the site in as many locations as the image has been inserted.

Adding a Smart Object   Because of the unique characteristic of the ability to have a native .psd file linked to a page, Dreamweaver must always be able to find the original .psd file. Following the best practice you have learned, the original .psd file you will want to use for a Smart Object should be placed in an *original graphics* (or *original.psds*) folder inside a site's umbrella folder, but not its root folder.

Following this procedure will assure that Dreamweaver will always be able to find it. If the site is transported to another computer, the master umbrella folder with the original graphics folder inside of it will be moved with it.

To learn how to use this feature, add the *butterfly.psd* file located in the *Chapter_13PracticeFiles* folder to the *original graphics* folder inside the umbrella folder of the SampleSite website. After you have done that, you are ready to add this image as a Smart Object in Dreamweaver.

Let's add this image to the *portsmouth_page.html* page of the SampleSite that we created in Chapter 11. After making the SampleSite the active site in the Files panel, open the *portsmouth_page.html* page. With the I-beam flashing, choose Insert>Image, or choose the Image option of the Common tab of the Insert panel. You will be asked to locate the native .psd file, which should have been added to the *original graphics* inside your Sample Umbrella folder.

After selecting the *butterfly.psd* file, you will enter the same Image Preview dialog box shown in Figure 13-5 to assign the optimization you want for the image. Choose an appropriate setting, keeping the native dimensions of the image. After you click OK, you are forwarded to the next dialog box, Save Web Image, through which you will need to locate the *images* folder inside your SampleRoot folder to save the image into it. In this dialog box, you can rename the image. However, it is easiest to keep the original name (updated with its new web file extension of .jpg) to avoid confusion. Lastly, you will want to assign some alt text, such as *butterfly photo*, and click OK. The image will be placed in Dreamweaver at your chosen insertion point, with its name listed in the Original section of the Property inspector when selected. It has been placed with one addition: it will contain a small icon in its upper-left corner consisting of a page, a square, and two arrows. At this point, your two arrows are green. Green is good. It indicates that Photoshop and Dreamweaver are *in sync* with each other; the file created in Photoshop matches the file placed in Dreamweaver. If you roll over the icon at this point, its tooltip will read *Images synched.* **FIGURE 13-10** illustrates this icon, as well as the icon when the two are not in sync.

Editing a Smart Object   Let's add a little more saturation to this image to add some brilliance to the flower and the butterfly. To do this, we will want to return to the native .psd file. With the image selected on the *portsmouth_page.html* page, you can click the Edit button in the Property inspector, or alternatively, right/Control-click and choose Edit Original With>Photoshop from the context-sensitive menu. You must choose Edit Original *not* Edit With, because Edit With will also bring you to Photoshop, but it will only allow you to edit the inserted .jpg file. By choosing the *Edit Original* option, you will return to the original .psd image.

Back in Photoshop, take a quick glance at the extension of the file that opened (checking that it is a .psd, not a .jpg) just to be sure that you did not accidentally choose the Edit With instead of Edit Original command if you used the right/Control-click method to return to Photoshop. Now choose Image>Adjustments>Hue/Saturation, increase the Saturation to +*20*, and then choose Save and close the file. When you return to Dreamweaver, sometimes the update is automatic, but sometimes you may

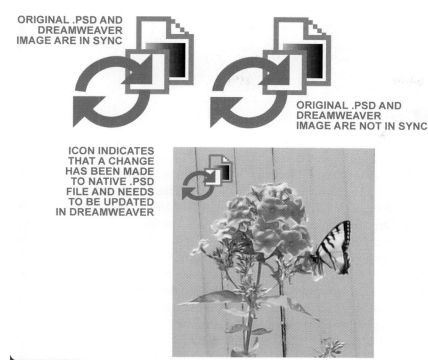

ORIGINAL .PSD AND
DREAMWEAVER
IMAGE ARE IN SYNC

ORIGINAL .PSD AND
DREAMWEAVER
IMAGE ARE NOT IN SYNC

ICON INDICATES
THAT A CHANGE
HAS BEEN MADE
TO NATIVE .PSD
FILE AND NEEDS
TO BE UPDATED
IN DREAMWEAVER

FIGURE 13-10 Smart Object icons.

need to click the image with the Select tool. However, after you do, the icon will update and change to warn you that the two are now not in sync by displaying the lower arrow in red, as shown in Figure 13-10. If you roll over the Smart Object icon this time, it will read *Original asset modified.* To *re-sync* the connection between Photoshop and Dreamweaver, select the image and then simply click the *Update from Original* icon in the Property inspector (looks just like the *in sync* icon), or right/Control-click and choose *Update from Original* from the context-sensitive menu.

You can also edit or update Smart Objects through the Assets panel. With the Images category active in the Assets panel, right/Control-click the image to choose the same commands from the context-sensitive menu when you are here. The advantage to updating here is that if the image that you are updating is used in multiple locations, they will all update automatically for you!

Just as in Photoshop, Smart Objects in Dreamweaver have two major advantages. First of all, changes made through this method can be global, updating the image in every use of it throughout your site. Second, optimization changes are made to a copy of the original image in the document by using the Image Preview dialog box and do not affect the original .psd. However, if you select a Smart Object on a page and click one of the Dreamweaver internal editing tools, such as the Brightness/Contrast one, the dialog box shown in **FIGURE 13-11** will appear.

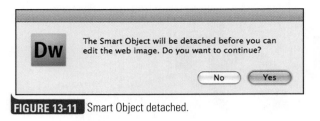

FIGURE 13-11 Smart Object detached.

If you click *Yes*, the Smart Object icon will disappear because the image will no longer be connected to the original Photoshop file. This is followed by the Undo message shown in Figure 13-7. Even though you will be able to undo a change made with one of the Dreamweaver internal editing tools, the Smart Object connection to the original .psd will have been permanently broken. If you should do this by accident, it's no problem; the original .psd file remains intact, allowing you to reinsert it as a Smart Object again! However, when an image is inserted as a Smart Object, the ability to return to Photoshop with a single click to make changes using its full image editing capabilities, rather than the basic ones included within Dreamweaver, makes the internal editing features unnecessary anyway.

13.3 Using Adobe Bridge with Dreamweaver

If you have used Adobe Bridge with Photoshop, you will find it handy with Dreamweaver as well. You can access Bridge directly from Dreamweaver by choosing File>Browse in Bridge. Although Bridge has many attributes, **FIGURE 13-12** provides an overview of its most common features.

1. From this pop-up menu, you can select the location of the file you want.
2. When an image is selected, an adjustable preview window lets you examine it more closely in an enlarged view.
3. The thumbnails can be enlarged with a slider for customized viewing of your images.
4. Many valuable properties are listed here (such as file size, date of creation, and dimensions) when an image has been selected in the Content section of Bridge.

Beyond these basics, there are some valuable features specific to its association with Dreamweaver. With the I-beam flashing in Dreamweaver, you can select an image in Adobe Bridge and then choose File>Place in Dreamweaver. If it is a .psd, you will be entered into the Image Preview dialog box, followed by the Save Web Image dialog box, and the Image Tag Accessibilities Attributes dialog box to apply alt text.

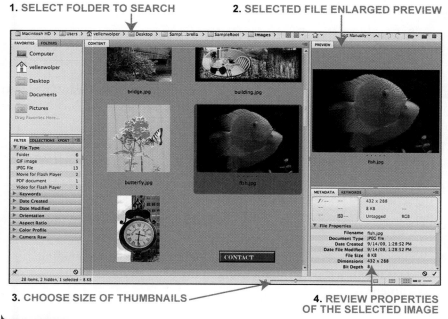

1. SELECT FOLDER TO SEARCH   **2. SELECTED FILE ENLARGED PREVIEW**

3. CHOOSE SIZE OF THUMBNAILS

4. REVIEW PROPERTIES OF THE SELECTED IMAGE

FIGURE 13-12 Bridge sample.

Then, the image will be placed in Dreamweaver as a Smart Object, as long as both your Bridge and your Dreamweaver versions are the same: they must both be version CS4 or both be version CS5. If an image you select is already in a web format (.jpg, .gif, or .png), the Image Tag Accessibilities Attributes dialog box will open to add alt text, followed by its placement on the page with a copy automatically added to the *images* folder of the site. Alternatively, with Bridge open and Dreamweaver open, you can drag and drop an image from Bridge directly into Dreamweaver, with the same sequence of dialog boxes opening, depending on whether it is already web ready or it is a native .psd image. To use the drag-and-drop option, unlike the Place command, the versions of Dreamweaver and Bridge do not have to be the same for this feature to work.

For CS3 Users

Both of the described features, the drag-and-drop method and the Place command from Bridge to Dreamweaver, also work with CS3. The only difference is that a native .psd file will not be placed in Dreamweaver as a Smart Object; it will simply be placed using the file format you choose in the Image Preview dialog box.

13.4 A Look at the Code in Split View: Insertion of a Favicon

FIGURE 13-13 illustrates the correlation between the information that was typed into the Link dialog box to add the favicon in Design view and the code Dreamweaver produced to create it.

1. The link element is added inside the `<head>` element of the document where, as you learned in Chapter 5, page titles and CSS are added.

2. Familiar to you by now, `href="` is followed by the location of the favicon in the *images* folder of the root folder of the site.

3. The `rel="` attribute is used to indicate how the link relates to the assigned page.

4. When a head tag is selected in the Split View mode, its corresponding code is identified with highlighting in the head element of the document.

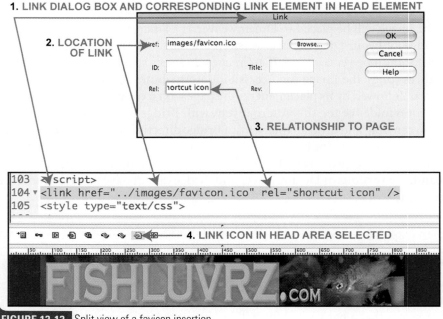

FIGURE 13-13 Split view of a favicon insertion.

13.5 What We Have Learned

Favicons are saved as favorites in your visitors' browsers. Therefore, we learned how to create one so your site will be listed there! We also explored the multiple ways that you can edit your images inside and outside of Dreamweaver. Within Dreamweaver, we explored its Image Preview dialog box, along with its small selection of internal editing tools. Outside of Dreamweaver, we learned how layers of a native Photoshop file can be selected and pasted directly into Dreamweaver and how native .psd images can be inserted as Smart Objects, which remain editable and are automatically updated to reflect those changes in Dreamweaver.

13.6 Reinforcing Your Knowledge

Project

1. Be sure your FishluvrzSite is the active site in the Files panel and open your *index.html* page. Let's add the heading text to this page. Place an I-beam inside the third row of the table, the cell just below the navigation bar. Type the following text:

   Welcome to Fishluvrz…Your one stop for all your fish and aquarium needs!

   After typing this sentence, add a soft return/line break (Shift+Enter/
   Return) and type the following sentence:

   Supplies? WE'VE GOT THEM!

   Insert another line break and type:

   Questions? WE'VE GOT ANSWERS!

2. Click anywhere inside the typed text and select *Heading 1* from the Format pop-up menu (HTML tab for CS4 and CS5 users) of the Property inspector. Because you have previously assigned the properties for it, and the line break kept all of the text within one paragraph, all of the text will automatically be converted to those specifications.

3. For the body text, we will insert some sample text. This time add a hard return after *ANSWERS!* to break and create a new paragraph. With the insertion point flashing, launch Microsoft Word and open the *index_body_text.doc* file (or the *index_body_text.rtf* file if needed) located in the *Chapter_13PracticeFiles* folder. Highlight all of the text and copy it to the Clipboard and then close and exit the application. Back in Dreamweaver, choose Edit>Paste Special and select the first option, *Text only.* (This will allow us to format it more specifically with CSS in Chapter 14.)

   As an alternative, also included in the *Chapter_13PracticeFiles* folder, is a version of the text saved as *index_body_text.txt.* If no formatting is required, as in this case, you can copy this file directly into the FishluvrzRoot folder, double-click it in the Files panel in Dreamweaver, copy it, close the window it automatically opened, place the I-beam where needed, and choose Paste. After the text has been placed on the page, choose Paragraph from the Format pop-up menu under the HTML category of the Property inspector.

   Regardless of the method you choose, don't worry if your table expands downward unexpectedly. We will adjust it later.

4. Let's insert a video into the index page. Place the I-beam at the end of the "Questions? WE'VE GOT ANSWERS!" sentence. With the I-beam flashing, choose Insert>Media>FLV. As you have learned, after you are in the Insert FLV dialog box, we will keep the type set to the default of *Progressive Download Video* and then browse to locate the video in the *Chapter_13PracticeFiles* folder. Choose to add it to your *images* folder of your FishluvrzRoot folder. Select *Clear Skin 1* and click the Detect Size button, being sure that Constrain is checked. After the size has been detected, change the width to 300; the corresponding height value should automatically update proportionately to 225 when you click it. Lastly, check *Auto play,* but do not check *Auto rewind.* (CS3 users should keep the *Prompt users to download Flash Player if necessary* option checked.) The video will be added to the page. However, the page must be previewed in a browser to watch the video. As you can see, it moved the line of text where it was added. Don't worry. We will adjust that with CSS in Chapter 14.

5. Place the I-beam in the left column of the three-column row below the row where you just added the text and video. Type the following items, being sure to add a hard return, creating a new paragraph

after each one *except* do not add a return after the last item on
the list:

Aquarium Essentials

Aquarium Kits

Aquarium Stands

Water Heaters

Water Pumps

6. Now, place the I-beam inside the middle column of this row and
type the following items, again being sure to add a hard return to
create a new paragraph after each one *except* the last item on the
list:

Aquarium Accessories

Water Treatment Products

Gravel Options

Fish Food

Thermometers

7. Complete this row by placing the I-beam in the third column and
typing the final list of items, again with a hard return to create a
new paragraph after each one *except* the last item on the list:

Aquarium Maintenance

Cleaning Supplies

Testing Equipment

Lighting Accessories

Aquarium Parts

8. Click an I-beam now inside the left column of the row below the
row of products you just added (the green row). We will add some
rollover navigation. Choose Insert>Image Objects>Rollover Image
and locate the *deals.gif* (original image) and *deals_dn.gif* (rollover
image) files in the *Chapter_13PracticeFiles* folder to complete the
Insert Rollover Image dialog box, as shown in **FIGURE 13-14**.

Notice that the *When clicked, Go to URL* field shows the hash symbol
(#). We will reassign this rollover to the products page after we create
it in Chapter 14. As you have learned, always choose to add a copy
to the *images* folder of your root folder when prompted. After it has
been inserted into the cell, and it is selected with selection handles,

Project (continued)

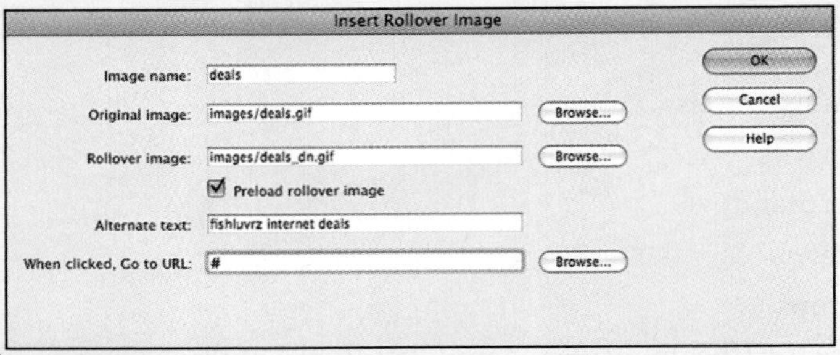

FIGURE 13-14 Fishluvrz deals rollover in the Insert Rollover Image dialog box.

click the right arrow of your keyboard to place the I-beam after it and press the Return/Enter key to create a new paragraph. Type the following sentence in lowercase text: *check out our internet specials of the week!* Add another hard return to create a new paragraph and insert the *fish_deals.jpg* image from the *Chapter_13PracticeFiles* folder into the cell, adding it to your *images* folder when prompted.

9. Using the Dreamweaver internal editing feature, apply the Sharpen tool to the *fish_deals.jpg* image to increase its sharpness by 5 in the Sharpen dialog box.

10. Place the I-beam in the middle column. Add another rollover image using *tips.gif* and *tips_dn.gif,* respectively, for the original and rollover images located in the *Chapter_13PracticeFiles* folder, and follow the same steps that you performed in step 8; however, this time, link the rollover to the *information_page.html* page you have already created. After inserting the rollover, again select the rollover with selection handles, place the I-beam after the image by clicking the right arrow key, add a hard return to create a new paragraph, and type the following lowercase text: *fish problems? get help from our experts!* Complete this cell by adding another hard return and inserting *fish_tips.jpg.*

11. We will add one more rollover to complete this row using the *blog.gif* and *blog_dn.gif* images, just as you did in step 8; this time, link the rollover to the *contact_page.html* page you already created. After inserting the rollover, again select the rollover with selection handles, place the I-beam after the image by pressing the right arrow key, add a hard return, and type the following lowercase text: *chat with other fishluvrz about your fish!*

12. For the last accompanying image, let's insert it as a Smart Object. Before we do that, place a copy of the *fish_blog.psd* image from the *Chapter_13PracticeFiles* folder into your *original fishluvrz graphics* folder inside your Fishluvrz umbrella folder. Now, add a hard return to create a new paragraph after the last sentence, choose Insert>Image, and locate the image in your *original fishluvrz graphics* folder. Set an appropriate optimization and set a matte color of #336600 in the Image Preview dialog box. After the image is inserted, if you are working in CS4 or CS5, it will display the in-sync icon. Choose to edit the Smart Object by clicking the Edit button in the Property inspector, or right/Control-click and choose Edit Original With>Photoshop from the context-sensitive menu. Lighten the image using either the Curves Levels, or Brightness/Contrast command from the Adjustments menu, or lighten it using the Dodge tool, and then sharpen it a little to your liking using Filter>Sharpen>Unsharp Mask. Save and quit Photoshop and return to Dreamweaver. When you return to Dreamweaver, your image will be out of sync with its original. Click the Update from Original icon in the Property inspector, or right/Control-click and choose Update from Original from the context-sensitive menu.

13. Add a rectangular hotspot covering most of the image area of each of the three fish photos you just inserted. Link the hotspots, one at a time, from left to right to # (for the products page only for now), *information_page.html*, and *contact_page.html*.

14. At this point, when viewed in Dreamweaver, your page should resemble **FIGURE 13-15**. Feel free to test it in a browser to play the video and test the cool rollovers. Don't worry if the layout and text still don't look right … the next stop is CSS in Chapter 14! We will apply CSS to finalize this page as part of our learning in the next chapter.

15. Let's add a favicon! Choose Insert>HTML>Head Tags>Link, or choose Link from the pop-up menu of the Head button located under the Common category of the Insert panel, to enter the Link dialog box to add the favicon. For the Href section, browse to locate it in the *Chapter_13PracticeFiles* folder and be sure to choose the *images* folder of the FishluvrzRoot folder for its destination. For the Rel section, type *shortcut icon*. That's it! Preview your index page in a browser again. You will be able to enjoy the video and the rollovers that you made, and perhaps get a peek at the favicon,

Project (continued)

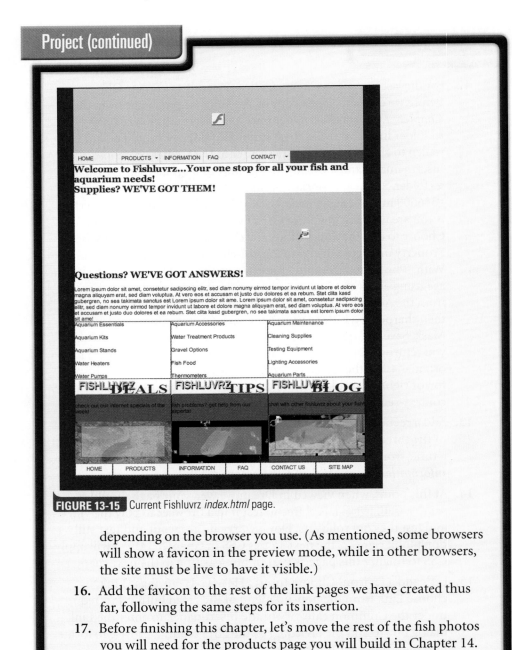

FIGURE 13-15   Current Fishluvrz *index.html* page.

depending on the browser you use. (As mentioned, some browsers will show a favicon in the preview mode, while in other browsers, the site must be live to have it visible.)

16. Add the favicon to the rest of the link pages we have created thus far, following the same steps for its insertion.

17. Before finishing this chapter, let's move the rest of the fish photos you will need for the products page you will build in Chapter 14. The photos are located in the *More Fish Photos* folder inside the *Chapter_13PracticeFiles* folder. Because they are native Photoshop files, copy them now into the *original fishluvrz graphics* folder of your Fishluvrz umbrella folder. We will optimize them using the Dreamweaver Smart Object feature when inserting them in the next chapter.

For step 12, you can edit the file prior to inserting it, or click it after it's inserted in Dreamweaver, and then click the Edit button in the Property inspector to open the native .psd in Photoshop. Make the changes, save it, return to Dreamweaver, delete the original, and insert the image again, as you did the original copy. Or, simply select the image and apply the Dreamweaver internal editing tools to lighten and sharpen the image.

13.7 Building Your Own Website

1. In this exercise, you will add a favicon to your index page. You will need to create your 16 x 16 px image first in Photoshop, and save it, typically as a .png file. Searching the Internet, you may want to download the .ico plug-in for Photoshop if you intend to use favicons on a regular basis for your web design work. Otherwise, you can use one of the many conversion services available on the Internet that allow you to upload your .png file to their site and have it instantly converted into the .ico format. Just remember that after you do that, it must be specifically renamed *favicon. ico* and added to your *images* folder.

2. Add favicons to any of the link pages you have created so far as well!

3. Using the image editing techniques you learned in this chapter, check each of your pages for images that could use tweaking. Adjust them using the Dreamweaver internal tools, copying and pasting from Photoshop, or selecting each one, clicking the Edit button in the Property inspector, and making your changes in Photoshop.

4. Add any needed text to your pages, because in the next chapter we will learn to format it using CSS.

5. Save and close your site.

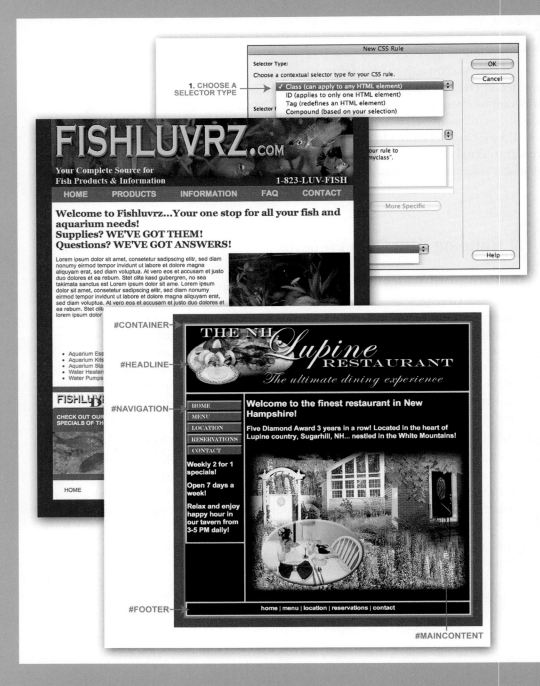

Working with Text and CSS in Dreamweaver

14

- Learn to create bulleted lists and other HTML formatting features
- Understand how the assignment of page properties relates to creating CSS rules
- Create, edit, and apply internal and external style sheets
- Customize a Spry Menu Bar
- Explore the use of div tags for structuring web pages

CSS offers text and layout formatting with global updating capabilities that graphic artists are familiar with in other programs and have come to rely on in their design work. In this chapter, you will learn how to format text using both HTML and CSS attributes, how to convert local formatting into site-wide formatting, and how to customize a Spry Menu Bar by reassigning its CSS styles. You will complete this chapter by learning the basic application of div tags for page structuring built from scratch, as well as an overview of the Dreamweaver application of div tags in its accompanying starter pages.

14.1 Formatting Text Without Entering the CSS Rule Definition Dialog Box

Some basic text formatting features can be assigned without knowing anything about CSS. Let's start this chapter by learning about these first and then ease our way into CSS!

14.1.1 HTML Formatting Features

Throughout this book thus far, the term Cascading Style Sheets (CSS) has been mentioned on numerous occasions, each time with the promise that in Chapter 14 we would learn about them. We are finally here! However, what you may not have realized is that you've actually already been using a little CSS since Chapter 9 when we learned to assign page properties! But, before we learn how you've been using CSS already and how you can now maximize their potential, let's cover some basic text formatting features available without having to enter the CSS panel. Applying a few features using the Format menu, the Text category of the Insert panel, the HTML option of the Insert application menu, or the HTML tab of the Property inspector, is a great way to be introduced to formatting text in Dreamweaver, because you are used to simply highlighting and choosing your desired text effect from the options bar or character palette in Photoshop. **FIGURE 14-1** details the features, what they do, and where they can be found.

With the exception of the Abbreviation, Acronym, and Characters features, all of the text features listed here are also available by clicking inside the text and then right/Control-clicking to select the option from the context-sensitive menu.

Although color, size, and font options appear in the CSS tab of the Property inspector in CS4 and CS5, when you click one of them, the CSS Rule dialog box will open and allow you to define the desired effect through CSS.

For CS3 Users

In CS3, as you have learned, the Format menu is called Text. You can also apply a font, color, and alignment to text under the Text category of the application menu, and through the Property inspector. Although Size and Size Change options are listed under the Text application menu, they will be grayed out because we assigned the *Use CSS instead of HTML tags* option under the General category of the Dreamweaver Preferences dialog box in Chapter 9. You can, however, assign a type size to selected text using the Property inspector. The single panel of the CS3 Property inspector is divided into two tabs in CS4 and CS5, as shown in **FIGURE 14-2**.

HTML TEXT FORMATTING FEATURES AND THEIR LOCATIONS

FEATURE	DESCRIPTION	LOCATION
FORMAT	APPLY AND REMOVE PARAGRAPH OR HEADING FORMAT	• FORMAT MENU • TEXT / INSERT PANEL (HEADINGS 1-3 ONLY) • INSERT>HTML>TEXT OBJECTS (HEADINGS 1-3 ONLY) • PROPERTY INSPECTOR (HTML)
STYLE	APPLY BOLD AND ITALIC STYLING	• FORMAT MENU • TEXT / INSERT PANEL • INSERT>HTML>TEXT OBJECTS • PROPERTY INSPECTOR (HTML)
INDENT OUTDENT	SAME AS BLOCK QUOTE: INDENTS INCREMENTALLY EACH TIME ASSIGNED, OUTDENT REMOVES INDENTING BY SAME PRESET INCREMENTS	• FORMAT MENU • TEXT / INSERT PANEL • INSERT>HTML>TEXT OBJECTS • PROPERTY INSPECTOR (HTML)
LIST	CREATE ORDERED, UNORDERED LISTS, AND DEFINITION STYLE LISTS	• FORMAT MENU • TEXT (INSERT PANEL) • INSERT>HTML>TEXT OBJECTS • PROPERTY INSPECTOR (HTML)
ABBREVIATION	DEFINE AN ABBREVIATION	• TEXT / INSERT PANEL • INSERT>HTML>TEXT OBJECTS
ACRONYM	DEFINE AN ACRONYM	• TEXT / INSERT PANEL • INSERT>HTML>TEXT OBJECTS
CHARACTERS	INSERT SPECIAL CHARACTERS, SUCH AS COPYRIGHT, TRADEMARK, AND REGISTERED TRADEMARK	• TEXT / INSERT PANEL • INSERT>HTML>SPECIAL CHARACTERS

FIGURE 14-1 HTML text formatting features.

CS3 TEXT OPTIONS

CS4 AND CS5 TEXT OPTIONS: HTML TAB

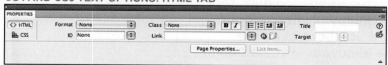

CS4 AND CS5 TEXT OPTIONS: CSS TAB

FIGURE 14-2 Text Property inspector CS3 vs. CS4 and CS5.

The Property inspector in CS4 and CS5 also has two additional options to assist you with CSS under its CSS tab. One is a pop-up menu called Targeted Rule. As shown in Figure 14-2, from this menu, you can choose to create a new rule, apply or remove an existing class, or create a new inline style. Right below this pop-up menu, there is also a button named EditRule. This button works in conjunction with the Targeted Rule pop-up menu. Select a rule using the Targeted Rule pop-up menu and then click the Edit Rule button to enter the Rule Definition dialog box to edit it. Additionally, if you choose to create a new rule by selecting the New Rule option from the Targeted Rule pop-up menu, you can then click the Edit Rule button to open the New CSS Rule dialog box to create one. We will explore all of these options later in this chapter.

Indent/Outdent/Block Quote Feature   Although the Format and Style options are already familiar to you, let's learn about the paragraph indent feature of Dreamweaver. After we learn about CSS, you will be able to assign a first-line indent to a paragraph. However, the Indent feature, also referred to as the Block Quote option, will indent an entire selected paragraph an equal amount from both its left and right sides by preset increments, as shown in **FIGURE 14-3**.

To reverse the action, choose the Outdent option. When applying this feature through the HTML tab of the Property inspector, it is represented by a small paragraph icon with a right arrow to apply an indent and one with a left arrow to apply an outdent.

Applying the List Feature to Selected Paragraphs   Lists can be created as an unordered list (bulleted list), an ordered list (numerical), and a definition list. When ordered or unordered lists are assigned through the HTML tab of the

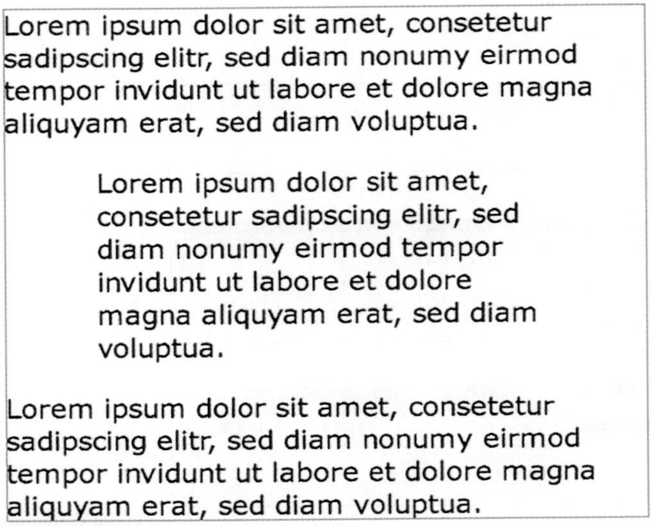

Lorem ipsum dolor sit amet, consetetur sadipscing elitr, sed diam nonumy eirmod tempor invidunt ut labore et dolore magna aliquyam erat, sed diam voluptua.

> Lorem ipsum dolor sit amet, consetetur sadipscing elitr, sed diam nonumy eirmod tempor invidunt ut labore et dolore magna aliquyam erat, sed diam voluptua.

Lorem ipsum dolor sit amet, consetetur sadipscing elitr, sed diam nonumy eirmod tempor invidunt ut labore et dolore magna aliquyam erat, sed diam voluptua.

FIGURE 14-3 Sample of a block quote.

ITEMS TYPED WITH A
RETURN BETWEEN THE TITLE
AND ITS DESCRIPTION

Item One

Lorem ipsum dolor sit amet, consetetur
sadipscing elitr, sed diam nonumy eirmod
tempor invidunt ut labore et dolore magna
aliquyam erat, sed diam voluptua.

Item Two

Lorem ipsum dolor sit amet, consetetur
sadipscing elitr, sed diam nonumy eirmod
tempor invidunt ut labore et dolore magna
aliquyam erat, sed diam voluptua.

Item Three

Lorem ipsum dolor sit amet, consetetur
sadipscing elitr, sed diam nonumy eirmod
tempor invidunt ut labore et dolore magna
aliquyam erat, sed diam voluptua.

DESCRIPTION WILL
AUTOMATICALLY BE
INDENTED FROM ITS TITLE

Item One
    Lorem ipsum dolor sit amet, consetetur
    sadipscing elitr, sed diam nonumy eirmod
    tempor invidunt ut labore et dolore magna
    aliquyam erat, sed diam voluptua.
Item Two
    Lorem ipsum dolor sit amet, consetetur
    sadipscing elitr, sed diam nonumy eirmod
    tempor invidunt ut labore et dolore magna
    aliquyam erat, sed diam voluptua.
Item Three
    Lorem ipsum dolor sit amet, consetetur
    sadipscing elitr, sed diam nonumy eirmod
    tempor invidunt ut labore et dolore magna
    aliquyam erat, sed diam voluptua.

FIGURE 14-4 Sample of a definition list.

Property inspector, they are selected by clicking icons displaying the respective type of bullet to the left of a miniature paragraph.

To create a list, each list item must be typed as its own paragraph by applying a hard return after each one and then highlighted to apply the style of list you want to use. Although you may not like the look of full paragraph spacing between your list items as you are typing them, as soon as you apply the list feature, they will be tightened up to be single spaced below each other. With any style of list you want to create, after you apply the option to at least one paragraph, as you continue to type, consecutive paragraphs will apply the list feature automatically until you press the Return/Enter key twice in succession to complete the list. In a definition list, the first paragraph is used for the item, with the following paragraph automatically indented for the description of the item typed in the previous paragraph. When you press the Return/Enter key again, the process will be repeated, as shown in FIGURE 14-4.

Although list characteristics, such as the style of bullets of an unordered list and the style of the numbering system of an ordered list (e.g., Roman numeral), can be customized through CSS, they can also be applied and customized as HTML text features.

To assign special HTML properties to a list, such as changing an ordered list to Roman numerals, select the list and choose Format>List>Properties, or right/Control-click and select List>Properties from the context-sensitive menu. In this dialog box, you can use a pop-up menu to assign changes to the ordered or unordered list format, change the style of either type, as well as switch from an ordered to an unordered list or vice versa.

Using the Abbreviation, Acronym, and Characters Features   To apply an abbreviation or acronym, highlight the word you want to affect and then choose the option from either the Text category of the Insert panel or the Insert>HTML>Text

Objects menu. You will be entered into a dialog box to detail the full name that the abbreviation or acronym represents. It will be automatically entered into the HTML code for you. The Characters option, also chosen from the Text category of the Insert panel or the Insert>HTML>Special Characters menu, provides the ability to add special characters (such as the copyright, trademark, and registered trademark symbols) to your text without having to know their HTML code equivalents. To apply one of these, simply place the I-beam where you want to insert the symbol, choose the feature under one of its locations, and then select the desired symbol from its fly-out menu.

Adding a Horizontal Rule   You can also add a horizontal line to a page by clicking Horizontal Rule in the Common category of the Insert panel (CS4 and CS5 only), or by choosing Insert>HTML>Horizontal Rule (CS3, CS4, and CS5). With an I-beam flashing, when you choose this option, the line will be added to the page at the designated location. When you select it, you can customize the line with a width, height, alignment, and a basic shading option using the Property inspector, with the ability to further customize it using CSS.

Using the Dreamweaver Spell Check Feature   Dreamweaver contains a spell check feature that is similar to that of other programs. Although you do not have to highlight text to use this feature, it will work only on the current active page. With the active page open, choose Commands>Check Spelling in CS4 and CS5, or Text>Check Spelling in CS3. If you highlight a specific word or words first, Dreamweaver will sequentially display each questionable word in the group of selected words, using a typical Adobe style Check Spelling dialog box, as shown in **FIGURE 14-5**. As Dreamweaver scans and locates possible errors, it automatically

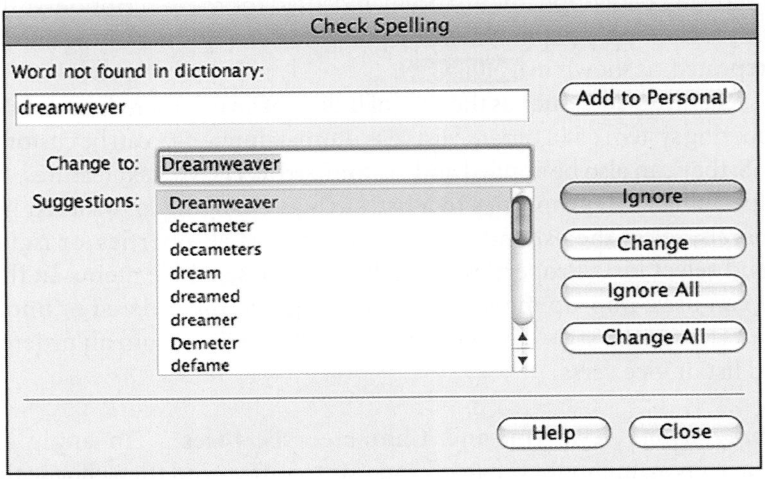

FIGURE 14-5   Check Spelling dialog box.

highlights them to identify their location in the document and offers suggested corrections.

If you do not have any text selected when you choose the Check Spelling option, a dialog box will display, "Dreamweaver has reached the end of the document. Do you want to continue checking from the start of the document?" Although this message may sound confusing, after you choose Yes, you will be brought to its Check Spelling dialog box. The first questionable word in the document is displayed with its suggested corrections. Your response will be followed by a sequential search for any additional possible errors.

Page Content Using CSS

When you learn how to use CSS to format your page content, its true value, potential, and strength will be unleashed, providing the tools you as an artist and designer have been craving.

14.2.1 Style Sheets for Page Layout vs. Style Sheets for Web Pages

If you have used style sheets in other graphic programs or in word processing programs, you already understand their major benefit. After they have been applied to your text, you can change one or more of the styles you have created, and the program used will automatically apply those changes throughout the entire document. This is an enormous time saver, especially with a multi-page document.

It is much the same when applying style sheets to web pages. When all of a website's pages have an external style sheet attached to them and a font, size, color, etc., is changed in the external style sheet, all instances of its application *throughout* the site are automatically updated. This is a huge convenience and time saver; as we have discussed throughout this text, "time is money" in web design.

14.2.2 The Automatic Application of CSS when Assigning Page Properties

As mentioned, you have already been using a little CSS without even entering the CSS panel. Let's explore how that happens. With your SampleSite as the active site in the Files panel, create a new blank page named *sample_css.html* and save it into the *pages* folder. (Once again, during this practice, it will not be necessary to add a title, keywords, and description text to this page. However, remember that you must start each page of a real site with these critical steps.) After you have done that, as we learned in Chapter 9, assign the font, size, text color, and page background color appearance properties using the Appearance (CSS) tab in the Page Properties dialog box, as shown in FIGURE 14-6. (Remember that when only three hexadecimal values are displayed when choosing a color, it is because the value is actually the displayed combination

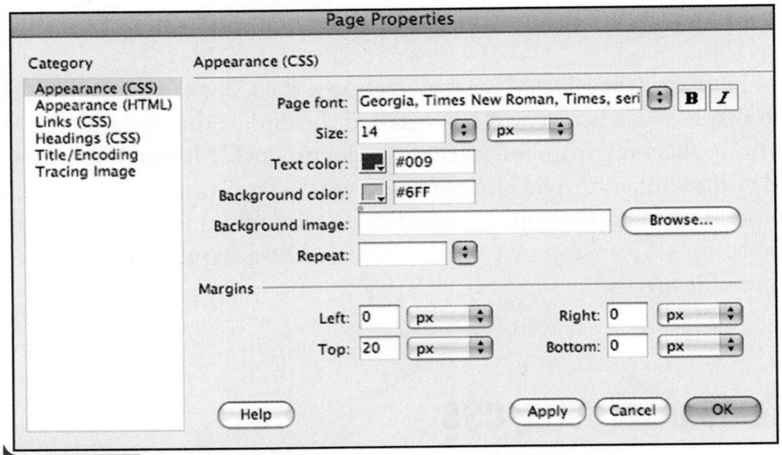

FIGURE 14-6 Basic CSS properties in the Page Properties dialog box.

of letters/numbers listed twice consecutively: the text color #009 is actually #000099. Always add the hash symbol [#] before the hexadecimal value to have browsers display your colors as intended.)

To view the CSS that you have just created, you will need to open the CSS panel. If you are working in the Designer workspace and it is not already showing, choose Window>CSS Styles, or choose Window>Workspace Layout>Reset 'Designer', which will dock it just above the Files panel in the Designer workspace. (In CS4 and CS5, you can also click the *CSS Panel* button in the Property inspector; in CS3 click the CSS button.) Once the panel is open, click the *All* tab. When the All tab is active, you will see *<style>* listed with an arrow next to it. When the arrow is clicked to the down position, the following two items will be visible: *body,td,th* and *body*. What do those terms mean and how did they get there? To answer those questions, we need to begin with an introduction to the anatomy of the CSS panel.

14.2.3 Anatomy of the CSS Panel

The CSS panel will contain any rules that have been created for the active document. A *rule* is like a style in other programs. In a program such as Adobe Illustrator or Adobe InDesign®, you can define a style containing multiple attributes. A CSS rule follows the same concept. In web design, multiple styling features can be contained in one rule. What is different about a rule in CSS vs. a style in another graphic program is its identification system. A *selector* in a CSS rule is like the Style type in a page layout program's style panel. If you are familiar with style sheets in print design, you know those programs typically contain two types: paragraph and character. In web design, there are four types: class, ID, tag, and compound. The definition of a CSS rule, containing the features you assign to the rule, like the style options of a style you assign in

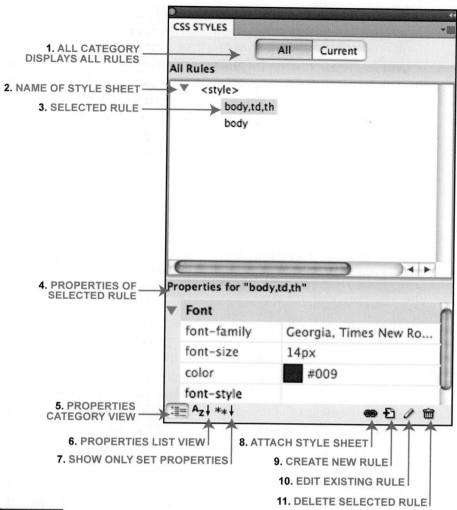

1. **ALL CATEGORY DISPLAYS ALL RULES**
2. **NAME OF STYLE SHEET**
3. **SELECTED RULE**
4. **PROPERTIES OF SELECTED RULE**
5. **PROPERTIES CATEGORY VIEW**
6. **PROPERTIES LIST VIEW**
7. **SHOW ONLY SET PROPERTIES**
8. **ATTACH STYLE SHEET**
9. **CREATE NEW RULE**
10. **EDIT EXISTING RULE**
11. **DELETE SELECTED RULE**

FIGURE 14-7 Anatomy of the CSS panel with the All tab selected.

a page layout program's style panel, becomes attached to that selector. **FIGURE 14-7** is a screen shot of the CSS panel, as it should be displayed now with the All tab selected, if your *sample_css.html* is the open active page of the SampleSite. It currently contains two rules: *body,td,th* and *body*.

1. The CSS panel has two viewing/accessibility options. The All tab will display all styles with their respective rules assigned to the page.

2. When a style sheet has been created, its name will display in this area of the panel; <style> is the default name applied by Dreamweaver for the style sheet that will be created when page properties are assigned in the Page Properties dialog box.

3. The rules created within the style sheet will be listed when the style's arrow is clicked into the down position. When you click a rule in the list, it will become highlighted and its properties will be displayed.

4. When a rule is selected, its properties are displayed with the ability to edit them in the Properties section of the CSS panel. When you click the item you want to change, such as the font size, a pop-up menu appears (based on your chosen display view), which allows you to scroll through all of the same default sizes that are listed in the Appearance (CSS) section of the Page Properties dialog box to choose a new selection, or type in your own custom size. (If this half of the CSS panel displays only the words "Properties for" followed by the name of the rule you have selected, you may need to drag up the bottom edge of the top half of the CSS panel to reveal the editing area of this lower half of the CSS panel section.)

5. As identified by its indented appearance, this is the current selected display view of the Properties section of the CSS panel. This view displays all the possible properties by categories: font, background, etc. When you click one of a selected rule's properties in the Properties section of the CSS panel in this view, a pop-up menu will appear to allow you to edit it.

6. This view will list all of the possible properties alphabetically. When you click one of the selected rule's properties in the Properties section of the CSS panel in this view, a pop-up menu will appear to allow you to edit the property.

7. This view will only list the properties assigned to the selected rule. When you choose this view, a clickable option is displayed at the bottom of the properties assigned: Add Property. When you select it, a pop-up menu will appear, allowing you to add more properties to the rule from an alphabetical listing of the available choices, or edit any existing property by clicking on the property and choosing from the pop-up menu that appears.

8. This "chain link" icon named *Attach Style Sheet* is used to attach an external style sheet to a page. When you click it, you will enter a dialog box to locate the style sheet you want to link to or import.

9. When you click this New CSS Rule icon, you will enter the New CSS Rule dialog box to define a new class, ID, tag, or compound rule.

10. With a rule selected in the CSS panel, when you click the Edit Rule button (pencil), you will be able to edit the properties you have previously assigned to the selected rule.

11. Just as the trash can allows you to delete features in various palettes of Photoshop, if a rule is selected when you click the trash can of the CSS panel, the rule will be deleted. You can also select and delete multiple rules at the same time. However, if you do select multiple rules, before they will be deleted, Dreamweaver will prompt you first: "You are trying to delete multiple CSS rules. Do you want to proceed?" If you click Yes, the rules will be deleted.

Making Changes Using the CSS Panel   Now that you have been introduced to the CSS panel, let's use it to alter the existing page properties. The appearance properties you have showing on your *sample_css.html* page were added using the Page Properties dialog box. Click the *Show only set properties* option, which is the third category view option at the lower-left corner of the CSS panel. Now, click the *body* property in the Properties section of the panel (not the *body,td,th*) and change its background color to *#FFFFCC*. Ahhh ... now *that* color is easier on your eyes!

Now select the *body,td,th* rule. In the Properties section of the CSS panel, change its color to *#006633*. Click *Add Property*, scroll down to select *font-weight*, and then assign *bold* in the pop-up menu that appears to its right. Choose *Add Property* one more time, select *padding*, and then type *10 px* for its width.

Now, we will add some more rules through the Page Properties dialog box by assigning the link properties shown in **FIGURE 14-8**.

Select the *Headings (CSS)* category. Assign a font collection of *Arial, Helvetica, sans-serif*, a size of *24 px*, and a color of *#000000* for Heading 1. For Heading 2, assign a size of *18 px* and a color of *#666666*. Click OK to exit the Page Properties dialog box. After you have done that, when the CSS panel *All* tab is active, you will notice two important additions. The four link states have been added individually to the CSS panel as: a:link, a:visited, a:hover, and a:active (in a very specific order that cannot be changed, if they are to work properly when viewed in a browser), plus an *a*.

Because links must be in the specified sequence to work properly in a browser, here's a little saying to help you remember the required order: a Little Very Handy Analogy. The start of each word represents the order required for the links: <u>a</u>, a:<u>l</u>ink, a:<u>v</u>isited, a:<u>h</u>over, a:<u>a</u>ctive.

Page Properties

Category	Links (CSS)
Appearance (CSS)	
Appearance (HTML)	Link font: Arial, Helvetica, sans-serif ⬍ **B** *I*
Links (CSS)	
Headings (CSS)	Size: 16 ⬍ px ⬍
Title/Encoding	
Tracing Image	Link color: ⬍ #FFF Rollover links: #636
	Visited links: #990 Active links: #636
	Underline style: Never underline ⬍

Help   Apply   Cancel   OK

FIGURE 14-8   Assigned CSS link properties in the Page Properties dialog box.

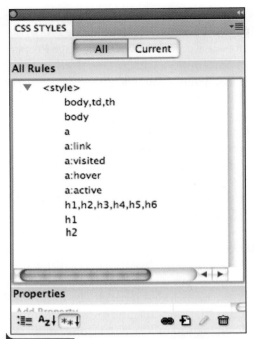

FIGURE 14-9   CSS panel displaying properties of body,td,th, body, and headings.

You will also notice that the CSS panel displays the h1 and h2 headings, plus an h1,h2,h3,h4,h5,h6 style for all heading properties that have not been otherwise specified. The reason for this is that a font was assigned to *all* headings, with additional separate settings of size and color for only headings 1 and 2. The top section of your CSS panel, if viewed using the *All* tab, should now resemble **FIGURE 14-9**.

When you click *body,td,th* in the CSS panel, its properties are displayed in the *Properties for* section of the panel. Notice when you click the style that the panel displays the font, size, color, font-weight, and padding properties. When you click *body*, the page background color and margins are displayed. When you make your initial selections in the Appearance (CSS) tab of the Page Properties dialog box, Dreamweaver automatically divides them for you into a *body* rule for the background and margins, and a *body,td,th* rule for the font properties of the body, as well as for any table cells or table headers in the body (td, th).

Before moving on to creating a CSS rule from scratch using the CSS panel, let's learn what's different about the Current tab of the CSS panel vs. the All tab. **FIGURE 14-10** shows the change we just made to the background of the page. The Current mode of the CSS Styles panel is divided into three sections: the top section displays the CSS properties for the current selection (whatever is *currently* selected *in the document itself*), a Rules section in the middle that details the rule containing the selected property, and a Properties section at the bottom (like the All tab has)

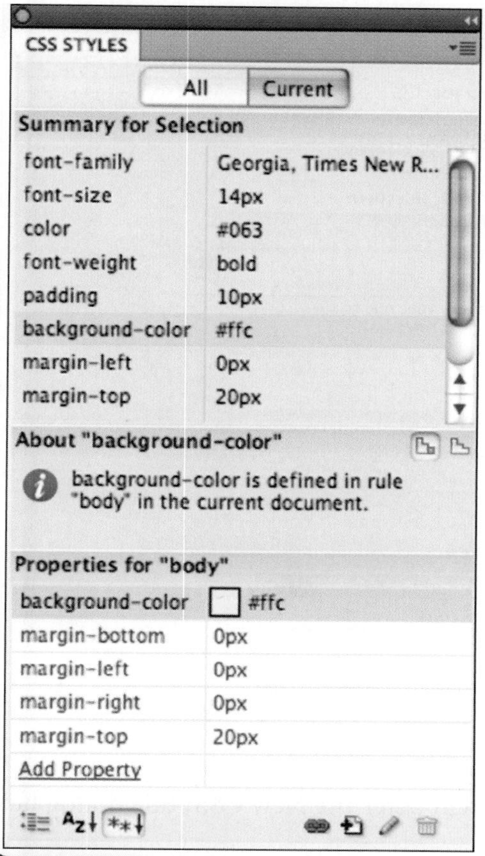

FIGURE 14-10 Current tab of the CSS panel.

that you can use to edit/add properties to the selected rule. In the top section of the panel, you cannot delete the property you select. However, when you click it, it will become highlighted simultaneously in the *Properties for* section below it, with the ability to edit or delete the property there.

14.2.4 Creating a New CSS Rule

We have created a rule using the Appearance (CSS) category of the Page Properties dialog box and altered that rule using the CSS panel. It is time now to learn to create a new rule from scratch. This can be done through the CSS panel by using the New CSS Rule icon (item 9 in Figure 14-7) or choosing New from the CSS panel's options menu; or by activating an I-beam on a page, right/Control-clicking, and choosing CSS Styles>New from the context-sensitive menu. In CS4 and CS5, using the CSS tab of the Property inspector, you can also select New CSS Rule from the Targeted Rule pop-up menu, and then click the Edit Rule button. After you have

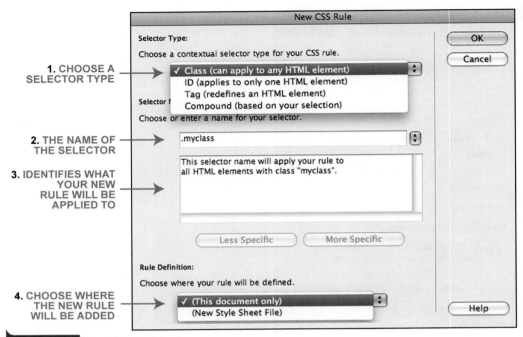

1. CHOOSE A SELECTOR TYPE

2. THE NAME OF THE SELECTOR

3. IDENTIFIES WHAT YOUR NEW RULE WILL BE APPLIED TO

4. CHOOSE WHERE THE NEW RULE WILL BE ADDED

FIGURE 14-11 New CSS Rule dialog box.

applied one of those commands, you will enter the New CSS Rule dialog box shown in **FIGURE 14-11**.

1. This pop-up menu allows you to choose one of the four types of selectors available.

2. If you choose the Class option, this area allows you to create its name, beginning with a period. If you choose the Tag option, it will provide a pop-up menu listing all the tag names to select from. Alternatively, if you choose the tag selector, you can enter the HTML tag here if you know it, such as h1 for Heading 1.

3. When you choose a selector, this text area will identify what your current selector will affect after it is created.

4. This pop-up menu allows you to determine whether the new rule you are creating will be included within the current document only, added to an existing style sheet, or attached to it as an external style sheet.

Types of Selectors   Before learning to assign properties, it is important to understand the differences between the three types of selectors: class, ID, and tag. As previously mentioned, the Compound option allows you to define one rule that, when applied, will affect a combination of two or more classes, IDs, or tags.

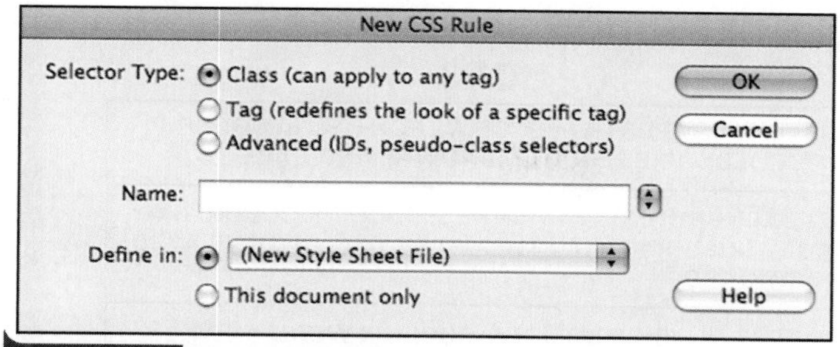

FIGURE 14-12 New CSS Rule dialog box in CS3.

For CS3 Users

The New CSS Rule dialog box shown in **FIGURE 14-12** contains some minor wording differences/exclusions that are contained in its CS4 and CS5 dialog box counterparts. For selectors, it offers the class, tag, and ID options, and although the descriptions are slightly different, their functions are the same. To create a rule affecting multiple tags, use the Advanced selector type. The only other difference is the absence of the text area explaining what your new rule will affect.

Class Selector   A class selector is similar to a character style in a page layout program. It can be applied multiple times, as needed, to images, entire paragraphs of text, or highlighted words only.

ID Selector   When you select this option from the pop-up menu, as shown in Figure 14-11, Dreamweaver will tell you that an ID can only apply to one element on the page. It is typically used with div tags to define sections of a page, such as the headline, navigation, and footer areas of a page. A basic introduction to the use of IDs and div tags will be covered later in this chapter.

Tag Selector   This type of selector allows you to choose an existing HTML tag and redefine its properties. For example, you can add more features to a Heading 1 tag, in addition to the basic features that you have the ability to assign using the Headings category of the Page Properties dialog box.

Creating a Rule Definition   After you have chosen the type of selector you want to define the properties for, you are entered into the multi-faceted CSS Rule Definition dialog box. Selecting your options here follows the same format as the Page Properties dialog box, except that it has additional categories and options to choose from for text and images. The categories have been summarized in **FIGURE 14-13**. The best way to learn them is through experimentation and application. We will be applying a number of them through this chapter; the rest are worth exploring on your own time to maximize your potential in CSS usage.

CSS RULE DEFINITION CATEGORIES

CATEGORY	OPTIONS
TYPE	ASSIGN TEXT PROPERTIES, SUCH AS FONT, SIZE, COLOR, WEIGHT (BOLD), LINE HEIGHT (LEADING), AND CASE
BACKGROUND	ASSIGN BACKGROUND PROPERTIES, SUCH AS COLOR AND AN IMAGE, INCLUDING HOW THE IMAGE WILL BE DISPLAYED AND POSITIONED
BLOCK	ASSIGN TEXT BLOCK FEATURES, SUCH AS WORD AND LETTER SPACING (TRACKING), TEXT ALIGNMENT WITHIN THE BLOCK, FIRST LINE INDENT, DISPLAY AND WHITE SPACE SETTINGS
BOX	ASSIGN DIMENSIONS, WRAP OPTIONS, AND INDIVIDUAL PADDING; ADD MARGIN SETTINGS FOR EACH SIDE OF THE BOX
BORDER	ASSIGN A STYLE, WIDTH, AND COLOR INDIVIDUALLY TO EACH SIDE OF THE BORDER
LIST	ASSIGN A LIST STYLE FROM THE AVAILABLE OPTIONS, OR CREATE ONE FROM YOUR OWN IMAGE, AND ASSIGN HOW THE TEXT WILL WRAP AROUND YOUR LIST OBJECT
POSITION	ASSIGN PLACEMENT, VISIBILITY, STACKING ORDER, AND CROPPING OPTIONS
EXTENSIONS	ASSIGN PAGE BREAKS FOR PRINTING OR ADD VISUAL EFFECTS WHEN ROLLED OVER, SUCH AS A QUESTION MARK FOR HELP OR A CLOCK TO SYMBOLIZE WAIT

FIGURE 14-13 CSS rule definition categories.

Let's create and apply a class selector. With your *sample_css.html* page open, choose to create a new CSS rule using one of the methods described. After you are in the New CSS Rule dialog box, choose *Class* from the Selector menu. When assigning a name to a class, naming it relative to its future use will help you keep track of the classes you create for later use. Title this one *.remindertext* (remember that a class must begin with a period and should be lowercase; it can contain numbers as well as letters with no spaces). For the *Choose where your rule will be defined* option (or *Define in* when using CS3), select *This document only* from the pop-up menu, and then click OK to enter the CSS Rule Definition dialog box.

In this dialog box, define the class with the following properties. In the Type category, assign the Font-family of *Trebuchet MS, Arial, Helvetica, sans-serif* (or *Verdana, Arial, Helvetica, sans-serif* in CS3); also assign Font-size: *16 pixels*, Font-weight: *Bold*, and Color: *#000000*. In the Background category, assign the Background-color: *#FFFFCC*. In the Block category, assign a Text-indent of *20 pixels*. In the Border category, assign a Style of *Dashed, Same for all*; assign a Width of *5 pixels, Same for all*; and assign a Color of *#006633, Same for all.*

Now click OK to exit the Rule Definition dialog box. After you have done that, with the *All* tab activated, peek at your new class using each of the three views: Category, List, and Only Set Properties. You will eventually find that one of the three views is your favorite view, but for now, you should experiment by viewing the CSS panel in different views to get familiar with each one's unique appearance and property editing method.

Applying a Rule   To test out the new class, we need some text and an image. Create a table with the following characteristics: 450 pixels wide, 1 row, 1 column, with zero for its padding, spacing, and border. Set the table alignment to *Center* and then set the Vertical alignment to *Top* for its single cell. Type *My CSS practice* and apply a hard return to create a new paragraph. Type *Creating my first rules* and then apply another hard return and type a couple of sentences about anything you like. Highlight your most recent paragraph and copy it to the Clipboard. Press the Enter/Return key to add one more hard return to begin another paragraph and then paste your text from the Clipboard into the table cell at the insertion point. We will apply our new *.remindertext* class to this paragraph. Place the I-beam anywhere inside this paragraph. You do not have to highlight all of the text. In fact, if you highlighted only a section of the text, the class would be applied only to the highlighted text (just like a character style sheet in page layout). However, for our purposes at this time, we will not select a specific part of the paragraph; by simply placing the I-beam randomly within the paragraph, we are signifying that we would like the class applied to the entire paragraph. Choose to assign the class using one of the following methods:

- With the I-beam placed in the text, right/Control-click and choose CSS Styles>.remindertext from the context-sensitive menu.
- Right/Control-click the rule in the top half of the CSS panel in the All view and choose Apply from the context-sensitive menu.
- Choose .remindertext from the pop-up menu in the CSS tab of the Property inspector under Targeted Rule (CS4 and CS5 only).
- Choose .remindertext from the Class category's pop-up menu under the HTML tab of the Property inspector.

After you have chosen to apply the class, it should immediately reflect the assigned definition!

For CS3 Users

In CS3, when using the Property inspector, choose .remindertext from the Style pop-up menu.

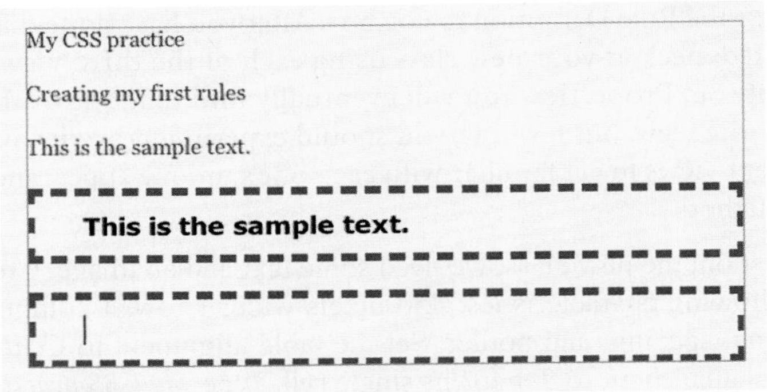

FIGURE 14-14 Class still applied to new paragraph.

Carrying this concept further, let's create another class named *.imageplacement* and again choose *This document only*. For this class, assign the following rule definition.

In the Border category, assign the Style *Solid, Same for all*; assign a Width of *10 pixels, Same for all*; and assign the Color a *#006633, Same for all*.

Create a new paragraph below the text with the .remindertext applied to it. If your new paragraph still has the .remindertext applied to it, as shown in **FIGURE 14-14**, you can right/Control-click and choose CSS Styles>None from the context-sensitive menu, or choose *Remove Class* from the Targeted Rule pop-up menu in the CSS tab of the Property inspector in CS4 or CS5, or choose *None* from the Style pop-up menu in CS3 or the Class pop-up menu under the HTML tab in CS4 and CS5. After you do that, you should simply see the I-beam flashing on the page, with no border around it.

Now, choose to insert the *bridge.jpg* image located in the *Chapter_14PracticeFiles* folder, being sure to add it to the *images* folder of the SampleRoot folder. With the image selected, choose to apply the .imageplacement rule to it. If you are applying styles using the Property inspector when working with images, the Class pop-up menu will appear at the right side of the panel when an image has been selected first.

Before we move on to external style sheets, let's redefine an existing HTML tag. Before entering the New CSS Rule dialog box again, select the table, being sure you are selecting the table, not the cell of the table. (Remember that you can use the tag selector located at the lower-left corner of the Document window for help!) After you have done that, choose to create a new rule; however, instead of selecting to create a class, choose *Tag (Redefines an HTML element)*. In the Selector Name section, notice that because you preselected the table, Dreamweaver assumed that you probably wanted to change the properties for the table tag. (It is the correct choice for us. However, if it wasn't the correct tag, you could simply scroll and select a different one from the alphabetized pop-up menu, or type it in.) Keep the *This document only* option to identify where the rule will be defined and click OK. In the Rule Definition dialog box, choose the *Background* category. For Background-image, browse and select the *background.jpg* image in the *Chapter_14PracticeFiles* folder. After you have done that, assign the *repeat* option for the *Background-repeat* section of the same category (by the way, if you do not choose an option, *repeat* is the default choice). In the *Border* category, assign the Style *Outset, Same for all*; assign a Width of *10 pixels, Same for all*; and assign a Color of *#999999, Same for all*. When you exit this dialog box, these reassigned properties will be immediately applied to the table.

To complete this exercise, apply Heading 1 to the first line, *My CSS practice*, and apply Heading 2 to the second line, *Creating my first rules*. When viewed in a browser, your table should resemble FIGURE 14-15.

FIGURE 14-15 Creating and applying CSS rules.

A great way to learn more about the effects of various CSS properties is to create more of your own "mini" pages, such as the one we just completed, assigning a myriad of different properties to the content on your pages.

Editing a Rule   To edit an existing rule, you need to enter the Rule Definition dialog box. To access this dialog box for editing, choose any one of the following methods:

- Select the rule and click the Edit Rule button (the pencil) at the lower-right edge of the CSS panel.
- Select the rule and choose Edit from the CSS panel's options menu.
- Select the rule, right/Control–click, and choose Edit from the context-sensitive menu.
- Select the rule in the Targeted Rule pop-up menu of the CSS tab of the Property inspector and then click the Edit Rule button below it (CS4 and CS5 only).

After you have entered the Rule Definition dialog box, simply make your desired changes, which will automatically be applied to all content on the page that has the rule applied to it. To test a "look" before leaving the dialog box and confirming your choice, you can click the Apply button.

14.2.5 Types of Styles

There are three types of styles: *internal* or *embedded* style sheets, *external* style sheets, and *inline* styles. Inline can be thought of as "in-content," built directly into the body content of the page. The two most widely used types are internal and external, which will be the two types we will focus on here. What differentiates the two main types is location and versatility. Internal style sheets reside in the head element of the page they are created on, and they are available to apply their features to only that page. As a graphic artist, you may be familiar with the term *embedded* from other programs, with regards to a graphic that has been "glued in" rather than linked, making the file larger; however, embedding eliminates issues of missing linked graphics. An embedded style sheet, the other name for an internal style sheet, has the same kind of relevance: it is included, not linked.

An external style sheet resides outside of the web page and is usually linked to it. This allows the page to have substantially less code, which allows the page to download faster. However, when uploading a site, a linked external style sheet must also be uploaded because its properties are not embedded. So far, we have chosen *This document only* in the *Choose where your rule will be defined* section of the New CSS Rule dialog box when creating our styles. All of the styles we have created thus far are internal embedded styles because of that. If you scroll in the pop-up menu where *This document only* is located, the alternative selection of *New Style Sheet File* will create an external style sheet instead.

The basic concept of the word *cascading* in the name Cascading Style Sheets refers to the application priority of a style: if there are conflicting style sheets, the closest style takes precedence. As you use style sheets in your website and incorporate both internal and external styles sheets in them, if a style conflict arises in the case of an external vs. an internal/embedded style, because the internal style is located in the <head> element of the page it is applied to, and therefore "closer," it will have a higher priority and override the external style sheet.

Creating an External Style Sheet   External style sheets can be created from existing internal styles or created from scratch. We will create them both ways, beginning with moving rules from an internal style sheet to an external one.

Creating an External Style Sheet from an Internal One   Before we do that, we will begin by editing the properties of some of our existing rules. With your *sample_css.html* page active, select the *body,td,th* rule in the CSS panel and click the Edit Rule button (the pencil) at the bottom of the panel to edit its properties, or try editing the properties using one of the three views of the properties in the bottom section of the CSS panel. Use the Rule Definition dialog box or the pop-up menus, which are available when you click the rule in the Properties section of the CSS panel, to make the following changes. In the Type category, change the Font-family from *Georgia, Times New Roman, Times, serif* to *Arial, Helvetica, sans-serif* and change the Color from *#006633* to *#FFFFFF*. In the Background category, add the Background-color: *#000000*. Click OK to complete the changes to the *body,td,th* rule, and then choose to edit the *body* rule.

For the *body* rule, make the following change. In the Background category, change the Background-color from *#FFFFCC* to *#663366*.

After you have made the changes, we are ready to move these rules to a new external style sheet. Any time you want to multi-select rules to move them, the process resembles selecting multiple layers in Photoshop. If they are consecutive, you can Shift-click them; if they are not consecutive, you can Command/Control-click to select them out of sequence. Be sure the arrow next to the word <style> is in the down position to reveal the rules contained in it. Select the following rules: *body,td,th; body; a; a:link; a:visited; a:hover;* and *a:active.* With all of these rules highlighted, right/Control-click and select *Move CSS Rules* from the context-sensitive menu, or choose the command from the CSS panel's options menu. After you have chosen this command, you will enter a dialog box to choose to either create a new style sheet or move the selected rules to one you have already defined. If you have other style sheets already defined, you can browse to locate the one that you want to add the selected rules to. We currently have no other style sheets already defined, so we will select the *A new sheet* radio button in this dialog box. Choosing this option will display a second dialog box, asking where you want to save the new style sheet, as shown in **FIGURE 14-16**.

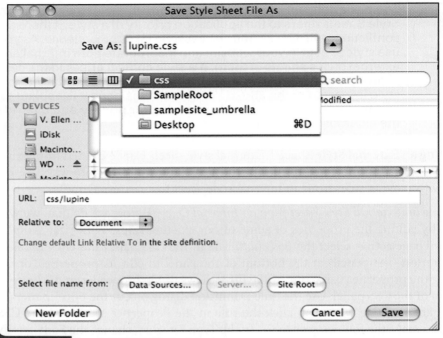

FIGURE 14-16 Save Style Sheet File As dialog box.

Finally, the reason you created a *css* folder for your site in Chapter 6 will make sense to you. Web pages can have multiple different style sheets applied to them. To keep your external style sheet files organized, we learned to create a *css* folder within the root folder of the site, specifically to store all of its applicable external CSS style sheets. When you start to build a site, you may not know how many style sheets you will need. Creating a folder to store them all ahead of time will keep you organized. In the Save Style Sheet File As dialog box, title the style sheet *lupine.css* and then use the pop-up menu to browse and locate the *css* folder you created within the SampleRoot folder of the SampleSite website. After you click the Save button and exit this dialog box, your CSS panel will automatically update with two style sheets displayed: the new one you just created and the original style sheet containing the rest of the styles, as shown in **FIGURE 14-17**.

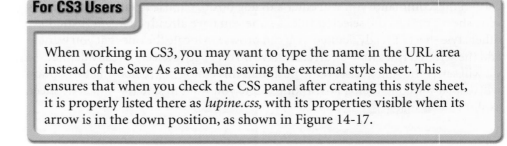

For CS3 Users

When working in CS3, you may want to type the name in the URL area instead of the Save As area when saving the external style sheet. This ensures that when you check the CSS panel after creating this style sheet, it is properly listed there as *lupine.css*, with its properties visible when its arrow is in the down position, as shown in Figure 14-17.

CSS STYLES

All   Current

All Rules

▼   <style>
        .remindertext
        .imageplacement
        table
        h1,h2,h3,h4,h5,h6
        h1
        h2
▼   lupine.css
        body,td,th
        body
        a
        a:link
        a:visited
        a:hover
        a:active

Properties

Add Property

FIGURE 14-17 Creating a new external style sheet from existing internal styles.

A page can have multiple style sheets. Style sheets can have one or more rules within them.

Attaching an External Style Sheet to Another Page   Now that you have created an external style sheet, we will attach it to another page. Open the *paste_sample. html* page you created in Chapter 13, which should be located in the *pages* folder of your SampleSite. With the arrow to the left of the <style> in the CSS panel in the down position, you will see that this page currently has the following rules: the *body,td,th* rule, the *body* rule, and the *h1* and *h2* rules. To attach the *lupine.css* external style sheet to this page, click the Attach Style Sheet icon (which resembles a chain link) at the bottom of the CSS panel; or click to highlight the CSS panel with no style selected, then choose *Attach Style Sheet* from the CSS panel's options menu; or right/Control-click and choose the option from the context-sensitive menu; or yet another option, choose Format>CSS Styles>Attach Style Sheet. The dialog box

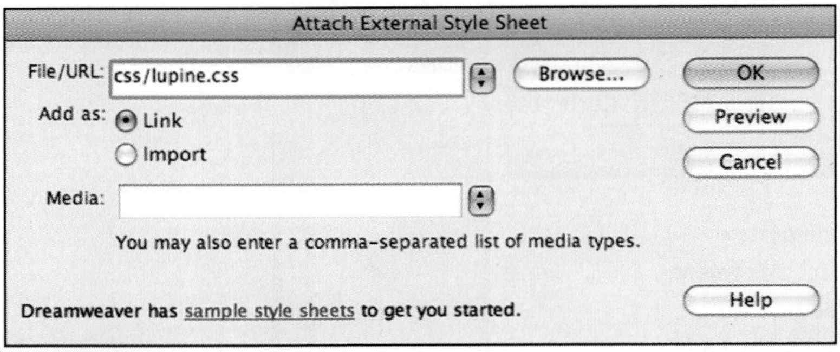

FIGURE 14-18 Attach External Style Sheet dialog box.

shown in **FIGURE 14-18** will open, allowing you to browse to locate the particular style sheet you want to attach. There are two ways you can attach an external style sheet to a page: link or import. As you can see, the Link option is the default; it is the most common method of attaching an external style sheet, and the one we will use because of its broader browser compatibility.

Browse to locate the *lupine.css* style sheet located in the SampleRoot folder. After you click OK—like magic, the page will reflect the attached styles!

When you attach an external style sheet to a page that has some of the same rules applied as part of an internal style sheet, it is important to select and delete the internal duplicate rules. In our case, the *body,td,th* and *body* rules are duplicated in the same original <style> style sheet. Click to highlight them and then click the trash can to delete those rules from the <style> internal style sheet. Alternatively, if you wanted to delete an entire internal style sheet, you could select the style sheet's name (<style>) and then click the trash can to delete the entire style sheet with all the rules included in it.

Let's finish the *paste_sample.html* page now that we have our newly attached styles. You may find it easier to work in Expanded Tables mode to see where the cells begin.

1. In the empty cell below the headline, type the following sentence and apply Heading 1 to it: *Welcome to the finest restaurant in New Hampshire!*

2. Create a new paragraph just below it. Type the following text and apply Heading 2 to it: *Five Diamond Award 3 years in a row! Located in the heart of Lupine country, Sugarhill, NH…nestled in the White Mountains!*

3. Select the contact navigation and then click the right arrow to place the I-beam to the right of it. Apply Return/Enter to create three paragraphs containing the following text and apply Heading 2 to each of them:

   Weekly 2 for 1 specials!

   Open 7 days a week!

   Relax and enjoy happy hour in our tavern from (add a soft return/line break) *3–5 PM daily!*

4. Select the remaining cell at the bottom of the table and check that its Horz and Vert options are both set to *Default*. Type the following text links, adding a space, a vertical line (\+Shift), and another space between each one as shown:

   home | menu | location | reservations | contact

   Highlight each one individually and add the hash symbol (#) in the link category of the Property inspector to again create the appearance of working links.

5. Complete the page by adding a class rule named *.footeralign*, being sure you add it to the *lupine.css* style sheet, not *This document only*. For its definition, choose the *Block* category and assign Text-align: Center. Highlight your footer navigation and apply this class to it. Notice that this time, we centered text using CSS, instead of the Horz: Center alignment option in the Property inspector for the table cell! The finished page, when viewed in a browser, should now resemble **FIGURE 14-19**.

Creating an External Style Sheet from Scratch or Adding Rules to an Existing One We have already learned how to create a new rule in the New CSS Rule dialog box. However, so far, each time we were there, we chose the *This document only*

FIGURE 14-19 Lupine page with CSS.

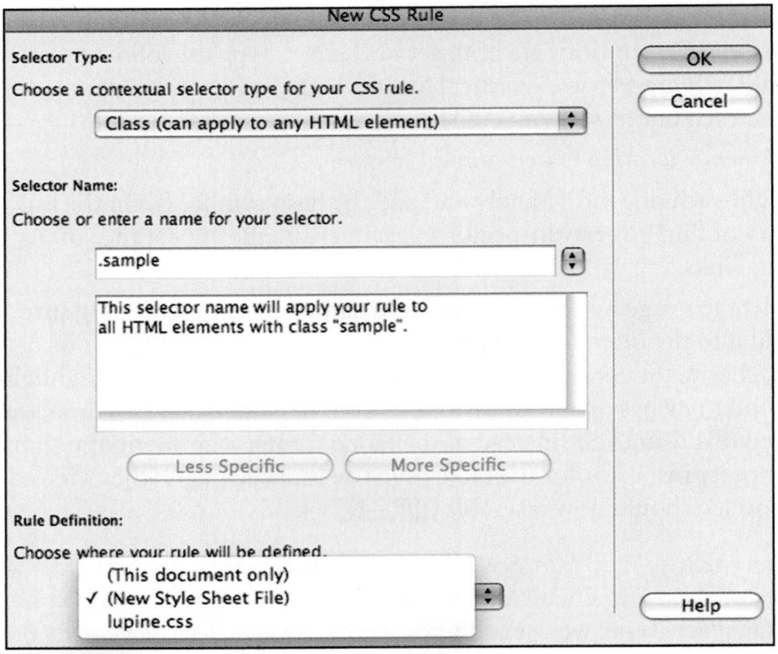

FIGURE 14-20 Choosing to create an external style sheet in the New CSS Rule dialog box.

option, which created an internal, embedded rule. When in this dialog box, if you click the pop-up menu at the bottom to choose where the rule will be defined, the alternative option is *New Style Sheet File* (in CS3, choose New Style Sheet File from the *Define in* pop-up menu). When you choose this option, before entering the Rule Definition dialog box, you are entered into the Save Style Sheet File As dialog box, identical to the one shown in Figure 14-16. However, if you have already created external style sheet(s), they will also be listed as alternatives in the pop-up menu to choose where your rule will be defined, as shown in **FIGURE 14-20**.

Making Changes to an External Style Sheet   Just as in style sheets for page layout, this is where the biggest advantage to external style sheets in web design lies. A change to a rule in an external style sheet updates every instance of that rule site-wide. To practice this, open the *rye_page.html* page of your SampleSite, one of the blank pages we made when learning to create rollovers in Chapter 11. You will notice in the CSS styles panel that it currently states "no styles defined" because we did not enter the Page Properties dialog box and assign any appearances to this particular page.

To learn how to change an external style sheet, begin by attaching the *lupine.css* style sheet to it. After you have done that, select the *a* rule and change the font size to *24 pixels*, changing the size of the links. Open your *paste_sample.html* page and notice that the font for all the footer links has been increased to 24 pixels automatically! Cool! Now, edit the *a* rule on any page with the external style sheet attached and return the size to *16 pixels* to dynamically return all links to their original defined size.

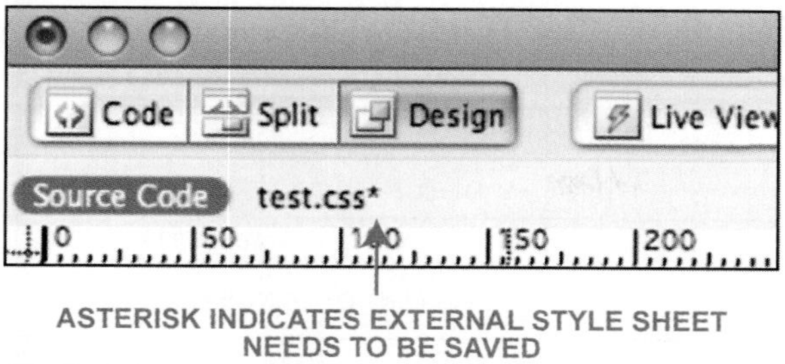

ASTERISK INDICATES EXTERNAL STYLE SHEET
NEEDS TO BE SAVED

FIGURE 14-21 CSS file.

Regardless of how an external style sheet is created, it is a separate document that must be saved for style changes to be available for future use. When one is created, in CS4 and CS5, it will display in your Document window, as shown in **FIGURE 14-21**.

Even though it will not display above the document in CS3, for all versions, be sure when closing for the day (or at any time while you work) that you choose File>Save to save its changes, or choose Save All to save the document page and its applicable external style sheet(s) simultaneously.

14.2.6 Customizing a Spry Menu Bar

Now that you have been introduced to CSS, let's learn to customize a Spry Menu Bar. When the feature was introduced in Chapter 11, we learned that Dreamweaver automatically generates CSS for the design of the menu bar, with the option for you, the designer, to customize it. We added a menu to the *index.html* page of the SampleSite: open the page now and display the CSS panel. In addition to the CSS that was generated by its page properties, you will also see a style sheet named SpryMenuBarHorizontal.css. When you click the down arrow, a host of premade styles appear. Don't let yourself be overwhelmed! There are only a few critical ones that you need to know to be able to customize the size, color, and font features for the various states, which are the ones we will examine. Under any particular rule, changes are noted; all other options for the rule will be left at the default settings. (Although we will discuss them as they relate to creating a horizontal menu, the options and customizing process is identical if a vertical menu has been inserted instead.) **FIGURE 14-22** provides an overview of those styling attributes.

The *ul.MenuBarHorizontal* rule defines the width of the bar and as-signs the type size relative to the existing CSS properties already defined. Select the rule and choose to edit it. In its Rule Definition dialog box, you will see under the Type category that the size is preset to *100%* (100% of the current assigned size); we will leave that as is for this menu. Under its Box category, it has a width assigned to *auto*. The table used to create this page has a width of 750 pixels. Let's change the width to echo the table's width by changing it to *750 pixels*.

The important features of the *ul.MenuBarHorizontal li* rule are its definition of the alignment for the type used in the menu items, as well as the width of the

SPRY MENU BAR CUSTOMIZATION

CSS RULE	MENU CUSTOMIZATION
ul.MenuBarHorizontal	• SIZE OF TYPE RELATIVE TO DEFINED PROPERTIES • WIDTH OF ENTIRE MENU BAR
ul.MenuBarHorizontal li	• WIDTH OF INDIVIDUAL UP STATES OF MENUS • ALIGNMENT OF MENU TYPE
ul.MenuBarHorizontal ul li	• WIDTH OF SUBMENU
ul.MenuBarHorizontal ul	• TEXT FEATURES FOR SUBMENU IF DIFFERENT FROM UP STATE • ADD BORDER AROUND SUBMENU
ul.MenuBarHorizontal a	• ASSIGN UP STATE BACKGROUND COLOR • ASSIGN UP STATE TYPE COLOR • OVERRIDE DEFINED FONT • ADD PADDING TO MENUS
ul.MenuBarHorizontal a:hover ul.MenuBarHorizontal a:focus ul.MenuBarHorizontal a.MenuBarItemHover ul.MenuBarHorizontal a.MenuBarItemSubmenuHover ul.MenuBarHorizontal a.MenuBarSubmenuVisible	• ASSIGN HOVER BACKGROUND COLOR • ASSIGN HOVER TYPE COLOR TO UP AND SUBMENU ITEMS
ul.MenuBarHorizontal a.MenuBarItemSubmenu ul.MenuBarHorizontal ul a.MenuBarItemSubmenu ul.MenuBarHorizontal a.MenuBarItemSubmenuHover ul.MenuBarHorizontal ul a.MenuBarItemSubmenuHover	• ASSIGN VARIOUS DIRECTIONAL ARROWS FOR SUBMENU CONTENT

FIGURE 14-22 Customizing a Spry Menu Bar.

individual menu up states. Change the text alignment, if you would like, or leave the default alignment of left under the Block category. However, under the Box category, we will change the width to *20%* (five menu items placed within a 750 pixel width); alternatively, type *150 pixels*, but keep the Float>left default. Notice that the menu immediately spreads from edge to edge of the table.

The *ul.MenuBarHorizontal ul li* rule defines the width of the submenu. Feel free to change its width under the Box category and then test the page in a browser to understand how the existing em measurement affects it. Or, change the measurement to a value in pixels (a width of 150 px will display the submenu the same as the main menu) and then test the page. In either case, make sure to assign a width that is wide enough for the text to display properly in the submenus (you must test the page in a browser to check this).

The *ul.MenuBarHorizontal ul* rule allows you to change the submenu's text features by overriding the up state text properties and change/remove the preassigned submenu border and border color, if desired.

The *ul.MenuBarHorizontal a* rule assigns type properties for the up state of the menu. Here, you assign the color of the type for the up state, assign the menu's up state background color, override the preexisting font page properties, if desired, and add padding to the width of the menus. Let's change the background color to

#000000 and the type color to *#FFFFFF*. Feel free to experiment by changing the rest of the mentioned features on your own.

The *ul.MenuBarHorizontal a:focus* and the *ul.MenuBarHorizontal a.MenuBarSubmenuVisible*, along with the three hover rules shown grouped together in Figure 14-22, affect the background and type colors when the menus are activated. As you can see in the CSS panel, they are grouped together under two rule definitions. Change the background to *#FFFFFF* and change the type color to *#000000* under each category. You will need to test the page in a browser to see these hover colors applied to the menu.

The last category of rules applies colored directional arrows to aid the visitor through the submenus. The arrows can be changed to one of the others provided, or to your own arrow created in Photoshop or Illustrator and optimized for the Web as a .gif. To test this, select the *ul.MenuBarHorizontal a.MenuBarItemSubmenu*. Under the *Background-image* option of the Background category in the Rule Definition dialog box, browse in the *Spry Assets* folder added to the *SampleRoot* folder. Replace its existing black graphic with *SpryMenuBarDownHover.gif*: the menu will immediately update with the new white arrow! After testing the menu in a browser, feel free to return to any of the rules listed here and experiment by changing their properties to further understand and reinforce your learning.

If you decide you want to start over and delete a Spry Menu Bar and the style sheet in the CSS panel and then create a new page... the old styles still remain! That's because the *Spry Assets* folder houses the CSS file. You will need to delete that file as well to start from scratch again.

14.3 An Introduction to the Use of Div Tags for Layout Using CSS

Now that you have some familiarity with creating styles for text and images using CSS, before closing our discussion of this powerful feature of web design, we will explore the basics of its application to the layout structure of a web page. When you learned about the types of selectors that are available for creating CSS rules, one of them was the ID selector that, as we discussed at the time, can only be applied to one element on a page. ID selectors can be used as one of the ways to define containers to house content on a web page when used in conjunction with the insertion of a div tag, because a web page will typically have only one headline area, one main navigation area, one main body content area, and one footer area. By defining a rule for the ID selector, a div tag can then be inserted with its assigned rule definition. FIGURE 14-23 shows the divs inserted using the ID selectors.

To introduce how the concept works, we will create a page built with div tags in our SampleSite using another set of lupine page images already prepared for you in a

#CONTAINER

#HEADLINE

#NAVIGATION

#FOOTER

#MAINCONTENT

FIGURE 14-23 Div layout.

folder named *lupine_div_images* located in the *Chapter_14PracticeFiles* folder. Locate the folder and add the entire folder to the *images* folder of the SampleRoot folder.

1. Create a new page named *div_sample.html* saved into your *pages* folder of the SampleSite. (Again, during this practice, it will not be necessary to add a title, keywords, and description text to this page. However, remember that you must start each page of a real site with these critical steps.)

2. Attach the *lupine.css* style sheet to the page.

3. Although you can access the option to create the rules for the ID selectors when you enter the Insert Div Tag dialog box, we will choose to create them ahead of time instead. Just as you have learned to create an umbrella table to house other tables within it, when creating a layout using divs, we will begin by creating an ID selector that will act as a "master umbrella" container to house the rest of the divs. Create a new CSS rule. For the selector type, choose *ID*. For the Selector Name category, type *#container* (all ID selectors must begin with the hash symbol (#)). Complete this dialog box by choosing *This document only* for where the rule will be defined

because this page will be the only one in the SampleSite that will use div tags for its layout.

When you have entered the Rule Definition dialog box, click the *Background* category and assign the background color *#000000*. After you have done this, select the *Box* category and assign a width of *750 pixels* and a *temporary* height of *300 pixels* (we will learn why it is temporary a little later). To make our layout a centered one, under the Margin category, uncheck *Same for all* and select *auto* from the pop-up menu for the right and left margins and assign *0 pixels* for the top and bottom margins. This will allow the layout to be centered, applying the "automatic" distance needed in relation to the viewer's monitor to fill the remaining space beyond the 750 pixels used for the container. Now, click OK to complete this first ID rule definition.

4. Now, we will create the rules for the page divisions that will be inside the master container. Create a new ID selector rule, name it *#headline*, and choose *This document only* for its location. Choose the *Box* category and assign a height of *183 pixels*. (We do not need to assign a width. Because it is left blank, it will default to the width provided by the master #container rule.) Click OK to complete the rule definition.

   Create the next ID selector rule named *#navigation* and choose *This document only* for its location. After you enter the Rule Definition dialog box, set the following properties. In the Box category, assign a Width of *144 pixels*. (No height is necessary. It will adjust as needed, based on our content.) Assign a Float of *Left*. Uncheck *Same for all* for the Padding and assign Top: *10 pixels*, Right: *5 pixels*, Bottom: *0 pixels*, and Left: *10 pixels*. Click OK to complete the rule definition.

   For the main content area, create an ID selector rule named *#maincontent* and select *This document only* for its location. After you enter the Rule Definition dialog box, set the following properties. In the Box category, uncheck *Same for all* for the Padding and assign Top: *5 pixels*, Right: *5 pixels*, Bottom: *0 pixels*, and Left: *5 pixels*. Uncheck *Same for all* for the Margin and assign Top: *0 pixels*, Right: *0 pixels*, Bottom: *0 pixels*, and Left: *160 pixels*.

   Click OK to complete the rule definition. Note that we did not assign a width or height this time. As you have learned, the height will flex as needed, and the width is defined by setting a margin relative to the width requirements of the #navigation rule. Alternatively, you could define a specific width, factoring in the width of the #navigation ID and its padding, when determining the width of the #maincontent ID.

   The last content area will be the footer navigation. Create one more ID selector rule named *#footer* and select *This document only* for its location. Assign the following properties in its rule definition. In the Block category, assign the Text-align to *Center*. In the Box category,

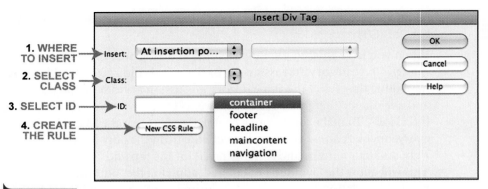

FIGURE 14-24 Insert Div Tag dialog box.

assign the Height of *30 pixels* and Clear: *both*. (This will place it below the rest of the divs within the-container div.) Uncheck *Same for all* for the Padding and assign Top: *10 pixels*, Right: *0 pixels*, Bottom: *0 pixels*, and Left: *0 pixels*. In the Positioning category, assign the Position of *relative*.

Before moving on to adding the div tags to our page, select all the new rules you have created (not your *lupine.css* style sheet) and choose to *Move CSS rules* to create a new style sheet titled *divs.css*. Save it inside the *css* folder of the SampleRoot folder. After you have done that, attach the new style sheet to the page and delete the original *<style>* style sheet.

5. We are ready to create the first div tag, our master container div tag that will encase the rest of our div content containers. You can enter the Insert Div Tag dialog box one of two ways. Using the Layout category of the Insert panel, you can click the *Insert Div Tag* icon. Alternatively, you can choose Insert>Layout Objects>Div Tag. After choosing to insert a div tag using either one of those methods, the dialog box shown in **FIGURE 14-24** will open.

   1. This pop-up menu offers a variety of insertion options. We will always choose to add them *At insertion point* because I believe it is the easiest method to understand where your new content will be entered when you are first learning about divs. Feel free to experiment with adding your div tags using the additional options from this pop-up menu when working on your own. If you choose one of the other options, you will also be prompted with the additional pop-up menu to the right of the insert one to choose where to insert the div tag in relation to others you have already inserted.

   2. We started to build a page using div tags by creating rule definitions for ID selectors. Alternatively, you could create classes to assign the div tags to instead.

   3. In our case, because we created the rules as ID selectors, all of the rules we have created for this page are now listed in the pop-up menu

for selection. Because IDs can only be used once, after you use one, the pop-up menu selection list will only display the remaining ID rules you have not yet applied to the page.

4. While we chose to create the rules before entering this dialog box, alternatively, you could enter this dialog box first, then click the New CSS Rule (or New CSS Style in CS3) button to enter the New CSS Rule dialog box to create a rule to use for a div tag. After you have created the rule definition for the class or ID, when you exit the definition dialog box you are returned to the Insert Div Tag dialog box to complete your entry.

6. Because we created our ID rules ahead of time, in this Insert Div Tag dialog box, select *At insertion point* for the Insert option and choose *container* from the ID pop-up menu. Click OK to add the div to the page. When it is selected on the page, you will notice that it is centered, with a toned area to the right and left of the div when the div is selected in the tag selector. This toned area represents our choice of *auto* for the *#container* margin settings, which adjusts the centering of the content based on the monitor viewing area provided. The div also contains some default text *Content for id "container" Goes Here.* Although we will now delete it, it is handy, because by deleting it, your I-beam will definitely be *inside* the container, which it needs to be to insert the next div tag.

7. After deleting this default text, with the I-beam still inside the div, choose to insert another div tag and select *headline* from the ID pop-up menu. Once again, it contains default text that will need to be deleted. However, after deleting it, this time we do not want our next div tag to be located inside the *#headline* one; we want it to be placed below it. Selecting the *#headline* div tag, not its content or the *#container* div tag, can be confusing. Here is a handy use of the tag selector. After deleting the default text inside the *#headline*, if the I-beam is still inside of it, it will be displayed in the tag selector at the lower-left corner of the Document window. When you click its name here, it will be highlighted and the outline of the div will be simultaneously highlighted for you on the page, as shown in **FIGURE 14-25**.

After you have deleted the text, press the right arrow on the keyboard to place the I-beam after the div, and insert the *#navigation* div tag (listed as *navigation* in the ID pop-up menu), again choosing *At insertion point* in the Insert Div Tag dialog box. After inserting it and deleting its default text, again move the insertion point after it by pressing the right arrow key, being sure its border has been highlighted in either yellow or blue, depending on the color of the page background where the div has been added. (In this page, yellow because our container div is black.)

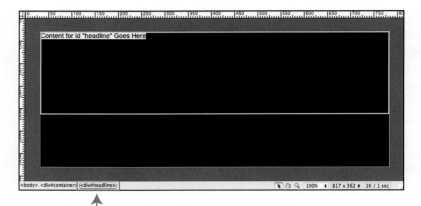

↑
TAG SELECTOR INDICATES THAT THE DIV TAG <DIV#HEADLINE> IS THE
CURRENTLY SELECTED DIV TAG

FIGURE 14-25 Tag selector.

8. Insert another div tag. Once again, choose *At insertion point* in the Insert Div Tag dialog box and select *maincontent* from the ID menu. This time, do not delete the default text. For now, select the div using the tag selector and press the right arrow on the keyboard to place the I-beam after the div, ready to insert the last div tag to complete the page structure.

 If you try to add a div tag inside a container div tag that is too large for the space provided, it will automatically be kicked down below the location you wanted to enter it, to where there is enough room for it to display, as shown in **FIGURE 14-26**.

9. Insert the *#footer* (the only ID left under its menu), choosing *At insertion point*, and notice its location after it's inserted. It will automatically be placed across the full distance of the *#container* div tag, below both the *#navigation* and *#maincontent* div tags, as shown in **FIGURE 14-27**.

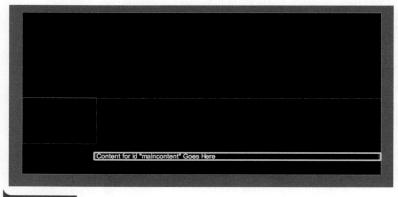

FIGURE 14-26 Size error.

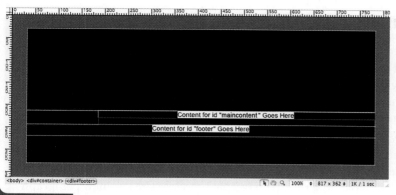

FIGURE 14-27 Footer with *Clear both* option applied.

The *Clear both* option that we applied to the Box category for this ID signified to Dreamweaver that you wanted the div tag to be below and span the distance of the two divs above it.

10. Let's tidy up our CSS panel first. Select all of the rules in the *lupine.css* style. Right/Control-click and choose *Move CSS Rules* from the context-sensitive menu. Select the *divs.css* style sheet to move them to and then delete the *lupine.css* style sheet from this page. Now, select the *body,td,th* rule and click the Edit Rule button (the pencil) to edit it, or practice editing it through the bottom Properties section of the CSS panel. Select the *Background* category and change the Background-color to *none* (choose the slash icon): our *#container* master container is already *#000000*, making this background rule color unnecessary.

    Finally, before adding any content to our div tags, we created the *#container* master div tag with a "temporary" height to make it easier to insert the rest of the div tags inside of it. Let's *delete* the height of the *#container* rule now before continuing, so that the container div will be able to flex and expand as needed for the divs it houses and the content that will be inserted inside of them. To do that, choose the *#container* rule, and in its Box category, simply delete the *300 pixels* height value, or highlight the height in the Properties section of the CSS panel with the rule selected and click the trash can icon to delete this property only.

11. We are ready now to add our text and images into the div tags. Place the I-beam inside the *#headline* div and insert the *lupine_headline.jpg* image into it (the *lupine_headline.jpg* is located in the *lupine_div_images* folder you added to the *images* folder of the SampleRoot). Add it using any of the methods you have learned to insert an image onto a page.

    Follow this by clicking inside the *#navigation div* to insert the *lupine_home.gif* image and then assign the *hash symbol (#)* in the Link category of the Property inspector to turn it into a link.

Add the remaining navigation images sequentially: *lupine_menu.gif, lupine_location.gif, lupine_reservations.gif,* and *lupine_contact.gif.* Because these need to be placed directly below each other, not as new paragraphs, you may find it easiest to insert each image by selecting the previous image, pressing the right arrow key, and then choosing the Insert>Image command. After you insert each navigation graphic, add the hash symbol (#) to each one, one at a time, in the Property inspector, to assign the link option to it.

12. Notice that the *#navigation* div tag continues to expand downward as needed. With the *lupine_contact.gif* button still selected, press the right arrow key, then apply a hard return this time to create a new paragraph, and type the following script: *Weekly 2 for 1 specials!* Create a new paragraph and type: *Open 7 days a week!* Create a new paragraph and type: *Relax and enjoy happy hour in our tavern from* (add a soft return/line break) *3–5 PM daily!* After you have done that, assign *Heading 2* to each paragraph.

    Place the I-beam inside the *#maincontent* div, checking the tag selector if necessary to be sure you are inside it (*<div#maincontent>* in the tag selector, not the *#container* div) and then highlight the default text and change it to: *Welcome to the finest restaurant in New Hampshire!* Create a new paragraph and type: *Five Diamond Award 3 years in a row! Located in the heart of Lupine country, Sugarhill, NH...nestled in the White Mountains!* Apply *Heading 1* to the first paragraph. Apply *Heading 2* to the second paragraph. Complete the *#maincontent* div by applying the Return key one more time, creating a new paragraph, and inserting the *lupine_building.jpg* image into the div.

    Place the I-beam inside the *#footer* div (*<div#footer>* in the tag selector), highlight its default text, and replace it with: *home | menu | location | reservations | contact.* Highlight each one individually and assign the hash symbol (#) in the Property inspector to give it the appearance of a link.

13. You may notice that the CSS panel currently does not display rules for the Heading 1 or Heading 2 formatting that we have applied to this page. Because we do not want the default assignment to rule our headings, we will redefine those two HTML tags. Create a new rule, choosing *Tag* for the selector type to redefine an HTML element. Scroll from the Selector name's pop-up menu to select *h1* as the tag to redefine. Select the *div.css* style sheet to define it in, and then, under the Type category, assign a size of *24 pixels.* Repeat this process for the *h2* tag, assigning a size of *18 pixels* to it. Your page will dynamically update to reflect the changes. Congratulations! You've learned the basics of structuring a page using CSS! When viewed in a browser, your page should now resemble FIGURE 14-28.

Margins vs. padding? Many times, you will find that the two options in the Box category of the Rule Definition dialog box will produce the same visual effect you are trying to create. However, sometimes you need to apply one over the other. FIGURE 14-29 illustrates the main difference between these two options.

The black represents the table cell or div the item is enclosed within. When you need to add space *outside* an item's border to push it away from an edge, you can add a margin (that is how we created the *#maincontent* div). When you want to bring content *in* from the edge of its border, you can add padding (such as the text and navigation buttons of the *#navigation* div).

FIGURE 14-28 Div page displayed in a browser.

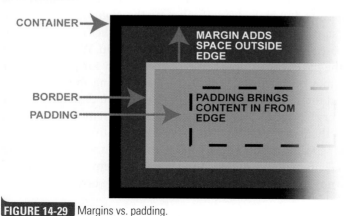

FIGURE 14-29 Margins vs. padding.

FIGURE 14-30 Illustration of the Code Navigator icon.

How about the "ship's wheel" icon? As promised in Chapter 9, let's explore its potential usability, depending on your work style. If you are comfortable editing code, you may find yourself loving this little ship's wheel icon, available only in CS4 and CS5. As you work on pages containing CSS, when the cursor hovers over an area or you click to create an insertion point, the icon illustrated in **FIGURE 14-30** pops up.

When you click it, the CSS rule applied to your selection appears in a little pop-up window that, when you select it, immediately brings you to that area of the CSS code to edit it. If editing code is not your bag, you can disable the ship's wheel by selecting the *disable* option from its pop-up menu. Later in your web design experience, if you decide you want it visible, with a page open simply Alt-click in Windows or Command/Option-click on the Mac and it will reappear for accessibility.

 ## 14.4   A Look at Dreamweaver Starter Page Layouts

Dreamweaver includes some starter pages, with basic divs already applied to them, to help you begin structuring your pages using CSS. You can select from a wide variety of column, header, sidebar, and footer combinations, each one with padding, width, etc., settings already applied to them, incorporated into fixed, liquid, and elastic layouts. To start with one of them, choose File>New. In the New Document dialog box, choose Blank page>HTML and then, instead of selecting the *None* option we have always chosen, select the starting page of your choice. When you click one, a diagram of the layout you have chosen is displayed to the right of the column. When you select one and choose *Create*, the page with sample text is opened, ready for you to edit its placeholder content. You may be thinking, "Why are we just learning about this now? Why didn't we learn about them in the beginning?" First, until you understood CSS, they wouldn't have been very beneficial. Second, they will have much more meaning to you if you choose to apply them in your future work, now that you understand how to customize them to fit your specific needs. Third, you are an artist! It was important to begin with your creative talents taking center stage and not allow them to be "confined" to starter pages that may not have allowed you to think outside the box.

In CS5, the starter pages are color coded and more intuitive, making them much more user friendly.

It will be very helpful to open some of the starter pages and simply study the CSS used for the page, starting with the fixed layout options. Click some of the rules created for the div tags and enter the Rule Definition dialog box to study the *Box* category for them. Studying the assigned properties and their effects on the starter page can expand your knowledge of structuring a page using div tags, while providing you with great ideas and design tips for your own layouts.

14.5 A Look at the Code in Split View: The Application of an External Style Sheet

FIGURE 14-31 illustrates the code of the source page and the code of the separate linked file. Let's take a closer look.

1. When an external style sheet has been attached to a page, two buttons become visible in the Document toolbar area when working in either CS4 or CS5. When you click the *Source Code* button, the source code for the page becomes visible in Split view. When a Spry Menu Bar or any other content has been added that requires JavaScript or CSS, they will be listed in this location as well.

2. Here, you can see that the `<head>` element does not contain any internal/embedded rules.

3. `<link href="../css/divs.css" rel="stylesheet" type="text/css" />` indicates that this page is linked to the external style sheet named *divs.css*.

4. When you click the *divs.css* button in the Document toolbar area, the attached style sheet appears ready for editing.

5. `@charset "UTF-8"` identifies that this is an attached external style sheet.

6. The selector begins the rule.

7. The left curly bracket opens the declaration.

8. All properties and values are listed, with a colon after each property and a semicolon after each value.

9. The right curly bracket closes the declaration.

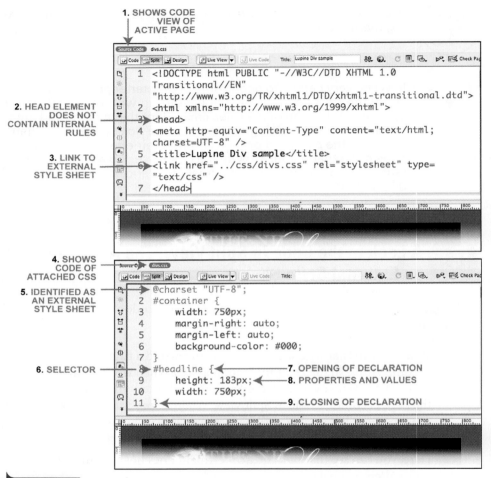

1. SHOWS CODE VIEW OF ACTIVE PAGE

2. HEAD ELEMENT DOES NOT CONTAIN INTERNAL RULES

3. LINK TO EXTERNAL STYLE SHEET

4. SHOWS CODE OF ATTACHED CSS

5. IDENTIFIED AS AN EXTERNAL STYLE SHEET

6. SELECTOR

7. OPENING OF DECLARATION

8. PROPERTIES AND VALUES

9. CLOSING OF DECLARATION

FIGURE 14-31 Split view of an external CSS style sheet.

14.6 What We Have Learned

Finally, we have learned to add pizzazz to the text and images on our web pages! We explored the text formatting features available through HTML and then moved on to the formatting features available through CSS. In addition to working with text, we learned how to apply style and customized positioning to inserted images. Our learning in CSS covered the creation, application, editing, and moving of rules, the customizing of a Spry Menu Bar, and included an introduction to the application of divs for page structuring. After applying div tags to page layout, we learned about the Dreamweaver starter pages and how using them or studying them can help us to continue to build our experience in CSS.

14.7 Reinforcing Your Knowledge

Project

1. Be sure your FishluvrzSite website is the active site in the Files panel and then open your *index.html* page. We will begin by styling the *index.html* page, including its Spry Menu Bar, move on to stylizing the *faq_page.html* page, and then build the *products_page.html* page from scratch. Lastly, we will unify the site by attaching our external style sheet to the *information_page.html* page and deleting its internal formatting.

2. With the *index.html* page open, let's begin by customizing the Spry Menu Bar. One at a time, select the rules and assign their properties as follows. For the **ul.MenuBarHorizontal** Type category, assign a Font size of *100%*. For the Box category, assign a Width of *750 pixels*; assign a Padding of *Same for all, 0 pixels*; and assign a Margin of *Same for all, 0 pixels*. In the **ul.MenuBarHorizontal li** Block category, assign a Text-align of *center*. In the Box category, assign a Width of *auto*; assign a Float of *left*; assign a Padding of *Same for all, 0 pixels*; and assign a Margin of *Same for all, 0 pixels*. In the Positioning category, assign the Position of *relative*. For the **ul.MenuBarHorizontal ul** Box category, assign a Width of *145 pixels*, a Float of *left*, and a Position of *absolute*. For the **ul.MenuBarHorizontal ul li** Box category, assign a Width of *145 pixels* and a Float of *left*. For the **ul.MenuBarHorizontal ul**, delete all border properties. In the **ul.MenuBarHorizontal a** Type category, assign a Font-size of *20 pixels*, a Font-weight of *bold*, and a Color of *#FFCC00*. In the Background category, assign a Background-color of *#336600*. In the Block category, assign the Display of *block*. In the Box category, assign the Padding: Top=8 px, Right=*30 px*, Bottom=*8 px*, and Left=*30 px*. For the **ul.MenuBarHorizontal a:hover, ul.MenuBarHorizontal a:focus, ul.MenuBarHorizontal a.MenuBarItemHover, ul.MenuBarHorizontal a.MenuBarItemSubmenuHover**, and **ul.MenuBarHorizontal a.MenuBarSubmenuVisible** Type category, assign the Color *#FFFFFF*. In the Background category, assign the Background-color *#000066*. We will leave the default colors for the submenu directional arrows.

3. Let's convert the items we typed in paragraph form in Chapter 13 into a bulleted list. Drag to highlight all the paragraphs in the first row of products that begins with *Aquarium Essentials* and apply an *unordered list* to them. Easy! Now do the same to the other two columns of products, one column at a time. After you have done this, turn them into links by highlighting each one and adding the hash symbol (#) for the link option in the Property inspector to simulate their linkage to another page. Before continuing, check and remove the I-beam if it is flashing *below* the last paragraph of each of these three bulleted lists. If it is, press the Backspace/Delete key to remove it. Extra paragraphs will affect the appearance of the page when viewed in a browser.

4. Now, we will redefine a couple of our existing CSS rules and create three additional ones, apply them, and then move some of them to an external style sheet to apply to other pages of the site.

   Select the *h1* rule to edit it. In the Box category, uncheck *Same for all* for Padding, and assign Right: *10 pixels*, Left: *10 pixels*. Leave all other options blank and click OK to complete the edit. You will notice that the text with the Heading 1 rule applied to it automatically updates to reflect the padding you have added to it.

   Select the *h2* rule. In the Type category, add Text-transform: *uppercase* (Case: *uppercase* in CS3). Select the *Box* category. Uncheck *Same for all* for the Margin and assign Right: *10 pixels* and Left: *10 pixels*. Leave all other options blank. Now, select the *Border* category and deselect the *Same for all* option for Style. Choose *solid* for the Bottom option. Deselect the *Same for all* options for Width and Color, assigning *5 pixels* for the Width Bottom option and *#336600* for the corresponding Color option. You will not see any changes in the page this time, because the h2 rule has not been applied to any text on this page.

   To complete the *index.html* page, we will create three class rules, which will be added to *This document only*. Create the first class rule named *.player*. For its definition, choose the *Box* category and select Float: *right*. For Margin, deselect *Same for all* and check Top: *10 pixels* and Left: *10 pixels*. Leave the other two margin options blank. After you have done that, let's apply it. Click the *fishluvrz_video.flv* to select it and then apply the *.player* class to it. To apply a class to an FLV file, the class option is at the top right of the Property inspector.

   Create another class rule named *.whitetext*. In the Type category of the Rule Definition dialog box, choose Font-weight: *bold*,

Text-transform: *uppercase*, and Color: *#FFFFFF*. In the Box category, choose *Padding*, uncheck *Same for all*, assign Left: *10 pixels*, and leave all other dimensions blank to complete this rule. Click anywhere inside each of the following paragraphs, one at a time, and apply the class to them:

check out our internet specials of the week!

fish problems? get help from our experts!

chat with other fishluvrz about your fish!

Lastly, create one named *.padding*. In the Rule Definition dialog box, select the *Box* category. Choose *Padding* and then uncheck *Same for all*. Assign Right: *10 pixels* and Left: *10 pixels* and leave all other options blank. Click OK to complete the rule. Click anywhere inside the body text of the page and assign the new *.padding* class to it.

5. Following best practice, we will move some of the rules to an external style sheet for application to the rest of the pages of our site. Command/Control-click to select the following rules: *body, body,td,th, a:link, a:visited, a:hover, a:active, h1, h2, h1,h2,h3,h4,h5,h6*, and the class *.padding* (we will not use the *.player* or *.whitetext* classes on our other pages) and then right/Control-click and choose *Move CSS Rules* from the context-sensitive menu. In the dialog box that follows, choose to create a new style sheet. Locate your *css* folder in your FishluvrzRoot folder as the destination for the style and name it *fishluvrz.css*. When you exit the dialog box, your CSS panel should look like **FIGURE 14-32**.

Before we move on to the *faq_page.html* page to assign our *fishluvrz.css* style sheet to it, let's take a peak at your hard work in a browser. If you have tightened up all your table cells and have no accidental added paragraphs, your index page should now resemble **FIGURE 14-33**. (Remember that your page should *resemble* the sample provided, but may not look exactly like the one shown: final appearance will vary based on browsers, settings, and platforms.)

6. Close your *index.html* page and open your *faq_page.html* page. With the CSS panel open, notice the *#headline1, #navBar1, #images1, #body1*, and *#footer1* (apDiv1 through apDiv5) rules in the style sheet. They were created behind the scenes because you created the page using AP Divs. Even though you converted them to a table, the internal rules that were created remained. Throw all of these into

Project (continued)

FIGURE 14-32 CSS panel with *fishluvrz.css*.

the trash before proceeding to add new styles to the page. Don't worry about your existing layout; by converting the AP Divs to a table, these rules are now just bloated, unused code. After you have done that, choose to attach the *fishluvrz.css* style sheet to this page and assign it to *link* when in the Attach Style Sheet dialog box. Now, select the original *<style>* style sheet on this page and delete it so that there will be no rule duplications, leaving only the *fishluvrz.css* and *SpryMenuBarHorizontal.css* external style sheets remaining in the CSS panel.

7. Click each paragraph of body text and apply the *.padding* class to it.

8. We will create a new internal style sheet containing one rule: we will not need to add it to the *fishluvrz.css* style sheet because it will only be used for this particular page. Create a new class rule named *.border*. In the New CSS Rule dialog box be sure to choose *This document only* for where the rule will be defined. In the Border category of the Rule Definition dialog box, keep *Same for all* checked for all

Project (continued)

FIGURE 14-33 Completed Fishluvrz index page.

three options in this category and assign the following features: Style: *solid*, Width: *5 pixels*, and Color: *#336600*. Select each of the images: *temperature.jpg*, *plants.jpg*, and *faucet.jpg* one at a time and assign the new *.border* class to them. Your *faq_page.html* page should now resemble **FIGURE 14-34** when viewed in a browser.

9. We will now build the *products_page.html* page from the ground up. Create a new blank HTML page. Before we think about styling the page, we will incorporate the 1, 2, 3 Go Checklist. Name the page *products_page.html* and save it into the *pages* folder of your

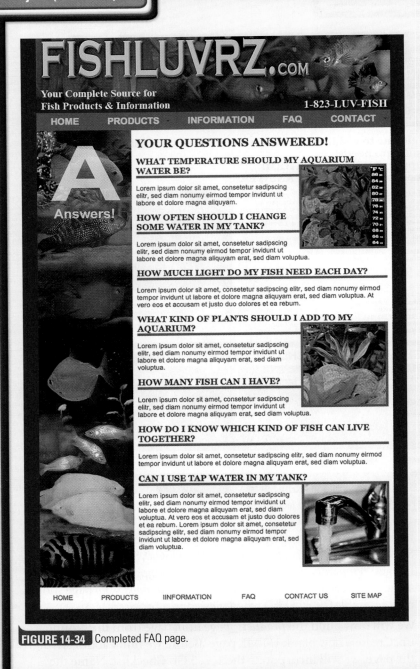

FIGURE 14-34 Completed FAQ page.

FishluvrzSite website. Add a title of *Tropical Fish for Your Fresh and Saltwater Aquariums*. Now add the following keywords: *Molly, Neon, Cichlid, Discus, Tropical fish, Freshwater aquarium fish, Saltwater aquarium fish*. Complete our starting checklist by adding the following sentences for description text: *We offer a wide variety of freshwater and saltwater tropical fish at prices you can afford. Tropical fish to fit your aquarium needs and budget.*

10. Now, we are ready to begin to build the page. Although we will add the content to this page using a table for its structure, feel free to try your hand at using div tags instead and rearranging the page content accordingly if you would like. Currently, the CSS panel lists *(no rules defined)*, because we did not assign any appearance properties using the Page Properties dialog box. We will attach our external style sheet instead. Locate the *fishluvrz.css* style sheet and attach it to the page, choosing to link it rather than import it. The page immediately acquires the background color of the rest of our site! Before creating the page structure, let's add a new internal style sheet with two class rules specific to this page.

    Create the first class named *.buynow*. Because it will be an internal style sheet specific to this page, be sure to choose *This document only* when creating the rule. For its rule definition, choose the *Type* category and apply Font-style: *italic* and Color: *#336600*.

    Name the second class *.fish*. In the Rule Definition dialog box, choose the *Box* category, uncheck *Same for all* for the Margin, and apply the following values: Top: *35 pixels*, Right: *10 pixels*, Bottom: *0 pixels*, Left: *10 pixels*.

11. To build its structure using tables, begin with an umbrella table: 1 row, 1 column, 750 pixels wide, with zero for its padding, spacing, and border. After it's inserted, align it to the *center* and choose Vert *Top* for its cell.

    Nest a table inside of it with 2 rows, 1 column, a width of 100%, and zero for its padding, spacing, and border. With the table selected, press the right arrow key to place the I-beam to the right of the table and insert another table below it with 8 rows, 2 columns, a width of 100%, and zero for its padding, spacing, and border.

12. To add the footer navigation, let's copy it from another page. Open your *index.html* page and select the footer navigation table

by using either the tag selector or the Expanded Tables mode to help. Copy it to the Clipboard and leave the *index.html* page open. Return to your new *products_page.html* page. Select the 8-row table you just created and then press the right arrow key to move the I-beam to the right edge of it, ready for the next insertion. Choose Edit>Paste. After your footer navigation has been added below the 8-row table, you will only need to adjust the links to be sure they are all assigned to their proper pages. A great tip for future sites!

13. In the first nested table at the top, insert the *fishluvrz_static_ headline.jpg* into the first row, then add an image map on top of the name to link back to the *index.html* page, as we did for the rest of the link pages. Return to the *index.html* page, click the cyan tab above the Spry Menu Bar to select it, choose Edit>Copy, and return to the *products_page.html* page. Place the I-beam in the cell below the headline in the top table, assign a background color of *#336600*, and then choose Edit>Paste. Now, before closing the *index.html* page, return to it and reassign the *deals.gif* rollover from the hash symbol (#) to link directly to the *products_page.html* page, and reassign the corresponding hotspot on the fish image below it to also link directly to the *products_page.html* page. Then, save and close the index page.

14. Return to the *products-page.html* page to finish it and for the 8 row, 2 column table, begin by selecting the entire table, assigning Vert *Top* and setting a background color of *#FFFFFF* to all of its cells. To complete the preparation for its content, drag to select all of the cells in the right column only and set their widths to *275 pixels*. To add the first four fish images to these cells, locate them in the *images* folder of the FishluvrzSite and insert them in the following order: *balloon_molly.jpg, blood_parrot.jpg, buffalo_head.jpg, convict_cichlid.jpg*. The remaining four fish images are native .psd files. When inserting them, you will need to locate them in the *original fishluvrz graphics* folder, where you moved them in Chapter 13, and optimize each one as you insert it, being sure to save it into the FishluvrzRoot *images* folder: *glow_fish.jpg, jack_dempsey.jpg, leopard_discus.jpg*, and *neons.jpg*.

   After importing all eight of the fish images, select each one at a time, assign the *.fish* class to it, and add the hash symbol (#) in the link option of the Property inspector to simulate the ability to theoretically link to a separate page to purchase the selected fish.

15. To add the content to the left cells of this table, begin by placing the I-beam in its top-left cell. Type: *balloon molly | buy now!* (no capitalization), and then create a new paragraph. For the product description, open the *product_text.doc* (or *product_text.rtf* if needed), which is located in the *Chapter_14PracticeFiles* folder, in Microsoft Word or another text editing program and copy it to the Clipboard. At your insertion point, choose *Paste Special* and select the *Text only* option.

16. To style the text we have just added, place the I-beam anywhere inside the fish name and assign *h2* to the paragraph. To complete this paragraph, drag to select the words *buy now!* and apply the *.buynow* class. Typically, a phrase like Buy now! would actually be a link to a purchasing page. So, with the text still highlighted, add the hash symbol (#) in the link option of the Property inspector to simulate the link action and add the same words in the Title area of the Property inspector to create a corresponding tooltip in CS4 and CS5.

    For the product description text, can you guess what you will need to do? Click anywhere inside it and apply the *.padding* class.

17. Highlight all of the text in this first cell (both its heading and its description text) and copy it to the Clipboard. Place the I-beam in the row just below it, choose Edit>Paste, and then paste it six more times, once in each of the successive cells below the one where you just pasted the text. Lastly, highlight and update the seven fish names you just pasted with the following names in the order listed: *blood parrot cichlid, buffalo head cichlid, convict cichlid, glow fish, jack dempsey, leopard snakeskin discus*, and *neons*. Remember that you have applied the *uppercase* option to the h2 tag, so each name will be capitalized automatically for you! Your completed *products_page.html* page should now resemble **FIGURE 14-35** when viewed in a browser.

18. Open the *information_page.html* page. Attach the *fishluvrz.css* style sheet to it and then delete the internal duplicate styles (do not delete the separate *SpryMenuBarHorizontal.css* style sheet). Because we created the appearance of a margin by the width of the table cells on this page, you will notice that the heading, *The fish facts you need to know*, now has extra padding on its left side. Rather than redesign the page, we will simply create one internal *This document only* style to override it. Create a new class rule named *.heading_override*, with Font-family: *Georgia, Times New Roman, Times, serif*, Size: *24 px*, and Color: *#000066*. Before assigning it, place the I-beam inside this text,

Project (continued)

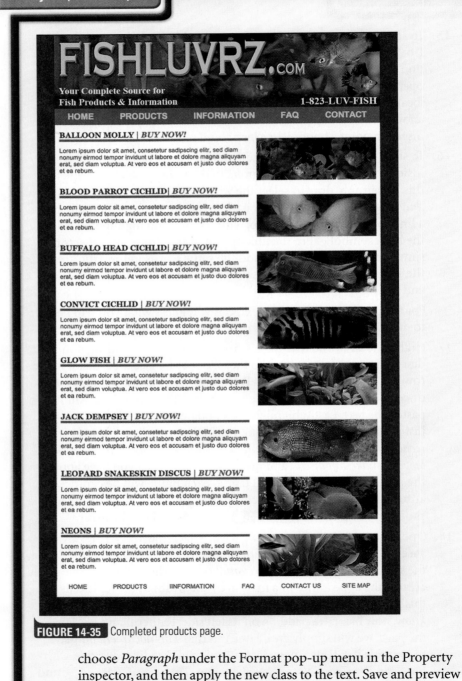

FIGURE 14-35 Completed products page.

choose *Paragraph* under the Format pop-up menu in the Property inspector, and then apply the new class to the text. Save and preview this page in a browser.

14.8 Building Your Own Website

1. Make your site active in the Files panel and open your *index.html* page. If you used a Spry Menu Bar for your navigation, begin by customizing it with your site colors, fonts, etc., test it in a browser, and make adjustments as needed after previewing your submenus.

2. In your CSS panel, notice the default rules created for your page through the Page Properties dialog box. Begin by creating class rules and/or adjusting existing HTML tags, with padding and margins as needed to create the space you need for the look you want around your text and your images. Apply the rules and then tweak them after testing the page in multiple browsers.

3. When you are satisfied with their look, select only the rules that will be applicable to other pages of your site and choose the *Move CSS Rules* command. When prompted, create a new style and be sure to save it to the *css* folder of your site root folder.

4. Close your *index.html* page and open one of your link pages. If it was created using the AP Divs to table method, begin by throwing away all the rules automatically created during that process, which will currently be displayed in your CSS panel.

5. Attach the external style sheet you created from the rules of your *index. html* page. Remember to complete this process by deleting any rules that are now internal, embedded duplicates.

6. In many cases, a link page may also need its own additional custom rules. Create them as needed, rather than changing an existing HTML tag, such as h1, your body rule, etc., unless you want the change to be sitewide! Remember that this is the beauty of CSS, but it can also be the nemesis of attaching an external style sheet!

7. Repeat this process for your remaining link pages, including attaching your external style sheet to your form page if your site is going to have one. You will learn how to create and add some additional rules specific to forms in the next chapter. Alternately, choose to create or recreate some of your pages by structuring them using div tags and CSS. You must be getting excited about your site. In Chapter 15, we will move on to learning to create a form and then the great finale … Chapter 16, learning to upload your site!

Input Tag Accessibility Attributes

1. ID FOR THE TEXT FIELD → ID: name

2. LABEL FOR THE FIELD → Label: Name:

Style: ○ Wrap with label tag

3. PLACEMENT OF THE LABEL → ● Attach label tag using 'for' attribute

○ No label tag

OK
Cancel
Help

6. TABBING ORDER IN FORM

FISHLUVRZ.COM

Your Complete Source for
Fish Products & Information   1-823-LUV-FISH

HOME   PRODUCTS   INFORMATION   FAQ   CONTACT

Please provide the following information so that we may better serve you!

TELL US ABOUT YOURSELF

First Name: Last Name:
Address: City/State/Zip:
Phone: Email:

You discovered us by:
○ Searching the Web
○ Friend's Referral
○ Flyer
○ Other
○ Radio

Your favorite fish is:
Balloon Molly
Blood Parrot Cichlid
Buffalo Head Cichlid
Convict Cichlid
Can't decide? Command/Control-click to choose multiple favorites!

HOW CAN WE HELP YOU

Select a department to contact: [Ask an expert ▾]

Fish problems? Live chat with an expert!
Chat with us 24/7

☑ Please add me to your weekly fish tips and product specials Email list!

(Reset form)   (Submit your inquiry now)

NO THANKS, TAKE ME RIGHT TO THE FISHLUVRZ BLOG!   FISHLUVRZ BLOG

HOME   PRODUCTS   INFORMATION   FAQ   CONTACT US   SITE MAP

OK
Cancel

Item Label	Value
Milliton Mountain	milliton
Aztec	aztec
Vantage Valley	vantage
Towertown Mountain	towertown
Landmark Hollow	landmark

3. ENTER THE LIST VALUES

Help

2. NUMBER OF VISIBLE SELECTIONS

PROPERTIES

List/Menu   Type ○ Menu   Height 4   List Values...   Class None

1. ID FOR THE LIST   skied   ● List   Selections ☑ Allow multiple   6. MULTIPLE SELECTIONS   7. APPLY CSS

Initially selected
Cannon Mo...
Killington
Stowe
Waterville V

4. CHOOSE THE LIST OPTION   5. ASSIGN AN INITIAL SELECTION

Creating a Form Using Dreamweaver

15

Chapter 15 is devoted exclusively to form building. We will begin with an overview of the various form-building tools provided in Dreamweaver, followed by the use of many of the most common form tools in the creation of a basic form. Along with understanding how to insert each type of form control, our practice will further reinforce our understanding of the typical usage of the form controls we will employ. Although we will not be able to perform a live test, we will learn what must be in place for data to actually be collected, as well as learn an informal method we can use to test a form. Lastly, we will learn how our newly acquired skills in CSS can be applied to forms to improve their readability and professional appearance.

15.1 Form Basics Using Dreamweaver

If you chose to include the optional Chapter 5 introduction to HTML in your web design learning, you explored the most common form elements (controls) and how to write the code for them. At that time, it was promised that in Chapter 15 you would learn more about the form elements that were introduced to you, learn about additional form objects available in Dreamweaver, learn how to build a form using them, and learn the server requirements that must be in place for a form to actually function. We're here!

15.1.1 An Introduction to the Dreamweaver Form Design Tools

We will begin our discussion with an introduction to the data input features of each of the Dreamweaver form objects, as shown in **FIGURE 15-1**. All of the form objects located under the Forms category of the Insert panel are also available by choosing Insert>Form from the application menu and then selecting the desired form object from its submenu. It will be helpful to think of them as form design tools. Just as you choose a tool in the Photoshop toolbox and assign specific features to its application in the Photoshop Options bar, selecting and applying a form object in Dreamweaver allows you to then customize its features in the Property inspector. Let's begin with a general introduction to each of the form objects available.

1. The *Form* object is a very special form object that defines the outer parameter of the form. Only data contained within its boundaries will be forwarded to the server for processing.

2. The *Text Field* object is probably the most common one, which we have all used on the Internet. It can be applied to any type of single-line text-entry requirement.

3. The *Hidden Field* object is one designed to work behind the scenes; it is not visible to the user.

4. The *Textarea* object provides multiple lines of text data entry.

5. A single *Checkbox* object allows an answer, such as a "Yes" response, without the user having to type any text.

6. A *Checkbox Group* object (CS4 and CS5 only) allows the user to have multiple checkboxes under the same entry category: multiple checkboxes allowing multiple checked responses.

7. A single *Radio Button* object allows an answer, such as a "Yes" response, without the user having to type any text entry, just as the single checkbox does.

8. Unlike a checkbox group, a *Radio Group* object will have multiple buttons; however, it will allow only one selection at a time within the

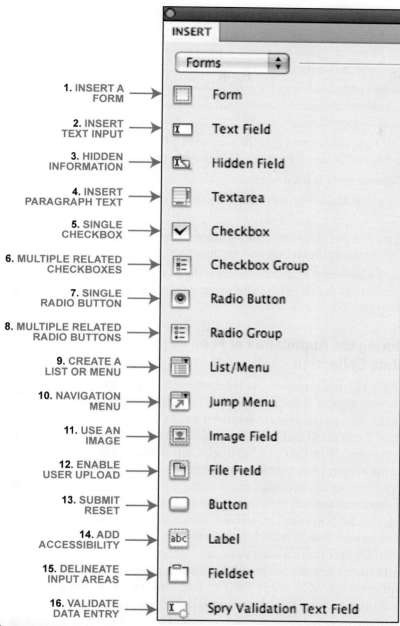

1. INSERT A FORM	Form
2. INSERT TEXT INPUT	Text Field
3. HIDDEN INFORMATION	Hidden Field
4. INSERT PARAGRAPH TEXT	Textarea
5. SINGLE CHECKBOX	Checkbox
6. MULTIPLE RELATED CHECKBOXES	Checkbox Group
7. SINGLE RADIO BUTTON	Radio Button
8. MULTIPLE RELATED RADIO BUTTONS	Radio Group
9. CREATE A LIST OR MENU	List/Menu
10. NAVIGATION MENU	Jump Menu
11. USE AN IMAGE	Image Field
12. ENABLE USER UPLOAD	File Field
13. SUBMIT RESET	Button
14. ADD ACCESSIBILITY	Label
15. DELINEATE INPUT AREAS	Fieldset
16. VALIDATE DATA ENTRY	Spry Validation Text Field

FIGURE 15-1 Form objects in Dreamweaver.

group. If another button is selected after one has been chosen, the original will automatically become deselected.

9. This object is called *List/Menu* (*Select/List Menu* in CS5) because, depending upon the settings you apply to it in the Property inspector,

the same form object is used to create either a list allowing multiple selections or a pop-up menu allowing only one choice from its multi-item list.

10. A *Jump Menu* navigational object is used to provide pop-up menu selection access to link pages.

11. An *Image Field* object is as it sounds. An image can be used in place of an ordinary Button object for tasks such as to reset the form or to initialize the form's submission.

12. The *File Field* object provides the user with a Browse button to locate a file on his/her computer to upload to the server.

13. The *Button* object is used to create both Submit and Reset buttons.

14. One way to add accessibility features to form objects is to insert the *Label* object.

15. Adding a *Fieldset* object sets the assigned form content apart from other areas of the form for styling and organization.

16. The *Spry Validation Text Field* object is the first of four entry validation form objects available in CS3 and seven validation form objects available in CS4 and CS5.

15.1.2 Exploring the Application of Form Objects for Data Collection

Although we have all used forms on the Internet, we have done it so much that the process has become almost automatic, without much thought to the structure of the form, just the data entry process required by the form. A brief return to the Web in search of form idea book samples will be very helpful at this stage of the form creation process. Now that you have been introduced to the wide variety of form objects available in Dreamweaver, searching the Web will provide you with numerous opportunities to recognize these form objects in action and how other web designers have customized the incorporation of these same form objects into their work. Examine a potpourri of website forms, citing the various ways they have adapted the form objects, which have just been introduced to you, to meet their data input requirements. Focus your exploration on how the form objects you can identify have been uniquely tailored to meet the needs of the site's data collection requirements. Also, study their styling and layout on the pages. This exploration will provide you with a better understanding of the typical data entry each of the main form elements commonly provides before we begin to learn how to create them.

15.1.3 Applying the Design Tools to Form Building

To understand the typical application of a variety of form objects and how to implement them in Dreamweaver, let's create a basic form.

Using the Form Object: The Important First Step in Creating a Workable Form Now that you have studied some forms, let's learn to build one. What you could not have discovered while you were searching the Internet is that all the form objects used in each of the forms you reviewed were enclosed within a master umbrella container, which is needed to be able to process the form. If you chose to include Chapter 5 in your learning, you already know that all form *controls*, the user interactive tools of a form (defined by Dreamweaver as *form objects*), must be enclosed within the opening and closing tag of the form element: the master umbrella container. The first form object you will need to use is the one named Form. (To avoid confusion, it will be referred to as the Form icon, rather than the Form form object.) By clicking the Form icon first, Dreamweaver will create the master umbrella container for you to insert all additional form objects inside of it when building a form, ensuring that the HTML form element will automatically encase the entire form for proper processing.

With your SampleSite website active in the Files panel, create a new page in its *pages* folder named *form_sample.html*. (Again, during this practice, it will not be necessary to add a title, keywords, and description text to this page. However, remember that you must start each page of a real site with these critical steps.) We will use this page to learn how to use the Form icon first and then learn how to insert and assign properties to the rest of the most common Dreamweaver form objects. Insert a table first to contain the form we will create. The table should have the following characteristics: 1 row; 1 column; 500 pixels wide; and zero for its cell padding, spacing, and border. Center it after it has been added to the page. Click inside the table and select the *Form* icon in the Forms category of the Insert panel or choose Insert>Form>Form. After you have done that, a red rectangle will appear inside the table, enclosing your insertion point.

 We have learned about the handy tag selector located in the lower-left corner of the Document window. Notice that it now reflects the addition of the form object on the page <form#form1>. While working with a form, the tag selector can help you activate the particular form object you need to select and will allow you to easily reselect this master umbrella form object at any time when clicked.

Notice in the tag selector that the inserted form is automatically named *form1*. Each form must have a unique identifier. When the form is selected, its default name displays in the Form ID area of the Property inspector where it can be highlighted and customized, and you can assign the rest of the options unique to this form object. This critical information determines if and how the form will be functional. Dreamweaver provides great tools to *create* a form. However, for a form to become functional, your Internet Service Provider (ISP) will supply you with the access needed, usually providing a *CGI-bin* (short for Common Gateway Interface) to process your forms. Let's take a look at what will be needed to add functionality beyond "good looks" to your form in **FIGURE 15-2**.

1. In the Form ID field, a form must have a unique lowercase name with no spaces. By default, Dreamweaver will name it *form1*. However, you can

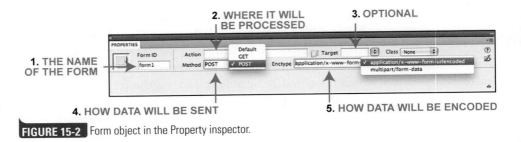

FIGURE 15-2 Form object in the Property inspector.

highlight this option and change it in the Property inspector any time you have selected <form#yourformnamehere> in the tag selector.

2. The Action field contains the address where the form will be processed. This will be provided for you by your ISP.

3. This optional pop-up menu, with its _blank, _parent, _self, and _top choices, can assign a target window to display the processed data.

4. The method for sending the data is assigned here, with three available options: Default, Get, and Post. *Default* will use the browser's prechosen sending method to forward its user's data to the processing location. The Get and Post methods each have individual advantages. The *Get* method is beneficial for user searches because it becomes attached to the URL and works well for short forms. The *Post* method embeds the data, making it somewhat more secure. It is designed to handle lengthier form data, and it is the default choice when using Dreamweaver. Consulting your ISP will determine which submission method is the best choice for transferring your type of data.

5. This box is optional. If you do not select an option, the default is *application/x-www-form-urlencoded*. Alternatively, you can type in *text/plain* for the Enctype, along with your own email address in the Action field, to test your form, which we will do before completing this chapter. Ultimately, however, you will want to work with your ISP and implement their processing script for the best, most reliable and secure method of data encoding for your form.

Before we move on to adding form objects inside this form container, it is important to note that if you do not add any information to the Property inspector when this form object is selected, you can still build, save, and preview your form in a browser. However, until this processing information has been added to the form, any data entered into it will not actually be sent anywhere. At any stage of the creation process, this form object can be reselected using the tag selector, and the processing information can then be added to make the form workable when uploaded.

Inserting Text Field and Textarea Form Objects   As we have learned, as long as all additional form objects are added inside the form created using the Form icon, the form will work properly after it has been configured with the server. We began our form by placing it inside a table to define its size and location on the page. Although not required, adding the rest of the form objects within the constraints of a table *inside* the master umbrella form created by the Form icon will add structure and organization to it: alternatively, it could be structured using CSS. Because our learning here will focus on form objects, the simplicity of using a table for its structure will allow us to focus our learning on the form's content. Before we finish the form, however, we will dress it up with a little CSS styling.

With the I-beam *inside* the form (Dreamweaver inserts it there automatically for you if you have selected the Form icon and then clicked on the page: in our case, inside of a table), insert a table with the following characteristics: 6 rows, 2 columns, a width of 100%, a cell padding of 5 pixels (adding breathing space around our content), and zero for its cell spacing and border. After it is inserted, select the left column of the table and assign a horizontal alignment of *Right* and a width of *150 pixels*.

Text Field Place the I-beam inside the upper-left cell of the table and select the *Text Field* form object from the Forms category of the Insert panel, or under the Form option of the Insert main menu. Because we followed best practice and assigned forms to be included in the Accessibility Preferences category of Dreamweaver, we are automatically entered into the dialog box shown in **FIGURE 15-3** for assigning accessibility features before the text field is added to the page.

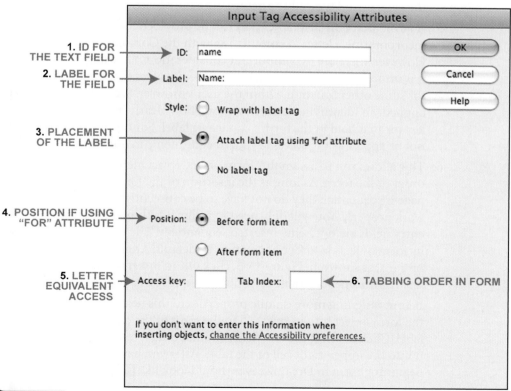

FIGURE 15-3 Input Tag Accessibility Attributes dialog box.

Although we are inserting a Text Field form object, this same dialog box will open when we insert most of the Dreamweaver form objects because of our accessibility preferences. Let's take a few minutes to understand its components.

1. The *ID* field assigns a name for the form object in the code. We will always choose to use lowercase letters with no spaces or special characters when naming an ID.

2. The *Label* field displays your instructions to the user on what information is requested in the corresponding input control (in this case, the Text Field form object), with any capitals, special characters, etc., as needed in its directions.

3. This is where you assign how the label will be attached to the form object. The *for* accessibility preference option allows the label to be moved to a separate cell, if using tables, and have the label still relate to its assigned form object. An extra benefit is the user's ability to click the label name (rather than only within the form field) to be able to activate the field for data entry. We will use the *for* option whenever applicable for accessibility. (In CS5, the *Attach label using "for" attribute* has been moved to the top of the Style list.)

4. This determines the position of the label if one is assigned. For text fields, the label would typically be before the form object.

5. A keyboard equivalent access key can be provided for a form field incorporating a letter in conjunction with the Command/Control key. However, there are two important considerations regarding this use. First, it is important to not assign a keyboard equivalent that is already in place for some other function within the user's browser. Second, if one has been applied, an identifying letter must somehow clearly indicate the access key for that field in the form's applicable label. For our purposes, we will not be applying any access keyboard equivalents in our forms.

6. This allows you to assign this form object's placement in the tabbing order of the form. As long as the insertion of the form objects of your page is sequential, they do not have to be consecutively numbered to work properly. You will only need to assign a tabbing index if your data entry fields are not being inserted sequentially. The form will tab through its form objects by order of creation by default. After assigning the options, as shown in Figure 15-3, click OK to insert this first form object inside the upper-left table cell of our sample form.

Before assigning more unique properties to this text field, we will move the form object into its own cell to the right of the cell containing its label. Click to select the text field only and drag it to the right, dropping it into the upper-right cell of the table. After you have done that, your beginning form in Dreamweaver should look like **FIGURE 15-4**.

Name:	

FIGURE 15-4 Form with text field.

When the form object (not its identifying label) is selected on the page, properties for the text field become active in the Property inspector, as shown in **FIGURE 15-5**.

1. The *TextField* option reflects the ID name given in the Input Tag Accessibility Attributes dialog box. Notice that it identifies this text field as *name*.

2. *Char width* determines the width of the field as it will display in the form. Experiment by setting it to different widths and noticing how the length of the text field expands and contracts, corresponding to the values you enter into this option, and then assign a character width for this text field of *30 characters*.

3. The *Single line* or *Multi line* option dictates the number of lines of text that can be entered. Because we chose *TextField* for the type of form object we inserted, the *Single line* option is prechosen as the Type, creating a single-line data entry area. By selecting *Multi line* instead, this text field will automatically be converted into a Textarea form object, providing a scroll bar and allowing you to determine the number of lines that will be visible in the form. For this name entry, keep this option set to single line.

4. To provide password protection your data entries, select the *Password* radio button. When you test it in a browser, only bullets or asterisks will display. Go ahead, try it if you'd like!

5. *Max chars* determines the maximum number of characters the user can enter into this field. It is important to understand that this number can

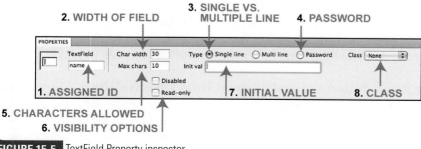

FIGURE 15-5 TextField Property inspector.

be larger than the Char width number; if it is larger, the letters will simply scroll as needed. If you define a limit on the number of characters that can be inserted, the user's browser will stop allowing entry when the limit is reached. Some browsers signify the limit with an alert tone. Let's test the limit feature by entering a maximum character limit of only *10.*

6. The *Disabled/Read-only* options allow visible text to be active only under certain scripting conditions (disabled) or visible and selectable, but not changeable (read-only). We will not apply either one of these options.

7. The optional *Init val* feature allows you to add explanatory words that will preexist in the field area, such as *Enter your name here.* We will not add any initial text to this field.

8. *Class,* which is located at the upper-right area of the Property inspector, enables you to apply some CSS styling to the form object. We will learn to apply some CSS styling to a form later in this chapter.

For CS3 Users

In CS3, the *Disabled* and *Read-only* options are not available. However, there are some text wrap options that become active if you choose to create a multiple line textarea: Default, Off, Virtual, and Physical. *Default* will wrap the text. *Off* will keep it in one long continuous scrolling single line. *Virtual* will wrap, but submit the data in one long line. *Physical* will wrap as well as submit the data wrapped.

Textarea   Place the I-beam in the left column of the second row and insert a *Textarea* form object. In the Input Tag Accessibility Attributes dialog box, assign an ID of *comments* and assign *We welcome your comments:* to the label. Leave the *for* attribute for Style and its Position at *Before form item* and do not assign Access or Tab values. After it has been entered into the form, as we did with the text field, highlight and drag it to the corresponding cell in the right column of the table. With it selected, set the *Char width* (length of the text area field) to *28* and *Num lines* (number of visible data entry lines) to *5.* As you can see, when the Textarea form object is selected, the Property inspector is identical to that of a text field form object, when the Multi line vs. Single line option has been selected.

Inserting Radio Button and Radio Group Form Objects   Using a single radio button vs. a radio group depends on your data entry needs. Two distinct form objects are available in Dreamweaver to accommodate these specific needs, and you can also use a single radio button to add more buttons to an existing radio group.

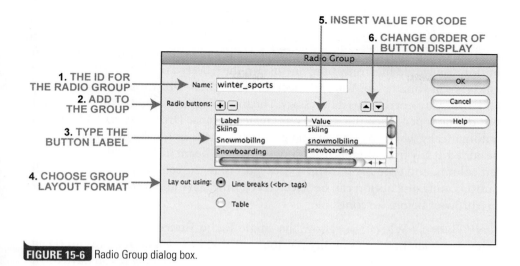

5. INSERT VALUE FOR CODE

6. CHANGE ORDER OF BUTTON DISPLAY

1. THE ID FOR THE RADIO GROUP

2. ADD TO THE GROUP

3. TYPE THE BUTTON LABEL

4. CHOOSE GROUP LAYOUT FORMAT

FIGURE 15-6 Radio Group dialog box.

Radio Group We will learn to add a radio group first. Place the I-beam in the third row of the right column and choose the *Radio Group* form object. This time, you are brought to the Radio Group dialog box to assign the properties for the group. Let's take a closer look at its options in **FIGURE 15-6**.

1. The *Name* option is the identifier for the code, which will ensure that all of its radio buttons function together as one group. As shown in the Figure 15-6 sample, name the practice radio group *winter_sports*.

2. This dialog box contains two labels and values, by default, to begin creating a radio button group. Clicking the *plus icon* will allow you to add selections to the group. With an entry selected, clicking the minus icon will delete it from the group.

3. When you click the word *Radio* under the Label column, it becomes active to customize the name for the button.

4. These two options determine how the buttons will be added to the form. We will choose to insert buttons using *Line breaks*. However, if you choose the *Table* option here, one will be added to the form, with each button placed in its own cell.

5. The *Value* is the response sent to the server for its corresponding label. Let's create a sample radio group by entering the label and value information, as shown in Figure 15-6.

6. The up and down arrows allow you to adjust the order of the display of the buttons. Because alphabetically *Snowboarding* should come before *Snowmobiling*, select it and click the up arrow to move it between *Skiing* and *Snowmobiling*.

When you click OK to leave this dialog box, the group is added to the form. After it's inserted, you can highlight one of the buttons in the group and then, in the Property inspector, assign it as *Checked* for a preselected option. Choose any button you would like (only one) and assign the *Checked* option to it. Do you have any typos in your group? You can select the text right in Dreamweaver Design mode and make your corrections if necessary. The Input Tag Accessibility Attributes dialog box did not open when this group was created because Dreamweaver adds labeling automatically when creating a radio group. Instructions for the user, however, can be added at any time after its insertion. Place the I-beam inside the third row in the left column and type *My favorite winter sport is:* in the cell. Remember, with radio buttons, only one option can be selected at a time. Save and test your sample form in a browser before we continue.

Radio Button   When you choose the single Radio Button form object, you will enter the Input Tag Accessibility Attributes dialog box, which requires an ID and a label. Dreamweaver automatically selects the *After form item* if you have the *for* Style attribute assigned, because it is the usual location of a single radio button's description. The Property inspector is identical in appearance when you select a single radio button on a page as when you select an individual button of a radio Button group. A typical use of a single radio button might be "Yes! Sign me up!" (Often, the button is already selected.)

Because it is identical, you can also use the single Radio Button form object to add more choices to an existing radio group. By clicking to the right of the last entry of an existing radio group on the page and applying a line break (soft return), you can click the single Radio Button form object to add another button to the group. However, for the button to function as part of the *existing* group, the name you assign when it's inserted must be the same as the group's name in the Property inspector. Click any of the original buttons you created for the *winter_sports* group. Notice that under the Radio Button section in the Property inspector, it displays *winter_sports*, the original identifier you typed as the name of the group. For a single radio button to be "joined onto" an existing group, you need to assign the exact same name in the Radio Button area of the Property inspector as the existing group's name and then assign a respective value for the button. To try this out, add a line break (Shift+Return) after *Snowmobiling* in your existing group and then click the Radio Button form object. In the Input Tag Accessibility Attributes dialog box, name it *snowshoeing*, with a label of *Snowshoeing*, and assign the *for* Style and Position to be *After form item* and do not assign Access or Tab values. After it's inserted on the page, select the button and change the name under the Radio Button section of the Property inspector to *winter_sports*. When tested in a browser, it should be added to the group. How will you know? Remember that only one button can be selected at any time in a radio group. When testing, it should become deselected when another one of the radio buttons in the same group is chosen. If it doesn't, check its radio button name in the left side of the Property inspector to be sure its name is identical to the rest of the buttons of the radio group *winter_sports*.

Inserting Checkbox and Checkbox Group Form Objects   Just as Dreamweaver provides individual form objects for a radio button vs. a radio group, it also provides individual form objects for single checkboxes vs. multiple checkboxes, with the ability to add to an existing checkbox group using the single checkbox form object. Let's take a look at these and how their content usages compare and contrast to those of single radio buttons vs. radio groups.

Checkbox   With the I-beam placed where you want to add it, the insertion and usage of a single checkbox is similar to that of a single radio button, except that after the checkbox has been inserted, be sure to add a *Checked value* identifying the data entry response.

Checkbox Group   When inserting a Checkbox Group form object, completion of its insertion dialog box is identical to that of a Radio Group form object. The important single difference between these two data entry form objects lies not in their creation, but in their application. While a radio group allows only one selection at a time to be chosen by the user, a checkbox group can be used for a request, such as "Check all that apply."

For CS3 Users

Although a Checkbox Group form object is not available in CS3, by following the same procedure used to add a single radio button to an existing Radio Group (using a line break and naming each checkbox with the same identifying name), the checkboxes will work together as a group when tested in a browser.

Inserting List and Menu Form Objects   Although the same form object is used to create either a list or a menu, there are two important differences between them as they relate to the use of this form object, which we will discuss individually.

List   A List form object is used to list all of the user's choices. The number of selections visible is defined in the Property inspector; the remaining options are available using a scroll bar, which will be created automatically if needed. When using the List/Menu form object as a list, multiple selections are possible. To add one to our form, click in the left cell of the next row and click the *List/Menu* form object (identified in CS5 as *Select List/Menu*) to enter the Input Tag Accessibility Attributes dialog box. Type *skied* for its ID. Type *I have skied at:* for its label. Keep the *for* Style attribute assigned, set the Position to *Before form item*, and do not assign Access or Tab values. After it has been added to the form, drag the list to the corresponding right cell of the table. When the List/Menu object is selected, the Property inspector allows you to assign this form object to be used as either a list

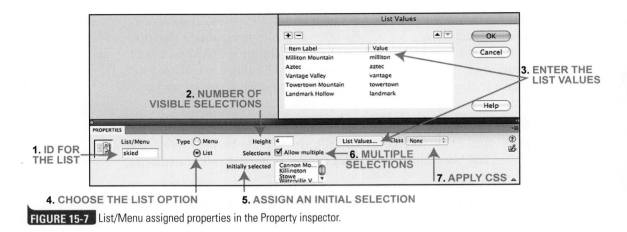

FIGURE 15-7 List/Menu assigned properties in the Property inspector.

or a menu, and add the selection choices to the list. Let's take a closer look at the Property inspector when creating a list, shown in **FIGURE 15-7**.

1. As we have learned, the ID assigned in the Input Tag Accessibility Attributes dialog box displays below the name of the type of form object chosen; in this case, it is *skied*.

2. When creating a list, this is where you define the number of selections that will be visible before the user will need to scroll to view other choices.

3. When you click the *List Values* button, you are entered into the List Values dialog box, which has a data entry process that echoes the process of creating a Radio Group object or a Checkbox Group object. What differs about accessing this data entry dialog box from the other two, however, is the ability to reselect the List Values button in the Property inspector any time you click an existing List/Menu form object in your layout, and re-enter the dialog box to add, delete, or edit its assigned values.

4. You must select the *List* radio button to create a list. *Menu* is the default selection.

5. If desired, you can select one of your entries to be prechosen.

6. When creating a list, this option allows the user to Command/Control-click for multiple selections.

7. Class rules can be applied to the list.

Complete the list by assigning its options, as shown in Figure 15-7. When you exit the List Values dialog box, you can choose an *Initially selected* option if desired. After you have assigned your desired options in the Property inspector, select the list in the form, add a soft return after it (line break), and then type *Command/Control-click for multiple selections*.

Now that the list has been added to the page, should the items be out of alphabetical sequence? Probably not. Reselect the list, click the *List Values* button in the Property inspector, and use the up/down arrows to arrange the ski areas alpha-betically: *Aztec, Landmark Hollow, Milliton Mountain, Towertown Mountain,* and *Vantage Valley.* Click OK to assign the changes.

Menu   There are two important differences if the Menu option is chosen instead of the List option in the Property inspector when using this same form object to create a menu. First, when viewed in a browser, unlike a list that will display the number of items you defined by its height with the ability to scroll to choose from the rest of its selections, a menu will display only one option until the user clicks its pop-up menu to reveal the rest of the available choices. Second, although a user can make multiple selections from a list, a menu will allow only one.

Let's insert a short menu to learn how it differs from a list. Click inside the left column of the next row of your table, and once again, select the *List/Menu* form object. In the Input Tag Accessibility Attributes dialog box, assign *live* for its ID, add *I ski all over New England, but live in:* for its label, keep the *for* attribute assigned for Style and *Before form item* for its Position and do not assign Access or Tab values. After it's inserted, drag the menu to the right column of the row, and with it still selected, assign the following options in the Property inspector, as shown in **FIGURE 15-8**.

1. Just as with the List option, our assigned ID displays on the left in the Property inspector.

2. Notice that you do not have to select the *Menu* option, even though the most recent use of this form object was for the creation of a list. The default choice is to create a menu.

3. Enter the labels and values as shown. Notice that the plus icon, minus icon, and arrows to move the position of the options are identical to these same features when creating Lists, Radio Groups, and Checkbox groups. After entering your labels and values, select and move the items to create an alphabetical listing: *Connecticut, Maine, Massachusetts, New Hampshire, Rhode Island,* and *Vermont.*

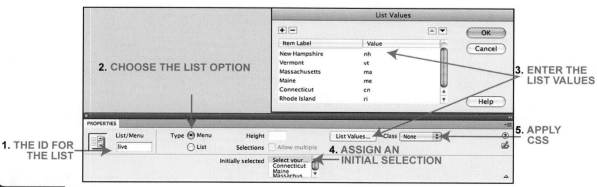

FIGURE 15-8 Menu settings in the Property inspector.

4. Notice that you can assign an initial selection and that the sample shows *Select your…* as an option that we currently do not have as a choice in the List Values dialog box. Open the List Values dialog box again by clicking the *List Values* button and add *Select your state:* as a label. You will not need to assign a value to it, but you will need to use the up arrow to move it to the top of the list. After you have exited the List Values dialog box, click to select this new entry in the *Initially selected* option of the Property inspector.

5. Just as when using this dialog box to create a list, class rules can be applied to the menu.

Inserting a Jump Menu Navigational Form Object   Our form is almost done. However, before we learn how to create reset and submit buttons for it, let's take a look at the Jump Menu form object. A *Jump Menu* is a navigational form object that allows the user to jump to a selected link page, without the designer having to assign a large amount of page space for the link navigation to occur. Although it functions and it is accessed and edited after insertion like a List/Menu form object, the dialog box used for its initial creation is similar to the Insert Navigation Bar dialog box in CS3 and CS4, as shown in **FIGURE 15-9**.

1. These plus and minus icons are ones you are familiar with by now, allowing you to add or delete entries, which are link pages in this case.

2. Also familiar at this point, after selecting one of your entries, these arrows will allow you to adjust the sequence of the links in the menu.

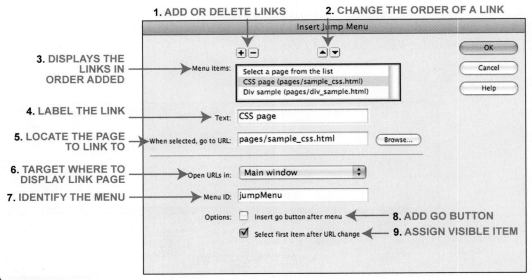

FIGURE 15-9 Insert Jump Menu dialog box.

3. Each time a link page is added to the menu, it is added to this *Menu items* list, allowing its deletion or listing order adjustment using the minus or arrow icons.

4. The identifying name for the link page is typed here, just as you would like it to be displayed in the jump menu's pop-up list.

5. Browse to locate the link page to jump to in your root folder, or type in a full URL to link to an external site page.

6. Choose the location (target) to display the link page.

7. Because we need an ID for all form objects, assign a name for the menu here, or accept the Dreamweaver default name *jumpMenu.*

8. When inserting a jump menu, you can also add an optional secondary step requiring the user to click a Go button after selecting a link page, before being able to proceed to the chosen page.

9. Although this sounds very similar to the *Initially selected* feature we have assigned to other form objects in the Property inspector, its function is quite different, and it is an important navigational feature of this dialog box. By adding a menu entry, named *Select a page from the list,* for example, as the first item in your jump menu list, the user will see those directions for the navigation without an additional descriptive label. Additionally, if this option is selected when the user has gone to a link page from the pop-up menu, returning to the initial page containing the jump menu will not display the last page visited. Instead, it will again display your directions; in the case of this sample, it displays *Select a page from the list.* It is important to remember that this option is based on the sequence of the items added to the menu, not on a selected item. As shown in Figure 15-9, even though the check mark is displayed when the CSS page is highlighted, when the jump menu is actually applied to the page, the *Select first item after URL change* option signifies that the first item listed in the menu list of this dialog box, which is *Select a page from the list* in this sample, is the one this option will affect.

To test a jump menu, we really would not want to add it to our existing form. Let's save and close this form page for a few minutes and open the *index.html* page of the SampleSite instead. On the index page, split one of the existing cells into two columns, place the I-beam inside of the empty cell, and click the *Jump Menu* form object. Insert the information, as shown in Figure 15-9, into the Insert Jump Menu dialog box that follows. What? No master umbrella Form object first? Is this breaking all the rules you have learned, or being added by mistake? When you exit the dialog box, you will discover that Dreamweaver automatically encased it within the required master form object for you. Is that cool or what? After it's inserted on the page, notice that when it's selected, the Property inspector options echo the List/Menu options, including the ability to click List Values to edit your link page entries. Before we return to finish the *form_sample.html* page, feel free to save your *index.html* page and test this jump menu, including applying the browser's Back button after navigating to a selected link page.

Inserting Validation   In addition to the form objects to create data input, the Forms category of the Insert panel and the Insert>Form menu also contain a variety of Spry Validation form objects that can be added to a form, such as *A value is required* or *Minimum number of characters not met*, which will block the submission of the form until the data requirement has been inserted. Let's convert one text field into a Spry Validation Text Field to explore this concept.

Close your *index.html* page and reopen your *form_sample.html* page. Click the *Text Field* form object in the upper-right cell of the table that we created initially for the form's name entry and then select the *Spry Validation Text Field* form object. This immediately transforms the existing text field into a validation text field. The Property inspector now reflects the available validation settings for this type of form object, as shown in **FIGURE 15-10**.

Here, you can assign minimum values that must be entered, or simply select the *Required* option from the *Preview states* pop-up menu. Under the *Type* pop-up menu are a variety of options you can select that will preassign typical restrictions. For example, if you select the *Email Address* option, it provides an error message of *Invalid format* if the user does not enter one with the necessary components of an email address. For our purposes, let's just select the *Required* option from the *Preview states* pop-up menu to test the form object, which will provide the error message of *A value is required* if the user does not add some kind of entry to the field.

When you attempt to save and preview the page with this new addition, the warning dialog box shown in **FIGURE 15-11** appears. Just as you learned when inserting a Spry Menu Bar, this warning states that when the Spry Validation form object was added, both a CSS file and a JavaScript file were created. They are required for the validation to work. Dreamweaver adds them to your site automatically. However, the message is a warning that unless these auxiliary files are also uploaded with the rest of your site files when it becomes live, the validation feature will not function properly. As promised, we will learn more about dependent files in our final chapter on the upload process.

Although we converted an existing text field, you can also insert Spry Validation fields directly through the Form or Spry categories of the Insert Panel. Selecting

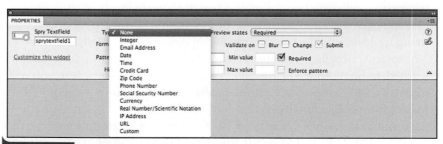

FIGURE 15-10 Spry Validation Text Field in the Property inspector.

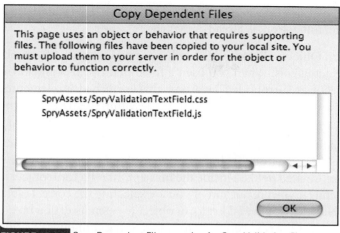

FIGURE 15-11 Copy Dependent Files warning for Spry Validation files.

to insert one using one of these methods will prompt the Input Tag Accessibility Attributes dialog box, and after you have exited that, will prompt you by asking *Add form tag?* If you choose Yes, when you exit the dialog box, your Spry field will automatically be housed inside a master Form object for you. When added in this manner, the validation field will be automatically selected, and the Property inspector will reflect the options to assign validation, as previously defined in this section.

Inserting Button Form Objects to Reset or Submit a Form   The Button form object is used to create both Reset and Submit buttons by simply assigning different properties to it in the Property inspector. We will learn how it is customized, depending on its usage, by inserting one of each into our sample form.

Reset Button   To insert both buttons, select the last row of the table and merge its cells, then set the Horizontal alignment to *Center* in the Property inspector. With the I-beam flashing in this cell, choose the *Button* form object. When the Input Tag Accessibility Attributes dialog box opens, we will assign an ID of *reset* this time. However, we will not assign a label. Under Style, we will choose *No label tag*, leave the default Position of *Before form item*, and choose not to add Access or Tab entries. Click OK to add the button into the cell. Notice that even though we chose an ID of reset, the wording on the button defaults to Submit. With the button selected, you simply need to make two changes in the Property inspector. The *Value* is what the button will have written on it; let's change it to *Reset the form*. Additionally, choose *Reset form* for the *Action* category. That's it!

Submit Button   Following the same format, place the I-beam to the right of your reset button and add another button next to it in the same cell. Give it an ID of *submit* and do not add a label. Leave the style as *No label tag*, leave the default Position of *Before form item*, and do not assign Access or Tab values. In the Property inspector, assign a value of *Click here to submit your survey now*. That's all there is to it; *Submit form*, the default action, is already selected.

Inserting a Fieldset Form Object   Before we learn how to add a Fieldset form object, let's learn what one actually is. When you used a form that had its content organized into named categories surrounded by a box, that form had implemented *fieldsets*: *containers* or *boxes* that housed related input fields within them in the form.

Adding a Fieldset Form Object to Enclose Existing Form Content   Following the logic that input areas of a fieldset are contained within a box, we need to select form fields to include in a fieldset (the "box"). Because we encased our form inside a table, select the table (our "related fields") inside the master umbrella form object to now select all of its content. (If you are not sure if you are selecting the correct table, check the tag selector.) Now, click the *Fieldset* form object to open its dialog box to assign its *Legend*. The legend is the title you want to assign to the container of fields. In our case, let's assign the name *my first form*. It will not be necessary to assign any capitalization because we will apply some CSS to it later. After this is done, the title displays in the upper-left corner of the form and the table has automatically been enclosed within the fieldset box. Although it will not look like much in Design view, if you take a minute to save the form and preview it in a browser, you will recognize the look as one you have seen in forms in other websites. You can edit the legend of an existing fieldset directly in design view at any time by highlighting its text.

If you are building a form without enclosing it in a table and realize that you want to move some or all of your fields into a fieldset, simply highlight the fields you want to enclose, click the *Fieldset* form object, title the legend in the dialog box that follows, and you will be done: the items you selected will be enclosed by the fieldset you assigned.

Beginning a Form with a Fieldset   If you have planned a form and know that you will want to build it inside of a fieldset, you can insert the fieldset as soon as you have added the initial master umbrella form object. By inserting a fieldset first and placing the I-beam inside the fieldset, all the form objects you add will automatically be enclosed in the fieldset you created.

Adding Styling to a Form with CSS

Let's begin to style this form by assigning a color to the legend. Although the text can be highlighted with a class assigned in the Property inspector, there is also a *legend* HTML tag that can be redefined. In the New CSS Rule dialog box, choose *Tag* for the *Selector type*, select *legend* from the *Selector name* pop-up menu, and add the rule to *This document only*. Assign the following properties to the legend in the Rule Definition dialog box that follows. In the Type category, assign the Font-family *Arial, Helvetica, sans serif*; also assign the Font-size *18 pixels*; the Font-weight *Bold*; Text-transform (Case) *Uppercase*; and the Color *#990000*. After you exit the Rule Definition dialog box, the legend automatically reflects the rule.

There is also a *fieldset* HTML tag that can be redefined. Choose to create another CSS rule, choose *Tag* again for the Selector type, select *fieldset* from the *Selector name* pop-up menu, and again choose *This document only*.

In the Rule Definition dialog box, assign the following properties. In the Type category, assign the Font-family *Arial, Helvetica, sans serif*; also assign the Font-size *14 pixels* and the Color *#990000*. In the Background category, assign the Background-color *#FFFFCC*. When you have exited this dialog box, you will see that the type and background of the form now reflect the attributes assigned to the fieldset.

The background of the text fields and the list, menu, and buttons, however, do not have the fieldset attributes assigned to them. You may remember that when we were adding them to the page, one of the options in the Property inspector was the ability to assign a CSS class. Let's try it out. Create a class rule named *.menus*, again selecting *This document only*. Assign the following properties. In the Type category, assign the Font-family *Arial, Helvetica, sans serif*; also assign the Font-size *14 pixels* and the Color *#990000*. In the Background category, assign the Background-color *#FFCC99*.

Support for colors assigned to menus and buttons varies across browsers. If the browser does not support it, the default will display instead. Let's apply it to the text and textarea fields, the list, the menu, and the buttons. In each case, select the form object on the page and then select *menu* from the Class pop-up menu. With the styling applied, when viewed in a browser, your form should now resemble **FIGURE 15-12**.

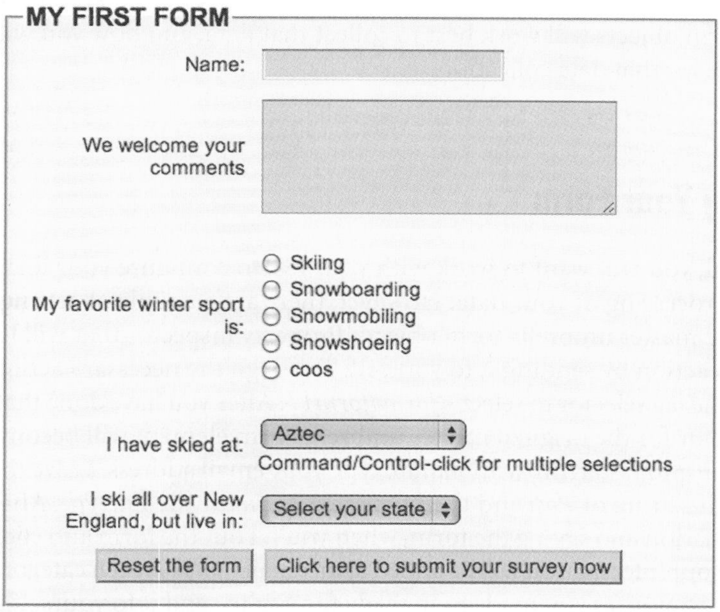

FIGURE 15-12 My first form.

Planning a Form Before Building It

We have learned to design a web page layout before attempting to create it and to design a navigational flowchart for a website before beginning to construct it. This is also the case in form design. You have searched the Internet and collected form samples, and you have learned how to build a form incorporating many of the most commonly used form objects. Each time you need to create a form in your future web design work, taking the time to plan out the form before starting to create it will save you time, and ultimately money. It will be very handy to start each form page by sketching out a design for the form first, asking yourself the following questions:

- What types of information do I want to collect?
- Which form objects will work best to collect that data? (As you have seen, certain types of data can be collected using more than one type of form object.)
- Will I want any of my fields to require validation?
- How should I lay out the form: A single column of form entries? Two columns of data entry? Maybe a combination? Do I need to incorporate a table or CSS for structure?
- Is my layout logical and easy for its future users to enter the data required in it?
- Would a fieldset (or multiple fieldsets) be useful to organize my form?

Your plan can be a simple pencil sketch, as long as it includes all of the data you need to collect, which form objects will work best to collect that data, and how you will lay out the structure for that data collection.

15.4 Testing Your Form

As you have learned, you will want to work with your ISP to configure your form for proper secure processing of your data. However, there are a couple of settings you can apply in the master umbrella form object's Property inspector that will let you see the form in action by sending it to yourself. To assign the necessary action and encoding, use the tag selector to select *<form#form1>*. After you have done that, the Property inspector for the original master umbrella form element will become active. For the *Action* entry, starting with *mailto:* type your email address. Leave the *Method* at its default setting of *Post* and then type *text/plain* for the *Enctype*. After entering this information and saving the form, when you fill out the form and click the submit button, your information will be added to an email that lists each category of the form and the responses you made to it, ready for you to send it to yourself!

15.5 A Look at the Code in Split View: The Application of the Form Element and Form Controls

FIGURE 15-13 illustrates the code Dreamweaver has written for a simple form.

1. The opening `<form>` tag, which includes the default name given by Dreamweaver, shows that it will be sent using `method="post"` (the default in Dreamweaver) and that currently no *action* has been applied to the form `action= ""`.

2. `<input` indicates the opening of a control.

3. `type="text"` indicates that this input control will be a text field.

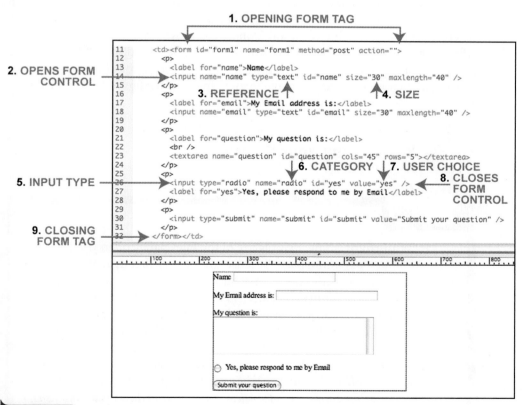

FIGURE 15-13 Split view of a form.

4. `size="30"` indicates the length of the area available for typing.
5. `input type="radio"` indicates that this is a radio button control.
6. `name="radio"` references the category of the radio button or radio button group.
7. `value="yes"` indicates the designated user response.
8. `/>` indicates the closing of a form control.
9. `</form>` is the closing tag of the form element.

15.6 What We Have Learned

Thanks to the many form objects in Dreamweaver, form building can be fun! By searching the Internet, we gained a clearer understanding of typical form objects used to gather the information requested at the sites we visited and learned how to apply that knowledge to the planning of a form before its construction. We learned that tables give structure and organization to a form, which can be further enhanced by the incorporation of a fieldset. We also reinforced our CSS skills from Chapter 14 by creating rules to define color and enhance text, which we applied to our form. After learning the critical information that must be added to our form for it to process data securely and efficiently, we learned a basic method of in-house form processing that we can use to test the form before it is configured with our ISP.

15.7 Reinforcing Your Knowledge

Project

1. With your Fishluvrz site active in the Files panel, open your *contact_page.html* page. Because this page is already named, our second step of the 1, 2, 3 Go Checklist is to change its existing title to *Contact Fishluvrz for Advice, Product Inquiries, and the Fishluvrz Blog!* Change the keywords to *fish care experts, fish questions answered, tropical fish products, aquarium products, contact an aquarium expert for advice, aquarium blog, tropical fish blog, fish information blog.* Lastly, delete the existing description text and add *Contact Fishluvrz for expert tropical fish advice and aquarium product requests. We offer a full line of aquarium products and services specializing in answers to your fish health and aquarium water quality problems.*

2. Attach the *fishluvrz.css* external style sheet to the page by choosing to link it and then delete its original internal one.

3. With the assistance of Expanded Tables mode if necessary, delete rows 3 through 5 of the top table.

4. Select the remaining top table (that has the navigation inside of it) and click the right arrow to place the I-beam to the right of the table. Insert a table with the following characteristics: 1 row, 1 column, a width of 100%, 5 pixels of padding, and zero for its cell spacing and border. After it's inserted, set the Vertical alignment to *Top* and set the Background color to *#FFFFFF*.

5. Click inside the table and type *Please provide the following information so that we may better serve you!* and then assign *Heading 1* to this text.

6. Create a new paragraph and click the Form icon to insert a master umbrella form object to encase the rest of our form objects. We will leave the default name of *form1* in the Property inspector, and we will not assign any Action, Target, or Enctype.

7. Insert a table inside this form object with the following characteristics: 4 rows, 4 columns, a width of 100%, 5 pixels of padding, and zero for its cell spacing and border. After it's placed, select its first and third columns, set the Horizontal alignment to *Right*, set the width to *15%*, and assign the width of its remaining two columns to *35%* each.

8. Select the upper-left cell of this table and click the *Text Field* form object to enter the Input Tag Accessibility Attributes dialog box. Type *first_name* for the ID and type *First Name:* for the Label. Select *Attach label tag using 'for' attribute* under Style and select *Before form item* for its Position, leaving the Access key and Tab Index blank. After you click OK to leave this dialog box, select the text field only and drag it to the second column. With it still selected, assign a *Char width* of *32* and *Max chars* of *40*. Keep the *Single line* setting and leave all other options of its Property inspector blank.

9. Placing the I-beam in the third column of the first row, insert another *Text Field* form object. Assign *last_name* for its ID and *Last Name:* for its Label. Keep the rest of the options the same as the first text field. After it's inserted, drag its text field to the column on its right and assign the same options in the Property inspector for this field that you did for the first one.

Project (continued)

10. Following this same format, continue to add four more text fields for the following categories: *Address:* (left in second row), *City/State/Zip:* (right in second row), *Phone:* (left in third row), and *Email:* (right in third row); each time, assign an appropriate ID for the category in the Input Tag Accessibility Attributes dialog box. Assign the rest of the options in the Input Tag Accessibility Attributes dialog box as you have learned and then apply the same options in the Property inspector for each text field after it has been inserted (as shown in Figure 15-15).

11. Place the I-beam inside the second column of the last row and insert a *Radio Group* form object. In its dialog box, name the group *discovered*. Add the first label *Searching the Web*, with a value of *web*. Add the remaining labels and values, as shown in **FIGURE 15-14**.

12. After the radio group is inserted, select the *Searching the Web* button and set its initial state to *Checked* in the Property inspector. To the left of the group in the first column of the same row, type *You* (soft return) *discovered* (soft return) *us by:* to finish this category.

13. Place the I-beam in the third column of the same row and insert a *List/Menu* form object. In the Input Tag Accessibility Attributes dialog box, assign *fish* for its ID, assign *Your favorite fish is:* for its label, choose the *for* attribute for its Style category, select a Position of *Before form item*, and leave the other options blank. After it's inserted on the page, add a line break after *Your* and *favorite* in the list's lable, then drag the list to the fourth column. In the Property inspector,

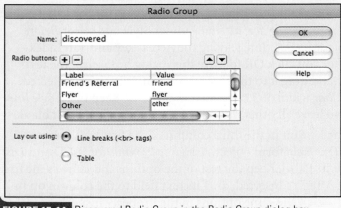

FIGURE 15-14 Discovered Radio Group in the Radio Group dialog box.

choose to create a *List*, set the *Height* to *4*, and set *Selections* to *Allow Multiple*. Click the *List Values* button to enter its dialog box and add the following labels/values:

> Balloon Molly/balloon
>
> Blood Parrot Cichlid/blood_parrot
>
> Buffalo Head Cichlid/buffalo
>
> Convict Cichlid/convict
>
> Glow Fish/glow
>
> Jack Dempsey/dempsey
>
> Leopard Snakeskin Discus/leopard
>
> Neon/neon

After exiting this dialog box, select the list and then press the right arrow key to move the I-beam to the right of the list. After a soft return, type *Can't decide? Command/Control-click to choose multiple favorites!*

In case you haven't done it yet, let's take a peek at this point in our form building by viewing it in a browser. When you do, your form should resemble **FIGURE 15-15**, remembering that the form's appearance may differ slightly among browsers.

FIGURE 15-15 Contact page form part one.

Project (continued)

14. Because we will be dividing this form into two main categories of data input, select this first table, click the right arrow to place the I-beam to the right of it, and insert one more table with the following characteristics: 3 rows, 4 columns, a width of 100%, a padding of 5 pixels, and zero for its cell spacing and border. After it's placed, select its first and third columns and set the Horizontal alignment to *Right*, set the width to *15%*, and set the width of its remaining two columns to *35%* each.

15. Place the I-beam in the first column of the first row of this new table and insert the *List/Menu* form object again. In the Input Tag Accessibility Attributes dialog box, assign *department* for its ID and *Select a department to contact:* for its label. Choose the *for* attribute for its Style, a Position of *Before form item*, and leave the other options blank. After you have clicked OK to exit the Input Tag Accessibility Attributes dialog box, drag the menu to the second column. In the Property inspector with the menu selected, leave the default choice of *menu* for the type and then click the *List Values* button to enter its dialog box, adding the following labels/values shown in **FIGURE 15-16**. In the Property inspector, choose *Ask an expert* to be initially selected when the menu displays.

16. Select the third column of the first row of this table and insert a *Textarea* form object. In the Input Tag Accessibility Attributes dialog box, assign *fish_problems* for its ID and *Fish problem? Live chat with an expert!* for its label. Choose the *for* attribute for its Style, a Position of *Before form item*, and leave the other options blank. After it's inserted, drag the textarea field to the fourth column of the row and set the Char width to *28*, Num lines to *4*,

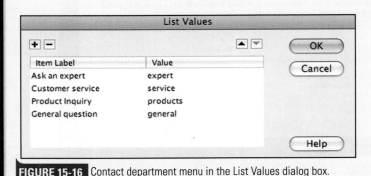

FIGURE 15-16   Contact department menu in the List Values dialog box.

and Init val to *Chat with us 24/7* in the Property inspector. If your table layout appears to be thrown off, check the width of each column and reassign the widths if needed: set the first column to *15%*, second column to *35%*, third column to *15%*, and fourth column to *35%*, or click the outer edge of the table to bounce it back into position.

17. Select the second row of this table, merge all of its cells, and then choose *Center* for its Horizontal alignment. Insert a *Checkbox* form object. In its Input Tag Accessibility Attributes dialog box, assign *fish_tips* for its ID and assign *Please add me to your weekly fish tips and product specials Email list!* for its label. Choose the *for* attribute for its Style, select a Position of *After form item*, and leave the other options blank. After it's inserted, choose an initial state of *Checked*, with the Checked value of *add* in the Property inspector.

18. Merge all the cells in the last row of this table and then choose *Center* for the Horizontal alignment. Insert a *Button* form object. In the Input Tag Accessibility Attributes dialog box, assign *reset* for its ID; however, this time, assign no label or label tag for the button and leave the rest of the options in this dialog box blank. With it selected in the Property inspector, type *Reset form* for its Value, and be sure to choose *Reset form* for its Action. With the I-beam to the right of the existing button in the form, insert one more button. In the Input Tag Accessibility Attributes dialog box, assign *submit* for its ID, assign no label or label tag for the button, and leave the rest of the options in this dialog box blank. With it selected in the Property inspector, type *Submit your inquiry now* for its value and leave the default selection of *submit form* for its action.

19. Using Expanded Tables mode if necessary, select the first table (the contact information, etc.) and add a *fieldset* to it. In the Legend dialog box, type *tell us about yourself* (no capitalization required). While still in Expanded Tables mode, select the second table and add its own *fieldset* with a legend of *how can we help you* (no capitalization required).

20. Our last step is to add styling to our form. Add a new CSS rule, choosing *Tag* for the Selector type, selecting *legend* for the Selector name from the pop-up menu, and choosing *This document only* for where this rule will be created. Each of the remaining rules that we create will be specific to *This document only*. After you have entered

Project (continued)

the Rule Definition dialog box for the legend, assign the following properties. In the Type category, assign the Font-family *Georgia, Times New Roman, Times, serif*. Also assign the Font-size *18 pixels*, Font-weight *Bold*, Text-transform *Uppercase*, and Color *#000066*.

Now create a class rule named *.categorytext* and assign the following properties. In the Type category, assign the Font-family *Arial, Helvetica, sans-serif*. Also assign the Font-weight *Bold* and the Color *#000066*. After you have created this class, assign this rule to all the form's text, including the text used in the radio group.

To add spacing between the two buttons, create a class named *.space* and assign the following properties in its Rule Definition dialog box. In the Type category, assign the Font-family *Arial, Helvetica, sans-serif*. Also assign the Font-weight *Bold* and the Color *#000066*. In the Box category, uncheck *Same for all* for the Margins, choose 5 pixels for the Right and Left margins, and leave the Top and Bottom margins blank. Assign this class to the reset and submit buttons of the form.

21. What about our promises on the home page to forward our visitors to the Fishluvrz blog? We will need to insert one more table to add that navigation to this page. Enter Expanded Tables mode to be sure you are selecting the second table on the page, the one which *encloses* the entire form, and then press the right arrow key to place the I-beam after it. Choose to insert a table with the following characteristics: 1 row, 2 columns, a width of 100%, and zero for its padding, spacing, and border. After it's inserted, assign a Horizontal alignment of *Right* and a Background-color *#336600* for both cells of the table. In the right cell, insert a rollover image, using the *blog.gif* for the original image, *blog_dn.gif* for the rollover image, and *Go to blog* for the alt text. Assign the hash symbol (#) for *When clicked go to URL*. After it's inserted on the page, select the cell and set its width to *250 pixels*. Lastly, place the I-beam in the left cell and type *no thanks, take me right to the fishluvrz blog!* Create its own CSS class rule named *.blogtext*, with the following properties. In the Type category, assign the Font-family *Arial, Helvetica, sans-serif*. Also assign the Font-size *16 pixels*, the Font-weight *Bold*, the Text-transform *Uppercase*, and the Color *#FFFFFF*. In the Box category, uncheck *Same for all* for the Padding, choose *10 pixels* for the Right and leave the other sides blank. Assign this rule to the text. Your finished page should now resemble **FIGURE 15-17**.

Project (continued)

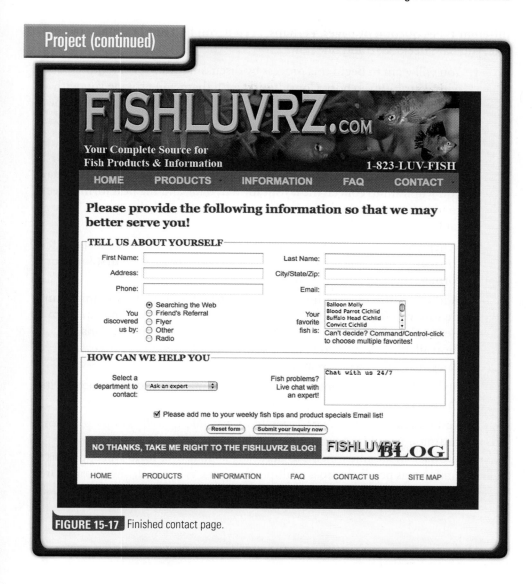

FIGURE 15-17 Finished contact page.

15.8 Building Your Own Website

Perhaps you have planned a form all along in your site design, or perhaps you had not originally expected to include one. However, after studying a variety of forms on the Internet, you may want to add one now. Although it could have its own page, as we have just done in the Fishluvrz site, a data entry area is often added to many different types of content pages. Perhaps, even if you had not originally planned one, you have decided to add one now.

1. You will want to begin this process by discussing your form requirements with your ISP/web host. Consultation with them will provide you with the information you need to activate your form securely, and assure you that before you start, your host will be able to accommodate your needs. If not, you will need to seek one that can.

2. When you are ready to begin to build your form, as we have learned, start with a plan. Sketch out your design with consideration for the data you will want to collect, the layout for that data, and the best form objects to use to collect it. In designing your form, decide whether you will use a table or CSS for its structure.

3. When you are ready to build your form, remember that you must create the master umbrella form object by clicking the Form icon first for your form to function after it is live.

4. Add your form objects, including fieldset(s) if desired, for organization. Be sure you follow best practice by including accessibility in your form. Remember that you can be assured that the accessibility options will be available to you if you have *form objects* checked in the Accessibility category of the Dreamweaver Preferences.

5. Style your form elements with CSS to coordinate their color scheme with the rest of your site.

6. Test it in as many browsers as you have available, as well as cross-platform testing if possible. As you will see, the form will vary from browser to browser. Make adjustments as necessary so that your form will appear as uniform as possible across multiple browsers. When your site becomes live in the next and final chapter, your form will be accessible to your visitors!

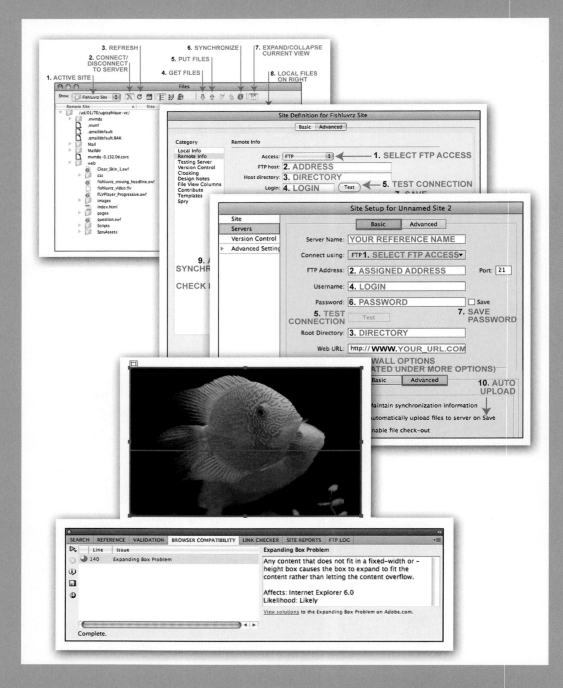

1. ACTIVE SITE

2. CONNECT/ DISCONNECT TO SERVER

3. REFRESH

4. GET FILES

5. PUT FILES

6. SYNCHRONIZE

7. EXPAND/COLLAPSE CURRENT VIEW

8. LOCAL FILES ON RIGHT

Files

Show: Fishluvrz Site

Remote Site · Size

/ud/01/7D/ugraphique~ve/
  .mvmda
  .mvmf
  .qmaildefault
  .qmaildefault.BAK
  Mail
  Maildir
  mvmda~0.132.0d.core
  web
    Clear_Skin_1.swf
    css
    fishluvrz_moving_headline.swf
    fishluvrz_video.flv
    FLVPlayer_Progressive.swf
    images
    index.html
    pages
    question.swf
    Scripts
    SpryAssets

Site Definition for Fishluvrz Site

Basic | Advanced

Category · Remote Info

Local Info
Remote Info
Testing Server
Version Control
Cloaking
Design Notes
File View Columns
Contribute
Templates
Spry

Access: FTP — **1. SELECT FTP ACCESS**

FTP host: **2. ADDRESS**

Host directory: **3. DIRECTORY**

Login: **4. LOGIN** (Test) — **5. TEST CONNECTION**

7. SAVE

9. A SYNCHR

CHECK I

Site Setup for Unnamed Site 2

Site
Servers
Version Control
Advanced Setting

Basic | Advanced

Server Name: **YOUR REFERENCE NAME**

Connect using: FTP **1. SELECT FTP ACCESS▾**

FTP Address: **2. ASSIGNED ADDRESS** Port: 21

Username: **4. LOGIN**

Password: **6. PASSWORD** ☐ Save

5. TEST CONNECTION (Test) **7. SAVE PASSWORD**

Root Directory: **3. DIRECTORY**

Web URL: http:// **WWW**.YOUR_URL.COM

WALL OPTIONS ATED UNDER MORE OPTIONS)

Basic | Advanced

10. AUTO UPLOAD

aintain synchronization information

automatically upload files to server on Save

able file check-out

SEARCH | REFERENCE | VALIDATION | BROWSER COMPATIBILITY | LINK CHECKER | SITE REPORTS | FTP LOG

Line | Issue

140 | Expanding Box Problem

Expanding Box Problem

Any content that does not fit in a fixed-width or -height box causes the box to expand to fit the content rather than letting the content overflow.

Affects: Internet Explorer 6.0
Likelihood: Likely

View solutions to the Expanding Box Problem on Adobe.com.

Complete.

Publishing Your Site

In This Chapter

- Learn how to acquire and register a domain name
- Learn how to select a web host for your site and assign your access settings
- Launch a final site review before uploading
- Explore the upload, download, and maintenance features of Dreamweaver

This final chapter will focus on the culmination of our hard work and our original goal set forth in Chapter 1—an artistic, professional presence on the World Wide Web! After learning how to secure a domain name and find the right host for our site, we will explore a "preflight" error checklist of steps that will ensure a successful upload before the world gets its first peek at it. After we have learned the site uploading and maintenance process, a final section of the chapter will be devoted to a few tips that will be helpful as you continue to expand your knowledge and artistic talent in web design.

Preparing for the Upload

Now that we have learned to construct a site, we need to learn how to upload it so that it will be visible on the Web for all of the world to enjoy. Before we can do that, however, several preparatory steps must be taken first.

16.1.1 Registering a Domain Name

If you chose to include Chapter 5 in your learning, you already know that a domain name is actually like your own "unique residence" or "personal space" on the Internet, different from every other website in the world. Although it presents contrastive challenges compared to those associated with building the site itself, finding the right domain name for your business is an integral part of an effective website that requires time, thought, research, and creativity to enhance, not detract from your site's overall success. A great site that no one sees except you is not a great site. Let's take a look at the considerations required to secure a successful, "search engine friendly," available domain name for your site.

Your Website Name vs. Search Engines   In addition to the considerations of page titles, keywords, description text, and alternate text, domain names are also an essential component of the search engine visibility process. If you have the luxury of choosing the domain name for your company, consider building keywords into it as one more way to help you be seen on the Web. Consider the name *nimblesque.com* for a dance studio vs. *nimblesquedancestudio.com* or *nimblesque-dance-studio.com*. The inclusion of the words "dance studio" in its name will significantly improve the Search Engine Optimization (SEO) of the site.

That said, with all the names already taken, how do you find one that is still available that will work for you?

The Name Game Brainstorming Process   As a graphic designer, you have brainstormed constantly as part of your career and have learned throughout this book to apply those skills to web design as well. This is also the case for the challenging quest for an available, searchable, domain name. What I recommend, which may initially seem daunting, is to use a comprehensive dictionary. Beginning with words associated with your type of products or services and then moving on to acronyms, synonyms, and applicable prefixes and suffixes that apply to words associated with your type of products or services will help you come up with a variety of possible domain names to begin your formal search. Building and prioritizing a considerable list, before even beginning to see what's available, will avoid disappointment and frustration when the domain name registration process begins.

If you have a company name already, consider adding keywords to its name when converting it to a domain name, such as the *Nimblesque* vs. *nimblesquedancestudio.com* sample, to increase its search engine visibility. Also, by testing some of your proposed names in search engines before you begin the registration process, you will eliminate much of the work of searching for a name through your chosen registrar. If you type it in as a web search and its name comes up in a wide variety of combinations already in use, cross it off your list and move on.

Searching for Your Domain   After you have populated your domain name priority list, the next step is to seek the assistance of an accredited domain registrar. Typing in "accredited web domain registrars" as a web search will provide you with a list of many accredited sites to pick from.

When you arrive at the site of the company you are going to use for your domain registration search, located somewhere on its home page will be the words "Start your search here" or "Search for your domain name here," allowing you to enter your potential name(s) and almost instantly receive results as to their availability. Often, if the name you searched for is not available, the registrar may suggest similar options. If you don't like any of their suggestions, don't despair! That's why you started with a creative list before you began the search! Just continue down your list until you secure a name that works for you.

Selecting a Domain Extension   Since .com is the most common domain extension, depending on the type of site the domain name will be used for, you may want to try to secure your name with it first. If you succeed at finding a workable name with an extension that works for you, the domain registrar you are using for your search will then politely offer to have you register it with them and offer additional possible domain names, incorporating a variety of other available extensions. You may want to consider purchasing a few of these as well, if you are concerned that someone else may want the same name in the future. The registration process is relatively inexpensive, making this option economically feasible, and potentially critical for retaining the uniqueness of search results for your site's products or services.

It is also important to remember that you are registering the domain name. You do not own it after you pay for a year, two years, five years, etc. It is not uncommon for someone new to the process to register once and think the domain is secure forever. Although the company you registered with will most likely send you numerous emails reminding you to renew (often months in advance of the expiration date), do not delete the messages without checking your actual expiration date. Be sure to renew your domain name before it expires—other people may actually have your name *reserved*—waiting for your domain name to expire so they can register it!

16.1.2 Finding a Web Host

The second step in the preparation of your site for the Internet is the acquisition of a web host for it. When purchasing your domain name, perhaps the company you registered the name with also offered web hosting services, with possible discount pricing when a domain name and subsequent domain hosting services were purchased simultaneously. Although it is tempting and easy to be lured into "one-stop shopping," the company that registered your domain may not be the best company to host your site.

Considerations When Choosing a Web Host   When choosing a web host, you will want to carefully examine the services provided by the host to ensure that they will fit your site's specific hosting requirements, as well as your budget.

Seeking a Recommendation   The first and best advice in the web host search is to begin by asking friends, relatives, and business associates who they use or recommend. When seeking advice, be sure you are comparing "apples with apples." The hosting requirements of those you ask for recommendations must be reasonably comparable to yours to be sure they are offering a plausible solution to your hosting needs.

Cost vs. Services   Comparative shopping will provide a "host" (pun intended!) of different pricing options. In each case, carefully review the following components of the price offered:

- available space provided vs. the price for it
- availability of an email account in addition to hosting your site
- CGI capabilities for form processing
- uptime information (percentage of the time the server is up and running)

Customer Service/Technical Support   Especially when asking for the advice or recommendations of others, be sure to ask about their satisfaction with the host's customer service/technical support when they uploaded their site for the first time and the company's availability and efficiency in handling technical support issues that may have surfaced since their initial upload.

Using a "Free" Host to Test Your Site   Although it is not recommended that your use of one of these for the long-term hosting of your site, there are an abundance of companies offering "free" web hosting. Along with that "free" hosting, the provider often includes an excessive amount of annoying advertising tagged onto your site or limits the length of time the hosting will be free before you must terminate the service or continue the service for a fee. These services, however, are great for testing your site and practicing the uploading process while doing so. To find one, simply type in a web search for "free web hosting services." Your search will even yield sites that will compare and rate the services the "free" sites provide. This will help you make your decision about which one to use. Be sure, however, to carefully read their terms of use agreement to be sure it will fit your needs and does not include any unexpected costs after its initial "free" luring introduction.

16.1.3 Assigning Your File Transfer Settings in Dreamweaver

Before being able to upload your files to the Web, your connection settings and file transfer preferences must be assigned and tested in Dreamweaver, using the information provided to you by your host.

FTP Settings   The most common method of accessing your host server to upload your files is through an FTP (File Transfer Protocol) connection, which will be the focus of our learning. After you have registered your domain name, and subsequently acquired your web host, you can complete the *Remote info* for your site. Although we waited until our site was built to learn how to do this step, it can actually be done at any stage of the site-building process once you have the two critical requirements: your domain name and your host.

> **Note:** *The server assignment process will be covered as it pertains to CS3 and CS4 first, followed by an explanation of the applicable changes when using CS5. In order to fully understand the process, CS5 users should read the following section first for a more thorough understanding of how the same information is entered when using CS5.*

Applying the settings provided by your host can be done in either the Basic or Advanced tab of the Site Definition dialog box. Use the one that has become the most comfortable to you. At any time during the site building process, when you choose *Manage sites* from the Files panel or from the Site application menu, you can enter the Site Definition dialog box to assign or edit the site's remote settings.

Although we have always used the *Local info* category when using its Advanced tab, assigning the server connection settings requires the *Remote info* category. If you are more comfortable with it, you may prefer to use the Site Definition dialog box's Basic tab; assigning the same information detailed in **FIGURE 16-1** by entering your URL in its first dialog box and then choosing *FTP* from the pop-up menu when you come to the dialog box with the question, "How do you connect to your remote server?" Using either its Basic or Advanced tab, the four or five critical settings you must apply (depending on your host) in order to be able to upload a site are access, host, directory (sometimes), login, and password. Let's take a closer look at these, as well as the rest of the available features of the *Remote info* category, which is located under its Advanced tab.

1. The FTP connection method is selected from this access pop-up menu. You must choose the FTP option before the remaining FTP remote information settings shown in Figure 16-1 will become available.

2. This address will be provided to you by your host.

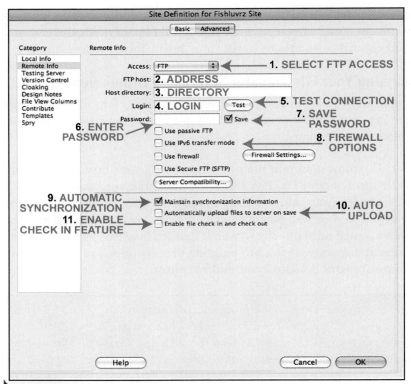

3. You may or may not actually need a directory. Your host will provide it for you if it's required.

4. The case-sensitive login in/username provided by your host is entered here.

5. After you enter your access information, you may click here to test your connection.

6. The case-sensitive password used between you and your host is entered here.

7. This option is chosen by default after your hosting information has been added and tested. Uncheck it if you do not want the information to be automatically saved for you. If you uncheck it, Dreamweaver will prompt you for your password each time you attempt to connect to the server.

8. A variety of firewall settings are available if applicable.

9. By default, Dreamweaver will maintain your synchronization information. The synchronization feature will be introduced later in this chapter.

10. If you would like, this option will automatically upload a file when it is saved.

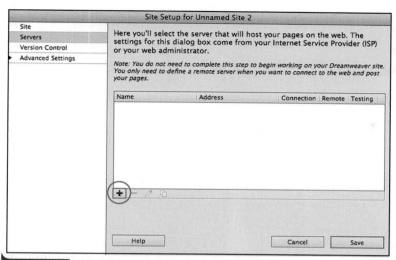

FIGURE 16-2 Add server screen in the Site Setup dialog box in CS5.

11. The Check in/Check out feature is useful for sites built and maintained by multiple web developers and is beyond the scope of this text. For our purposes, we will leave the option unchecked, which is the default for this feature.

In CS5, you must first select the *Servers* tab from the Site Setup dialog box. After you do that, click the *plus* icon to enter the dialog box to assign your settings, as shown in **FIGURE 16-2**. As you can see in **FIGURE 16-3**, when you have clicked to add a server after inserting your own reference name for the site, although some of their locations have been moved (which is why some of them are out of numerical order), the same essential features of CS3 and CS4 (itemized in Figure 16-1) are shown in their corresponding locations in CS5. If you skipped the previous section of the text that described this dialog box using CS3 and CS4, you can refer to it now for an explanation of each category based on its number. Just as the site definition was divided into two panels, you can see that the server information is divided into a Basic and an Advanced tab. The Web URL category available under its Basic tab is the same as the *http address* optional category located under the Advanced tab in the Site Definition dialog box in CS3 and CS4.

Testing Your Connection   Using any version, when you have entered the settings supplied by your host and clicked the Test option, Dreamweaver will attempt to connect with the remote server. If you have your settings and want to try it, go for it. Don't worry if you are not ready to upload. This is not part of the upload process. It is simply testing your connection to your host. If the connection fails, the "Failed connection" dialog box will appear, as shown in **FIGURE 16-4**.

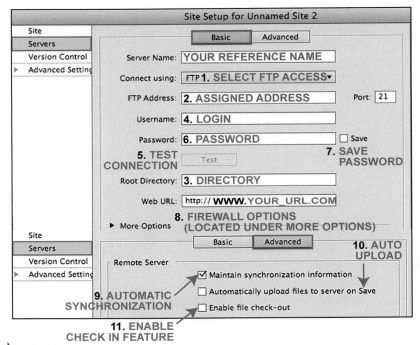

FIGURE 16-3 Server setup in CS5.

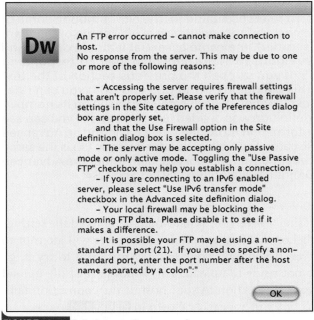

FIGURE 16-4 Failed connection occurred.

If you receive this message when you test your connection, don't get discouraged. Just contact your host to report the problem and ask a service representative to walk you through the connection process. It may be that they require firewall settings or a different FTP port, but they should welcome the opportunity to assist you—that's why you chose one with a good technical support record!

Assigning Site File Transfer Preferences   The Dreamweaver Preferences dialog box includes a category named Site, which offers customization of the uploading process. As you can see in FIGURE 16-5, it is not used to assign the connection settings to your host; it is used to assign the preferences for the actual transferring of files to your remote site, including an option to be forwarded to manage/assign/edit your remote information if desired.

1. By default, Dreamweaver displays the Local files (the appearance of the Files panel as you have worked with it thus far) on the right, with the Remote files on the left when viewed in the Files panel's expanded view. This will make more sense to you when we learn how to actually upload files later in this chapter. After you understand the process, you can return to the Preferences dialog box at any time to reverse the display position of these two panel windows if desired.

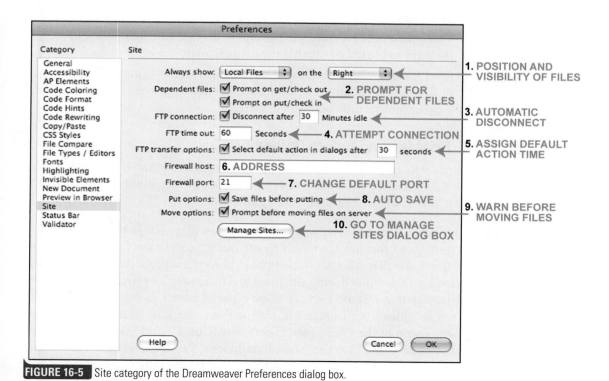

FIGURE 16-5   Site category of the Dreamweaver Preferences dialog box.

2. *Dependent files* are all your images, videos, etc., included on the web pages (files that the pages "depend on" to display properly). Although we will discuss this in more detail when learning the upload process, the default option is to prompt you, which is the safe solution. If these are unchecked, your dependent files will not be automatically transferred after your initial upload and may create problems when updating your site with changes.

3. This option assigns the time frame to have Dreamweaver automatically disconnect from the server because of a lack of activity.

4. Although this may seem like item 3, it actually refers to something very different. This is the amount of time you allow Dreamweaver to attempt to make a connection with the server before it gives up and displays the "Failed connection" message shown in Figure 16-4.

5. If checked, this option allows you to assign the amount of time you want Dreamweaver to wait before it selects the default transfer option when a dialog box appears during a file transfer and you do not respond.

6. If using a firewall, the address is entered here.

7. The usual port is 21. This would only be changed if required by your host.

8. This convenience feature will assure that all files have been saved prior to uploading.

9. This convenience feature will prompt you when you are moving files on the remote site to be sure that the move is what you want to do.

10. After making your selections in this dialog box, this button allows you to be forwarded directly to the Manage Sites dialog box to create or edit the local or remote information for a site.

16.1.4 Final Review Before Uploading

Are you ready to upload? We are almost ready to learn to do that. However, it will be very helpful, and an excellent habit to practice each time you build a site, to perform a final site review before beginning the upload process.

Checking Links Sitewide   As you build a site, you may change the names of link pages, create pages that are not linked to any other pages in the site, add images to your *images* folder that you later decide not to use, etc., without deleting, adjusting, or reassigning their links during the process. Dreamweaver provides a great *Link Checker* feature that will alert you of these types of errors so that you can correct them prior to uploading. To access it, choose Site>Check Links Sitewide; or from the options menu of the Files panel, choose Site>Check Links Sitewide; or choose Window>Results>Link Checker; or on an individual page basis, choose File>Check Page>Links. In each case, the command will activate the Link Checker panel and

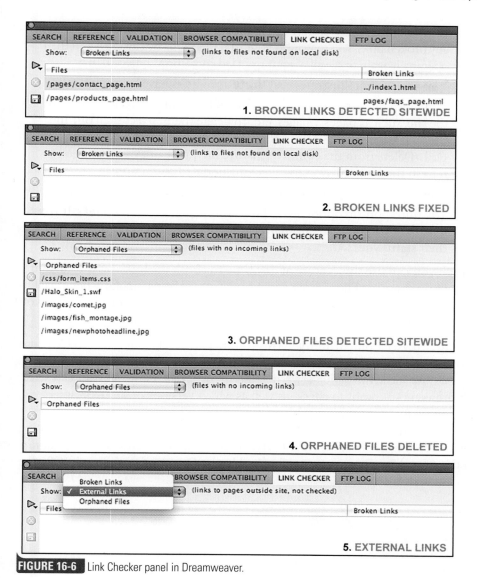

FIGURE 16-6 Link Checker panel in Dreamweaver.

display three options under its pop-up menu: Broken links, Orphaned links, and External links. **FIGURE 16-6** illustrates how this feature works.

1. When *Broken Links* is selected from the pop-up menu, any broken links and the pages containing the link(s) will be listed. When you double-click a broken link in this panel, it will become highlighted in the document and allow you to browse and repair the link right through the Link Checker. Sometimes, when you check a link that Dreamweaver indicates is broken, it may appear to

be assigned correctly: simply delete and reassign the link anyway. After fixing any broken links, you may need to refresh this panel by closing it and then opening it again to see all of your updated corrections reflected in it.

2. This screen shot illustrates that the broken links have been corrected.

3. *Orphaned links* are any files that have no links connected to them within the site, such as pages, images, etc. To delete them, select each one in the Files panel, one at a time, then right/Control-click, and choose Edit>Delete from the context-sensitive menu. Again, you may need to refresh the Link Checker to reflect the updated corrections.

4. This screen shot illustrates that all orphaned files have been deleted.

5. The third pop-up option available in this panel is *External Links*. If you have external links, Dreamweaver will only list them here. You must check their status yourself.

Although you can use this feature at any time to check the links on the currently open page by choosing File>Check Page>Links, it will be particularly beneficial to use the Check Links Sitewide feature when you are ready to upload, just in case you may have made changes after you checked an individual page earlier.

Checking Browser Compatibility   This feature will check your page's HTML and CSS for compatibility with the browsers and versions you select in its Target Browsers dialog box. As shown in **FIGURE 16-7**, defaults are in place. However, you can select which browsers you want to check, as well as which versions of those browsers you want to check for compatibility with your page.

To access this feature, select *Check Browser Compatibility* by either choosing File>Check Page>Browser Compatibility, or selecting *Check Browser Compatibility* from the *Check Page* pop-up menu located in the Document toolbar. In CS5 the

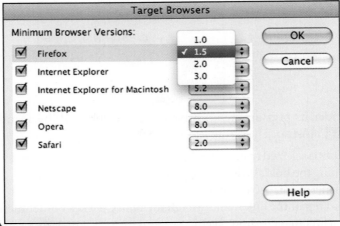

FIGURE 16-7   Target minimum browser versions in the Target Browsers dialog box.

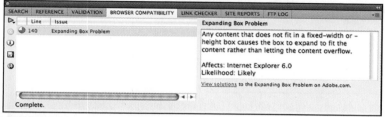

FIGURE 16-8 Browser Compatibility panel in Dreamweaver.

icon is the same: the page with a check mark. It is just not additionally labeled with the words *Check page* next to it, as it is in CS3 and CS4. When chosen, the Browser Compatibility panel opens, as shown in **FIGURE 16-8**.

The arrow at the upper-left corner provides a menu with the option to check the page, as well as the ability to access the dialog box shown in Figure 16-7, by choosing *Settings*. The window on the right opens by explaining how to use the feature, but will be converted to an explanation of the issue, if one is detected, with a list of the browser(s) affected by it. Compatibility issues, if found, may be one of three possible types: an error, which should definitely be fixed for the page to display properly; a warning, meaning that the page may not display correctly, but the error will not have a major effect on its appearance; and informational, which indicates that a code discrepancy may have been detected that will have no visual impact when viewed in the targeted browser(s). If no issues are found, the words *No issues detected* will be displayed at the bottom after the check has been performed. The degree of suspected incompatibility is indicated by a red circle: the amount of the circle's *fill* determines the predictability and severity of possible browser issues: a quarter, half, three-quarter, or completely filled circle indicates the likelihood of discrepancy. The more completely filled the circle is, the greater the probability of a browser compatibility conflict. Notice the problem the AP Div is warned to have if viewed in an older version of Internet Explorer, as shown in Figure 16-8.

Running Reports   Located under the Site menu is a command named Reports. As shown in **FIGURE 16-9**, its dialog box is divided into two sections: Workflow and

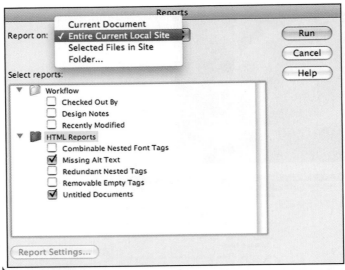

FIGURE 16-9   Reports command dialog box with Entire Current Local Site option selected.

HTML Reports. Under its HTML category, two options are particularly helpful when preparing to upload: *Missing Alt Text* and *Untitled Documents.* When you select *Entire Current Local Site* before you choose one of these options and click Run, Dreamweaver will check whether you have any missing alt text or any documents without titles, depending on which option you selected in the Reports dialog box. Although you have learned to use the 1, 2, 3 Go Checklist for adding titles, and you have assigned Accessibility preferences to prompt you to add alt text—just in case—this is a great tool to use before uploading. The results will appear, and problems can be fixed in the Site Reports panel, which will automatically open if it was not already visible. The panel works just like the Link Checker and Browser Compatibility panels; its arrow at the upper-left returns you to the initial dialog box you started from, the one shown in Figure16-9, allowing you to select another report from its menu to run.

Using the Top Ten Final Checklist   So … are we finally ready to upload yet? Not quite. In addition to the three "final check" options built into Dreamweaver that we have just learned about, there are more "final double-checks" we should review: important steps we have learned that are easy to forget when the excitement (or stress!) of the actual upload is imminent.

To help you to remember, I have included the following checklist as a printable .pdf file in the *Chapter_16PracticeFiles* folder on the accompanying CD that you can print each time you are ready for the first upload for every site you create. Although you have learned each of these steps by now, let's take a look at each of them one more time, as shown in **FIGURE 16-10**.

1. As we learned as part of the 1, 2, 3 Go Checklist, double-check now that your home page is named *index.html* and that all of your link page names do not include any spaces and all have the required extension.

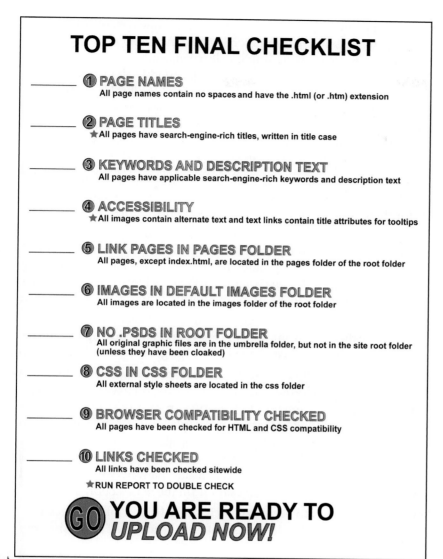

TOP TEN FINAL CHECKLIST

____ ① PAGE NAMES
All page names contain no spaces and have the .html (or .htm) extension

____ ② PAGE TITLES
★ All pages have search-engine-rich titles, written in title case

____ ③ KEYWORDS AND DESCRIPTION TEXT
All pages have applicable search-engine-rich keywords and description text

____ ④ ACCESSIBILITY
★ All images contain alternate text and text links contain title attributes for tooltips

____ ⑤ LINK PAGES IN PAGES FOLDER
All pages, except index.html, are located in the pages folder of the root folder

____ ⑥ IMAGES IN DEFAULT IMAGES FOLDER
All images are located in the images folder of the root folder

____ ⑦ NO .PSDS IN ROOT FOLDER
All original graphic files are in the umbrella folder, but not in the site root folder
(unless they have been cloaked)

____ ⑧ CSS IN CSS FOLDER
All external style sheets are located in the css folder

____ ⑨ BROWSER COMPATIBILITY CHECKED
All pages have been checked for HTML and CSS compatibility

____ ⑩ LINKS CHECKED
All links have been checked sitewide
★ RUN REPORT TO DOUBLE CHECK

GO YOU ARE READY TO *UPLOAD NOW!*

FIGURE 16-10 Top Ten Final Checklist.

2. Also learned as part of the 1, 2, 3 Go Checklist, double-check now that you remembered to add a title for each page (run the Site>Reports command if you would like) and that you remembered that the title should be in title case (with each major word beginning with a capital letter).

3. The third component of the 1, 2, 3 Go Checklist, especially if pages were created by choosing the *Save As* command, is to be sure that you have adjusted your keywords and description text to reflect the unique content of each link page.

4. It is easy, when inserting images, navigation, or rollovers, to ignore the Input Tag Accessibility Attributes dialog box, including adding tooltip titles for Spry navigation. As you have learned, you can select a Spry Menu Bar at any time to add/edit its tooltips, modify alt text in a navigation bar in CS3 or CS4 at any time by choosing Modify>Navigation, or select an image on a page at any time to assign or reassign its alternate text in the Property inspector. Remember that you can also use the Site>Reports command to help you check a variety of issues, including the ability to check for missing alt text.

   Check all of your alternate text now, and if you are working in CS4 and CS5, also check your text link tooltips, which were created by assigning a title for them in the Title area of the Property inspector.

5. Organizing your site makes uploading and maintaining your site easier. Double-check that all link pages added to your site are located within your *pages* folder of the root folder. If not, in the Files panel, simply drag them into it, and click *Update* when prompted by Dreamweaver to update the links to the page(s) that have been moved.

6. Just as in step 5, if any of the images are not in your *images* folder, you can still move them safely through the Files panel and click *Update* when prompted regarding the pages linked to the images that need to be updated.

7. As long as you do not upload them, your site will work with original native file graphics stored in its root folder. However, as you have learned, keeping them in an *original graphics* folder stored in your site umbrella, but not in its root folder, will assure that you can easily locate them at any time to work on them if necessary, without worrying about accidental uploads. Although I recommend keeping them in an originals folder outside of the root folder, if any of them are located in it, alternatively, you can assigned them to be *cloaked*, which we will examine in the next section of this text.

8. You have been taught to begin each new site with a *css* folder: check to be sure that all external style sheets that have been added to the site are stored within it.

9–10. As you can see, the final two items on this top ten list are two of the three new check features you have just learned about here in Chapter 16: the commands to check links and check browser compatibility.

Cloaking Files   When you think of the word *cloak*, you may think of a coat or cover. Another definition of this word is to "hide." The *Cloak* feature of Dreamweaver will add a red slash across a file or folder that you want to cover or hide temporarily from the upload process at any particular time, for whatever reason. To apply it, select the file or folder and then right/Control-click and choose Cloaking>Cloak or reverse it by choosing Cloaking>Uncloak or Cloaking>Uncloak All from the context-sensitive menu. Under the Cloaking category of the Advanced tab of the Site Definition dialog box, you can also assign specific types of files that you may want to cloak (such as files ending in .psd), as well as disable the feature if desired, because it is available by default.

> Assigning a type of file (such as a .psd) to be cloaked will ensure that if any of them are located in your active root folder, they will not be accidentally uploaded! Why are we just learning about this option now? As you have learned, best practice is to keep them in an original graphics folder within the site umbrella folder, but not the root folder. Here, it is introduced as a way to protect any that you added into the root folder by accident.

16.2 Uploading and Maintaining Your Site

Uploading and maintaining a site utilizes features of the powerful Files panel that we have not yet employed. We are finally ready to examine its upload icons, learn how to use them to upload a site initially, and how to use them to maintain a site after it is live.

16.2.1 The Upload Icons of the Files Panel

Before learning how to use them, let's examine the Files panel's essential upload/download icons and their associated functions, as shown in **FIGURE 16-11**.

1. In order to upload, the site to be uploaded must be selected from the Files panel's pop-up menu first.

2. If you have entered your FTP settings and tested the connection after entering them, you will be able to click the Connect to remote host icon (which resembles a "plug") to connect to your host's server. To disconnect, click the same icon again to "unplug" your connection.

3. Sometimes, you may need to refresh the view of both the local and remote sites in the Files panel to see changes you have made to either one.

4. After your site has been initially uploaded, you can select any file in the remote site when connected to your server and then click the *Get* button to download it. You will be asked if you want its dependent files (images, etc., included on the page). However, if you already have those, you do not have to download them as well. Alternatively, you could select the file in the remote site, right/Control-click, and choose *Get* from the context-sensitive menu. This feature is most valuable for sites with multiple developers.

5. When the site folder or an individual page is selected, clicking this button will upload it to the server. Just as with the Get option, alternatively, you could select the file in the local site, right/Control-click, and choose *Put* from the context-sensitive menu.

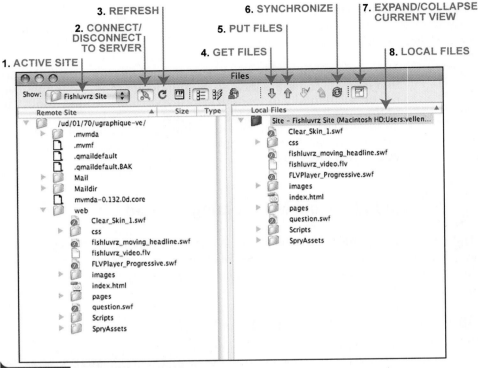

FIGURE 16-11 Upload icons in the Files panel.

6. Clicking this icon will launch the Synchronize feature of Dreamweaver, helping to assure that your local and remote sites are in sync. We will explore this option in more detail later in this chapter.

7. Clicking this icon expands/contracts the current view of the Files panel from working in Local view to displaying both Local and Remote views (renamed Remote server in CS5) for uploading purposes. Alternatively, in the Local view, you can choose View>Expand Files Panel from the Files panel's options menu to display both views simultaneously.

8. By default, when the Files panel is in Expanded view, the local site will be on the right, with the remote site displayed on the left. As you have learned, in the Site category of the Dreamweaver preferences, you can select to reverse the display locations of these two views, as shown in Figure 16-5.

16.2.2 Uploading Your Site the First Time

Let's learn to upload! If you tested your connection when you entered your FTP settings and received confirmation from Dreamweaver that your connection was successful, as shown in **FIGURE 16-12**, then you are ready to perform the initial upload.

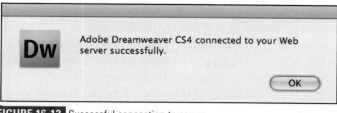

FIGURE 16-12 Successful connection to server.

In the Files panel, with the site active that you wish to upload, the first step is to click the *Connect to remote host* icon to "plug in" to your server. After you have done that, highlight the root folder in the Files panel and then click the *Up* arrow to begin the uploading process. Dreamweaver will then ask you whether you want to upload the entire site. When you click OK, the process will begin. A Background File Activity message will display as the files are being uploaded, as shown in **FIGURE 16-13**.

As a graphic designer, you are most likely familiar with the term *background printing*, meaning that your printer will perform its task while you continue to work. The Dreamweaver background activity feature follows that same basic concept. Depending on the size of the site you are initially uploading, it could take a few minutes, making the ability to resume work appealing. However, if working in Dreamweaver, you should not try to work on the same site, or perhaps not even open another application if you have RAM concerns. You may want to just sit back, relax, and enjoy watching your files scroll through the Background File Activity dialog box and dream of the site's appearance live on the Web a few minutes later!

16.2.3 Uploading Changes to Your Published Site

Just as you have probably had happen to you with your print design work, until you saw a hard copy of the file, you did not detect errors in it. Often, even though you have previewed pages in browsers as you created them, this same scenario can happen in web work, after it is "on the Web." As soon as your upload has been completed (you can stay connected to your host if you would like), you can type in your web address in a browser and immediately be able to see your site live. At last! In reviewing it, however, perhaps you will discover errors or things you realize you should or want to change.

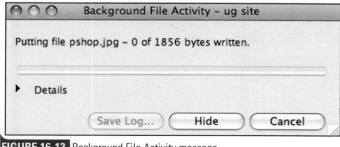

FIGURE 16-13 Background File Activity message.

No problem. Simply open the page in your local site (with or without a live connection to your host) and make your change. When you are ready to upload it, if you had chosen to "unplug" your connection, click to plug it back in, select the file, and click the *Up* arrow; or, as a graphic artist used to the drag-and-drop world, yes, just drag it to the remote site (server). If you decide to drag and drop, however, be sure to drop it onto the correct folder. If it is a link page, drag it on top of the *pages* folder of the remote site (or drag an image onto the *images* folder). If simply added to the remote site, Dreamweaver will not automatically know where it needs to go within the site. If it is a page, Dreamweaver will recognize that it is a page and prompt you regarding its dependent files. Although you only need to add dependent files again if you made changes to them on the page in question, when in doubt, it never hurts to have Dreamweaver reload them to be sure.

16.2.4 Synchronizing Your Site

Have you ever worked off your laptop and your desktop on a print design project and accidentally saved over the new version with the old one? Don't be ashamed to say yes; we've all done it at one time or another. One way Dreamweaver can help you avoid this is its option to choose Edit>Select Newer Remote, Edit>Select Newer Local, or Edit>Select Recently Modified from the Files panel's options menu. All applicable files under the category you have selected will become highlighted, helping you to keep track of your activity. A more sophisticated solution is to employ the Dreamweaver *Synchronization* feature, which is particularly helpful in avoiding that error with your website after it is live. When you are connected to your host and your site is active, you can click the *Synchronize* icon in the Files panel. When you do, the Synchronize Files dialog box shown in **FIGURE 16-14** will appear.

Two synchronize options will appear, with three possible synchronization directives. Whether it displays *Selected Remote Files Only* or *Selected Local Files Only* will depend on where you have selected the file(s) in question, or, if in doubt, simply choose to synchronize the entire site. The first two of its directives are self-explanatory. However, the third option, *Get and Put newer files* may be confusing. This option will

FIGURE 16-14 Synchronize Files dialog box.

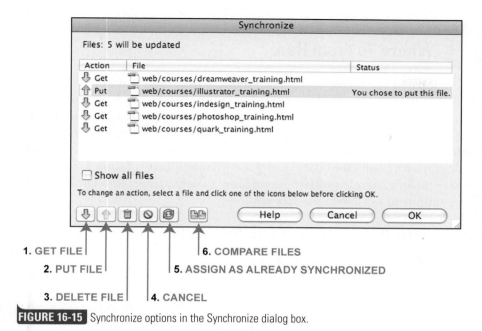

FIGURE 16-15 Synchronize options in the Synchronize dialog box.

assure that the latest versions of all files are up to date on both the local and remote sites. When you choose to synchronize your site, a dialog box will display the status of your files, with options for the files found. Those options are shown in **FIGURE 16-15**.

When a file is selected in this list, you may choose an action other than the one you have defined, such as the *Put* action in Figure 16-14.

1. Because a file is selected to be *Put* instead of *Get*, the *Get* option is available to change its status.

2. The selected file has been chosen to *Put*. Therefore, the *Put* alternative is currently grayed out.

3. Here, you could choose to delete the selected file.

4. This *Cancel* option will allow you to disengage the selected file from the process altogether.

5. This option allows you to define the selected file as already synchronized.

6. This feature will be grayed out unless a third-party file comparison software has been installed. Under the File Compare category of the Dreamweaver Preferences dialog box, you can browse to locate your installed third-party software, or click the *Help* option to be forwarded to a page of the Dreamweaver Resources that will suggest some comparison software options and how to use them.

16.3 Where To From Here?

You have learned about color, type, layout, image preparation, and how to incorporate all of these into website design using Dreamweaver. You have also learned that sometimes, just as in Photoshop and other graphic programs familiar to you, a design effect can be achieved through a variety of techniques or processes that yield the same final visual appearance when viewed in a browser. The goal of this text is to provide you with a solid foundation, including a multiplicity of tools for your web designer's toolbox, coupled with the confidence to delve deeper into Dreamweaver as you continue to work with the program.

16.3.1 Further Organization of Your Sites with the Addition of an Assets Folder

As you gain experience and build larger sites, when creating their umbrella site folders, you may want to design their structure to further organize their dependent files. It may become beneficial to place individual file types, such as images, media, etc., into their own specific folders, all enclosed within an *assets* folder inside the root folder, especially as the number of dependent files increase relative to the sizes of your sites. It will be one more organizational tool that you may want to employ. While other web training sources may suggest making an *assets* folder first, because Dreamweaver has its own Assets panel, I believe it can be confusing working with an *assets* folder vs. the Assets panel until you have a solid understanding of how Dreamweaver handles files. Now that you do, feel free to incorporate an *assets* folder into your future sites to further organize them.

16.3.2 More CSS and Use of Divs

We were introduced to these two web design tools at a basic level. As your experience in Dreamweaver expands, you may want to continue to expand your knowledge and application of these powerful web design features.

16.3.3 Dreamweaver Help

If you have a question, a great resource at any time is the Help feature in Dreamweaver, with an access button often conveniently located within the dialog box you are using at the time, but it is always available at any time by choosing Help>Dreamweaver Help. Especially in CS4 and CS5, choosing this menu option will always provide a wealth of Adobe *Community Help* on your subject in question.

16.3.4 Build, Build, Build

Lastly, just as in using any other graphics software you have learned, experience and your own little tricks of the trade come with usage. Moving from print design to web design is challenging and, initially, often frustrating with the limitations it contains by its very nature. I hope you are ready and excited to forge on with this medium, maximizing its potential, with the world (the World Wide Web, that is) at your fingertips.

16.4 What We Have Learned

Before we can upload a site, we must first obtain our own personal domain in the world—the World Wide Web. We learned how to brainstorm for a name, test its availability, and secure it through registration. FTP connection settings, provided by the host of our choice, can be tested as soon as they have been entered into Dreamweaver. A final "preflight" review, including the application of the Link Checker, Browser Compatibility, Reports commands, and the rest of the items on the Top Ten Final Checklist, can ensure that we will have a smooth and hassle-free site upload. Our chapter culminated with a walk through the initial upload and update processes of website creation and its subsequent maintenance using Dreamweaver.

16.5 Reinforcing Your Knowledge

Project

Although you will not be able to actually upload the Fishluvrz site on your end, we can reinforce the final review process by tweaking the Fishluvrz site, experiencing the "preflight" stage of the uploading process for future applications.

1. Following the Top Ten Final Checklist, begin by double-checking your naming of all the link pages of the Fishluvrz site. Their names should all be as follows: *products_page.html*, *information_page.html*, *faq_page.html*, and *contact_page.html*. All names should be lowercase and include the .html extension, with no spaces in their names.

2. In addition to checking that you have added the titles supplied for each page, remembering that the Reports panel can help you with this, also check now that each page title has been typed in title case. As you have learned, you can check and make page title changes if needed in multiple locations: changing the title in the title area of the Document tool bar; changing it in the title area of the Page Properties dialog box's Title/Encoding category; or choosing View>Head Content, selecting its icon in the Head content area of the Document window and then making your corrections in the Property inspector.

3. You were supplied with keywords and description text for each page of the site. As you have learned, they can be edited when the Head content is visible by clicking the respective icons and editing them in the Property inspector. Can you think of any additions or changes to the ones provided that would be appropriate for the type of pages they represent? As you check each page for typing errors or missing words, feel free to modify or add to them as you think appropriate, based on the page's content.

4. Select each graphic in the site, including those used for navigation with image hot spots and check their assigned alternate text in the Property inspector, remembering that the Reports panel can help you with this. It should be representative of the graphic, allowing the user to clearly understand what it represents if the graphic were not visible. Also, check the tooltips assigned for each Spry navigation menu item. For CS4 and CS5 users, check the tooltip titles assigned to all of your text links (including the lists on the index page) under the Title area of the Property inspector.

5. Now, it's time to check the organization of your root folder. While working exclusively through the Files panel in Dreamweaver, verify that all the link pages are in the *pages* folder, except for the *index.html* page. Are all of the images in the *images* folder? If any of them are outside of their respective folders, move them into the appropriate folder and choose to update the corresponding pages when prompted. Are all external CSS style sheets in the *css* folder? Did you insert any native graphic files accidentally? If you did, have you cloaked them? When the FLV video was added to the *index.html* page, Dreamweaver automatically generated two files placed in a *script* folder, as well as the *Clear_Skin_1.swf* and the *FLVPlayer_Progressive. swf* files (all four of these are dependent files of the video). To display properly in multiple browsers, if you did not add them specifically to the *images* folder when you inserted them, it is best to *not* move those files into it now.

6. How about the favicon? Did you remember to add it to each page of the site? It should be located in the *images* folder and should have been added to each page by choosing: Insert>HTML>Head Tag>Link, browsing for it in the *Href* category, and assigning *shortcut icon* for the *Rel* category of the Link dialog box. Check each page and add it if needed now.

Project (continued)

7. Before continuing, take a few minutes and check the following:
   - the links in all of your Spry navigation on all pages are assigned properly (for our purposes, the product and contact submenu items should link to the same pages as their main navigation)
   - all of your footer text links have been reassigned as needed to function properly
   - on the index page: the *deals* rollover and the fish image map below it have been assigned to the *products_page.html*; the *tips* rollover and fish image map below it have been assigned to the *information_page.html*; and the *fishluvrz blog* rollover and fish image map below it have been assigned to the *contact_page.html* page
   - all product text links located on the *index.html* page have the hash symbol (#) assigned to them to simulate a link
   - all fish images and their respective *Buy Now!* text on the *product_page.html* page have the hash symbol (#) assigned to them to simulate a link
   - the *fishluvrz blog* rollover added to the *contact_page.html* page has the hash symbol (#) assigned to it to simulate a link
   - all of your link pages have the image map over their headline graphic assigned to link back to the *index.html* page
8. Now that you have done that, perform a final test of your work by running both the Dreamweaver Link Checker and Browser Compatibility commands, fixing any errors that Dreamweaver identifies.

The site theoretically is now ready to upload.

16.6 Building Your Own Website

1. If you have not yet registered your website's domain name, you must begin by brainstorming for an available, applicable name. Remember that you can informally test your ideas by searching for the names you come up with, using your favorite search engine.
2. When you have your name(s) ready, choose a registrar and begin your formal search. When you are registering your domain name, decide if

you want to register the same name with other extensions as well and how long you will want the name to be registered before completing the process with your registration payment.

3. Using either the same company you registered your domain name with, or another recommended host, enter the FTP settings provided by the host into the Site Definition dialog box shown in Figure 16-1 and then click the *Test* button to test your connection. If you receive the "Failed connection" dialog box shown in Figure 16-4 contact your provider and have one of their service representatives walk you through the process.

4. Before beginning the upload process, use the Top Ten Final Checklist to be sure you remembered all the steps to properly prepare your site for the upload, including running the Link Checker, Browser Compatibility, and Reports commands, and cloaking any files if necessary, as detailed individually in its list.

5. With your site active in the Files panel, click the *Expand* icon to display both the local and remote site (server) simultaneously and then click the *Connect to remote host* (the plug) icon to connect to your host. You may see a few folders in your remote site that the host supplied for you. However, one of them most likely will be named *html* or *web*. Upload your site into that folder. If in doubt, check with your provider first. Now, select your root folder and then click the *Put* icon (Up arrow) to begin the upload process. Click OK when prompted to add all dependent files when performing this initial upload.

6. When the upload has finished, feel free to leave your connection "plugged in," test your site by typing its address in a browser, and enjoy the fruits of your labor when it displays. Carefully check each page, all links, etc., and ask friends, relatives, and colleagues to do the same. Any time that you discover something you want to change, simply make the change to the page, reconnect to your host if you are not still connected, and then drag the updated page into its appropriate folder within your host-assigned folder of your remote site, or use the Put icon (Up arrow). If your change requires an updated image as well, by always choosing to upload the dependent files, you will be assured that Dreamweaver has accounted for these updates with the associated page. Feel free to experiment with the synchronization feature of Dreamweaver when making your updates: become more familiar with this feature and decide whether you will want to incorporate it into your regular site maintenance routine.

7. Congratulations! Your site has been added to the world—and you did it all yourself!

Index